Cooking Light

COOKBOOK 1993

Cooking Light

COOKBOOK 1993

Oxmoor House®

Copyright 1992 by Oxmoor House, Inc.
Book Division of Southern Progress Corporation
P.O. Box 2463, Birmingham, Alabama 35201

Library of Congress Catalog Number: 87-61020
ISBN: 0-8487-1104-1
ISSN: 1043-7061

Manufactured in the United States of America
First Printing 1992

Editor-in-Chief: Nancy J. Fitzpatrick
Senior Foods Editor: Susan Carlisle Payne
Senior Editor, Editorial Services: Olivia Kindig Wells
Director of Manufacturing: Jerry R. Higdon
Art Director: James Boone

Cooking Light® Cookbook 1993

Editor: Cathy A. Wesler, R.D.
Assistant Foods Editor: Anne C. Chappell, M.S., R.D.
Copy Editor: Diane Lewis Swords
Assistant Copy Editor: Holly Ensor
Editorial Assistant: Whitney Wheeler
Director, Test Kitchens: Vanessa Taylor Johnson
Assistant Director, Test Kitchens: Gayle Hays Sadler
Test Kitchen Home Economists: Michele Brown Fuller, Elizabeth Luckett,
    Christina A. Pieroni, Kathleen Royal, Angie Neskaug Sinclair, Jan A. Smith
Senior Photographer: Jim Bathie
Photographer: Ralph Anderson
Senior Photo Stylist: Kay E. Clarke
Photo Stylist: Virginia R. Cravens
Designer: Faith Nance
Production Manager: Rick Litton
Associate Production Manager: Theresa L. Beste
Production Assistant: Pam Beasley Bullock
Recipe and Menu Developers: Susan S. Bradley, Patricia Coker, Marilyn Wyrick Ingram,
    Marjorie Johnston, Trish Leverett, Debby Maugans, OTT Communications, Inc.,
    Jane Ingrassia Reinsel, Elizabeth J. Taliaferro, Grace Wells
Text Consultants: Maureen Callahan, M.S., R.D.; Office of the Vice President of Health
    Affairs, University of Alabama at Birmingham: Julius Linn, M.D., Executive Director;
    Lisa Latham, Associate Editor
Exercise Model: Judith A. Mason

Cover: *Shrimp and Asparagus Medley (page 127)*
Back Cover: *Pepper-Topped Focaccia (page 112) and Fresh Chive Buttermilk Biscuits
    (page 107)*
Frontispiece: *Orange Marmalade Cheesecake (page 243)*

Contents

Living Well Is The Best Reward

Sit back and relax as you enjoy a peaceful start to your day. And as you do so, enjoy a nutritious variety of warm breads including (clockwise from top) Citrus-Cranberry Twists (page 116), Lemon-Raspberry Sweet Rolls (page 115), and Whole Grain-Pumpkin Muffins (page 107).

Research continues on the relationship between nutrition, fitness, and health, and *Cooking Light Cookbook 1993* will help you understand this new and timely information. Good health is not a fad or craze. Instead, it's something to achieve and maintain for a lifetime—a lifetime of living well.

Cooking Light shows you how to put the latest nutrition advice to work to get all the nutrients you need while reducing the risk of chronic illness. Build a diet around grains, fruits, and vegetables, all of which can provide fiber. Eat moderate quantities of lean meats and low-fat dairy products. Use fats and sweet sparingly. This is the message the government hopes its Food Guide Pyramid will convey.

Several years of research have given us a clearer picture of fat. We now know more about the type and amount of fat in the diet that contributes to heart disease and certain types of cancer. And evidence is strengthening to support the idea that lifestyle changes not only slow progression of heart disease but also reverse the process to some extent. No longer is there any doubt that people who eat less fat, especially saturated fat, and exercise regularly decrease their risk of developing heart disease and other common health problems.

Living well with *Cooking Light* means healthy living. Along with recipes and menus, you will find an abundance of information on nutrition and fitness and the role they play in bringing about a healthier lifestyle. Enjoy this all-new volume and reap the benefits that good health, good food, and fitness bring to you and your family.

Update '93

Americans are getting the message that reducing fat intake and exercising regularly pay off. According to an American Dietetic Association survey, more than one-fourth of the men questioned reported that they ate less fat last year, a step only 14 percent reported in 1991.

Evidence for the need to reduce fat in the diet continues to unfold. Last year, scientists further reinforced the connection between too much fat in the diet, elevated blood cholesterol levels, and heart disease risk. For every 1 percent rise in blood cholesterol, the risk of coronary heart disease jumps 3 percent. Additional studies strengthened the links between high-fat diets and increased cancer risks and between high-fat diets and weight gain.

The Importance of HDLs

National Institutes of Health (NIH) experts have concluded that having low levels of high-density lipoprotein (HDL) cholesterol increases heart disease risk. HDLs carry cholesterol away from blood vessel walls, reducing the chance of plaque buildup in arteries. This information helps explain why almost as many heart attacks occur among people with a "desirable" total cholesterol level of less than 200 milligrams per deciliter (mg/dL) as among those with a level over 300 mg/dL. Such people may have a low HDL cholesterol level—one below 35 mg/dL.

This means it's no longer enough to know just your total cholesterol level. You need to know your level of HDL cholesterol. Also, learn your ratio of total cholesterol to HDL cholesterol level. A ratio of less than 4.5 means, cholesterol-wise, you're in good shape.

If your HDL is low, begin a regular exercise program. Researchers at The Cooper Institute for Aerobic Research in Dallas have shown that strolling as few as three miles five days a week can increase HDL levels.

A Stanford University study of both men and women on low-fat, low-cholesterol diets showed that those on diets alone lost weight and lowered total cholesterol levels. But those who added exercise to their regimens not only lost more weight but also increased protective HDL levels.

In addition to exercise, a NIH panel also recommends using weight control and smoking cessation rather than drug treatment to raise HDL levels.

Simply substituting lean meats and low-fat dairy products for high-fat meats and regular dairy products can reduce total and low-density lipoprotein (LDL) cholesterol levels. LDL cholesterol is the one that builds up on arterial walls.

The fight against cholesterol problems and heart disease needs to start early in life. To combat the buildup of plaque in arterial walls that can begin in childhood, the National Cholesterol Education Program recommends a dual approach. All children over the age of two should eat a low-fat, low-saturated fat diet like the one recommended for adults by the American Heart Association. Children with a parent or grandparent who had heart disease or a stroke before age 55 should have a cholesterol screening.

Breakfast Breaks

Eating breakfast—a sensible breakfast, that is—is another way to reduce your chances of heart attack and stroke, according to researchers. The reason: Platelets, blood cells that stick together to form clots that can plug narrowed blood vessels, are stickier in the morning. And skipping breakfast makes platelets even stickier.

Another boon to breakfast-loving cholesterol watchers has been proven by researchers analyzing 30 years of conflicting data concerning the oat bran-cholesterol connection. The researchers found that eating 3 grams of soluble fiber from oat bran a day lowers high cholesterol levels by 2 to 3 percent. This equates to eating a large bowl of a dry oat bran cereal or three packets of instant oatmeal.

In addition, University of Kentucky researchers showed it was the soluble fiber (oat bran) that lowered cholesterol. Insoluble fiber (wheat bran) did not. Because scientists believe that beta-glucan, a soluble fiber in oat bran, is the reason oat bran lowers cholesterol, you may soon see a host of products "fortified" with beta-glucan.

If you favor a breakfast that includes eggs, a study found that blood cholesterol levels were no different among people who ate 3, 7, or 14 eggs a week along with high-fat breakfast foods. Thus, reducing saturated fat-rich bacon and butter proved more important in lowering cholesterol than reducing the number of eggs in the diet.

Breakfast foods may play an important role in cholesterol for both adults and children. A study of 530 children by the American Health Foundation found that children who skipped breakfast had higher cholesterol levels. Those eating ready-to-eat cereal with at least 2 grams of fiber per ounce had the lowest cholesterol levels.

Not a Paradox at All

How can the French eat their pâté and rich cream sauces, and smoke more than Americans, and still have such a low risk of heart disease? Is the answer the red wine they drink? Well, maybe partly.

After looking at the figures, scientists say it's not a paradox at all but rather a time-warp phenomenon. Until recently, the French didn't consume excessive amounts of fat. In 1961, fat supplied just 28 percent of calories in their diets. By 1988, it had jumped to 39 percent, primarily because the French were eating more meat and dairy products. Yet Americans were getting that many calories from fat as early as 1923. Scientists predict that if the French continue to consume this greater amount of fat, their blood vessels will become just as clogged as those of Americans.

Red wine is not a panacea. Studies have shown that people who drank one or two beers or glasses of wine or one or two ounces of hard liquor a day had a lower risk of dying from heart disease than those who didn't drink at all. The main reason appears to be that small amounts of alcohol increase the level of protective HDL cholesterol.

Drinking too much alcohol, however, can contribute to heart disease. And because of alcohol's link to cirrhosis, social problems, accidents, and cancer, it's not recommended as a viable option for the prevention of heart disease.

Controlling Blood Pressure

High blood pressure means the diastolic measure (bottom number) is consistently at least 90 millimeters of mercury (mm Hg) or the systolic pressure (top number) exceeds 140 mm Hg. But one-third of heart attacks and strokes occur in people who have high-normal blood pressures defined by diastolic values between 80 and 89 mm Hg. Mild high blood pressure has been previously defined as 90 to 104 mm Hg.

Researchers studying a group of people with blood pressures in the high end of the normal range found that among weight loss, salt restriction, and stress reduction, weight loss worked best to lower blood pressure. The weight loss didn't have to be that drastic. An average weight loss of 8½ pounds over 18 months did the trick.

Don't overlook the ability of regular, moderate exercise to lower blood pressure. Even though a study made news last year because it failed to show that exercise lowers blood pressure, the majority of studies confirm that it does. In fact, it's an essential part of any effective weight reduction program. A person who exercises regularly generally has a lower resting blood pressure, and their blood pressure tends to rise less during stressful situations.

Research from England has shown that moderate exercise reduced the risk of stroke by 50 percent, even in men with normal blood pressures. Walking on a regular basis reduced the risk by 40 percent, and jogging, by 60 percent.

More Fiber and Exercise, Less Fat Equals Less Cancer

Dietary factors contribute to one-third of the 500,000 deaths from cancer each year, according to the American Cancer Society. Scientists have found more evidence confirming that fat promotes cancer, and fiber protects against it.

The National Cancer Institute says that by following its guidelines for a low-fat, high-fiber diet rich in fruits and vegetables, Americans can reduce rates of colon cancer by 50 percent and breast cancer by 25 percent. Evidence also is mounting that antioxidants (vitamins A, C, E, and beta carotene) in the diet provide additional cancer protection.

A new study confirms that eating more fruits, vegetables, and grains and substituting fish and poultry for red meat can substantially reduce the risk of developing colon and rectal cancer. A Harvard researcher showed that a low-fat, high-fiber diet stopped development of colon polyps in people who had an inherited tendency to develop them. Polyps are precancerous lesions that appear some 10 years before colon cancer develops in them.

Conversely, the researchers found that people who ate a lot of fat but little fiber were nearly four times as likely to develop polyps in the colon. Researchers concluded that saturated fat in the diet increases the chance of developing polyps while fiber decreases it.

Fiber also gets high marks for reducing the risk of breast cancer, perhaps because it lowers estrogen levels. And the type of fiber may make a difference. One study showed that wheat fiber reduced estrogen levels but oat bran and corn bran did not.

The controversy continues over whether eating less fat lowers the risk of breast cancer. To resolve the question and assess other effects of low-fat diets in women, NIH hopes to begin a 15-year study of 45,000 women who will agree to eat a diet containing only 20 percent of calories as fat.

Exercise cuts the risk of colon cancer as well. A Harvard study showed that physical activity that burned 1,000 calories a week decreased the risk of colon cancer by 50 percent. In fact, since 1980 seven of eight major studies have confirmed that physical activity reduces the risk of colon cancer. This probably is because exercise speeds waste material through the intestines, thus reducing the time that cancer-causing agents stay in contact with the intestines.

The ABCs of Vitamins

A 10-year health survey of 11,000 adults showed that those who consumed the most vitamin C, up to 300 milligrams a day, lived longer. In the study conducted by the University of California at Los Angeles, women showed less dramatic results. But for men and women alike, the risk of heart disease decreased as the intake of vitamin C increased. Some nutrition experts say it's not the vitamin C itself but the fact that those who had the highest levels of vitamin C probably took better care of themselves. They ate more fruits and vegetables, weighed less, smoked less, and exercised more.

Several vitamins garnered attention in 1992 for their antioxidant

properties. Oxidation, the processing of oxygen, is essential for life. And when oxidation occurs, the body's cells produce highly charged oxygen molecules called free radicals. Scientists are just beginning to discover the damage out-of-control free radicals can cause. It is likely that they play a harmful role in a host of disease processes, including atherosclerosis, cancer, arthritis, and cataracts. They may even affect how fast the body ages.

The good news is that cells have an orderly system to deal with free radicals and repair any damage they cause. An important part of that system involves antioxidants. Although some antioxidants are manufactured by body cells, others are found in foods. The most common antioxidants in foods are vitamins C, E, and beta carotene.

The Nurses' Health Study (the largest long-term study of women in the world) reports that beta carotene, which the body converts into vitamin A, decreases women's risk of heart disease.

In the study, women who consumed more than 15 to 20 milligrams of beta carotene a day had a 40 percent lower risk of stroke and a 22 percent lower risk of heart attack than those who consumed less than 6 milligrams a day. This equals one serving of apricots, carrots, spinach, or sweet potatoes, or two servings of broccoli, cantaloupe, kale, or yellow squash. In addition, those who ate foods rich in vitamin A also decreased their risk of breast cancer by 20 percent.

Studies also have shown that people who consume little beta carotene are at greater risk of developing lung cancer. And those who don't get enough vitamin C increase their chances of developing esophageal, oral, and stomach cancers.

Antioxidants also show up in the latest information on aging. Preliminary evidence suggests that antioxidants may slow the development of chronic diseases that occur with increased age. It is recommended that you get your antioxidants from food, especially fruits and vegetables, rather than from supplements. The National Academy of Sciences recommends a balanced diet that includes five ½-cup servings of fruits and vegetables daily.

If you choose to get antioxidants and vitamins primarily from supplements, you are shortchanging yourself. Foods contain a host of other nutrients and substances that are just as important as vitamins and antioxidants. For example, broccoli, brussels sprouts, cabbage, cauliflower, kale, kohlrabi, and mustard greens get high marks as cancer fighters. This is not only because they contain fiber, beta carotene, and vitamin C but also because they contain a natural chemical called sulforaphane. This chemical generates special enzymes in body cells that ward off cancer-causing agents.

Building a Food Pyramid

In 1991, the U.S. Department of Agriculture (USDA) halted release of a pyramid-shaped food guide until more testing of the graphic could be done with the public. Government officials believe the newly released Food Guide Pyramid reflects the current dietary guidelines.

To help you make the proper food choices, the Food and Drug Administration (FDA) has proposed new food labeling regulations. The USDA has joined the effort that will make nutrition labeling on processed foods mandatory in 1993. The reforms will regulate health claims, establish standard serving sizes for

131 specific foods, and standardize language by defining commonly used terms such as low-fat. These changes will cost the food industry at least $1.6 million initially, but the changes could save $100 billion in health care costs over the next 20 years.

Food Technology in the News

Irradiation gets the nod as an effective means of eliminating salmonella from poultry. Irradiation of food also kills insects, parasites, and germs that cause food poisoning and food spoilage. In addition, irradiation benefits fruits such as figs, bananas, mangoes, and strawberries by delaying ripening and spoilage. Other fruits—apples, pears, and citrus fruits, for example—actually spoil faster following irradiation.

Irradiation does not make food radioactive and therefore it does not increase human exposure to radiation. Although most scientists label it a safe process, others say more testing is required to know the consequences of eating irradiated food.

Opening a new era in designer foods, the FDA has declared that bioengineered plants used for food are generally recognized as safe. The response recognizes new technology that allows the insertion of genes into plants to provide a host of changes that, among other things, may improve shelf life and increase insect resistance.

Strolling to Success

Researchers have concluded that the largest health gains come with the transition from inactivity to moderate exercise. In one exercise-related study, the death rate fell 55 percent from the least-active group to the next-to-least active.

Active men are half as likely as sedentary ones to develop diabetes. According to a study reported in *The New England Journal of Medicine*, the risk of developing diabetes declined with an increase in activity. Each 500 calories burned during exercise on a weekly basis (equal to jogging one hour a week) reduced the risk by 6 percent. Those most likely to benefit were overweight men who had the greatest chance of developing diabetes.

Harvard researchers studying more than 87,000 middle-aged women found that those who exercised vigorously at least once a week also reduced their risk of developing diabetes.

Researchers at the USDA Human Nutrition Research Center on Aging at Tufts University say the more physically active you are as you grow older, the slower your body and mind will age. Directors of the center say that although inactivity doesn't necessarily shorten life span, it definitely shortens "health span." If you stay active through the years, you're less likely to develop heart disease, diabetes, osteoporosis, and cancer.

Exercise for Children

Encourage your children to exercise. A recent Youth Risk Behavior Survey found that only 37 percent of students in grades 9 through 12 were vigorously active three or more times a week. When encouraging children to exercise, remember that the main reason youngsters exercise is for fun.

Regular exercise increases youngsters' strength and coordination, boosts self-confidence, and relieves stress. Physical activity can also help control a child's weight and lower cholesterol and blood pressure.

The National Association for Sports and Physical Education recommends 30 minutes a day of physical activity with a qualified instructor in elementary school and at least 50 minutes a day in junior and senior high school.

The development of special programs and health clubs for kids is a positive trend. Find a program based on fun games and recreation that involves lots of movement and positive reinforcement. Beware of those that stress competition or segregate kids by ability. The club's staff should be trained professionals, and programs and equipment should be specific to each age group.

Never Say Diet

Many dieters say it's impossible to stay on a diet long term. Fortunately, the trend today is toward healthy eating for a lifetime. But the essential ingredient for a healthy life and for controlling weight is regular exercise.

No matter how hard you try, you can't get around the fact that to lose weight, you must use more calories than you take in. If you try losing weight only by cutting calories, your body sees hard times ahead and burns fewer calories to conserve its resources. Break the dieting cycle by adding exercise. It's the best way to increase the number of calories you burn.

Remember, food is not the enemy; it is a necessary fuel for the body and one of life's greatest pleasures. You can eat all types of food in moderation as part of a life built around a well-balanced, low-fat, high-fiber diet and regular exercise. Preparing foods the *Cooking Light* way helps you take advantage of today's move toward a healthier, more active life.

The Food
& Fitness
Connection

Take positive steps toward good health by participating in leisure-time physical activities and decreasing the fat in your diet. Hit the trails of the great outdoors, and pack low-fat, high-carbohydrate snacks such as (clockwise from top) Miniature Brown Bread Loaves (page 109), Nutty Cereal Snack (page 201), Spicy Pita Chips (page 201), and low-fat snack crackers. For added energy, tuck a few pieces of fresh fruit into your backpack.

In *Healthy People 2000: National Health Promotion and Disease Prevention Objectives*, the U.S. Public Health Service and the Department of Health and Human Services present a strategy for improving the health of the nation over the next decade. This document contains a set of health objectives to be achieved by the year 2000. To help you reach some of the nutrition and fitness goals, *Cooking Light* continues to show that making small changes in the way you eat and exercise can result in big health benefits.

Exercise is just as important as diet when you are taking steps to improve your health, and this exercise doesn't have to be grueling or painful. Take note of a study of Harvard University alumni. It found that people who participated in regular leisure-time physical activities, such as walking, cycling, bowling, dancing, and gardening, increased their life spans by one to two years. Another study from The Cooper Institute for Aerobic Research showed that people who only slightly increased their levels of physical activity greatly improved their health. Over and over, fitness experts are saying the same thing about exercise—it needs to be regular, it needs to be varied, and it needs to be fun.

If you are looking for a physical activity to keep you challenged and motivated, try step aerobics. It continues to grow in popularity as people step to the music at home as well as in health clubs. Not only does this low-impact aerobic workout provide cardiovascular benefits but it also includes muscle-strengthening and toning exercises for the upper and lower body. Beginners enjoy step aerobics because the basic moves are simple; advanced steppers enjoy it because it continues to offer a challenge as they increase the height of the step and the complexity of the movements.

To start you on your way to healthier eating, turn to "The *Cooking Light* Kitchen" and see how you can trim fat and add fiber to your menus and still attain great-tasting results. And let "What's New in the Marketplace" guide you to some of the newest low-fat products on the grocery shelves and help you understand the labels on these products.

Throughout *Cooking Light*, you will find nutrition and fitness information that will help you achieve your goals for a healthier lifestyle. Share these tips with family and friends as you all become more interested in improving your health. You'll find the tips flagged with the following symbols:

NUTRITION  FITNESS

Nutrition Basics for *Cooking Light*

For Americans who don't drink alcohol or smoke, eating habits probably shape long-term health more than any other personal choice, according to the 1988 *Surgeon General's Report on Nutrition and Health.* Undoubtedly, you've heard the "good diet promotes good health" message before and vowed immediately to change your not-so-healthful eating habits.

But despite good intentions, planned diet changes often go unfulfilled. Impatient for immediate results, many people set impossible-to-achieve goals and end up making no changes at all. A better approach is to set attainable goals and revamp eating habits step by step.

SETTING GOALS

In *Healthy People 2000: National Health Promotion and Disease Prevention Objectives,* government health experts provide an extensive list of lifestyle goals that can help prevent disease and enhance health. Two of the nutrition goals in the document bear particular mention. One calls for Americans to eat less fat, especially saturated fat. Another nutrition goal is for people to eat more complex carbohydrates—fruits, vegetables, and whole grains. Because these starchy foods are naturally low in fat, this goal complements the "less is better" approach to fat.

The new Food Guide Pyramid from the USDA graphically communicates the same message: Eat less fat, and build your diet upon a base of complex carbohydrates. The placement of the food groups in the pyramid conveys the government's recommendations to eat more grains, fruits, and vegetables; eat moderate quantities of lean meats and dairy products; and use sweets, fats, and oils sparingly. The recommended number of daily servings from each food group is listed, and symbols are used to indicate which food groups contain added sugar and/or fat. The graphic shows that all food groups are important to the total diet and helps illustrate how to turn dietary guidelines into food choices.

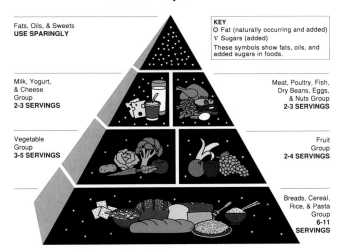

Food Guide Pyramid
A Guide to Daily Food Choices

Fats, Oils, & Sweets
USE SPARINGLY

KEY
○ Fat (naturally occurring and added)
▽ Sugars (added)
These symbols show fats, oils, and added sugars in foods.

Milk, Yogurt, & Cheese Group
2-3 SERVINGS

Meat, Poultry, Fish, Dry Beans, Eggs, & Nuts Group
2-3 SERVINGS

Vegetable Group
3-5 SERVINGS

Fruit Group
2-4 SERVINGS

Breads, Cereal, Rice, & Pasta Group
6-11 SERVINGS

FIGURING OUT FATS

It's not difficult to understand the concept that fats are fattening. Fat contributes 9 calories per gram compared to the 4 calories found in equal weight portions of carbohydrate and protein. So a diet high in fat can increase the risk for obesity. And medical researchers point to a number of other potential health problems that can result from too much fat in the diet. Solid evidence links a high-fat diet to several types of cancer, gallbladder disease, and heart disease.

In *Healthy People 2000,* government officials urge Americans to trim fat levels from the current average of 36 percent of total calories to 30 percent or less. Because checking fat percentages for every food can be time consuming, it is more realistic to translate the 30 percent figure into grams of total fat and set a fat budget for the day. The recommended maximum number of fat grams for the day is calculated by multiplying the total daily calorie requirement by .30 and dividing by 9. Saturated fat should account for no more than one-third of the total daily fat allowance.

ADDING UP THE SATURATES

Scientific evidence clearly associates a high intake of saturated fat with an increased risk for cardiovascular disease, so it's important to be familiar with foods that contain saturated fat. These foods, mainly from animal products, include butter, lard, fatty meats, whole-milk cheeses, cream, whole milk, and 2% milk. Two vegetable fats—coconut oil and palm kernel oil—are also highly saturated.

Currently, saturated fat levels in the typical American diet comprise about 13 percent of the total calories. Health experts say a drop to 10 percent would be a reasonable, healthful change. However, for people already plagued with high blood cholesterol levels, a drop to 7 percent or less would be wiser. That lower figure may be necessary because studies indicate that saturated fats can raise blood cholesterol levels and thereby act as a risk factor for heart disease. Keep in mind that simply trimming total fat from the diet will likely bring saturated fat within the 10 percent range.

LOW-FAT MEALS GET RAVES

Contrary to popular opinion, eating foods that contain less fat can be a quite pleasurable dining experience. Take the crew of a U.S. Navy destroyer, for instance. Although some of the sailors were meat-and-potato lovers, when their chef trimmed the fat from meals (less meat, more potatoes) in accordance with nutritional guidelines from the American Cancer Society, the sailors admitted they actually enjoyed the leaner cuisine. After six months, these sailors also enjoyed trimmer physiques (they lost an average of 12 pounds each) and lower cholesterol levels.

The same scenario occurred when researchers at Cornell University added low-fat versions of muffins, casseroles, and beverages to the diets of a group of mildly overweight adults. Study participants who received the leaner 20 to 25 percent fat diet lost an average of 7 pounds each without realizing how they had lost the weight.

NOTHING COMPLEX ABOUT CARBOHYDRATES

Shifting the focus from high-fat foods to low-fat carbohydrates offers health benefits other than weight control. Fruits, vegetables, and whole grains come packaged with fiber and a variety of other beneficial nutrients.

In new studies from China, researchers speculate that a high-fiber diet may be protecting the people in that country from certain types of cancer. Most Chinese eat about 35 grams of fiber per day, while Americans eat about 11 grams. The National Cancer Institute recommends 25 to 35 grams per day. Water-insoluble fiber, like that found in wheat bran, adds bulk to the diet and helps prevent constipation and may reduce the risk of colon cancer. Water-soluble fiber, the kind found in oats, dried beans, and apples, can help lower cholesterol levels in the blood.

New studies reveal that vitamin C, which is found in citrus fruits and juices, strawberries, broccoli, cauliflower, and peppers, may help keep the immune system healthy. This nutrient may also ward off cataracts as well as protect against heart disease. Grains rich in vitamin E, such as wheat germ, may also hold a key to immunity. Preliminary reports also suggest that this fat-soluble vitamin is capable of repairing some of the muscle damage that can occur during exercise.

Beta carotene, the plant pigment in dark green or deep yellow-orange vegetables and fruits, converts into vitamin A and appears to protect against certain types of cancer and heart disease. The best sources of beta carotene are carrots, sweet potatoes, squash, spinach, greens, and broccoli.

Health experts at the USDA and the Department of Health and Human Services urge Americans to eat at least five servings of fruits and vegetables each day and a minimum of six servings of breads, cereals, or grain products. Whole grain products, with their large fiber contribution, are an even better selection.

If you can make only two changes in your diet, eat less fat and more fiber. Choose whole grain breads and cereals, rice, and pasta for the base of your diet. Top this base with a variety of fruits and vegetables. By making these additions, you can easily reduce your intake of high-fat foods. Throughout the pages of *Cooking Light*, you will find ways to prepare and enjoy a bounty of nutrient-packed fruits, vegetables, and grains—all low in fat and high in flavor.

Computing Nutrition

Your Daily Needs

To estimate your daily calorie requirement, multiply your current weight by 15. Remember that this is only a rough guide because calorie requirements vary according to age, body size, and level of activity. If a change of weight is desired, add or subtract 500 calories per day to allow for weight gain or loss of 1 pound a week. However, a diet of less than 1,200 calories a day is not recommended unless medically supervised. For more information concerning your requirements, consult a registered dietitian.

Implement the *Cooking Light* 50-20-30 guidelines (page 30) by calculating the amount of carbohydrate, protein, and fat needed for optimal health. Multiply your calorie requirement by the percentages 50, 20, and 30 for the number of calories to be provided by each nutrient. Divide the carbohydrate and protein calories by 4 (4 calories per gram) and the fat by 9 (9 calories per gram) to determine how many grams of each nutrient you need.

For example, here's how to calculate the distribution for a 2,000-calorie diet:

50% carbohydrate = 2,000 calories x .50 = 1,000 calories ÷ 4 = 250 grams carbohydrate

20% protein = 2,000 x .20 = 400 calories ÷ 4 = 100 grams protein

30% fat = 2,000 x .30 = 600 calories ÷ 9 = 67 grams fat

Therefore, for a person eating 2,000 calories a day, at least 1,000 calories should be from carbohydrate. No more than 400 calories should be from protein, and no more than 600 calories should be from fat.

Every Recipe Analyzed

Calories and a nutrient breakdown per serving accompany every recipe. The nutrients listed include grams of protein, fat, saturated fat, carbohydrate, and fiber, along with milligrams of cholesterol, iron, sodium, and calcium.

When planning meals, refer to the daily amounts of nutrients listed below to make the most of the values that follow *Cooking Light* recipes. The amounts listed for fiber, cholesterol, and sodium are suggested daily intakes; the amounts of iron and calcium are the Recommended Dietary Allowances (RDAs) for these nutrients:

Fiber	25 to 35 grams
Cholesterol	300 milligrams or less
Iron	15 milligrams
Sodium	3,300 milligrams or less
Calcium	800 milligrams

Determining Calorie Percentages

Use *Cooking Light* nutrient breakdowns to calculate the percentage of calories contributed by carbohydrate, protein, and fat. Let's say you are looking at the recipe for Robust Vegetable Stew (complete recipe on page 228), and you want to determine the percentage of fat in one serving.

First, find in the analysis the number of grams of fat per serving. This recipe has 2.2 grams fat. To find the percentage of calories from fat, multiply grams of fat by 9 (the number of calories per gram of fat) to get fat calories per serving. Then divide this number by the total calories. Fat contributes about 11 percent of the calories.

Robust Vegetable Stew

PROTEIN 9.0 FAT 2.2 (Saturated Fat 0.8) CARBOHYDRATE 31.2
FIBER 4.6 CHOLESTEROL 0 IRON 2.9 SODIUM 302 CALCIUM 108

To calculate the calories contributed by carbohydrate and protein, multiply grams of carbohydrate or protein per serving by 4 (the number of calories per gram of carbohydrate or protein). Divide the number by total calories.

Meeting the 50-20-30 Guidelines

All recipes will not fall so neatly within the guidelines. When this occurs, combine these foods with other foods to meet the recommended percentages: more than 50 percent carbohydrate, about 20 percent protein, and no more than 30 percent fat. Saturated fat is part of the total fat content and should be no more than one-third of the daily fat grams. The goal is to achieve the recommended balance of nutrients on a daily basis, taking into consideration three meals and a snack.

How the Recipes Are Analyzed

The recipes are developed for people interested in lowering their intake of calories, fat, cholesterol, and/or sodium to maintain healthy eating patterns. If you are following a medically prescribed diet, consult a registered dietitian to see how *Cooking Light* recipes can fit into your specific meal plan.

The calorie and nutrient breakdown of each recipe is derived from computer analysis, based primarily on information from the U.S. Department of Agriculture. The nutrient values are as accurate as possible and are based on these assumptions:
- All nutrient breakdowns are listed per serving.
- All meats are trimmed of fat and skin before cooking.
- When a range is given for an ingredient (for example, 3 to 3½ cups flour), the lesser amount is calculated.
- A percentage of alcohol calories evaporates when heated, and this reduction is reflected in the calculations.
- When a marinade is used, only the amount of marinade used (not discarded) is calculated.
- Garnishes and optional ingredients are not calculated.
- Fruits and vegetables listed in the ingredients are not peeled unless specified.

Exercise—The Perfect Partner

For some people, the definition of true physical fitness is a well-sculpted body or the ability to do 100 push-ups at a time. Others are comfortable with a body that can walk a neighborhood mile without shortness of breath. The American College of Sports Medicine defines total fitness as the ability to perform moderate to vigorous levels of physical activity without exhaustion and to maintain this level of physical activity throughout life. Nowhere in this definition is there a word about grueling physical activity that requires above average skill or commitment.

The message is simple: To achieve physical fitness, just start moving. As part of *Healthy People 2000*, government officials have placed physical activity and exercise among the nation's top health priorities. By saying exercise is just as important as diet when it comes to health promotion and disease prevention, experts hope to persuade Americans to live as actively as possible.

BASIC TRAINING

One of the fitness objectives in *Healthy People 2000* is to encourage health-care providers to get an exercise history from their patients and to give prescriptions for exercise as well as diet. The basic prescription for a total workout has the following three key components:
• Aerobic fitness—to improve the function and efficiency of the heart, lungs, and blood vessels.
• Muscle strength and endurance—to build muscle tone and strength.
• Flexibility—to reduce the risk of muscle strain and injury.

Although figuring out how much aerobic and strength training is right for you is an individual process, the American College of Sports Medicine has some basic guidelines. The aerobic component encourages three to five sessions (lasting 20 to 60 minutes, depending on the intensity) of heart-strengthening activities such as walking, jogging, or aerobic dance per week. Individuals should exercise at a steady, comfortable pace within their target heart rate zones. (To figure out your target heart rate, refer to the chart on page 63.) Fitness experts say that 60 to 90 percent of maximum heart rate is the most beneficial zone for most people, although a lower intensity may still burn some fat.

For strength training, the minimum recommended frequency is two sessions of 8 to 10 exercises per week. Workouts need to include major muscle groups such as the chest, shoulders, arms, back, abdomen, and legs.

To maintain flexibility, stretching exercises should be a part of every workout. Stretches should be performed slowly and evenly and when muscles are warm. Muscles should be stretched to the point of tension, not pain.

EXERCISE MORE, LIVE LONGER

Bodies physically age at different rates, and the chronological age and the physical age can be as much as 30 years apart. Credit heredity for some of this longevity. Lifestyle factors, particularly the degree of activity throughout the life span, also seem to play a major role in the physical aging process. A case in point involves an 84-year-old jogger who still runs marathons after 61 years. His doctors say his body is physically 20 years younger.

Numerous research studies support the anti-aging benefits of exercise. For example, studies have found that older adults who exercise can build and maintain denser bones than can those who are sedentary. As for muscles, overwhelming evidence shows that much of the decline in muscle tone that occurs with age is due to inactivity, not aging. And according to studies at the University of Washington, regular exercise can also improve aerobic capacity in older adults.

In a group of previously sedentary men aged 61 to 81 years, aerobic capacity jumped 20 percent after a six-month aerobic fitness program. Researchers say that this change gave participants aerobic capacities of people 15 to 20 years younger. In view of all the studies that support a link between physical activity and longevity, there's little doubt that many of the negative effects of aging can be delayed with a regular fitness and strengthening program.

EXERCISE MYTHS AND MISCONCEPTIONS

To present a clearer picture of what exercise can do for the body, several common exercise misconceptions need to be dispelled.

MYTH	TRUTH
Muscle that is not used turns to fat.	Muscle tissue cannot be converted to fat. Active people who stop exercising can become flabby because fat deposits fill up the space formerly occupied by muscles.
No pain, no gain.	You do have to overload muscles to make them grow stronger, but not to the point of pain. Exercise does not have to be strenuous to be beneficial. A low-intensity workout of longer duration can accomplish the same fitness goals as a high-intensity workout with less risk of injury.
Spot-reducing exercises can trim fat from thighs and abdomens.	50 leg lifts and 75 sit-ups will not get rid of fat. It takes aerobic exercise to burn body fat, and even then the fat comes from all over the body, not just one place. Exercise can tone muscles in problem areas and make them appear sleeker.
Exercise increases the appetite.	A 40-minute aerobic dance class or a 3-mile jog is more likely to suppress the appetite than increase it. Short-term (less than an hour) exercise tends to boost body temperature and suppress hormones that trigger hunger.
Cellulite is more difficult to get rid of than other types of fat.	The fat that causes dimpling on the thighs and arms is no more difficult to get rid of than the fat surrounding internal organs. Dimpling results when compartments of body fat grow so full that they stretch the connective tissue that links them together. The prescription for losing excess body fat is aerobic exercise and a low-fat diet.

OTHER BENEFITS OF EXERCISE

A recent publication from the National Institute on Aging stated: "If exercise could be packed into a pill, it would be the single most widely prescribed and beneficial medicine in the nation." Although exercise is not a cure-all, it can improve health in measurable ways.

Regular exercise can lower high blood pressure by toning the heart muscle and making it pump blood more efficiently.

Studies show that exercise can help control blood sugar for some people with diabetes and can reduce or eliminate their need for insulin.

Medical reports also confirm that weight-bearing exercises such as walking, jogging, and aerobic dancing can increase bone density and help prevent osteoporosis.

Researchers at the Baylor College of Medicine found that overweight adults who exercised regularly (even when they did not diet) were able to lose weight and keep it off for at least two years.

While exercise can help lower LDL cholesterol, a regular walking routine can increase the level of "good" cholesterol (HDL) in the blood by as much as 6 percent. That increase equates to an 18 percent drop in the risk of heart disease.

MUSCLING OUT THE FAT

A recent report on the "fattening of America" cites inactivity as one of the most likely causes of obesity. But numbers on a scale are not what determine whether a body is fit or fat. Health experts now talk of healthy bodies and healthy weights in context of the proportion of lean body mass (muscle and bone) to fat tissue. Low-intensity exercise has been shown to decrease total body fat and increase lean body mass. Lean body mass uses up more energy than does fat tissue. This means that a more muscular person, even without dieting or exercising, has an easier time of controlling weight than does a person with a greater percentage of body fat. Also, high levels of body fat are associated with an increased risk of chronic illnesses such as high blood pressure, heart disease, and diabetes. To be fit, not fat, embrace active pursuits as well as healthy eating habits.

Getting in Step

Step aerobics, a high-intensity, low-impact aerobic workout, continues to be the rage at health clubs across the country. Stepping up and down on a platform while simultaneously performing upper body movements works all major muscle groups in the lower body and also tones the upper body. Because it is a high-intensity aerobic exercise, stepping can also burn body fat and strengthen the heart. And it's easily adaptable to all fitness levels.

Beginners can start off on a low step and perform no arm movements. Advanced steppers can increase intensity by increasing step height, using hand-held weights, and stepping for longer periods of time.

A total workout on the step should include a warm-up, stretches, cardiovascular movements, conditioning (muscle-strengthening) exercises, and a cool-down. Be sure to check with your physician before beginning this or any other fitness program.

SAFETY TIPS

Step directly on the center of the step, placing entire foot on the step.

Do not overstep the step.

Stand up straight. Keep your back straight, not arched.

Do not lean over from your back.

STRETCHES

Calf Stretches—Place both feet on the step and drop left heel off the edge of step. Keep legs straight and body lifted. Hold for 8 counts. Repeat with opposite heel.

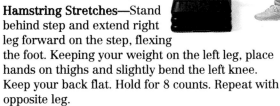

Hamstring Stretches—Stand behind step and extend right leg forward on the step, flexing the foot. Keeping your weight on the left leg, place hands on thighs and slightly bend the left knee. Keep your back flat. Hold for 8 counts. Repeat with opposite leg.

CARDIOVASCULAR MOVEMENTS

End Lunges—Stand on the end of the step with feet together and arms down at sides. Lunge back with left leg, with only the toe touching the floor. Keep right knee over center of foot on the step. Extend both arms forward as left foot goes back. Return left foot to step, and return arms to sides. Repeat with opposite leg. Repeat sequence 8 times.

CONDITIONING EXERCISES

Tricep Dips—Move to the front of the step and get into a sitting position with the heels of hands on edge of step, lining up shoulders with the hips. Keep your back toward step and your heels on the floor. Roll shoulders slightly forward and inhale. Bend elbows and drop hips to floor. Exhale as you straighten arms and push up. Repeat 10 times.

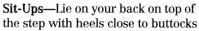

Sit-Ups—Lie on your back on top of the step with heels close to buttocks and arms crossed over chest. Inhale. As you exhale, slowly curl your head, shoulders, and upper back off the step, keeping lower back pressed against the step. Inhale as you slowly roll back to the starting position. Repeat 10 times. To increase intensity, lower one end of the step and do incline sit-ups with feet on the step and arms crossed. These sit-ups can also be done with legs raised and knees bent at a 90-degree angle.

Incline Push-Ups—Kneel on the floor with feet crossed at ankles. Place hands on step, lining up chest with heels of hands. Pitch weight slightly forward; keep the back straight and drop chest to step by bending elbows. Inhale. Exhale while pushing up to starting position. Repeat 10 times.

Leg Lifts—Hold the step upright and center yourself behind it. Keeping the left foot flexed, slowly lift left leg to the side, raising the leg to a 45-degree angle. Lower the left leg to starting position; repeat 8 times. Repeat with opposite leg.

Set Yourself Up for Success

Advice and directions for pursuing a healthy lifestyle can sometimes be overwhelming. But don't feel compelled to make overnight changes in the way you eat and live. The trick, say experts, is to revamp your lifestyle slowly. When government officials devised objectives for the nation as part of *Healthy People 2000*, they allowed a time frame of 10 years for the population to accomplish health goals. The report recognized that as people make gradual changes in their health behaviors, the health status of the nation will improve. A fuller measure of health and a better quality of life are within your grasp. You just need to take the first step. To start, concentrate on one area of your lifestyle at a time. If you choose to make diet changes first, the overall strategy for improvement is to eat less fat. To accomplish that general goal, begin by changing specific eating habits one at a time.

LESS FAT, MORE FLAVOR

Making meal-by-meal adjustments is one approach to changing your diet, especially when you are trying to decrease fat. At breakfast, replace the whole milk that you pour on cereal with lower-fat skim milk. Try that change once or twice per week until you are comfortable with the switch. Other changes you could make at breakfast include spreading toast or English muffins with fruit preserves instead of butter or replacing a high-fat pastry or doughnut with a cinnamon-raisin bagel. At lunch, prepare tuna salad with nonfat mayonnaise, put turkey instead of bologna on your sandwich, or eat pretzels rather than potato chips.

A low-fat diet prescription is often met with dismay by many Americans. Unfortunately, the concept that low-fat cuisine can taste good is hard for many people to believe. But chefs and dietitians are working together to prove that low fat and good flavor are not mutually exclusive terms. Adding flavor without adding fat does not require sophisticated culinary skills, only a little knowledge of how to make the most of the natural flavors of fresh foods.

More professional chefs are adding low-fat techniques to their repertoires and are creating dishes that have even the restaurant critics cheering. At the top of a chef's list of ways to jazz up low-fat dishes are flavor enhancers such as citrus juices, flavored vinegars, balsamic vinegar, wine, and apple cider. All of these liquids are acidic in nature and can enhance the taste of everything from soups to casseroles to vegetables. For example, adding a splash of lemon juice to a pan of sautéed carrots takes the flavor from bland to more complex. Sprinkling a fresh or dried herb such as dill on those same carrots adds another layer to that flavor complexity. In fact, liberal use of herbs is another culinary secret of food professionals. Learning to cook with herbs and spices opens a whole new horizon of tastes.

SLOW AND STEADY WINS THE RACE

When you decide to take on the challenge of increasing your level of physical activity, there is no need to jump into a grueling daily fitness regimen. Even a modest increase in activity can produce substantial health benefits, according to researchers at The Cooper Institute for Aerobic Research in Dallas. When these scientists studied the physical fitness levels of more than 13,000 adults, they found a low risk of death from all causes among people who were active—even when the level of activity was low. Surprisingly, the people who benefited most from exercise were those individuals who were only slightly more active than the sedentary ones.

Researchers at the Institute recommend starting with a low-intensity activity, such as walking, and working up to a plan that includes 20 minutes of that activity three days per week. Building small incremental activities into your daily schedule is the way to improve total fitness and reduce your risk factors for cardiovascular disease and cancer.

FUN, NOT PERFORMANCE

In attempts to focus on the correct way to exercise, fitness experts sometimes forget to mention one important part of any fitness program—the fun factor. Too many Americans still believe that they must maintain a grueling training schedule in order to be physically fit. But studies show just the opposite. You do not have to perform like a marathon runner, a distance cyclist, or a triathlon competitor to achieve health benefits from exercise.

According to one group of researchers, frequent participation in leisure-time physical activities is associated with increased longevity. A study of Harvard University alumni found that adults who regularly participated in walking, yard work, or light sports increased their life spans by one to two years. Another study found that leisure activity can protect against cardiovascular disease. In other words, activities you do for fun—a softball game, a bicycle ride, a walk around the park—can promote good health just as efficiently as a rigid fitness routine.

To maintain an active lifestyle, experts recommend that people pursue activities that make them feel good. When exercise becomes something you feel you must do whether you like it or not, your chances of staying physically active are lowered. If you find yourself counting every minute you spend on an exercise cycle and wishing you were finished, switch to another activity. Try one that gives you more pleasure. Professional athletes may work until they are the best in their sport, but exercising for health requires no performance standards. The goals are to keep active and, at the very least, have some fun.

KEYS TO PERMANENT WEIGHT LOSS

In a recent report from the National Institutes of Health, experts note the high failure rate of weight-loss diets. Statistics show that as many as 90 to 95 percent of dieters who successfully lose weight end up regaining lost pounds within five years. As dismal as these numbers may sound, health professionals say this high failure rate can be easily turned around if dieters employ these basic strategies:

• Set realistic goals. Dropping 10 pounds in a week may be possible if you starve yourself. But health experts say it is a slow, steady loss (1 to 2 pounds per week) that leads to permanent weight change. Reasonable, moderate changes in food intake are easier to live with than are "quick fix" deprivation diet plans.

• Opt for a long-term commitment. Because it's either too much food or too little activity (or a combination of both) that causes weight gain, successful weight loss requires the development of new behaviors. Too many dieters follow a weight-loss or exercise program for only a short time.

Changes need to be permanent if weight loss is to be permanent.

• Learn to deal with stress. Stressful situations may cause you to fall back into old eating and lifestyle habits. Because it is nearly impossible to avoid worries about job, family, and finances, find ways to diffuse those stresses. Exercise is one of the best ways.

• Seek support. Sharing your frustrations and accomplishments with others who understand your goals can help you keep a positive attitude. Some people benefit from a diet support group. Others need the support of a professional counselor or to read inspirational articles about people who have successfully lost weight. Find out what fulfills your needs and seek social and emotional support.

• Learn to self-monitor your progress. There are no diet police to tell you when you have had enough to eat or to prompt you to exercise regularly. You must make the effort to check up on yourself periodically.

The *Cooking Light* Kitchen

You can increase fiber and decrease fat in family menus by making a few simple modifications. The Patio Dinner menu (recipes and analysis for each begin on page 50) is a perfect example of how using low-fat cooking techniques, substituting low-fat ingredients, and adding fresh vegetables and fruits can change a meal from being high in fat and humdrum to being light, lean, and out of the ordinary.

Instead of barbecuing a whole chicken with skin, grill boned, skinned chicken breasts for maximum flavor and minimum fat. Instead of brushing grilled vegetables with oil, add sliced vegetables to the foil packets and grill them along with the chicken. Substitute light process cream cheese product and low-fat yogurt for whipped topping in frozen fruit salad to cut the fat by more than half. Replace traditional garlic bread with Spicy Grilled Bread. Its flavor comes from nonfat mayonnaise and spicy mustard instead of butter.

Also, you can decrease fat and add fiber to your dessert by serving Oatmeal Snack Cake instead of oatmeal cookies. Reduced-calorie margarine, skim milk, and egg substitute all help reduce the fat, and raisins increase the fiber.

Decreasing fat and increasing fiber in your diet does not have to be a chore. When you follow the *Cooking Light* guidelines, you'll see how easy it is to prepare healthy, satisfying meals.

Cooking Light	Traditional
TOTAL CALORIES PER SERVING: 617	TOTAL CALORIES PER SERVING: 1,069
Calories from Fat: 14%	Calories from Fat: 52%
PROTEIN 37.7 FAT 9.6 (Saturated Fat 2.9) CARBOHYDRATE 96.6 FIBER 3.7 CHOLESTEROL 77 IRON 4.1 SODIUM 729 CALCIUM 193	PROTEIN 36 FAT 61.4 (Saturated Fat 22.9) CARBOHYDRATE 101 FIBER 2.1 CHOLESTEROL 129 IRON 4.1 SODIUM 641 CALCIUM 114
Chicken and Vegetable Packets *(1 serving)*	Barbecued chicken *(3 ounces)*
Frozen Orange Salad *(1 serving)*	Grilled zucchini *(½ cup)*
Spicy Grilled Bread *(1 slice)*	Frozen fruit salad *(½ cup)*
Oatmeal Snack Cake *(1 serving)*	Garlic bread *(1 slice)*
Cherry Lemonade *(1 cup)*	Oatmeal cookies *(3 cookies)*
	Old-fashioned lemonade *(1 cup)*

Cardamom has a pungent, sweet, slightly camphoric flavor and is associated with Scandinavian cooking. It is available whole or ground and is used in pastries, breads, cookies, coffee, and hot spiced wines.

Chinese five-spice powder is a blend of equal parts of cinnamon, cloves, fennel seed, star anise, and Szechwan peppercorns. It has a pungent, slightly sweet licorice flavor and is used in Oriental cuisine, especially for meat and fish.

Cumin has a strong pungent flavor and is available whole or ground. Cumin is one of the main ingredients of curry powder and is used in a wide variety of dishes in Indian, Middle Eastern, and African cuisines.

Ginger has a hot, spicy-sweet flavor and is available whole, ground, or crystallized. It is a mainstay of Oriental and Indian cooking. Ginger is used minced or grated in marinades and sauces, ground in cookies, and crystallized in candies and desserts.

Mace, the red, web-like covering of the nutmeg shell, has a warm, spicy flavor. It is available ground or whole and is used in cakes, apple dishes, pies, breads, soups, and pastries. Mace can be substituted for nutmeg in some dishes.

Nutmeg is a dried, oval-shaped seed with a sweet, spicy, slightly bitter flavor. It is available whole or ground. Nutmeg is used ground or freshly grated in eggnog, warm beverages, fruits, puddings, cakes, breads, and custards.

Peppercorns are available in green (fresh, unripe berries), black (dried green berries), white (dried cores of red berries), and mixed. They have a pungent flavor and are available whole, cracked, or ground.

Red pepper is from the dried fruit of the capsicum pepper plant and has no relation to peppercorns. It has a hot, pungent flavor and is available whole, crushed, or ground. It is used in sausage, pizza, and Mexican food.

Saffron has a distinctive aroma and a bitter, highly aromatic flavor. It is available ground or in threads. Saffron is used to add flavor and bright yellow color to rice, chicken and seafood dishes, soups, and sauces.

What's New in the Marketplace?

The marketplace today holds hundreds more healthier food choices than it did just a year ago. Manufacturers are reformulating traditional products at such a rapid pace that shopping for low-fat foods takes no special effort. Now appearing in local supermarkets are fat-free cheeses, low-fat snack crackers, no-oil chips, nonfat dips, and fat-free cookies. To accompany these new products, companies are revamping food labels to reflect current nutrition concerns: total fat, saturated fat, percentage of calories from fat, cholesterol, complex carbohydrate, and fiber.

In November 1990, the Nutrition Labeling and Education Act was signed by the president. This act mandated that the FDA revise its food-labeling guidelines. Although it probably will be one to two years before the final guidelines are approved, the revisions will reflect the most comprehensive changes in food labeling in 50 years.

Until the final labeling regulations have been passed, learn to read between the lines and make wise choices based on the updated information now appearing on labels.

Enjoy the convenience of snack foods without the guilt with low-fat and fat-free chips, dips, cheeses, crackers, and cookies.

With the abundance of "light," "fat-free," and "nonfat" products on grocery shelves, it takes a savvy shopper to determine which products really are healthy. And labels sometimes only add to the confusion. To help clear up the confusion, the FDA has proposed the following definitions for common label terms:

Sugar-free—less than 0.5 grams of sugar (any type) per serving.

Calorie-free—less than 5 calories per serving.

Low-calorie—40 calories or less per serving.

Low-sodium—140 milligrams or less of sodium per serving and per 100 grams.

Cholesterol-free—less than 2 milligrams of cholesterol and 2 grams or less of saturated fat per serving.

Low-cholesterol—20 milligrams or less of cholesterol per serving and per 100 grams, and 2 grams or less of saturated fat per serving.

Fat-free—less than 0.5 grams of fat per serving, providing that it has no added fat or oil.

Low-fat—3 grams or less of fat per serving and per 100 grams.

Low saturated fat—1 gram or less of saturated fatty acids per serving and not more than 15 percent of calories from saturated fatty acids.

Reduced-fat—no more than half the fat of an identified comparison; the reduction must exceed 3 grams of fat per serving.

(Percent) Fat-free—may only describe foods that meet the FDA definition of low-fat.

Light or lite—at least a one-third reduction in calories (a minimum reduction of 40 calories and more than 3 grams of fat; if fat contributes 50 percent or more of calories, fat must be reduced by 50 percent compared with reference food).

Fresh—raw food that has not been frozen, processed, or otherwise preserved.

MONITORING YOUR BODY FAT

Until recently, most health professionals gauged healthy body weight by having patients step on a scale. A person was judged to be too fat if the number on the scale was higher than the range listed in standard height/weight tables. Now, experts are emphasizing a healthy body composition—the percentage of lean tissue versus fat tissue.

Although there are a myriad of techniques available to estimate body fat percentage, one new piece of equipment is the bioelectric impedance (BEI) monitor. Used in hospitals, sports medicine clinics, and health clubs, the BEI monitoring device offers a noninvasive, accurate, and relatively inexpensive way to estimate body fat percentage.

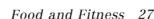

To use the monitor, technicians attach wires with small coin-sized patches to the hand and foot and pass a tiny surge of electric current through the body. The electric current meets resistance when it goes through water, and because water is usually found in fat-free tissue, the amount of resistance reflects how much fat-free lean tissue is present. The percentage of body fat can then be calculated using the resistance quotient and the client's height and weight. The technique is simple, requires little time, and causes no discomfort.

As long as fluid levels of the body are normal, BEI figures are comparable in accuracy to underwater weighing, a costly technique that scientists sometimes use to assess body fat levels. Of course, there are a few limitations to accuracy. People with abnormal fluid retention or dehydration cannot be accurately tested. Also, the height/weight tables used by BEI monitors don't apply to some groups of people such as athletes or the elderly who have lean and fat body masses that may be dramatically different from the average person.

Some health clubs offer another innovative measuring method using infrared waves as an alternative to BEI monitoring. Manufacturers of the infrared tools (there is a hand-held model and a larger clinic-size machine) contend that they are as accurate as underwater weighing. However, the hand-held model is used only on the bicep area and does not measure body fat levels around the abdomen or hips.

At present, no single device is the perfect tool for measuring body fat, and results should be interpreted appropriately depending on age, sex, and other factors that affect body water content.

READ THEM AND WALK

One of the new trends among walkers and joggers is audiocassette books on tape. Rather than getting bored with the same old scenery on a walking route, many fitness buffs are letting their minds escape to another dimension as they exercise.

The latest best-selling novels, self-help books, and literary classics, as well as several current magazines, are available on audiotape. Executives in the publishing industry say that the most popular audiocassette books are the abridged, or shortened, versions of popular books. Because they are condensed onto two cassette tapes and last only about three hours, you can finish a book in three to six exercise sessions. Mail-order companies and audiocassette shops also sell and rent unabridged books to walkers. An exercise program with *War and Peace*, which covers 40 tapes, is guaranteed to give your heart a workout and burn some body fat.

Walking with audiocassette book tapes can provide pleasure for the soul and a push for the body. With well-known actors and actresses, or the authors themselves, reading with mood-setting background music and dramatic sound effects, listening to some taped books can be almost like going to the theater. The characters come alive; the suspense heightens; the action intensifies. (Be careful not to get so caught up in the action that you fail to pay attention to traffic, pedestrians, and road hazards.) Once swept up in the drama of an historical epic or the intrigue of a murder mystery, walkers may be more motivated to return to the next scheduled workout, or to walk for longer periods of time. What better reason to do another mile than to find out if the butler did it?

Healthy American Meals

Entertain simply yet elegantly with
Mustard-Crusted Rack of Lamb and
Rosemary Potatoes. Tender spears of
asparagus and crusty dinner rolls are
choice accompaniments for the meal.
(Menu begins on page 87.)

Each menu has been carefully developed for your enjoyment, and each meets the *Cooking Light* guidelines for healthy eating. At least 50 percent of the total menu calories are derived from carbohydrate, about 20 percent from protein, and less than 30 percent are contributed by fat. Each menu also has less than 10 percent of the calories coming from saturated fat. Use this 50-20-30 ratio as a guide when planning your own menus.

The four menu chapters reflect the growing interest in decreasing fat in the diet along with a desire for freshness and good flavor. Regional favorites and international dishes add to the variety. Whether you need ideas for an elegant brunch, a quick-to-prepare lunch, or a hearty meal for a crowd, look to these sections for your menu needs.

Breakfast and Brunch. Say hello to morning with recipes that will delight your family and friends. For a family-style breakfast, try A Passion for Pancakes or A Feast on the Fourth. Offer the gift of good food by surprising a friend with Gift Basket Breakfast or entertaining with the hearty New Neighbor Brunch or the elegant Mother's Day Brunch.

Quick and Easy. Cooking healthy meals doesn't have to take a lot of time. Most of the preparation for Sewing Club Luncheon and Game Night Supper can be done ahead. For a cozy dinner for two, try the English Pub Supper. Or present a holiday menu with a twist. Christmas in July features traditional foods of the season prepared with summertime ease.

Microwave It Light. Use your microwave oven to make the most of the flavors, textures, and colors of regional foods. For a taste of the islands, try the Caribbean Dinner with its tropical fruits and vegetables. Capture the robust flavors of tomatoes, garlic, and oregano with Italian Dinner. Create a special mood and feature fresh herbs, tender vegetables, and juicy fruits with An Elegant French Dinner.

That's Entertaining. Show your flair for hospitality by entertaining anywhere from the back porch to the picnic grounds. Let guests enjoy the Come for Cards menu while seated at card tables. Use the outdoors as a dining room with Music and Dinner Alfresco or An Indian Summer Supper. Or bring out your best table linens and china, and usher your guests into the dining room for a sophisticated dinner party. Whatever the location, your family and friends will enjoy being entertained with *Cooking Light* menus.

A mouth-watering stack of pancakes with an assortment of toppings is a switch from the usual breakfast fare. Serve Pineapple-Yogurt Pancakes with Pineapple Topping. Cherry Sauce offers another choice in this pancake breakfast menu. (Menu begins on page 34.)

Breakfast & Brunch

Ham Spread, Apricot-Kumquat Conserve, Cinnamon Pears, and French Vanilla Coffee Mix are creatively packed in a gift basket for an out-of-the-ordinary breakfast.

Gift Basket Breakfast

Ham Spread
Apricot-Kumquat Conserve
Commercial English Muffins
Cinnamon Pears
French Vanilla Coffee Mix

SERVES 4
TOTAL CALORIES PER SERVING: 431
(Calories from Fat: 13%)

Nothing will light up the eyes of a friend like a gift basket brimming with culinary surprises. On the next special occasion, offer a hand-crafted basket filled with everything needed for a ready-made leisurely breakfast.

Include your favorite brand of commercial English muffins to go with the Ham Spread and the Apricot-Kumquat Conserve. Menu calories include 1 English muffin, 2 tablespoons ham spread, 2 tablespoons conserve, and ¾ cup coffee per serving.

Be sure to attach the recipes for all of the food items in the basket, along with directions for storage. The ham spread, conserve, and pears should all be refrigerated.

HAM SPREAD

½ cup 1% low-fat cottage cheese
⅔ cup finely chopped lean cooked ham
3 tablespoons (¾ ounce) shredded low-fat
  Swiss cheese
1½ teaspoons minced fresh parsley
¼ teaspoon prepared horseradish
¼ teaspoon Dijon mustard
⅛ teaspoon poppy seeds

Place cottage cheese in container of an electric blender or food processor; top with cover, and process until smooth. Transfer cottage cheese to a small bowl. Stir in ham, Swiss cheese, parsley, horseradish, mustard, and poppy seeds. Cover and chill thoroughly. Yield: 1 cup (15 calories per tablespoon).

PROTEIN 2.1 FAT 0.5 (Saturated Fat 0.2) CARBOHYDRATE 0.3
FIBER 0 CHOLESTEROL 3 IRON 0.1 SODIUM 99 CALCIUM 26

APRICOT-KUMQUAT CONSERVE

¾ cup no-sugar-added apricot spread
3 kumquats, sliced and seeded
2 tablespoons finely chopped pecans
1 tablespoon golden raisins
2 teaspoons lemon juice

Combine all ingredients in a small saucepan. Cook over low heat 5 minutes or until apricot spread melts, stirring constantly. Remove from heat, and let cool to room temperature. Spoon mixture into an airtight jar; cover and chill overnight. Store in the refrigerator. Yield: 1 cup (40 calories per tablespoon).

PROTEIN 0.1 FAT 0.6 (Saturated Fat 0.1) CARBOHYDRATE 10.1
FIBER 0.2 CHOLESTEROL 0 IRON 0 SODIUM 0 CALCIUM 2

CINNAMON PEARS

3 medium-size ripe pears (about 1¼ pounds),
  peeled, cored, and sliced
½ cup water
2 tablespoons red cinnamon candies
2 teaspoons sugar
¼ teaspoon ground cinnamon

Combine all ingredients in a medium saucepan; bring to a boil. Cover, reduce heat, and simmer 10 to 15 minutes or until pears are tender, stirring occasionally. Remove from heat, and let cool. Transfer mixture to an airtight jar. Cover and chill. Serve with a slotted spoon. Yield: 2 cups (114 calories per ½-cup serving).

PROTEIN 0.4 FAT 0.4 (Saturated Fat 0) CARBOHYDRATE 29.1
FIBER 2.9 CHOLESTEROL 0 IRON 0.5 SODIUM 3 CALCIUM 16

FRENCH VANILLA COFFEE MIX

¾ cup instant nonfat dry milk powder
¾ cup instant coffee granules
½ cup sugar
1 vanilla bean, split lengthwise

Combine first 3 ingredients in container of an electric blender or food processor; top with cover, and process until powdered. Transfer mixture to an airtight container. Add vanilla bean. Cover tightly, and store at least 5 days. Remove vanilla bean before using.
To serve, spoon 1 tablespoon coffee mixture into a mug. Add ¾ cup hot water, and stir well. Yield: 32 servings (25 calories per serving).

PROTEIN 1.2 FAT 0.0 (Saturated Fat 0) CARBOHYDRATE 4.6
FIBER 0 CHOLESTEROL 1 IRON 0.1 SODIUM 16 CALCIUM 37

A Passion for Pancakes

Maple-Pumpkin Pancakes
Pineapple-Yogurt Pancakes
Black Forest Pancakes
Skim Milk
Orange Juice

Pancakes, hotcakes, flapjacks, or silver dollars—whatever you call them, they are a great way to start the day.

Select any one of these pancake recipes when you need a change-of-pace breakfast for your family. Or prepare all three recipes and invite your friends to stop by for a pancake party.

Be adventurous and mix and match pancakes and toppings. There's a flavor to suit everyone's taste. Round out the meal with glasses of skim milk and fresh orange juice.

Try Maple-Pumpkin Pancakes for an eye-opening breakfast.

MAPLE-PUMPKIN PANCAKES

¾ cup quick-cooking oats, uncooked
1½ cups skim milk
2 eggs, lightly beaten
½ cup cooked, mashed pumpkin
3 tablespoons reduced-calorie maple syrup
1 tablespoon vegetable oil
1¼ cups all-purpose flour
2 teaspoons baking powder
½ teaspoon salt
½ teaspoon pumpkin pie spice
½ teaspoon ground cinnamon
Vegetable cooking spray
Maple Topping

Combine oats and milk in a medium bowl; let stand 5 minutes. Add eggs, pumpkin, maple syrup, and oil to oat mixture, stirring well.

Combine flour and next 4 ingredients in a large bowl; make a well in center of mixture. Add oat mixture to dry ingredients, stirring just until dry ingredients are moistened.

For each pancake, pour ¼ cup batter onto a hot griddle or skillet coated with cooking spray. Turn pancakes when tops are covered with bubbles and edges look cooked. Top each pancake with 1 tablespoon Maple Topping. Yield: 16 servings (86 calories per serving).

Maple Topping

¾ cup vanilla nonfat frozen yogurt, softened
¼ cup reduced-calorie maple syrup
⅛ teaspoon ground cinnamon

Combine all ingredients in a small bowl; stir well. Cover and chill. Yield: 1 cup.

PROTEIN 3.4 FAT 2.0 (Saturated Fat 0.4) CARBOHYDRATE 13.9
FIBER 0.8 CHOLESTEROL 27 IRON 0.8 SODIUM 139 CALCIUM 74

PINEAPPLE-YOGURT PANCAKES

1½ cups all-purpose flour
1½ teaspoons baking powder
½ teaspoon baking soda
¼ cup unprocessed oat bran
1 teaspoon sugar
½ teaspoon salt
¾ cup unsweetened pineapple juice
¾ cup pineapple low-fat yogurt
1 egg, lightly beaten
Vegetable cooking spray
Pineapple Topping

Combine first 6 ingredients; make a well in center. Combine juice, yogurt, and egg; add to dry ingredients, stirring just until dry ingredients are moistened.

For each pancake, pour ¼ cup batter onto a hot griddle or skillet coated with cooking spray. Turn pancakes when tops are covered with bubbles and edges look cooked. Top with Pineapple Topping. Yield: 12 servings (102 calories per serving).

Pineapple Topping

1 tablespoon cornstarch
2 tablespoons water
1 (15¼-ounce) can crushed pineapple in juice, undrained
1 tablespoon sugar
½ teaspoon grated orange rind

Combine cornstarch and water in a saucepan, stirring until smooth. Add pineapple, sugar, and orange rind; stir well. Bring to a boil, stirring constantly; cook until mixture is thickened. Yield: 1¾ cups.

PROTEIN 3.1 FAT 0.9 (Saturated Fat 0.3) CARBOHYDRATE 20.4
FIBER 0.8 CHOLESTEROL 18 IRON 0.9 SODIUM 183 CALCIUM 61

BLACK FOREST PANCAKES

1 cup all-purpose flour
1½ teaspoons baking powder
½ teaspoon baking soda
3 tablespoons sugar
2 tablespoons unsweetened cocoa
¼ teaspoon salt
1 cup 1% low-fat chocolate milk
1 egg, lightly beaten
1½ tablespoons margarine, melted
Vegetable cooking spray
Cherry Sauce

Combine first 6 ingredients; make a well in center of mixture. Combine chocolate milk, egg, and margarine; add to dry ingredients, stirring just until dry ingredients are moistened.

For each pancake, pour 2 tablespoons batter onto a hot griddle or skillet coated with cooking spray. Turn pancakes when tops are covered with bubbles and edges look cooked. Top with Cherry Sauce. Yield: 16 serving (75 calories per serving).

Cherry Sauce

2 tablespoons sugar
2 teaspoons cornstarch
¼ cup water
¼ teaspoon lemon juice
½ (16-ounce) package frozen unsweetened cherries, thawed

Combine sugar, cornstarch, and water in a saucepan, stirring until smooth. Add lemon juice and cherries; stir well. Cook over medium heat, stirring constantly, until thickened and bubbly. Yield: 1 cup.

PROTEIN 1.9 FAT 1.8 (Saturated Fat 0.5) CARBOHYDRATE 12.9
FIBER 0.2 CHOLESTEROL 14 IRON 0.6 SODIUM 117 CALCIUM 47

A Feast on the Fourth

Red, White, and Blue
French Toast
Star-Spangled Bacon
Strawberry Fruitsicles
Iced Hazelnut Coffee

SERVES 10
TOTAL CALORIES PER SERVING: 304
(Calories from Fat: 9%)

Before your neighborhood Fourth of July parade begins, invite another family or two over for a patriotic breakfast.

Keep menu preparation simple on a busy morning. Spoon the red and blue fruit mixture over sweet slices of French toast. Let the children help cut Canadian bacon into stars before heating it in a tangy sauce.

Good food, good friends, and a day that's fun from breakfast to fireworks make the Fourth of July one of the best holidays of the year.

Celebrate your independence with Red, White, and Blue French Toast along with Star-Spangled Bacon and Iced Hazelnut Coffee.

RED, WHITE, AND BLUE FRENCH TOAST

1 cup fresh raspberries
1 cup coarsely chopped fresh red plums
1 cup fresh blueberries
2 tablespoons sugar
1½ cups frozen egg substitute, thawed
1 cup skim milk
¼ cup plus 2 tablespoons sifted powdered sugar, divided
1¼ teaspoons ground cinnamon
1¼ teaspoons vanilla extract
10 (1-ounce) slices whole wheat bread
Vegetable cooking spray

Combine first 4 ingredients in a medium bowl; toss gently. Cover and chill thoroughly.

Combine egg substitute, milk, ¼ cup powdered sugar, cinnamon, and vanilla in a shallow bowl, beating well. Dip each slice of bread, 1 at a time, in egg mixture, coating well.

Coat a large nonstick skillet with cooking spray; place over medium heat until hot.

Arrange 2 to 4 bread slices in skillet, and cook 4 to 5 minutes on each side or until browned. Repeat procedure with remaining bread slices. Sprinkle remaining 2 tablespoons powdered sugar evenly over toast; top evenly with fruit mixture. Yield: 10 servings (140 calories per serving).

PROTEIN 7.4   FAT 1.1   (Saturated Fat 0.2)   CARBOHYDRATE 26.4
FIBER 2.8   CHOLESTEROL 1   IRON 1.4   SODIUM 199   CALCIUM 74

STAR-SPANGLED BACON

20 (½-ounce) slices Canadian bacon
¼ cup unsweetened apple juice
2 tablespoons water
2 tablespoons honey
1½ tablespoons vinegar
1½ teaspoons dry mustard

Cut bacon slices into stars with a 3-inch star-shaped cookie cutter. Reserve bacon trimmings for other uses. Place bacon in a 13- x 9- x 2-inch baking dish.

Combine apple juice, water, honey, vinegar, and mustard in a small bowl, stirring well; pour over bacon. Cover and bake at 350° for 15 minutes or until thoroughly heated. Transfer bacon to a serving platter using a slotted spoon. Yield: 10 servings (38 calories per serving).

PROTEIN 3.8 FAT 1.3 (Saturated Fat 0.4) CARBOHYDRATE 2.5
FIBER 0 CHOLESTEROL 9 IRON 0.1 SODIUM 260 CALCIUM 2

STRAWBERRY FRUITSICLES

3½ cups sliced fresh strawberries
1 cup unsweetened orange juice
1 cup strawberry low-fat yogurt
3 tablespoons honey
10 (5-ounce) paper cups
10 wooden sticks

Combine strawberries, orange juice, yogurt, and honey in container of an electric blender; top with cover, and process until smooth. Pour mixture evenly into paper cups. Cover tops of cups with aluminum foil, and insert a stick through foil into center of each cup. Freeze until firm.

To serve, remove foil, and peel paper cup away from fruitsicle. Yield: 10 fruitsicles (70 calories each).

PROTEIN 1.4 FAT 0.5 (Saturated Fat 0.2) CARBOHYDRATE 16.2
FIBER 1.6 CHOLESTEROL 1 IRON 0.3 SODIUM 13 CALCIUM 42

ICED HAZELNUT COFFEE

6 cups strong brewed coffee
7 cups strong brewed hazelnut-flavored coffee, chilled
3 cups skim milk
¼ cup plus 1 tablespoon sugar

Pour 6 cups brewed coffee into ice cube trays; freeze until firm.

Combine hazelnut-flavored coffee, milk, and sugar; stir until sugar dissolves. Pour over coffee ice cubes, and serve immediately. Yield: 2½ quarts (56 calories per 1-cup serving).

PROTEIN 2.8 FAT 0.1 (Saturated Fat 0.1) CARBOHYDRATE 11.0
FIBER 0 CHOLESTEROL 1 IRON 1.3 SODIUM 45 CALCIUM 97

 FEEDING CHILDREN LIKE CHILDREN Limiting fat and calories may be safe diet advice for adults, but it's not always appropriate for growing children, especially those under age two. Youngsters have high calorie needs, particularly during their first few years. Moreover, their stomach capacity is small. These are good reasons why children need calorie-dense foods, including foods that contain some fat. All children need some fat and cholesterol, particularly for normal development of the brain and nervous system.

When considering fiber, sugar, and salt, the watchword for children is moderation. Encourage children to eat fresh fruits, vegetables, and grains. These foods supply a healthy dose of fiber, making it unnecessary to dish up foods extra high in fiber.

When it comes to sugar, the only caution with children is to not let sugary indulgences crowd out more nutritious foods.

In essence, this advice in some ways mimics the advice for adults. It's just that limits for children are a bit more lenient. Research shows that parents who are too strict about fat and calories early in their child's life run the risk of stunting the child's growth. Indeed, there's time enough in later childhood years to fine-tune eating habits to make them more in line with adult guidelines. First, let children eat to grow.

New Neighbor Brunch

Turkey Sausage Casserole
Thyme-Scented Tomatoes
Miniature Blueberry
Muffins
Orange Juice
Coffee Nog à la Mode

SERVES 6
TOTAL CALORIES: 524
(Calories from Fat: 17%)

Make new friends immediately by honoring a new neighbor with a casual brunch.

After your guests have enjoyed the hearty sausage casserole, warm blueberry muffins, and freshly-squeezed orange juice (2 muffins and ½ cup juice per person), clear the table and settle back for lively conversation and mugs of Coffee Nog à la Mode. What could make a neighbor feel more welcome?

Turkey Sausage Casserole, Thyme-Scented Tomatoes, Miniature Blueberry Muffins, and Coffee Nog à la Mode make an ideal brunch menu for welcoming a neighbor.

TURKEY SAUSAGE CASSEROLE

Vegetable cooking spray
½ pound ground turkey sausage
3 tablespoons chopped green onions
3 cups cubed French bread
1 cup (4 ounces) shredded 40% less-fat mild
    Cheddar cheese
1⅓ cups skim milk
¾ cup frozen egg substitute, thawed
1 teaspoon prepared mustard
¼ teaspoon pepper

Coat a large nonstick skillet with cooking spray; place over medium-high heat until hot. Add sausage and green onions; cook over medium heat until meat is browned, stirring to crumble. Drain and pat dry with paper towels. Set aside.

Place bread cubes in an 8-inch square baking dish coated with cooking spray. Layer sausage mixture and cheese over bread. Combine milk and remaining ingredients; stir well. Pour over sausage and cheese. Cover and refrigerate at least 8 hours.

Bake, covered, at 350° for 30 minutes. Uncover and bake an additional 15 to 20 minutes or until set. Let stand 5 minutes before serving. Yield: 6 servings (201 calories per serving).

PROTEIN 16   FAT 7.0   (Saturated Fat 3.0)   CARBOHYDRATE 19.4
FIBER 0.6   CHOLESTEROL 33   IRON 1.7   SODIUM 494   CALCIUM 223

THYME-SCENTED TOMATOES

¾ cup bite-size shredded whole wheat cereal
    biscuits, finely crushed
1½ tablespoons minced fresh parsley
2½ teaspoons minced fresh thyme
¼ teaspoon garlic powder
1 tablespoon commercial oil-free Italian dressing
3 medium tomatoes (about 1½ pounds)

Combine first 4 ingredients in a small bowl; add Italian dressing, and stir well. Set aside.

Cut tomatoes in half crosswise. Place tomato halves, cut-side up, on rack of a broiler pan. Broil 5½ inches from heat 6 minutes.

Sprinkle tomato halves evenly with cereal mixture; broil 1 to 2 minutes or until cereal mixture is lightly browned. Transfer tomatoes to a serving platter. Yield: 6 servings (48 calories per serving).

PROTEIN 1.7 FAT 0.5 (Saturated Fat 0.1) CARBOHYDRATE 10.7
FIBER 2.0 CHOLESTEROL 0 IRON 0.8 SODIUM 37 CALCIUM 9

MINIATURE BLUEBERRY MUFFINS

1 cup all-purpose flour
¼ cup sugar
¾ teaspoon baking powder
⅓ cup skim milk
1 tablespoon vegetable oil
¼ teaspoon grated lemon rind
¼ teaspoon vanilla extract
1 egg, lightly beaten
¾ cup fresh blueberries
Vegetable cooking spray
1 tablespoon sugar

Combine flour, ¼ cup sugar, and baking powder in a medium bowl; make a well in center of mixture.

Combine milk, oil, lemon rind, vanilla, and egg in a small bowl; stir well. Add to dry ingredients, stirring just until dry ingredients are moistened. Fold in fresh blueberries.

Spoon batter into miniature (1¾-inch) muffin pans coated with vegetable cooking spray, filling each three-fourths full.

Sprinkle evenly with 1 tablespoon sugar. Bake at 375° for 18 to 20 minutes or until muffins are golden. Remove from pans immediately. Yield: 21 muffins (46 calories each).

PROTEIN 1.0 FAT 1.1 (Saturated Fat 0.2) CARBOHYDRATE 8.1
FIBER 0.4 CHOLESTEROL 10 IRON 0.3 SODIUM 16 CALCIUM 14

COFFEE NOG À LA MODE

1 cup strong brewed coffee
½ cup frozen egg substitute, thawed
¼ cup sugar
3 cups skim milk
1½ cups vanilla nonfat frozen yogurt
¼ teaspoon ground nutmeg

Combine coffee, egg substitute, and sugar in a large saucepan; stir well. Gradually add milk, stirring well.

Cook over low heat until thoroughly heated, stirring constantly (do not boil). Pour ¾ cup coffee mixture into each of 6 mugs. Top each serving with ¼ cup frozen yogurt; sprinkle evenly with ground nutmeg. Serve immediately. Yield: 6 servings (127 calories per serving).

PROTEIN 7.9 FAT 0.2 (Saturated Fat 0.2) CARBOHYDRATE 23.8
FIBER 0 CHOLESTEROL 2 IRON 0.6 SODIUM 125 CALCIUM 223

Chicken-Vegetable Strudel and Marinated Asparagus (page 42) set the stage for a brunch to honor Mother.

Mother's Day Brunch

**Chilled Cantaloupe Soup
Chicken-Vegetable Strudel
Marinated Asparagus
Creamy White Chocolate Dessert
Iced Tea**

SERVES 6
TOTAL CALORIES PER SERVING: 557
(Calories from Fat: 25%)

Busy lives have diminished many family traditions, but the second Sunday in May is still held in high esteem. Mother's Day is a ritual which honors a most special family member, and this beautiful springtime menu is a perfect match for the occasion. It is elegant in presentation, but simple in preparation.

Begin with bowls of Chilled Cantaloupe Soup. Vanilla yogurt gives the soup its creamy texture while keeping the fat content low. Flaky sheets of phyllo are rolled around a filling of chicken and vegetables for the entrée, Chicken-Vegetable Strudel.

Asparagus is the vegetable that heralds the warm weather. Marinated Asparagus, featuring a tangy vinaigrette and crumbled blue cheese, is an ideal accompaniment for the chicken strudel.

Smooth as silk, Creamy White Chocolate Dessert is a perfect ending for a memorable meal. Spoon the dessert into heart-shaped molds for a special touch of love.

CHILLED CANTALOUPE SOUP

6 cups cubed cantaloupe (about 1 large)
½ cup unsweetened orange juice
1 (8-ounce) carton vanilla low-fat yogurt
3 tablespoons lemon juice
2 teaspoons powdered sugar
Edible flowers (optional)

Place half of cantaloupe and orange juice in container of an electric blender or food processor; top with cover, and process until smooth. Transfer mixture to a medium bowl. Repeat procedure with remaining cantaloupe and orange juice.

Combine yogurt, lemon juice, and powdered sugar; add to cantaloupe mixture, and stir well. Cover and chill thoroughly. To serve, ladle soup into individual bowls. Garnish with edible flowers, if desired. Yield: 1½ quarts (107 calories per 1-cup serving).

PROTEIN 3.5   FAT 1.0   (Saturated Fat 0.6)   CARBOHYDRATE 23.4
FIBER 2.0   CHOLESTEROL 2   IRON 0.4   SODIUM 41   CALCIUM 86

CHICKEN-VEGETABLE STRUDEL

½ cup diced carrot
½ cup diced sweet red pepper
¼ cup unsweetened orange juice
Butter-flavored vegetable cooking spray
2 cups chopped fresh mushrooms
¼ cup chopped green onions
2 cups shredded cooked chicken breast (skinned before cooking and cooked without salt)
1 tablespoon Dijon mustard
½ teaspoon dried whole basil
¼ teaspoon grated orange rind
¼ teaspoon salt
¼ teaspoon pepper
6 sheets commercial frozen phyllo pastry, thawed
1 tablespoon fine, dry breadcrumbs
Fresh basil sprigs (optional)

Combine carrot, sweet red pepper, and orange juice in a small saucepan. Bring to a boil; cover and cook 5 to 7 minutes or until crisp-tender. Drain well. Place vegetables in a medium bowl, and set aside.

Coat a large nonstick skillet with cooking spray; place over medium-high heat until hot. Add mushrooms and green onions; sauté until tender. Add mushroom mixture, shredded chicken, mustard, dried basil, orange rind, salt, and pepper to vegetable mixture; stir well to combine.

Place 1 sheet phyllo pastry on a damp towel (keep remaining phyllo covered). Lightly coat phyllo with vegetable cooking spray. Layer remaining 5 sheets phyllo on first sheet, lightly coating each sheet with cooking spray.

Spoon chicken mixture lengthwise down half of phyllo stack, leaving a ½-inch margin. Roll up phyllo, jellyroll fashion, starting with long side containing chicken mixture. Tuck ends under; place diagonally, seam side down, on a baking sheet coated with cooking spray. Lightly coat top of pastry with cooking spray, and sprinkle with breadcrumbs. Make 12 (¼-inch-deep) diagonal slits across top of pastry, using a sharp knife. Bake at 375° for 20 minutes or until golden. Let stand 5 minutes before serving. Transfer to a serving platter, and slice. Garnish with fresh basil sprigs, if desired. Yield: 6 servings (186 calories per serving).

PROTEIN 16.8   FAT 4.3   (Saturated Fat 1.0)   CARBOHYDRATE 19.5
FIBER 1.0   CHOLESTEROL 42   IRON 1.7   SODIUM 227   CALCIUM 20

MARINATED ASPARAGUS

1½ pounds fresh asparagus
3 tablespoons white wine vinegar
2 tablespoons water
2 tablespoons lemon juice
1 tablespoon vegetable oil
¾ teaspoon dry mustard
¾ teaspoon grated lemon rind
⅛ teaspoon pepper
1 (2-ounce) jar diced pimiento,
  drained
3 tablespoons crumbled blue cheese

Snap off tough ends of asparagus. Remove scales with a knife or vegetable peeler, if desired. Arrange asparagus in a vegetable steamer over boiling water. Cover and steam 4 to 5 minutes or until crisp-tender. Place asparagus in a shallow dish.

Combine white wine vinegar, water, lemon juice, vegetable oil, dry mustard, lemon rind, pepper, and diced pimiento in a jar. Cover tightly, and shake mixture vigorously.

Pour vinegar mixture over asparagus; cover and chill 1 hour. Just before serving, sprinkle asparagus evenly with crumbled blue cheese. Yield: 6 servings (58 calories per serving).

PROTEIN 3.5 FAT 3.9 (Saturated Fat 1.3) CARBOHYDRATE 3.8
FIBER 1.6 CHOLESTEROL 4 IRON 0.7 SODIUM 69 CALCIUM 43

CREAMY WHITE CHOCOLATE DESSERT

¾ cup evaporated skimmed milk
½ cup sugar
3 ounces white chocolate, grated
2 teaspoons unflavored gelatin
¼ cup cold water
2 teaspoons vanilla extract
⅔ cup plain nonfat yogurt
¼ cup low-fat sour cream
Vegetable cooking spray
Fresh whole strawberries (optional)

Combine first 3 ingredients in a saucepan. Cook over medium heat, stirring constantly with a wire whisk, until chocolate melts. Transfer to a bowl; cool.

Sprinkle gelatin over cold water in a saucepan; let stand 1 minute. Cook over low heat, stirring until gelatin dissolves. Add gelatin mixture and vanilla to white chocolate mixture; stir well. Chill 30 minutes or until mixture reaches the consistency of unbeaten egg white, stirring occasionally. Fold in yogurt and sour cream. Spoon into 6 (½-cup) molds coated with cooking spray. Cover and chill at least 8 hours. Unmold; garnish with fresh strawberries, if desired. Yield: 6 servings (205 calories per serving).

PROTEIN 6.0 FAT 6.3 (Saturated Fat 3.8) CARBOHYDRATE 31.1
FIBER 0.1 CHOLESTEROL 6 IRON 0.1 SODIUM 69 CALCIUM 153

Peppered Raspberry Lamb Chops, Blue Cheese Potatoes, Tarragon Brussels Sprouts, and Beer Bread reflect the simple heartiness of English fare. (Menu begins on page 52.)

Quick & Easy

Take a break from stitching and enjoy Spicy Tuna-Pasta Toss, Zucchini Corn Muffins, and Sparkling Lemon-Mint Tea.

Sewing Club Luncheon

Spicy Tuna-Pasta Toss
Zucchini Corn Muffins
Gingered Peach Sundaes
Sparkling Lemon-Mint Tea

SERVES 6
TOTAL CALORIES PER SERVING: 599
(Calories from Fat: 26%)

Invite the ladies to sew away the morning without having to worry about lunch. This noontime meal can be prepared ahead and served on a quilt tablecloth when the sewing needles are returned to the pincushions.

Toss tri-colored pasta, tuna, and salsa together for a main-dish salad with punch. Add Zucchini Corn Muffins and glasses of Sparkling Lemon-Mint Tea, and everyone will have the energy to continue sewing for the rest of the afternoon.

Serve delicious Gingered Peach Sundaes in your prettiest dessert dishes for a grand finale before everyone goes home with their newly stitched creations.

SPICY TUNA-PASTA TOSS

6 ounces tri-colored corkscrew pasta, uncooked
2 (6⅛-ounce) cans chunk white tuna in spring
  water, drained
½ cup sweet yellow pepper strips
½ cup quartered cherry tomatoes
¼ cup diced celery
¾ cup no-salt-added salsa
½ cup reduced-calorie mayonnaise
½ teaspoon ground red pepper
Curly leaf lettuce leaves (optional)
2 tablespoons sliced green onions

Cook pasta according to package directions, omitting salt and fat. Drain; rinse under cold water, and drain. Combine pasta, tuna, and next 3 ingredients.
Combine salsa, mayonnaise, and red pepper. Add to pasta mixture; toss. Cover and chill. Serve in a lettuce-lined bowl, if desired; sprinkle with green onions. Yield: 6 servings (236 calories per 1-cup serving).

PROTEIN 16.9 FAT 7.2 (Saturated Fat 0.7) CARBOHYDRATE 24.8
FIBER 0.9 CHOLESTEROL 26 IRON 0.7 SODIUM 341 CALCIUM 9

ZUCCHINI CORN MUFFINS

¾ cup all-purpose flour
¼ cup yellow cornmeal
¾ teaspoon baking powder
¼ teaspoon baking soda
⅛ teaspoon salt
⅛ teaspoon ground cumin
1 cup shredded zucchini
2 tablespoons vegetable oil
2 tablespoons honey
1 egg white, lightly beaten
1 teaspoon skim milk
Vegetable cooking spray

Combine first 6 ingredients; stir. Add zucchini to flour mixture; make a well in center of mixture. Combine oil, honey, egg white, and milk; add to dry ingredients, stirring just until dry ingredients are moistened. Spoon batter into a muffin pan coated with cooking spray,

filling two-thirds full. Bake at 375° for 20 minutes or until golden. Yield: 6 muffins (148 calories each).

PROTEIN 3.0 FAT 5.1 (Saturated Fat 0.9) CARBOHYDRATE 23.1
FIBER 0.8 CHOLESTEROL 0 IRON 1.1 SODIUM 129 CALCIUM 39

GINGERED PEACH SUNDAES

3 medium-size fresh peaches, peeled and sliced
2 tablespoons chopped almonds
1 tablespoon brown sugar
1 tablespoon minced crystallized ginger
1 tablespoon lemon juice
1 tablespoon reduced-calorie margarine, melted
3 cups vanilla ice milk

Combine first 6 ingredients in a large nonstick skillet. Cook over medium heat 8 to 10 minutes or until peaches are tender, stirring frequently. Scoop ½ cup ice milk into each of 6 dessert dishes. Top each with ¼ cup peach mixture. Serve immediately. Yield: 6 servings (156 calories per serving).

PROTEIN 3.5 FAT 5.3 (Saturated Fat 2.0) CARBOHYDRATE 25.4
FIBER 1.3 CHOLESTEROL 9 IRON 0.7 SODIUM 73 CALCIUM 103

SPARKLING LEMON-MINT TEA

3 mint-flavored tea bags
3 cups boiling water
1 (6-ounce) can frozen lemonade concentrate,
  thawed and undiluted
2¼ teaspoons sugar
2½ cups sparkling mineral water, chilled
Fresh mint (optional)

Combine tea bags and water; cover and steep 20 minutes. Discard tea bags. Add lemonade concentrate and sugar; stir well. Cover and chill. Stir in mineral water; serve over ice. Garnish with mint, if desired. Yield: 1½ quarts (59 calories per 1-cup serving).

PROTEIN 0.1 FAT 0.1 (Saturated Fat 0) CARBOHYDRATE 15.3
FIBER 0.1 CHOLESTEROL 0 IRON 0.2 SODIUM 25 CALCIUM 2

Game Night Supper

Ham and Swiss Pinwheels
Fruit Kabobs with
Creamy Strawberry Dip
Kahlúa Cookies
Strawberry Tea

SERVES 8
TOTAL CALORIES PER SERVING: 592
(Calories from Fat: 24%)

Invite the crowd over to play board games, and use our meal-planning strategy. Stay ahead of the game by making the creamy strawberry dip, fruit kabobs, Kahlúa Cookies, and Strawberry Tea early in the day. Let the Ham and Swiss Pinwheels rise while the guests arrive, and pop them into the oven after the first roll of the dice.

Players won't even have to leave the excitement of the game to enjoy this winner's circle menu. Serve the hand-held pinwheels, kabobs, and cookies right at the game table. Menu calories include 2 pinwheels and 3 cookies per person.

Be a winner by serving Ham and Swiss Pinwheels and Fruit Kabobs with Creamy Strawberry Dip.

HAM AND SWISS PINWHEELS

2 teaspoons all-purpose flour
1 (1-pound) loaf frozen white bread dough, thawed
3 tablespoons Dijon mustard
1 tablespoon honey
2 cups (8 ounces) shredded reduced-fat Swiss cheese
8 (1-ounce) slices lean cooked turkey ham
2 tablespoons chopped pepperoncini, drained
Vegetable cooking spray

Sprinkle flour evenly over work surface. Turn dough out onto floured surface, and roll to a 12-inch square.

Combine mustard and honey in a small bowl; brush mixture over dough. Sprinkle evenly with cheese; top with ham slices. Sprinkle with pepperoncini.

Roll up dough, jellyroll fashion; pinch seam to seal (do not seal ends). Cut roll into 16 slices. Place slices, cut side down, on a baking sheet coated with cooking spray. Cover and let rise in a warm place (85°), free from drafts, 45 minutes. Bake at 350° for 15 to 18 minutes or until golden. Serve immediately. Yield: 16 pinwheels (135 calories each).

PROTEIN 9.8 FAT 4.3 (Saturated Fat 1.9) CARBOHYDRATE 13.9
FIBER 0.7 CHOLESTEROL 9 IRON 0.9 SODIUM 424 CALCIUM 184

FRUIT KABOBS WITH CREAMY STRAWBERRY DIP

1 (8-ounce) carton vanilla low-fat yogurt
½ cup light process cream cheese product, softened
2 tablespoons no-sugar-added strawberry spread
1 teaspoon grated lemon rind
1 medium pear, cored and cut into 8 wedges
1 firm, ripe nectarine, cut into 8 wedges
8 grapefruit sections
8 (½-inch-thick) banana slices (about 1 small)
8 seedless green grapes
1 kiwifruit, peeled and cut into 8 wedges
8 large fresh strawberries
1 tablespoon lemon juice

Spoon yogurt onto several layers of heavy-duty paper towels; spread to ½-inch thickness. Cover with additional paper towels; let stand 5 minutes. Scrape yogurt from paper towels, using a rubber spatula.

Beat cream cheese at medium speed of an electric mixer until creamy. Add yogurt, strawberry spread, and lemon rind; beat well. Cover; chill at least 2 hours.

Thread 1 piece of each fruit onto 8 (6-inch) skewers; brush with lemon juice. Yield: 8 servings (103 calories per kabob and 2 tablespoons dip).

PROTEIN 2.8 FAT 2.9 (Saturated Fat 1.6) CARBOHYDRATE 18.1
FIBER 2.1 CHOLESTEROL 9 IRON 0.3 SODIUM 89 CALCIUM 55

KAHLÚA COOKIES

¼ cup margarine, softened
½ cup sugar
3 tablespoons Kahlúa or other coffee-flavored liqueur
1 egg
2 cups all-purpose flour
1½ tablespoons instant coffee granules
½ teaspoon ground cinnamon
¼ teaspoon salt
2 tablespoons powdered sugar
½ teaspoon unsweetened cocoa
Vegetable cooking spray

Cream margarine in a medium bowl; gradually add ½ cup sugar, beating at medium speed of an electric mixer until light and fluffy. Add liqueur and egg, beating well.

Combine flour and next 3 ingredients, stirring well. Gradually add flour mixture to creamed mixture, beating at low speed of an electric mixer until well blended. Cover and chill dough 15 minutes.

Combine powdered sugar and cocoa. Shape dough into 1-inch balls; roll each ball in sugar mixture. Place on cookie sheets coated with cooking spray. Flatten each with a fork in a crisscross pattern. Bake at 400° for 9 minutes. Cool on wire racks. Store in an airtight container. Yield: 40 cookies (47 calories each).

PROTEIN 0.8 FAT 1.4 (Saturated Fat 0.3) CARBOHYDRATE 7.8
FIBER 0.2 CHOLESTEROL 5 IRON 0.3 SODIUM 30 CALCIUM 3

STRAWBERRY TEA

8 strawberry-flavored tea bags
6½ cups boiling water
½ cup sugar
1½ tablespoons lemon juice
1½ cups cranberry-strawberry drink, chilled

Combine strawberry-flavored tea bags and boiling water in a large pitcher; cover and steep 10 minutes. Remove and discard tea bags. Add sugar and lemon juice, stirring until sugar dissolves. Cover and chill thoroughly.

Stir in cranberry-strawberry drink. Serve over ice. Yield: 2 quarts (78 calories per 1-cup serving).

PROTEIN 0.0 FAT 0.0 (Saturated Fat 0) CARBOHYDRATE 20.3
FIBER 0 CHOLESTEROL 0 IRON 0.1 SODIUM 8 CALCIUM 0

Country Cooking

Skillet Beef Casserole
Spinach-Apple Salad
Strawberry Shortcake
à la Mode
Chocolate-Pecan Coffee

SERVES 6
TOTAL CALORIES PER SERVING: 530
(Calories from Fat: 22%)

Home-style cooking is updated in this hearty menu with old-time flavor. The skillet casserole is full of chunks of lean beef, golden potatoes, and garden-fresh vegetables.

A spinach salad is a quick and easy way to feature the flavor of fresh spinach. This new version of strawberry shortcake is sweet, delicious, and low in fat. Enjoy it with a warm cup of chocolate-flavored coffee.

Skillet Beef Casserole, topped with golden potato slices, is prepared completely in one skillet.

SKILLET BEEF CASSEROLE

2 (8-ounce) baking potatoes, peeled and cut into
  ⅛-inch slices
1 pound lean boneless beef sirloin steak
Vegetable cooking spray
½ cup thinly sliced carrot
1 cup thinly sliced onion
½ cup thinly sliced celery
2 cloves garlic, minced
2 tablespoons all-purpose flour
1 teaspoon coarsely ground pepper
¾ teaspoon dried whole thyme
1 (16-ounce) can no-salt-added green beans,
  drained
1 (14-ounce) can no-salt-added whole tomatoes,
  drained and chopped
1 (5½-ounce) can no-salt-added vegetable juice
  cocktail
2 teaspoons reduced-calorie margarine, melted

Cook potatoes in boiling water to cover 3 minutes or until crisp-tender. Drain and set aside.

Trim fat from steak; cut steak into 1-inch pieces. Coat a 10-inch ovenproof skillet with cooking spray; place over medium-high heat until hot. Add steak; cook, turning occasionally, until browned on all sides. Remove from pan, and set aside. Wipe drippings from skillet with a paper towel.

Coat skillet with cooking spray. Add carrot, and sauté 4 to 5 minutes, stirring frequently. Add onion, celery, and garlic; sauté until vegetables are tender. Combine flour, pepper, and thyme; stir well. Stir flour mixture into vegetable mixture; cook 1 minute, stirring constantly. Add beef, green beans, tomato, and vegetable juice cocktail. Bring to a boil; reduce heat, and simmer 5 minutes, stirring occasionally.

Remove skillet from heat; arrange potato slices over beef mixture to cover completely. Brush potato with melted margarine. Broil 5½ inches from heat 15 minutes or until golden. Yield: 6 servings (197 calories per serving).

PROTEIN 18.4 FAT 5.5 (Saturated Fat 1.9) CARBOHYDRATE 19.2
FIBER 3.3 CHOLESTEROL 43 IRON 5.1 SODIUM 77 CALCIUM 74

SPINACH-APPLE SALAD

6 cups torn fresh spinach
½ cup chopped Red Delicious apple
¼ cup golden raisins
2 tablespoons slivered almonds, toasted
¼ cup plus 1 tablespoon unsweetened apple juice
3 tablespoons cider vinegar
1 teaspoon Dijon mustard
1 teaspoon vegetable oil
¼ teaspoon garlic powder
¼ teaspoon pepper

Combine spinach, apple, raisins, and almonds in a large bowl; toss gently.

Combine apple juice and remaining ingredients in a small jar; cover tightly, and shake vigorously. Pour over spinach mixture, and toss gently. Yield: 6 servings (61 calories per 1-cup serving).

PROTEIN 1.5 FAT 2.0 (Saturated Fat 0.3) CARBOHYDRATE 10.8
FIBER 2.1 CHOLESTEROL 0 IRON 1.1 SODIUM 49 CALCIUM 40

STRAWBERRY SHORTCAKE À LA MODE

3 cups fresh strawberries, sliced
2 tablespoons sugar
1¾ cups plus 2 teaspoons all-purpose flour, divided
2 teaspoons baking powder
¼ teaspoon baking soda
¼ teaspoon salt
2 teaspoons sugar
3 tablespoons reduced-calorie margarine
½ cup plus 2 tablespoons plain nonfat yogurt
¾ cup vanilla ice milk, softened

Combine sliced strawberries and 2 tablespoons sugar in a medium bowl; stir gently. Cover and chill at least 45 minutes.

Combine 1¾ cups flour, baking powder, baking soda, salt, and 2 teaspoons sugar in a medium bowl; cut in margarine with a pastry blender until mixture resembles coarse meal. Add yogurt, stirring just until dry ingredients are moistened.

Sprinkle remaining 2 teaspoons flour evenly over work surface. Turn dough out onto floured surface and knead 4 or 5 times.

Roll dough to ⅝-inch thickness; cut dough into 6 rounds with a 3-inch biscuit cutter. Place rounds on an ungreased baking sheet. Bake at 425° for 8 to 10 minutes or until biscuits are golden. Remove from baking sheet, and let cool on a wire rack.

Cut each biscuit in half horizontally; place each bottom half on an individual dessert plate. Spoon half of strawberry mixture evenly over bottom halves of biscuits.

Place tops of biscuits on strawberries, cut side down, and top evenly with remaining strawberry mixture. Spoon 2 tablespoons ice milk over each serving, and serve immediately. Yield: 6 servings (240 calories per serving).

PROTEIN 5.9 FAT 5.3 (Saturated Fat 1.2) CARBOHYDRATE 43.0
FIBER 3.0 CHOLESTEROL 4 IRON 1.9 SODIUM 318 CALCIUM 153

CHOCOLATE-PECAN COFFEE

½ cup medium-grind pecan-flavored coffee
1 tablespoon unsweetened cocoa
½ teaspoon ground cinnamon
5 cups water
3 tablespoons chocolate-flavored syrup

Combine first 3 ingredients in basket of a drip coffee maker or electric percolator. Place water in pot. Prepare coffee according to manufacturer's instructions. Stir in chocolate syrup. Yield: 4½ cups (32 calories per ¾-cup serving).

PROTEIN 0.7 FAT 0.3 (Saturated Fat 0.1) CARBOHYDRATE 6.8
FIBER 0 CHOLESTEROL 0 IRON 1.1 SODIUM 10 CALCIUM 9

Patio Dinner

Chicken and Vegetable
Packets
Frozen Orange Cups
Spicy Grilled Bread
Oatmeal Snack Cake
Cherry Lemonade

SERVES 4
TOTAL CALORIES PER SERVING: 617
(Calories from Fat: 14%)

For many people, summer
means leisure-filled days and
simple food preparation. You
can use the grill to create a
memorable meal with little fuss.

Early in the day, prepare the
salad and the cake (menu calories include 1 slice per person).
Assemble the chicken packets
and the bread so that they will
be ready to put on the grill just
before serving time. Then, relax
and enjoy a cool glass of lemonade while the food is on the grill.

*Enjoy outdoor dining with Chicken and Vegetable Packets, Spicy
Grilled Bread, and Cherry Lemonade.*

CHICKEN AND VEGETABLE PACKETS

1 teaspoon salt-free lemon-pepper seasoning
½ teaspoon onion powder
½ teaspoon garlic powder
¼ teaspoon dried whole thyme
1 small sweet red pepper, sliced
1 medium zucchini, sliced
1 medium carrot, scraped and sliced
Vegetable cooking spray
4 (4-ounce) skinned, boned chicken breast halves
½ cup Chablis or other dry white wine

Combine first 4 ingredients in a small bowl; stir well.
Combine sweet red pepper, zucchini, and carrot
in a medium bowl. Add 1¼ teaspoons seasoning
mixture to vegetable mixture, and toss gently to coat.
Cut 4 (18- x 12-inch) pieces of heavy-duty aluminum foil; coat foil with cooking spray. Place 1 chicken
breast half on one end of each piece of foil; sprinkle
chicken evenly with remaining 1 teaspoon seasoning mixture. Spoon one-fourth of vegetable mixture
over each chicken breast half; sprinkle 2 tablespoons
wine over each. For each packet, fold end of foil over
chicken, bring edges together. Fold edges over to seal;
pleat and crimp edges of foil to make an airtight seal.
Place grill rack over medium coals. Place chicken
packets on rack, and cook 15 minutes or until packets are puffed and chicken is done. Remove packets
from grill. Cut an opening in the top of each packet,
and fold foil back. Spoon chicken and vegetables onto
individual serving plates, and top with remaining
juices. Yield: 4 servings (159 calories per serving).

PROTEIN 27.5   FAT 2.1   (Saturated Fat 0.4)   CARBOHYDRATE 6.8
FIBER 1.7   CHOLESTEROL 66   IRON 1.9   SODIUM 88   CALCIUM 36

FROZEN ORANGE CUPS

⅔ cup orange low-fat yogurt
2 ounces light process cream cheese product,
    softened
1 tablespoon sugar
1 (11-ounce) can mandarin oranges in light syrup,
    drained and chopped
Leaf lettuce leaves (optional)

Combine first 3 ingredients; beat at medium speed
of an electric mixer until smooth. Stir in oranges. Spoon
mixture evenly into 4 muffin cups lined with paper
liners. Freeze 1 hour or until firm.
Remove from muffin cups; peel away paper liners,
and place salads on individual lettuce-lined salad
plates, if desired. Yield: 4 servings (110 calories per
serving).

PROTEIN 3.0 FAT 2.8 (Saturated Fat 1.7) CARBOHYDRATE 18.4
FIBER 0.1 CHOLESTEROL 10 IRON 0.1 SODIUM 103 CALCIUM 71

SPICY GRILLED BREAD

¼ (16-ounce) loaf Italian bread
1 tablespoon nonfat mayonnaise
2 teaspoons spicy brown mustard
¼ teaspoon onion powder
2 tablespoons minced fresh parsley
1 tablespoon grated Parmesan cheese
Vegetable cooking spray

Slice bread in half lengthwise, leaving one side
attached. Open bread, butterfly fashion.
Combine mayonnaise, mustard, and onion pow-
der in a small bowl, stirring well. Spread over cut sides
of bread; sprinkle with parsley and cheese. Reassemble
loaf, and wrap in heavy-duty aluminum foil coated
with cooking spray. Place on grill rack over medium
coals; cook 10 minutes, turning after 5 minutes. Cut
bread into 4 slices. Serve warm. Yield: 4 servings (92
calories per serving).

PROTEIN 3.3 FAT 0.9 (Saturated Fat 0.2) CARBOHYDRATE 17.2
FIBER 0.9 CHOLESTEROL 1 IRON 0.8 SODIUM 272 CALCIUM 28

OATMEAL SNACK CAKE

⅓ cup raisins
3 tablespoons hot water
1½ cups all-purpose flour
½ cup plus 2 tablespoons sugar
3 tablespoons regular oats, uncooked
1 teaspoon baking soda
½ teaspoon ground cinnamon
¼ teaspoon salt
¾ cup skim milk
¼ cup reduced-calorie margarine, melted
¼ cup frozen egg substitute, thawed
Vegetable cooking spray
1 tablespoons regular oats, uncooked

Combine raisins and water; let stand 10 minutes.
Drain. Combine flour and next 5 ingredients; make
a well in center of mixture. Combine milk, margarine,
and egg substitute; add to dry ingredients, stirring just
until dry ingredients are moistened. Fold in raisins.
Spoon batter into an 8-inch square pan coated with
cooking spray. Sprinkle with 1 tablespoon oats. Bake
at 375° for 20 to 25 minutes or until a wooden pick
inserted in center comes out clean. Yield: 9 servings
(184 calories per serving).

PROTEIN 3.9 FAT 3.7 (Saturated Fat 0.5) CARBOHYDRATE 34.9
FIBER 1.0 CHOLESTEROL 0 IRON 1.3 SODIUM 227 CALCIUM 55

CHERRY LEMONADE

½ cup fresh lemon juice
⅓ cup superfine sugar
3¼ cups cherry-flavored sparkling mineral water
Lemon slices (optional)
Fresh cherries (optional)

Combine lemon juice and sugar; stir until sugar
dissolves. Cover and chill. Stir in mineral water. Serve
over ice. If desired, garnish with lemon slices and
cherries. Yield: 4 cups (72 calories per 1-cup serving).

PROTEIN 0.1 FAT 0.0 (Saturated Fat 0) CARBOHYDRATE 19.2
FIBER 0 CHOLESTEROL 0 IRON 0 SODIUM 39 CALCIUM 2

English Pub Supper

Peppered Raspberry Lamb
Chops
Blue Cheese Potatoes
Tarragon Brussels Sprouts
Beer Bread
Layered Blackberry Dessert
Hot Tea

SERVES 2
TOTAL CALORIES PER SERVING: 650
(Calories from Fat: 20%)

Good times and good cheer—
the essence of an English pub.
Recreate that atmosphere at
home with stimulating conversation and traditional pub fare.

To capture the essence of a
pub, add beer to an easy quick
bread (menu calories include 1
slice per person).

Lamb is a favorite meat in England, and here it is served with a
peppery raspberry sauce. The
brussels sprouts can simmer
while the lamb chops broil.

The blackberry dessert is a
low-fat version of the traditional
English fool and is a perfect ending for this hearty meal.

*Layered Blackberry Dessert is a jolly-good way to enjoy plump, juicy
fresh blackberries.*

PEPPERED RASPBERRY LAMB CHOPS

4 (4-ounce) lean lamb loin chops (1 inch thick)
½ teaspoon cracked pepper
Vegetable cooking spray
3 tablespoons low-sugar raspberry spread
2 teaspoons low-sodium Worcestershire sauce
1½ teaspoons raspberry-flavored vinegar
Fresh raspberries (optional)

Trim fat from chops. Press pepper onto both sides
of each chop. Place chops on a rack in a roasting pan
coated with cooking spray.

Broil 5½ inches from heat 6 to 7 minutes on each
side or to desired degree of doneness. Transfer to a
serving platter, and keep warm.

Combine raspberry spread, Worcestershire sauce,
and vinegar in a saucepan; cook over medium heat
until spread melts, stirring constantly. Spoon evenly
over chops. Garnish with fresh raspberries, if desired.
Yield: 2 servings (239 calories per serving).

PROTEIN 26.3   FAT 8.7   (Saturated Fat 3.0)   CARBOHYDRATE 12.5
FIBER 0.1   CHOLESTEROL 83   IRON 1.9   SODIUM 117   CALCIUM 20

BLUE CHEESE POTATOES

Butter-flavored vegetable cooking spray
1 medium baking potato, cut into ¼-inch slices
¼ cup chopped green pepper
¼ cup chopped onion
1 tablespoon crumbled blue cheese
2 teaspoons minced fresh chives

Coat a large nonstick skillet with cooking spray; place over medium-high heat until hot. Add potato; cook 7 to 8 minutes or until browned, turning occasionally. Add green pepper and onion. Cover, reduce heat, and cook 20 minutes or until tender, turning occasionally. Sprinkle with cheese; cover and cook 1 minute or until cheese melts. Sprinkle with chives, and serve immediately. Yield: 2 servings (98 calories per ½-cup serving).

PROTEIN 3.3   FAT 1.4   (Saturated Fat 0.7)   CARBOHYDRATE 18.8
FIBER 2.2   CHOLESTEROL 3   IRON 1.5   SODIUM 57   CALCIUM 36

TARRAGON BRUSSELS SPROUTS

1 cup small fresh brussels sprouts (about
   ¼ pound)
2 tablespoons chopped onion
½ teaspoon minced fresh tarragon
½ cup canned low-sodium chicken broth,
   undiluted
1½ teaspoons reduced-calorie margarine,
   melted

Wash brussels sprouts thoroughly, and remove discolored leaves. Cut off stem ends, and cut a shallow X in bottom of each sprout.
Combine brussels sprouts, onion, tarragon, and chicken broth in a medium saucepan; bring to a boil. Cover, reduce heat, and simmer 10 to 12 minutes or until brussels sprouts are tender. Drain well. Drizzle margarine over brussels sprouts, and toss gently. Yield: 2 servings (51 calories per ½-cup serving).

PROTEIN 2.2   FAT 2.0   (Saturated Fat 0.3)   CARBOHYDRATE 6.9
FIBER 2.6   CHOLESTEROL 0   IRON 0.9   SODIUM 43   CALCIUM 30

BEER BREAD

2 cups all-purpose flour
1½ cups whole wheat flour
1 tablespoon baking powder
3 tablespoons brown sugar
2 teaspoons caraway seeds
½ teaspoon salt
3 tablespoons golden raisins, chopped
1 (12-ounce) can light beer, at room temperature
¼ cup frozen egg substitute, thawed
Vegetable cooking spray

Combine first 7 ingredients; make a well in center of mixture. Add beer and egg substitute, stirring just until dry ingredients are moistened.
Spoon batter into an 8½- x 4½- x 3-inch loafpan coated with cooking spray. Bake at 375° for 45 to 50 minutes or until a wooden pick inserted in center comes out clean. Let cool in pan 10 minutes. Remove from pan; let cool completely on a wire rack. Yield: 16 servings (116 calories per ½-inch slice).

PROTEIN 3.6   FAT 0.4   (Saturated Fat 0.1)   CARBOHYDRATE 23.8
FIBER 1.9   CHOLESTEROL 0   IRON 1.3   SODIUM 138   CALCIUM 49

LAYERED BLACKBERRY DESSERT

¾ cup fresh blackberries
1 tablespoon sugar
1 (8-ounce) carton vanilla low-fat yogurt
⅛ teaspoon brandy extract
Additional fresh blackberries (optional)
Fresh mint sprigs (optional)

Combine ¾ cup blackberries and sugar in container of an electric blender; top with cover, and process until smooth. Press puree through a sieve to remove seeds.
Combine yogurt and extract; stir. Layer blackberry mixture and yogurt mixture evenly in 2 (6-ounce) parfait glasses. If desired, garnish with blackberries and mint. Yield: 2 servings (146 calories per serving).

PROTEIN 5.9   FAT 1.6   (Saturated Fat 0.9)   CARBOHYDRATE 27.8
FIBER 3.4   CHOLESTEROL 6   IRON 0.3   SODIUM 75   CALCIUM 209

Cranberry-Wine Spritzers, Glazed Turkey Kabobs, Savory Potato Salad (page 56), and Maple-Mustard Carrots (page 56) feature holiday-food flavor with a summertime twist.

Christmas in July

Cranberry-Wine Spritzers
Glazed Turkey Kabobs
Maple-Mustard Carrots
Savory Potato Salad
Pumpkin-Frozen Yogurt Sandwiches

SERVES 4
TOTAL CALORIES PER SERVING: 560
(Calories from Fat: 8%)

Why wait until December to enjoy the traditional flavors of the holiday season? Celebrate Christmas in July with a menu that will take your mind off the hot weather.

Rather than heat up the kitchen while roasting a turkey, prepare quick-cooking turkey kabobs. Transfer the flavor of traditional stuffing into a cool potato salad filled with the seasoning of thyme and sage.

Coat baby carrots with a mixture of maple syrup and mustard for an uncommonly good accompaniment.

Keep the summer theme with frozen yogurt sandwiches—frosty treats that feature the flavor of your favorite holiday pie. Enjoy the taste of cranberries in a refreshing spritzer. Instead of using your best holiday china, use casual red or green dinnerware and serve the meal outdoors.

CRANBERRY-WINE SPRITZERS

1⅔ cups cranberry juice cocktail
1⅓ cups Riesling or other sweet white wine
1 cup sparkling mineral water

Combine cranberry juice cocktail and wine in a pitcher; mix well. Cover mixture and chill thoroughly.

Just before serving, stir in sparkling mineral water. Serve spritzers over crushed ice. Yield: 4 cups (114 calories per 1-cup serving).

PROTEIN 0.2   FAT 0.1   (Saturated Fat 0)   CARBOHYDRATE 17.0
FIBER 0   CHOLESTEROL 0   IRON 0.5   SODIUM 22   CALCIUM 9

GLAZED TURKEY KABOBS

½ cup apricot nectar
1 tablespoon honey
⅛ teaspoon ground red pepper
1 clove garlic, minced
1 pound boneless turkey breast, skinned and cut into 1-inch cubes
2 medium-size green peppers, cut into 1-inch pieces
8 large cherry tomatoes
8 medium-size fresh mushrooms
¼ cup no-sugar-added apricot spread, melted
2 tablespoons Kahlúa or other coffee-flavored liqueur
Vegetable cooking spray

Combine first 4 ingredients; stir. Place turkey in a zip-top heavy-duty plastic bag; add nectar mixture. Seal and marinate in refrigerator at least 8 hours.

Drain turkey, discarding marinade. Thread turkey and vegetables on 8 (10-inch) skewers. Combine apricot spread and liqueur.

Coat grill rack with cooking spray; place on grill over medium-hot coals. Place kabobs on rack, and cook 15 to 20 minutes or until turkey is done, turning and basting frequently with liqueur mixture. Yield: 4 servings (205 calories per serving).

PROTEIN 26.8   FAT 1.2   (Saturated Fat 0.3)   CARBOHYDRATE 22.6
FIBER 1.5   CHOLESTEROL 71   IRON 2.4   SODIUM 51   CALCIUM 18

MAPLE-MUSTARD CARROTS

1 pound baby carrots, scraped
1½ tablespoons reduced-calorie maple syrup
1 tablespoon reduced-calorie margarine, melted
2 teaspoons Dijon mustard

Place carrots in a saucepan; cover with water. Bring to a boil; cover, reduce heat, and simmer 20 to 25 minutes or until tender. Drain well. Combine syrup and remaining ingredients; stir well. Pour syrup mixture over carrots; toss gently to coat. Yield: 2 cups (57 calories per ½-cup serving).

PROTEIN 0.9 FAT 2.1 (Saturated Fat 0.3) CARBOHYDRATE 9.5
FIBER 2.7 CHOLESTEROL 0 IRON 0.4 SODIUM 133 CALCIUM 23

SAVORY POTATO SALAD

10 ounces round red potatoes
¼ cup chopped celery
2 tablespoons chopped fresh parsley
1 (2-ounce) jar diced pimiento, drained
¼ cup nonfat mayonnaise
3 tablespoons nonfat sour cream
1½ tablespoons canned low-sodium chicken broth,
    undiluted
¼ teaspoon rubbed sage
¼ teaspoon pepper
¼ teaspoon dried whole thyme

Wash potatoes. Cook in boiling water to cover 15 minutes or until tender; drain and cool completely. Peel potatoes, and cut into ½-inch cubes. Combine potato, celery, parsley, and pimiento.
Combine mayonnaise and remaining ingredients in a small bowl; stir well. Add mayonnaise mixture to potato mixture; toss gently to coat. Cover and chill. Yield: 4 servings (76 calories per ½-cup serving).

PROTEIN 2.4 FAT 0.1 (Saturated Fat 0) CARBOHYDRATE 16.5
FIBER 1.3 CHOLESTEROL 0 IRON 1.0 SODIUM 213 CALCIUM 15

PUMPKIN-FROZEN YOGURT SANDWICHES

¼ cup cooked, mashed pumpkin
2 tablespoons unsweetened applesauce
1 tablespoon sugar
¼ teaspoon pumpkin pie spice
1⅓ cups vanilla nonfat frozen yogurt, softened
8 (2-inch) gingersnap cookies

Combine pumpkin, applesauce, sugar, and pumpkin pie spice in a small bowl. Fold softened frozen yogurt into pumpkin mixture. Spread ⅓ cup frozen yogurt mixture onto each of 4 gingersnaps. Top with remaining 4 gingersnaps. Place on a baking sheet; freeze until firm. Wrap sandwiches individually in heavy-duty plastic wrap, and store in freezer. Yield: 4 servings (108 calories per serving).

PROTEIN 2.9 FAT 1.3 (Saturated Fat 0.3) CARBOHYDRATE 22.1
FIBER 0.3 CHOLESTEROL 3 IRON 0.5 SODIUM 51 CALCIUM 103

Create your own tropical paradise with a Caribbean dinner. The finest flavors of the islands are featured in Hearts of Palm Vinaigrette, Island Chicken and Papaya, and Tropical Mixed Vegetables. (Menu begins on page 67.)

Microwave It Light

Strips of peppery chicken are served on a bed of tangy greens in Spicy Chicken Salad.

New Orleans Jazz Lunch

Creamy Sweet Potato Soup
Spicy Chicken Salad
Banana Bread
Praline Peach Compote
Iced Tea

SERVES 6
TOTAL CALORIES PER SERVING: 571
(Calories from Fat: 26%)

Nowhere are good food, good music, and good times so skillfully combined and readily available as they are in New Orleans. Create the ambiance of lunch in a French Quarter courtyard with this easy menu that is rich in flavor and tradition.

Get lunch off to a delicious beginning with Creamy Sweet Potato Soup, a golden soup made from a regional favorite. Use the microwave oven to quickly cook the sweet potatoes.

You can cook the chicken for Spicy Chicken Salad a day ahead and refrigerate it. Chop the vegetables for the salad and make the dressing ahead as well. Accompany each salad with 1 slice of sweet, tender Banana Bread.

Pralines, a familiar New Orleans treat, lend their unique flavor to a fruit dessert. Praline Peach Compote boasts much of the praline flavor but few of the calories. Let the good times roll.

CREAMY SWEET POTATO SOUP

3 cups peeled, diced sweet potato (about
   4 medium)
2½ cups canned no-salt-added chicken broth,
   undiluted and divided
1 cup evaporated skimmed milk
1 tablespoon bourbon
1 tablespoon brown sugar
½ teaspoon apple pie spice
⅛ teaspoon ground ginger
1½ teaspoons vanilla extract

Place sweet potato and ½ cup chicken broth in a 3-quart casserole. Cover with heavy-duty plastic wrap, and vent. Microwave at HIGH 12 to 14 minutes or until sweet potato is tender, stirring after 5 minutes.

Transfer to container of an electric blender or food processor; top with cover, and process until smooth. Return mixture to casserole.

Stir in remaining 2 cups broth, milk, bourbon, brown sugar, apple pie spice, ginger, and vanilla. Cover and vent. Microwave at HIGH 3 to 5 minutes or until thoroughly heated. Yield: 1½ quarts (127 calories per 1-cup serving).

PROTEIN 5.1 FAT 1.1 (Saturated Fat 0.4) CARBOHYDRATE 23.1
FIBER 2.0 CHOLESTEROL 2 IRON 0.6 SODIUM 114 CALCIUM 141

SPICY CHICKEN SALAD

½ teaspoon garlic powder
½ teaspoon onion powder
¼ teaspoon dry mustard
¼ teaspoon paprika
¼ teaspoon ground red pepper
⅛ teaspoon ground white pepper
6 (4-ounce) skinned, boned chicken
   breast halves
3½ cups shredded lettuce
1½ cups shredded red cabbage
1 cup shredded carrot
½ cup sliced green onions
⅓ cup white wine vinegar
1 tablespoon chopped fresh parsley
1 tablespoon Dijon mustard
2 teaspoons vegetable oil
1 teaspoon chopped fresh basil
¼ teaspoon salt
¼ teaspoon freshly ground black pepper

Combine first 6 ingredients in a small bowl; blend well. Rub spice mixture over both sides of each chicken breast. Place chicken in an 11- x 7- x 2-inch baking dish with thickest portions toward outside of dish. Cover with wax paper, and chill 1 hour.

Microwave chicken, covered, at HIGH 8 to 10 minutes or until chicken is tender, rotating a half-turn after 4 minutes. Let cool; slice into ¼-inch-wide strips.

Combine lettuce, cabbage, carrot, and green onions; toss well. Combine vinegar, parsley, mustard, oil, basil, salt, and black pepper in a small bowl; stir well with a wire whisk. Add vinegar mixture to lettuce mixture; toss well. Divide lettuce mixture evenly among 6 individual serving plates. Arrange chicken strips evenly over each serving. Yield: 6 servings (169 calories per serving).

PROTEIN 25.3 FAT 4.7 (Saturated Fat 1.1) CARBOHYDRATE 4.9
FIBER 1.5 CHOLESTEROL 66 IRON 1.4 SODIUM 244 CALCIUM 42

BANANA BREAD

Vegetable cooking spray
2 tablespoons fine, dry breadcrumbs
¾ cup all-purpose flour
¾ cup whole wheat flour
½ cup sugar
1 teaspoon baking soda
⅛ teaspoon salt
½ cup margarine, softened
½ cup frozen egg substitute, thawed
⅓ cup skim milk
½ teaspoon vanilla extract
1½ cups mashed ripe banana (about 3 medium bananas)

Coat a 6-cup microwave-safe ring mold with cooking spray; sprinkle with breadcrumbs. Combine flours and next 7 ingredients. Blend at low speed of an electric mixer until moistened. Beat 2 minutes at medium speed; stir in banana. Pour into prepared mold. Microwave at MEDIUM HIGH (70% power) 11 to 13 minutes or until a wooden pick inserted near center comes out clean, rotating mold after 5 minutes. Let stand 10 minutes. Invert onto serving plate. Yield: 16 servings (145 calories per serving).

PROTEIN 2.6   FAT 6.0   (Saturated Fat 1.1)   CARBOHYDRATE 21.1
FIBER 1.6   CHOLESTEROL 0   IRON 0.7   SODIUM 156   CALCIUM 27

PRALINE PEACH COMPOTE

Vegetable cooking spray
3 tablespoons chopped pecans
½ cup unsweetened orange juice
¼ cup firmly packed dark brown sugar
2 teaspoons grated orange rind
6 large peaches, peeled and sliced

Coat a 10-ounce custard cup with cooking spray. Spread chopped pecans in custard cup, and microwave, uncovered, at HIGH 2 to 4 minutes or until pecans are lightly toasted. Set aside.

Combine orange juice, brown sugar, and orange rind in a 1-cup glass measure. Microwave at HIGH 1 to 2 minutes or until sugar dissolves. Place peaches in a bowl. Pour orange juice mixture over peaches; stir gently. Cover and chill 1 hour.

To serve, spoon peach mixture evenly into individual dessert dishes. Sprinkle pecans evenly over each serving. Yield: 6 servings (128 calories per serving).

PROTEIN 1.5   FAT 4.9   (Saturated Fat 0.4)   CARBOHYDRATE 22.1
FIBER 2.3   CHOLESTEROL 0   IRON 0.5   SODIUM 2   CALCIUM 16

 ## THE PASSIVE APPROACH TO EXERCISE

Some health clubs and tanning salons are offering the use of equipment called continuous passive motion (CPM) exercise tables. The premise is simple. Just sit or lie back, and the machine will do your exercise for you. Advertisements tout this no-sweat style of conditioning as a painless way to trim extra inches from arms, thighs, and waistlines.

These motorized machines move your body's muscle groups through a full range of motion, but they don't make you lose weight nor do they tone muscles. CPM tables were designed to rehabilitate muscles of polio patients and are widely used in hospital physical therapy departments.

Typically, CPM tables help paraplegics, stroke victims, and people with neuromuscular problems who cannot exercise on their own. The tables also can reduce a patient's recovery time following orthopedic surgery. But these benefits are quite different from the results that advertisements claim these machines can produce. If you want to get in better shape, don't rely on CPM tables. Active movement, not passive, is the only way to tone up and trim down.

Clockwise from top: Begin the new year with Quick Cassoulet, Pickled Vegetable Salad, Waldorf Cheese Spread, and Hot Holiday Toddy (recipes on page 62).

New Year's Day Buffet

Hot Holiday Toddy
Waldorf Cheese Spread
Celery Sticks
Quick Cassoulet
Pickled Vegetable Salad
Steamed Cranberry Pudding with Citrus Sauce
Sparkling Mineral Water

SERVES 8
TOTAL CALORIES PER SERVING: 588
(Calories from Fat: 16%)

What better way to spend the first day of the new year than in the company of good friends. Gather around the television for bowl game excitement, and set out a hearty buffet when the armchair quarterbacks get hungry.

All of the dishes in this menu can either be prepared quickly in the microwave oven or made ahead of time so that you, too, can enjoy the games. Calories for the buffet menu have been calculated to include 2 tablespoons cheese spread, 2 celery sticks, and 1 slice pudding per person.

The microwave oven makes entertaining easy. Resolve to make it an essential part of every party that you plan.

HOT HOLIDAY TODDY

6 cups cranberry-apple drink
1 teaspoon apple pie spice
2 cups rosé or blush wine
8 (3-inch) sticks cinnamon (optional)

Combine cranberry-apple drink and apple pie spice in a 2-quart glass measure. Microwave at HIGH 8 to 10 minutes or until thoroughly heated, stirring after 4 minutes. Stir in wine. Garnish with cinnamon sticks, if desired. Serve immediately. Yield: 2 quarts (164 calories per 1-cup serving).

PROTEIN 0.3　FAT 0.1　(Saturated Fat 0)　CARBOHYDRATE 32.4
FIBER 0　CHOLESTEROL 0　IRON 0.4　SODIUM 8　CALCIUM 20

WALDORF CHEESE SPREAD

Vegetable cooking spray
2 tablespoons chopped walnuts
½ cup (2 ounces) shredded 40% less-fat Cheddar cheese
¼ cup light process cream cheese product, softened
1 tablespoon nonfat mayonnaise
2 tablespoons skim milk
¼ cup finely chopped apple
3 tablespoons finely chopped celery
2 tablespoons finely chopped raisins

Coat a 10-ounce custard cup with vegetable cooking spray. Spread chopped walnuts in custard cup, and microwave, uncovered, at HIGH 3 to 4 minutes or until walnuts are toasted, stirring after each minute. Set walnuts aside.

Combine Cheddar cheese, cream cheese, mayonnaise, and milk in container of an electric blender; top with cover, and process until smooth. Transfer cheese mixture to a small bowl; stir in walnuts, apple, celery, and raisins. Serve with celery sticks. Yield: 1 cup (30 calories per tablespoon).

PROTEIN 1.3　FAT 1.6　(Saturated Fat 0.7)　CARBOHYDRATE 3.2
FIBER 0.3　CHOLESTEROL 2　IRON 0.1　SODIUM 53　CALCIUM 33

QUICK CASSOULET

1 cup chopped carrot
½ cup chopped onion
½ cup canned no-salt-added beef broth, undiluted
2 (15.8-ounce) cans black-eyed peas, rinsed and drained
1 (14½-ounce) can no-salt-added whole tomatoes, undrained and chopped
1½ cups chopped cooked lean pork
1 cup chopped cooked chicken breast
¼ cup dry vermouth
1 teaspoon dried whole thyme
½ teaspoon garlic powder
½ teaspoon ground allspice
¼ teaspoon pepper
3 tablespoons toasted fine, dry breadcrumbs
2 tablespoons chopped fresh parsley

Place carrot, onion, and broth in a 3-quart casserole. Cover with heavy-duty plastic wrap, and vent. Microwave at HIGH 8 minutes. Add peas and next 8 ingredients; stir well. Cover with heavy-duty plastic wrap, and vent. Microwave at MEDIUM HIGH (70% power) 13 to 15 minutes or until thoroughly heated, stirring after 7 minutes. Sprinkle with breadcrumbs and parsley. Yield: 8 servings (224 calories per serving).

PROTEIN 21.1　FAT 5.1　(Saturated Fat 0.4)　CARBOHYDRATE 23.2
FIBER 2.7　CHOLESTEROL 42　IRON 2.3　SODIUM 103　CALCIUM 62

PICKLED VEGETABLE SALAD

4 cups shredded cabbage
1 cup thinly sliced cucumber
¾ cup thinly sliced radishes
¾ cup shredded carrot
½ cup chopped purple onion
¼ cup white vinegar
1 tablespoon brown sugar
3 tablespoons prepared mustard
1 tablespoon low-sodium Worcestershire sauce
½ teaspoon salt
¼ teaspoon crushed red pepper

Combine shredded cabbage, cucumber, radishes, carrot, and onion; toss gently, and set aside.

Combine vinegar, brown sugar, mustard, Worcestershire sauce, salt, and pepper in a 2-cup glass measure. Cover with heavy-duty plastic wrap, and vent. Microwave at HIGH 45 seconds to 1 minute or until sugar dissolves. Stir well. Pour over cabbage mixture, tossing gently to coat. Cover and chill. Yield: 8 servings (29 calories per ½-cup serving).

PROTEIN 0.9   FAT 0.4   (Saturated Fat 0)   CARBOHYDRATE 6.2
FIBER 1.3   CHOLESTEROL 0   IRON 0.4   SODIUM 239   CALCIUM 28

STEAMED CRANBERRY PUDDING WITH CITRUS SAUCE

½ cup hot water
½ cup unsweetened orange juice
½ cup dried cranberries
2 tablespoons margarine, softened
½ cup molasses
¼ cup sugar
1 egg
1½ cups all-purpose flour
1 teaspoon baking soda
½ teaspoon ground cinnamon
¼ teaspoon salt
⅛ teaspoon ground ginger
Vegetable cooking spray
Citrus Sauce

Combine hot water and orange juice. Place cranberries in a small bowl. Pour orange juice mixture over cranberries, and let stand 15 minutes.

Cream margarine and molasses; gradually add sugar, beating well at medium speed of an electric mixer. Add egg; beat well. Combine flour, baking soda, cinnamon, salt, and ginger. Add flour mixture to creamed mixture; beat well.

Spoon batter into a 1½-quart microwave-safe ring mold coated with vegetable cooking spray. Cover with heavy-duty plastic wrap. Microwave at MEDIUM HIGH (70% power) 10 to 12 minutes or until pudding is set, rotating mold a quarter-turn after 5 minutes. Cut into slices, and top each slice with 1 tablespoon Citrus Sauce. Serve warm. Yield: 16 servings (109 calories per serving).

Citrus Sauce

1 cup unsweetened orange juice
1 tablespoon cornstarch
1 teaspoon grated orange rind
1 teaspoon grated lemon rind

Combine orange juice and cornstarch in a 2-cup glass measure, stirring well. Microwave, uncovered, at HIGH 3 to 4 minutes or until thickened and bubbly, stirring every minute. Stir in orange rind and lemon rind. Yield: 1 cup.

PROTEIN 1.7   FAT 1.9   (Saturated Fat 0.4)   CARBOHYDRATE 21.6
FIBER 0.4   CHOLESTEROL 13   IRON 1.1   SODIUM 111   CALCIUM 35

 COUNTING THE BEATS
To determine your heart rate, locate your radial artery (on the thumb side of your wrist) and take your pulse during your exercise session. Count your pulse for 10 seconds and multiply that number by 6 to get your actual heart rate. If that number is above your target heart rate (THR) zone, slow down the intensity of your workout. If the number is below the zone, step up the pace.

AGE	PREDICTED MAXIMUM HEART RATE	TARGET HEART RATE ZONE		NUMBER OF HEARTBEATS IN 10 SECONDS	
	(in minutes)	60%	– 90%	60%	– 90%
20	200	120	180	20	30
25	195	117	176	20	29
30	190	114	171	19	29
35	185	111	167	19	28
40	180	108	162	18	27
45	175	105	158	18	26
50	170	102	153	17	26
55	165	99	149	17	25
60	160	96	144	16	24

MATHEMATICAL FORMULA
Maximum Heart Rate (MHR) – 220 minus ago
MHR x 60% and 90% = THR in minutes

Enjoy Key West Lime Parfaits (page 66) served in frosted glasses and topped with chocolate wafer crumbs.

Florida Flair

Sunshine Marys
Citrus and Greens Orlando
Coastal Seafood Medley
Spiced Brown Rice
Key West Lime Parfaits
Sparkling Mineral Water

SERVES 6
TOTAL CALORIES PER SERVING: 573
(Calories from Fat: 18%)

This menu features some of the Sunshine State's finest. Sunshine Marys resemble an old standard but offer a new twist—orange juice.

The creamy sauce in Coastal Seafood Medley complements the fresh seafood and is easy to prepare in the microwave oven. The delectable flavor of fresh oranges and grapefruit in Citrus and Greens Orlando is heightened with a cooked citrus dressing.

Lime sherbet and chocolate wafers are key ingredients in Key West Lime Parfaits. Cool and refreshing, they are a perfect ending for the meal.

SUNSHINE MARYS

4⅔ cups no-salt-added tomato juice
1 cup unsweetened orange juice
⅓ cup vodka
½ teaspoon salt-free lemon-pepper seasoning
¼ teaspoon onion powder
¼ teaspoon hot sauce

Combine all ingredients in a large pitcher; stir well. Cover and chill. Serve over ice. Yield: 1½ quarts (86 calories per 1-cup serving).

PROTEIN 2.2 FAT 0.0 (Saturated Fat 0) CARBOHYDRATE 14.1
FIBER 0.8 CHOLESTEROL 0 IRON 1.2 SODIUM 23 CALCIUM 5

CITRUS AND GREENS ORLANDO

½ cup apricot nectar
3 tablespoons lemon juice
1 tablespoon unsweetened orange juice
1 teaspoon cornstarch
⅛ teaspoon ground ginger
Dash of ground nutmeg
1 teaspoon grated lemon rind
1½ cups torn iceberg lettuce
1½ cups torn green leaf lettuce
2 medium-size oranges, peeled and sectioned
2 medium grapefruit, peeled and sectioned

Combine first 6 ingredients in a 1-cup glass measure; stir well. Microwave at HIGH 2 minutes or until slightly thickened, stirring after 1 minute. Cool slightly; stir in lemon rind. Cover and chill.

Combine iceberg lettuce and leaf lettuce; toss well. Place ½ cup lettuce mixture on each of 6 salad plates. Arrange orange and grapefruit sections on lettuce; drizzle 2 tablespoons juice mixture over each serving. Yield: 6 servings (68 calories per serving).

PROTEIN 1.3 FAT 0.2 (Saturated Fat 0) CARBOHYDRATE 17.1
FIBER 2.7 CHOLESTEROL 0 IRON 0.3 SODIUM 3 CALCIUM 35

COASTAL SEAFOOD MEDLEY

¾ pound medium-size fresh shrimp, peeled and deveined
2 quarts hot water
¾ pound bay scallops
1 (14-ounce) can artichoke hearts, drained and sliced in half
½ cup sliced water chestnuts
2 tablespoons finely chopped onion
1 tablespoon plus 1 teaspoon reduced-calorie margarine
1½ tablespoons all-purpose flour
¼ teaspoon salt
¼ teaspoon ground white pepper
1 cup skim milk
¼ cup dry sherry
1 (2-ounce) jar sliced pimiento, drained
2 tablespoons chopped fresh parsley
3 tablespoons grated Parmesan cheese

Combine shrimp and water in a 3-quart casserole. Cover with heavy-duty plastic wrap, and microwave at HIGH 2 minutes. Add scallops; microwave, covered, at HIGH 3 minutes or until shrimp turn pink and scallops are opaque. Drain well. Combine shrimp, scallops, artichoke hearts, and sliced water chestnuts in an 11- x 7- x 2-inch baking dish; set aside.

Place chopped onion and margarine in a 1-quart casserole; microwave, uncovered, at HIGH 1 minute. Add flour, salt, and pepper; stir until smooth. Gradually add milk and sherry, stirring until smooth. Microwave, uncovered, at HIGH 3 to 4 minutes or until mixture is thickened, stirring after every minute. Stir in pimiento and parsley.

Pour sauce over shrimp mixture, and sprinkle with Parmesan cheese. Microwave at HIGH 3 to 4 minutes or until mixture is thoroughly heated, rotating a half-turn after 2 minutes. Yield: 6 servings (156 calories per serving).

PROTEIN 17.8 FAT 3.5 (Saturated Fat 1.1) CARBOHYDRATE 13.2
FIBER 0.7 CHOLESTEROL 90 IRON 2.3 SODIUM 379 CALCIUM 144

SPICED BROWN RICE

½ cup sliced celery
½ cup chopped green pepper
½ cup chopped onion
1 clove garlic, minced
2 tablespoons low-sodium soy sauce
2 teaspoons brown sugar
1 teaspoon reduced-calorie margarine
½ teaspoon ground allspice
¼ teaspoon ground ginger
¼ teaspoon ground cardamom
2¼ cups cooked brown rice (cooked without salt or fat)

Combine celery, green pepper, onion, garlic, soy sauce, brown sugar, margarine, allspice, ginger, and cardamom in a 2-quart casserole. Cover with heavy-duty plastic wrap, and vent. Microwave at HIGH 3 to 4 minutes or until vegetables are crisp-tender, stirring after 2 minutes.

Stir in cooked brown rice; microwave at HIGH 1 to 2 minutes or until thoroughly heated. Yield: 6 servings (82 calories per ½-cup serving).

PROTEIN 1.8   FAT 1.0   (Saturated Fat 0.2)   CARBOHYDRATE 16.2
FIBER 1.6   CHOLESTEROL 0   IRON 0.5   SODIUM 149   CALCIUM 16

KEY WEST LIME PARFAITS

Vegetable cooking spray
¼ cup finely chopped macadamia nuts
½ cup plus 2 tablespoons chocolate wafer cookie crumbs, divided
3 cups lime sherbet, softened
1 tablespoon grated lime rind

Coat a 1-quart casserole with cooking spray. Spread nuts in casserole, and microwave, uncovered, at HIGH 6 to 7 minutes or until lightly toasted, stirring every 30 seconds. Combine toasted nuts and ½ cup chocolate cookie crumbs; stir well, and set aside.

Combine lime sherbet and lime rind in a medium bowl; stir well.

Spoon 1 tablespoon chocolate cookie crumb mixture into each of 6 (6-ounce) parfait glasses; top each with ¼ cup sherbet mixture. Spoon 1 tablespoon crumb mixture over each; top each with ¼ cup sherbet mixture. Sprinkle each serving with 1 teaspoon cookie crumbs. Cover and freeze until firm. Yield: 6 servings (181 calories per serving).

PROTEIN 1.9   FAT 6.6   (Saturated Fat 1.1)   CARBOHYDRATE 30.1
FIBER 0.1   CHOLESTEROL 8   IRON 0.3   SODIUM 104   CALCIUM 53

TWILIGHT WORKOUTS

Nature turns the lights out early during winter months. If this change in schedule means you'll be outdoors for a workout in the dark, take extra care. Joggers, cyclists, and walkers who take to the streets at night or during the predawn hours are less likely to be seen by motorists. But if you heed the following precautions, you'll reduce the risks.

• Dress in light colors. Add reflective tape to outfits, or wear fluorescent vests and head-, wrist-, and anklebands. Equip your bike with reflective materials on the seat, front, sides, rear, and pedals.

• Carry a flashlight or a flashing device that operates on batteries. Anchor generator- or battery-powered headlights and taillights to your bike.

• Move against the flow of traffic when running or walking. That way, you'll see oncoming cars. (Just make sure to look away from approaching headlights; they can temporarily blind you.) When biking, ride with the flow of traffic. A mirror will help you see cars approaching from the rear.

• Skip the music headphones. It's crucial to be able to tune in to the sounds around you. You may hear a car before you see it.

Serve Pineapple-Mango Ice Milk (page 69) in baby pineapple shells for an island paradise dessert.

Caribbean Dinner

Island Chicken and Papaya
Tropical Mixed Vegetables
Hearts of Palm Vinaigrette
Pineapple-Mango Ice Milk
Spiced Coffee

SERVES 4
TOTAL CALORIES PER SERVING: 436
(Calories from Fat: 12%)

Caribbean cuisine is based on the treasures of the region's soil—extravagantly colored fruits and richly textured vegetables. This cuisine lends itself to cooking in the microwave oven so the foods will retain their fresh flavor, texture, and eye-appealing color.

Chicken stays tender in Island Chicken and Papaya, yet it cooks in about half the time needed for conventional methods. The vegetables in Tropical Mixed Vegetables are beautifully bright with just the right amount of crunch. (Menu calories include ½ cup ice milk per person.)

ISLAND CHICKEN AND PAPAYA

2 teaspoons reduced-calorie margarine
¼ cup honey
¼ cup lime juice
¼ teaspoon ground nutmeg
⅛ teaspoon ground cinnamon
Dash of ground allspice
4 (4-ounce) skinned, boned chicken breast halves
1 papaya, peeled, seeded, and sliced
Lime rind curls (optional)

Place margarine in an 11- x 7- x 2-inch baking dish; microwave at HIGH 20 seconds or until margarine melts. Stir in honey and next 4 ingredients. Place chicken in dish with thickest portions toward outside of dish. Cover with wax paper, and microwave at HIGH 10 to 12 minutes or until chicken is tender, rotating a half-turn after 5 minutes.

Add papaya to chicken; cover with wax paper, and microwave at HIGH 1 to 2 minutes or until thoroughly heated. Garnish with lime rind curls, if desired. Yield: 4 servings (213 calories per serving).

PROTEIN 22.3   FAT 2.6   (Saturated Fat 0.6)   CARBOHYDRATE 26.6
FIBER 1.4   CHOLESTEROL 54   IRON 0.9   SODIUM 83   CALCIUM 33

TROPICAL MIXED VEGETABLES

¼ pound fresh green beans
1 cup sliced carrot
¼ cup canned low-sodium chicken broth, undiluted
2 tablespoons Chablis or other dry white wine
¼ teaspoon curry powder
⅛ teaspoon ground white pepper
½ small sweet red pepper, cut into julienne strips
⅓ cup chopped onion
1 tablespoon unsweetened shredded coconut, toasted

Wash beans; trim ends, and remove strings. Cut into 1-inch pieces. Combine beans and next 5 ingredients in a 2-quart casserole. Cover with heavy-duty plastic wrap, and vent. Microwave at HIGH 6 minutes. Add sweet red pepper and onion. Cover and microwave at HIGH 4 to 5 minutes or until vegetables are crisp-tender. Sprinkle with coconut. Yield: 4 servings (43 calories per ½-cup serving).

PROTEIN 1.2   FAT 1.3   (Saturated Fat 1.0)   CARBOHYDRATE 7.4
FIBER 2.1   CHOLESTEROL 0   IRON 0.7   SODIUM 15   CALCIUM 23

HEARTS OF PALM VINAIGRETTE

¼ cup unsweetened orange juice
1 tablespoon Dijon mustard
2 tablespoons white wine vinegar
1 teaspoon olive oil
1 clove garlic, crushed
½ teaspoon dried whole thyme
¼ teaspoon salt
¼ teaspoon pepper
4 lettuce leaves
1 (14.4-ounce) can hearts of palm, drained, rinsed, and cut into ½-inch slices
½ small red onion, sliced and separated into rings
2 tablespoons chopped fresh parsley

Combine orange juice, Dijon mustard, white wine vinegar, olive oil, crushed garlic, thyme, salt, and pepper in a small bowl, stirring well with a wire whisk. Set mixture aside.

Place 1 lettuce leaf on each of 4 individual salad plates. Arrange hearts of palm and sliced onion evenly on lettuce leaves. Sprinkle evenly with chopped parsley. Drizzle 2 tablespoons orange juice mixture over each salad. Serve immediately. Yield: 4 servings (94 calories per serving).

PROTEIN 2.1   FAT 1.6   (Saturated Fat 0.2)   CARBOHYDRATE 19.9
FIBER 1.5   CHOLESTEROL 0   IRON 1.5   SODIUM 270   CALCIUM 26

PINEAPPLE-MANGO ICE MILK

1¼ cups chopped fresh pineapple
1 cup chopped ripe mango
½ cup sugar
1 cup evaporated skimmed milk
¾ teaspoon lime juice
¼ teaspoon rum extract
4 baby pineapple shells (optional)
Edible flowers (optional)

Combine first 3 ingredients in container of an electric blender. Top with cover; process until smooth. Add milk, lime juice, and rum extract; process until blended.

Pour mixture into freezer can of a 4-quart hand-turned or electric freezer. Freeze according to manufacturer's instructions. Let ripen 1 hour, if desired. If desired, scoop ½-cup portions of ice milk into baby pineapple shells, and garnish with edible flowers. Serve immediately.

Transfer remaining ice milk to an airtight container; cover and freeze. Yield: 6½ cups (64 calories per ½-cup serving).

PROTEIN 1.6 FAT 0.2 (Saturated Fat 0) CARBOHYDRATE 14.8
FIBER 0.5 CHOLESTEROL 1 IRON 0.2 SODIUM 23 CALCIUM 60

SPICED COFFEE

4¼ cups water
2 tablespoons instant coffee granules
2 tablespoons brown sugar
¼ teaspoon ground cinnamon
⅛ teaspoon ground nutmeg
⅛ teaspoon ground allspice
⅛ teaspoon ground cloves

Combine water, instant coffee granules, brown sugar, ground cinnamon, nutmeg, allspice, and cloves in a 2-quart glass measure. Cover with heavy-duty plastic wrap, and vent. Microwave at HIGH 5 to 6 minutes or until mixture is thoroughly heated; strain coffee mixture.

To serve, pour warm coffee mixture into individual mugs, and serve immediately. Yield: 4 cups (22 calories per 1-cup serving).

PROTEIN 0.2 FAT 0.1 (Saturated Fat 0) CARBOHYDRATE 4.6
FIBER 0.1 CHOLESTEROL 0 IRON 0.3 SODIUM 2 CALCIUM 9

WORKING IN A WORKOUT

Although lack of time is probably the most common excuse for avoiding exercise, there are many reasons people make but don't stick to exercise resolutions. Here are a few commonsense suggestions to short-circuit those behaviors.
• Take the slow-but-steady approach to fitness, especially in the beginning. Overdoing it (hopping on a bicycle every night after a few months of inactivity) is the surest route to burnout, not to mention injury.
• Start in the morning. Many people are tired at the end of the day and use this as an excuse for not exercising. Studies show that three out of four people who rise and shine and work out in the early morning stick with the regimen. Only one out of four

afternoon or evening exercisers stay with a program for the long haul.
• Give your workout high priority. If you have to, make an appointment for exercise. It's much harder to ignore something you've planned than something that isn't on your daily schedule.
• Stick by the rule of two. Everyone gets bored doing the same thing over and over. Find two activities you like, preferably at least one indoor pursuit for when the weather is bad, and alternate them.
• Plan for success. You know your schedule, your lifestyle, and your preferences. That makes you the best person to set up a fitness regimen that will be effective and flexible enough to suit you.

Italian Dinner

Garlic Pasta Appetizer
Italian Veal Cutlets
Mixed Squash with Mint
Soft Breadsticks
Wine-Poached Pears with
Vanilla Custard Sauce
Red Wine

SERVES 4
TOTAL CALORIES PER SERVING: 597
(Calories from Fat: 17%)

Create the atmosphere of your favorite Italian bistro in your dining room with a menu that highlights the region's cuisine. Begin with a pasta appetizer and follow with a robust veal entrée. End with fruit for a typical Italian feast. Menu calories include 1 commercial breadstick and 6 ounces red wine per person.

Garlic Pasta Appetizer, Mixed Squash with Mint, and Italian Veal Cutlets provide a taste of Italy.

GARLIC PASTA APPETIZER

¼ cup thinly sliced celery
¼ cup canned no-salt-added chicken broth, undiluted
2 tablespoons thinly sliced green onions
1 teaspoon garlic powder
2 teaspoons olive oil
1⅓ cups cooked spaghetti (cooked without salt or fat)
2 tablespoons sliced ripe olives
16 arugula leaves

Combine first 5 ingredients in a glass bowl; microwave at HIGH 1 minute. Add spaghetti and olives; toss well. Divide evenly among arugula-lined plates. Yield: 4 appetizer servings (53 calories per serving).

PROTEIN 1.4 FAT 3.1 (Saturated Fat 0.5) CARBOHYDRATE 5.4
FIBER 1.2 CHOLESTEROL 0 IRON 0.5 SODIUM 66 CALCIUM 34

ITALIAN VEAL CUTLETS

¼ cup chopped onion
½ teaspoon olive oil
1 clove garlic, minced
1 cup no-salt-added tomato sauce
2 teaspoons chopped fresh basil
¼ teaspoon salt
1 pound veal cutlets (¼ inch thick)
¼ cup plus 1 tablespoon all-purpose flour
1 tablespoon chopped fresh oregano
¼ teaspoon pepper
1½ tablespoons freshly grated Parmesan cheese
2 teaspoons chopped fresh parsley

Combine chopped onion, olive oil, and garlic in a 1-quart casserole. Cover with heavy-duty plastic wrap, and vent. Microwave at HIGH 1 to 2 minutes or until onion is tender. Stir in tomato sauce, basil, and salt. Cover and vent. Microwave at HIGH 3 to 4 minutes or until mixture is thickened, stirring after 2 minutes. Set aside, and keep warm.

Trim fat from cutlets. Place cutlets between 2 sheets of heavy-duty plastic wrap, and flatten to ⅛-inch thickness, using a meat mallet or rolling pin.

Combine flour, oregano, and pepper in a medium bowl; stir well. Dredge cutlets in flour mixture.

Place a 10-inch browning skillet in microwave oven; preheat, uncovered, at HIGH 6 minutes. Place cutlets in skillet, overlapping, if necessary. Microwave, uncovered, at HIGH 1 minute. Turn cutlets, and microwave, uncovered, at HIGH 3 to 4 minutes or until veal is tender.

Pour tomato sauce mixture over cutlets; sprinkle with Parmesan cheese and chopped parsley. Microwave, uncovered, at MEDIUM HIGH (70% power) 1 to 2 minutes or until cheese melts. Yield: 4 servings (186 calories per serving).

PROTEIN 22.7 FAT 4.3 (Saturated Fat 1.4) CARBOHYDRATE 13.1
FIBER 1.4 CHOLESTEROL 84 IRON 2.1 SODIUM 289 CALCIUM 60

MIXED SQUASH WITH MINT

1⅓ cups sliced zucchini (about 2 small)
1⅓ cups sliced yellow squash (about 2 small)
¼ cup water
1 teaspoon lemon juice
½ teaspoon sugar
1½ teaspoons minced fresh mint

Place sliced zucchini, yellow squash, water, lemon juice, and sugar in a 1½-quart casserole. Cover with heavy-duty plastic wrap, and vent.

Microwave at HIGH 5 to 7 minutes or until tender; drain well. Sprinkle with minced fresh mint. Serve with a slotted spoon. Yield: 4 servings (18 calories per serving).

PROTEIN 1.1 FAT 0.2 (Saturated Fat 0) CARBOHYDRATE 4.0
FIBER 1.0 CHOLESTEROL 0 IRON 0.4 SODIUM 2 CALCIUM 17

WINE-POACHED PEARS WITH VANILLA CUSTARD SAUCE

2 large firm pears (about 1 pound)
1¼ cups Pinot Noir or other sweet red wine
¾ cup water
2 tablespoons sugar
1½ teaspoons grated lemon rind
1 vanilla bean, split lengthwise
Vanilla Custard Sauce

Peel and core pears, leaving stem ends intact. Slice each pear in half lengthwise, leaving stem intact on one side. Place pear halves in a 1-quart casserole.

Combine wine and next 4 ingredients; pour over pear halves. Cover with wax paper, and microwave at HIGH 8 minutes or until tender, rotating dish a half-turn after 4 minutes. Cover and chill at least 4 hours. Drain pears, discarding wine mixture.

Place pear halves, cut side down, on a flat cutting surface. Cut lengthwise slits in pears to within ½ inch of stem end, forming a fan. Spoon Vanilla Custard Sauce evenly onto 4 dessert plates. Arrange fanned pear halves over sauce. Yield: 4 servings (139 calories per serving).

Vanilla Custard Sauce

¾ cup skim milk
1 (2-inch) piece vanilla bean, split lengthwise
3 tablespoons sugar
1 egg

Combine milk and vanilla bean in a 2-cup glass measure. Microwave, uncovered, at HIGH 2 minutes or until hot (do not boil). Let stand 5 minutes. Remove and discard vanilla bean.

Combine sugar and egg, stirring well with a wire whisk. Gradually stir about one-fourth of hot milk mixture into egg mixture; add to remaining hot mixture, stirring constantly with a wire whisk. Microwave, uncovered, at MEDIUM HIGH (70% power) 2 minutes, stirring after 1 minute. Cover and chill thoroughly. Yield: 1 cup.

PROTEIN 3.5 FAT 1.7 (Saturated Fat 0.5) CARBOHYDRATE 29.3
FIBER 2.4 CHOLESTEROL 54 IRON 0.5 SODIUM 41 CALCIUM 75

Serve a romantic dinner in French fashion with Chicken Tarragon, Green Beans with Gruyère, and Crisp Green Salad (page 74).

An Elegant French Dinner

Easy Vichyssoise
Chicken Tarragon
Green Beans with Gruyère
Crisp Green Salad
Commercial French Bread
Fresh Berries with Brandied Custard Sauce
White Wine

SERVES 4
TOTAL CALORIES PER SERVING: 759
(Calories from Fat: 15%)

French cuisine is noted for its artful use of the freshest ingredients and for perfect flavor combinations that are pleasing to the palate.

Vichyssoise sets the mood for this elegant dinner. This microwave version of a French classic can be prepared with ease. Chicken Tarragon upholds the French passion for using fresh vegetables and herbs, and the microwave oven plays an important role in bringing out their full flavors.

Crisply-cooked green beans topped with a sprinkling of Gruyère cheese and a simple green salad complement this menu's variety of textures and flavors. White wine from the region and fresh French bread round out the meal.

Fresh berries topped with a creamy custard sauce will say "finis" deliciously. (Menu calories have been calculated to include 6 ounces wine and 1 slice bread per person.)

EASY VICHYSSOISE

2 cups canned low-sodium chicken broth,
  undiluted
2 cups peeled, diced potato
½ cup finely chopped onion
1 cup evaporated skimmed milk
¼ teaspoon salt
⅛ teaspoon ground white pepper
⅛ teaspoon ground nutmeg
Chopped fresh chervil (optional)

Combine first 3 ingredients in a deep 3-quart casserole. Cover with heavy-duty plastic wrap, and microwave at HIGH 14 to 16 minutes or until vegetables are tender.

Pour mixture into container of an electric blender or food processor; top with cover, and process until smooth. Transfer to a medium bowl. Add milk, salt, pepper, and nutmeg; stir well. Cover and chill thoroughly. To serve, ladle soup into individual bowls. Garnish with chopped fresh chervil, if desired. Yield: 4 cups (131 calories per 1-cup serving).

PROTEIN 6.9 FAT 0.3 (Saturated Fat 0.1) CARBOHYDRATE 24.2
FIBER 1.6 CHOLESTEROL 3 IRON 0.8 SODIUM 228 CALCIUM 196

CHICKEN TARRAGON

4 (4-ounce) skinned, boned chicken breast halves
1 small onion, sliced
¾ cup peeled, seeded, and chopped tomato
½ cup sliced fresh mushrooms
½ cup sliced celery
½ cup Chablis or other dry white wine
½ cup canned low-sodium chicken broth,
  undiluted
1 tablespoon finely chopped fresh tarragon,
  divided
¼ teaspoon salt
¼ teaspoon pepper
1 tablespoon cornstarch
1 tablespoon water
Fresh tarragon sprigs (optional)

Place chicken in a 3-quart casserole with thickest portions toward outside of dish. Cover with wax paper, and microwave at HIGH 2 minutes; drain.

Return chicken to casserole; add onion, tomato, mushrooms, and celery. Combine wine, chicken broth, 2 teaspoons tarragon, salt, and pepper; pour over chicken mixture. Cover with wax paper, and microwave at HIGH 8 to 10 minutes or until chicken is done and vegetables are crisp-tender, rotating a half-turn after 4 minutes. Transfer chicken and vegetables to a serving platter, using a slotted spoon; keep warm.

Combine cornstarch and water; stir well. Add to wine mixture; stir in remaining 1 teaspoon tarragon. Microwave at HIGH 2 to 3 minutes or until slightly thickened, stirring after every minute. Spoon over chicken and vegetables. Garnish with fresh tarragon sprigs, if desired. Yield: 4 servings (200 calories per serving).

PROTEIN 31.9 FAT 3.8 (Saturated Fat 1.0) CARBOHYDRATE 7.8
FIBER 1.4 CHOLESTEROL 84 IRON 1.7 SODIUM 241 CALCIUM 37

GREEN BEANS WITH GRUYÈRE

1 pound fresh green beans
½ cup water
¼ cup finely chopped onion
¼ teaspoon salt
¼ teaspoon salt-free lemon-pepper seasoning
½ cup (2 ounces) shredded Gruyère cheese

Wash beans; trim ends, and remove strings.

Combine beans, water, onion, salt, and lemon-pepper seasoning in a 1½-quart casserole. Cover with heavy-duty plastic wrap, and vent. Microwave at HIGH 5 to 6 minutes or until crisp-tender, stirring after 4 minutes. Sprinkle with Gruyère cheese. Serve immediately. Yield: 4 servings (96 calories per ½-cup serving).

PROTEIN 6.3 FAT 4.7 (Saturated Fat 2.7) CARBOHYDRATE 8.6
FIBER 2.5 CHOLESTEROL 16 IRON 1.1 SODIUM 201 CALCIUM 186

CRISP GREEN SALAD

1 tablespoon chopped shallots
3 tablespoons white wine vinegar
2 tablespoons Dijon mustard
2 tablespoons water
1 teaspoon olive oil
½ teaspoon sugar
¼ teaspoon chicken-flavored bouillon granules
¼ teaspoon pepper
2 cups torn Boston lettuce
2 cups torn radicchio

Combine shallots, vinegar, mustard, water, olive oil, sugar, bouillon granules, and pepper in a small bowl; stir well with a wire whisk until blended.

Combine lettuce and radicchio in a medium bowl; add vinegar mixture, and toss well. Arrange on individual salad plates. Yield: 4 servings (31 calories per 1-cup serving).

PROTEIN 0.5   FAT 1.8   (Saturated Fat 0.2)   CARBOHYDRATE 2.6
FIBER 0.7   CHOLESTEROL 0   IRON 0.1   SODIUM 280   CALCIUM 4

FRESH BERRIES WITH
BRANDIED CUSTARD SAUCE

½ cup skim milk
2 tablespoons sugar
1 teaspoon cornstarch
1 egg, lightly beaten
1 tablespoon brandy
½ teaspoon vanilla extract
1 cup fresh raspberries
1 cup fresh sliced strawberries
1 cup fresh blueberries

Combine milk, sugar, and cornstarch in a 2-cup glass measure. Microwave, uncovered, at HIGH 2 minutes or until thickened, stirring every 30 seconds.

Gradually stir about one-fourth of hot milk mixture into beaten egg; add to remaining milk mixture, stirring constantly with a wire whisk. Stir in brandy and vanilla extract. Microwave at MEDIUM (50% power) 1 minute or until thickened, stirring after 30 seconds. Cover and chill thoroughly.

Combine raspberries, strawberries, and blueberries. Spoon ¾ cup berry mixture into each of 4 individual dessert dishes; top evenly with custard sauce. Yield: 4 servings (109 calories per serving).

PROTEIN 3.3   FAT 1.7   (Saturated Fat 0.5)   CARBOHYDRATE 21.2
FIBER 4.7   CHOLESTEROL 54   IRON 0.6   SODIUM 35   CALCIUM 57

Enjoy music and dinner under the stars with this elegant outdoor meal. Grilled and Chilled Chicken-Rice Salad, Chocolate Pound Cake, and Concert Coolers surpass the usual picnic fare. (Menu begins on page 81.)

That's Entertaining

Come for Cards

Card Game Crunch
Stack-the-Deck Ribbon
Sandwiches
Sugar Snap Roll-Ups
Fresh Strawberries
Sugared Amaretto Bites
Coffee

SERVES 8
TOTAL CALORIES PER SERVING: 574
(Calories from Fat: 25%)

Card games have long been a
reason to invite friends over on
a regular basis. With each meet-
ing, strategies sharpen, conversation gets spicier, and good
foods abound.

Let your games begin with a
crunchy snack mix placed at
each table. Then deal each
player a plate of ribbon sandwiches, roll-ups, and fresh
strawberries.

Before the final hand, pour
the coffee and pass around a
platter of cookies. Menu calories
include 4 roll-ups, ½ cup strawberries, and 3 cookies per person.

Show your winning hand with Card Game Crunch, Stack-the-Deck Ribbon Sandwiches, and Sugar Snap Roll-Ups.

CARD GAME CRUNCH

1 cup plain croutons
1 cup small unsalted pretzels
1 cup cheese-flavored Melba rounds
1 cup bite-size crispy wheat cereal squares
2 tablespoons reduced-calorie margarine, melted
1 tablespoon Dijon mustard
1 tablespoon water
2 teaspoons low-sodium Worcestershire sauce
½ teaspoon chili powder
¼ teaspoon garlic powder
Vegetable cooking spray

Combine croutons, pretzels, Melba rounds, and cereal squares in a medium bowl. Combine marga-rine and next 5 ingredients, stirring well. Pour mar-garine mixture over crouton mixture, tossing to coat. Place in a 15- x 10- x 1-inch jellyroll pan coated with cooking spray. Bake at 350° for 10 to 12 minutes, stirring twice. Yield: 4 cups (115 calories per ½-cup serving).

PROTEIN 2.8 FAT 4.1 (Saturated Fat 0.6) CARBOHYDRATE 17
FIBER 0.6 CHOLESTEROL 0 IRON 1.5 SODIUM 289 CALCIUM 8

STACK-THE-DECK RIBBON SANDWICHES

1½ cups shredded Red Delicious apple
1½ cups shredded carrot
¾ cup (3 ounces) finely shredded 40% less-fat
  Cheddar cheese
¼ cup plus 2 tablespoons nonfat mayonnaise
¼ cup crushed pineapple in juice, drained
2 tablespoons light process cream cheese product
12 (1-ounce) slices whole wheat bread
8 (1-ounce) slices white bread

Combine first 6 ingredients in a medium bowl; stir well. Spread 2½ tablespoons apple mixture on each of 8 whole wheat bread slices. Top each with 1 white bread slice; spread 2½ tablespoons apple mixture over each. Stack to make 4 sandwiches. Top with remaining 4 whole wheat bread slices. Wrap each in plastic wrap; chill at least 2 hours. Unwrap sandwiches, and remove crusts, using an electric knife; discard crusts. Cut each sandwich into fourths, using the electric knife. Yield: 8 servings (161 calories per serving).

PROTEIN 6.0 FAT 3.4 (Saturated Fat 1.5) CARBOHYDRATE 28.8
FIBER 2.3 CHOLESTEROL 9 IRON 1.0 SODIUM 413 CALCIUM 117

SUGAR SNAP ROLL-UPS

32 fresh Sugar Snap peas
2 tablespoons Dijon mustard
2 teaspoons honey
1 tablespoon diced pimiento, drained
8 (1-ounce) slices lean cooked ham

Cook peas, covered, in a small amount of boiling water 1 minute or until crisp-tender. Rinse with cool water; drain and set aside. Combine mustard, honey, and pimiento; stir well. Brush evenly over ham slices. Cut each slice into 4 equal strips. Place 1 pea pod on end of each strip; roll up, jellyroll fashion. Cover and chill thoroughly. Yield: 32 roll-ups (13 calories each).

PROTEIN 1.5 FAT 0.4 (Saturated Fat 0.1) CARBOHYDRATE 0.8
FIBER 0.1 CHOLESTEROL 4 IRON 0.2 SODIUM 128 CALCIUM 2

SUGARED AMARETTO BITES

3 tablespoons amaretto
3 tablespoons light corn syrup
1 tablespoon unsweetened orange juice
2 cups vanilla wafer crumbs
½ cup plus 2 tablespoons sifted powdered sugar,
  divided
2 tablespoons unsweetened cocoa

Combine amaretto and corn syrup in a small saucepan; bring to a boil, stirring until blended.

Combine orange juice, vanilla wafer crumbs, ½ cup powdered sugar, and cocoa in a medium bowl; stir until blended. Add amaretto mixture to crumb mixture, stirring well. Shape mixture into 1-inch balls. Roll balls in remaining 2 tablespoons powdered sugar. Store in an airtight container. Yield: 2 dozen (72 calories each).

PROTEIN 0.6 FAT 2.2 (Saturated Fat 0.1) CARBOHYDRATE 12.3
FIBER 0 CHOLESTEROL 0.1 IRON 0.3 SODIUM 44 CALCIUM 5

 CEREAL SMARTS
Dishing up a generous helping of cereal may help lower your cholesterol level while it satisfies your appetite. Researchers at Saint Joseph's University in Pennsylvania found that people who ate cereal for breakfast had cholesterol levels that averaged 6.6 mg/dL lower than those of people who skipped breakfast.

Which substance in cereal acts as a cholesterol-lowering agent? None of them, say researchers. Instead, what elevates breakfast skippers' cholesterol is nibbling on high-fat foods, which is often done to make up for calories missed at breakfast.

High-fiber cereal may help control that nibbling, say researchers at the University of Minnesota in a separate report. After tabulating breakfast and lunch calorie totals of cereal eaters, researchers noticed that people who ate a high-fiber cereal ate fewer calories at lunch than those who ate a low-fiber variety. Dieters, take note.

Round up a crowd for Three Bean-Turkey Soup, Broccoli-Cauliflower Tossed Salad, and Whole Wheat and Rye Bread (page 80).

Western Roundup Supper

Three Bean-Turkey Soup
Broccoli-Cauliflower Tossed Salad
Whole Wheat and Rye Bread
Fruited Rice Pudding
Coffee

SERVES 10
TOTAL CALORIES PER SERVING: 634
(Calories from Fat: 12%)

Pull out the cowboy hats, lassos, chaps, and spurs, and invite the crowd over for a western theme night.

Serve this menu on trays in front of a big-screen television, and show your favorite episodes of old westerns.

A steaming bowl of Three Bean-Turkey Soup will satisfy even the heartiest appetite. Serve the soup with Broccoli-Cauliflower Tossed Salad and 1 wedge of bread per person.

Before the cowhands leave, offer warm rice pudding to give them energy for the next roundup.

THREE BEAN-TURKEY SOUP

1 cup dried red kidney beans
1 cup dried Great Northern beans
1 cup dried black beans
8 cups water
Vegetable cooking spray
1 pound freshly ground raw turkey
1 cup chopped onion
¾ cup chopped green pepper
4 cloves garlic, minced
2 (14½-ounce) cans no-salt-added whole tomatoes,
  undrained and coarsely chopped
1 (8-ounce) can no-salt-added tomato sauce
1½ cups sliced carrot
2 teaspoons dried whole oregano
1 teaspoon dried whole thyme
½ teaspoon chicken-flavored bouillon granules
½ teaspoon salt
½ teaspoon pepper

Sort and wash beans; place in a large Dutch oven. Cover with water to a depth of 2 inches above beans; let soak overnight. Drain well. Combine beans and 8 cups water in pan; bring to a boil. Cover, reduce heat, and simmer 1 hour. Drain beans, reserving 3 cups water. Transfer ⅓ cup beans to a small bowl; mash beans with a fork, making a paste.

Coat pan with cooking spray; place over medium-high heat until hot. Add ground turkey, chopped onion, chopped green pepper, and minced garlic; cook until turkey is browned and onion is tender, stirring frequently to crumble turkey. Drain turkey mixture, and pat dry with paper towels. Wipe drippings from pan with a paper towel.

Return turkey mixture to pan. Add drained beans, reserved 3 cups water, bean paste, tomato, and remaining ingredients; bring to a boil. Cover, reduce heat, and simmer 1 hour and 15 minutes or until beans are tender. Yield: 15 cups (297 calories per 1½-cup serving).

PROTEIN 25.2 FAT 2.7 (Saturated Fat 0.8) CARBOHYDRATE 44.6
FIBER 14.3 CHOLESTEROL 29 IRON 5.0 SODIUM 217 CALCIUM 138

BROCCOLI-CAULIFLOWER TOSSED SALAD

2½ cups fresh broccoli flowerets
2½ cups fresh cauliflower flowerets
5 cups torn Bibb lettuce
1 cup chopped sweet red pepper
¼ cup canned low-sodium chicken broth,
  undiluted
¼ cup water
1 clove garlic, minced
2 tablespoons lemon juice
1 tablespoon olive oil
1 to 1½ teaspoons crushed red pepper
¼ teaspoon salt
¼ teaspoon freshly ground pepper

Arrange broccoli and cauliflower in a vegetable steamer over boiling water. Cover and steam 4 to 5 minutes or until vegetables are crisp-tender. Transfer vegetables to a large bowl. Add lettuce and sweet red pepper; toss gently.

Combine chicken broth and remaining ingredients in a small jar; cover tightly, and shake vigorously to blend. Pour over vegetable mixture; toss gently. Serve immediately. Yield: 10 servings (32 calories per 1-cup serving).

PROTEIN 1.5 FAT 1.6 (Saturated Fat 0.2) CARBOHYDRATE 3.9
FIBER 1.2 CHOLESTEROL 0 IRON 0.5 SODIUM 68 CALCIUM 21

WHOLE WHEAT AND RYE BREAD

2 packages dry yeast
1 cup warm water (105° to 115°)
1 cup nonfat buttermilk
½ cup molasses
¼ cup vegetable oil
2¼ cups whole wheat flour
¾ cup rye flour
3 tablespoons unsweetened cocoa
1 teaspoon caraway seeds
1 teaspoon salt
2¼ cups bread flour, divided
Vegetable cooking spray

Dissolve yeast in warm water in a large bowl; let stand 5 minutes. Add buttermilk, molasses, and vegetable oil; beat at medium speed of an electric mixer until well blended. Add whole wheat flour, rye flour, cocoa, caraway seeds, and salt; beat until well blended. Gradually stir in 2 cups plus 2 tablespoons bread flour to make a soft dough.

Sprinkle 2 remaining tablespoons bread flour evenly over work surface. Turn dough out onto floured surface, and knead until dough is smooth and elastic (about 5 minutes). Place dough in a large bowl coated with cooking spray, turning to coat top. Cover and let rise in a warm place (85°), free from drafts, 1 hour or until doubled in bulk.

Punch dough down; divide in half. Shape each portion into a round loaf. Let rest 10 minutes. Place each round on a baking sheet coated with vegetable cooking spray.

Cover and let rise in a warm place, free from drafts, 30 minutes or until doubled in bulk. Bake at 350° for 30 minutes or until loaves sound hollow when tapped. Remove loaves from baking sheets; cool on wire racks. Cut each loaf into 12 wedges. Yield: 24 servings (132 calories per wedge).

PROTEIN 3.9 FAT 2.9 (Saturated Fat 0.6) CARBOHYDRATE 23.4
FIBER 2.3 CHOLESTEROL 0 IRON 1.6 SODIUM 112 CALCIUM 40

FRUITED RICE PUDDING

4 cups plus 1 tablespoon skim milk, divided
¾ cup sugar
½ cup short-grain rice, uncooked
1 tablespoon cornstarch
2 eggs, lightly beaten
1½ cups canned pears in juice, drained and
    chopped
1½ teaspoons vanilla extract
Vegetable cooking spray
1 tablespoon brown sugar
½ teaspoon ground cinnamon

Combine 4 cups milk, sugar, and rice in a large saucepan; bring to a boil. Cover, reduce heat, and simmer 15 minutes, stirring occasionally. Combine cornstarch and remaining 1 tablespoon milk. Add to rice mixture, stirring constantly. Bring to a boil; cook 1 minute. Remove from heat. Gradually stir about one-fourth of rice mixture into eggs; add to remaining rice mixture, stirring constantly. Stir in pear and vanilla.

Pour mixture into a 2-quart baking dish coated with cooking spray. Combine brown sugar and cinnamon; sprinkle over rice mixture. Bake at 350° for 45 minutes. Yield: 10 servings (173 calories per serving).

PROTEIN 5.3 FAT 1.3 (Saturated Fat 0.4) CARBOHYDRATE 34.6
FIBER 0.2 CHOLESTEROL 44 IRON 0.7 SODIUM 65 CALCIUM 130

Begin this elegant outdoor meal with chilled Savory Carrot Soup (page 82).

Music and Dinner Alfresco

Savory Carrot Soup
Grilled and Chilled Chicken-Rice Salad
Commercial French Bread
Chocolate Pound Cake
Concert Coolers

SERVES 6
TOTAL CALORIES PER SERVING: 687
(Calories from Fat: 15%)

Music sets the mood for an evening at an outdoor concert under the stars. Make it a special occasion by using a festive tablecloth, cloth napkins, and your finest china. Chill the mixture for the Concert Coolers in a silver wine bucket and serve the coolers in graceful stemmed glasses.

Begin the meal with Savory Carrot Soup and French bread. You will get rave reviews with Grilled and Chilled Chicken-Rice Salad, a main-dish salad that is easy to pack and transport. For the encore, offer slices of Chocolate Pound Cake. Menu calories include 1 slice of bread and cake per person.

SAVORY CARROT SOUP

Vegetable cooking spray
2 teaspoons reduced-calorie margarine
1½ cups chopped onion
2¾ cups sliced carrot
1½ cups diced red potato
3 cups canned no-salt-added chicken broth,
    undiluted
¾ cup unsweetened orange juice
½ teaspoon dried whole thyme
¼ teaspoon salt
¼ teaspoon pepper
Fresh thyme sprigs (optional)

Coat a large saucepan with cooking spray; add margarine, and place over medium-high heat until margarine melts. Add onion and carrot; sauté until crisp-tender. Add potato and chicken broth; bring to a boil. Cover, reduce heat, and simmer 25 minutes or until carrot is tender.

Position knife blade in food processor; add carrot mixture in batches. Process 1 minute or until mixture is smooth.

Return carrot mixture to saucepan; add orange juice, dried whole thyme, salt, and pepper. Cook, uncovered, until thoroughly heated. Serve warm or chilled. Garnish with fresh thyme, if desired. Yield: 1½ quarts (112 calories per 1-cup serving).

PROTEIN 3.2 FAT 2.1 (Saturated Fat 0.5) CARBOHYDRATE 20.6
FIBER 3.7 CHOLESTEROL 0 IRON 1.2 SODIUM 206 CALCIUM 37

GRILLED AND CHILLED CHICKEN-RICE SALAD

4 (4-ounce) skinned, boned chicken breast halves
1 tablespoon low-sodium soy sauce
½ teaspoon salt-free lemon-pepper seasoning
Vegetable cooking spray
1 cup chopped Red Delicious apple
2 teaspoons lemon juice
¾ cup sliced celery
⅓ cup raisins
2½ cups cooked long-grain rice (cooked without
    salt or fat)
¼ cup plus 2 tablespoons nonfat mayonnaise
¼ cup plain nonfat yogurt
¼ cup unsweetened apple juice
Lettuce leaves (optional)
¼ cup thinly sliced green onions

Brush chicken breast halves with soy sauce, and sprinkle with lemon-pepper seasoning.

Coat grill rack with vegetable cooking spray, and place on grill over medium-hot coals. Place chicken breasts on rack, and cook 5 to 6 minutes on each side or until chicken is tender. Remove chicken from grill, and let cool slightly. Cut chicken into 1-inch pieces.

Combine chopped apple and lemon juice in a large bowl. Add chicken, sliced celery, raisins, and cooked rice to apple mixture; toss well.

Combine mayonnaise, yogurt, and apple juice in a small bowl; stir well. Pour mayonnaise mixture over chicken mixture, and toss gently to combine. Cover and chill thoroughly.

Just before serving, spoon mixture into a lettuce-lined bowl, if desired. Sprinkle with green onions. Yield: 6 servings (232 calories per 1-cup serving).

PROTEIN 19.8 FAT 2.5 (Saturated Fat 0.7) CARBOHYDRATE 33.3
FIBER 1.6 CHOLESTEROL 47 IRON 1.7 SODIUM 318 CALCIUM 47

CHOCOLATE POUND CAKE

Vegetable cooking spray
2¼ cups plus 1 teaspoon sifted cake flour, divided
½ cup margarine, softened
¾ cup sugar
3 egg whites
2 teaspoons vanilla extract
¼ cup unsweetened cocoa
¾ teaspoon baking soda
¼ teaspoon salt
1 (8-ounce) carton vanilla low-fat yogurt
1 teaspoon powdered sugar
Fresh strawberries (optional)

Coat bottom and sides of an 8½- x 4½- x 3-inch loafpan with cooking spray; sprinkle with 1 teaspoon flour, and set aside.

Cream margarine. Gradually add sugar; beat well at medium speed of an electric mixer. Add egg whites; beat 4 minutes or until well blended. Stir in vanilla.

Combine remaining 2¼ cups flour, cocoa, soda, and salt; add to creamed mixture alternately with yogurt, beginning and ending with dry ingredients.

Pour batter into prepared pan. Bake at 350° for 55 to 60 minutes or until a wooden pick inserted in center comes out clean. Cool in pan 10 minutes; remove from pan. Let cool completely on a wire rack. Sift powdered sugar over cooled cake. Garnish with fresh strawberries, if desired. Yield: 16 servings (160 calories per ½-inch slice).

PROTEIN 2.9   FAT 6.2   (Saturated Fat 1.2)   CARBOHYDRATE 23.1
FIBER 0   CHOLESTEROL 1   IRON 1.3   SODIUM 162   CALCIUM 39

CONCERT COOLERS

1 cup unsweetened orange juice
1 cup cranberry juice cocktail
2 tablespoons sugar
2 cups Chablis or other dry white wine, chilled
2 cups club soda, chilled
Fresh mint sprigs (optional)

Combine first 4 ingredients in a pitcher; stir well. Cover and chill. Just before serving, stir in club soda. Serve over ice. Garnish with mint sprigs, if desired. Yield: 1½ quarts (110 calories per 1-cup serving).

PROTEIN 0.4   FAT 0.0   (Saturated Fat 0)   CARBOHYDRATE 15.5
FIBER 0.1   CHOLESTEROL 0   IRON 0.5   SODIUM 21   CALCIUM 16

 YO-YO DIETING

Low-calorie diets can actually make you more likely to gain weight. Research suggests that on-again, off-again dieting sets up a person to put on extra pounds in the long run. To make matters worse, initial weight loss on rapid weight reduction diets tends to be a combination of muscle and some fat, but the weight gained back is all fat.

It seems that the body interprets severe calorie restriction as starvation. To compensate, metabolism slows down. Fewer calories are needed to function, and so weight loss becomes more difficult. It sounds like a cruel trick, but to the "starved" body it is a defense mechanism. To short-circuit this response, dieters need to take a more balanced approach to weight loss.

The best way to diet is to make a permanent change in eating habits, not to endure a short-term fast. Aim for a moderate cut in calories rather than a severe cut. A good rule for dieters is to estimate 10 calories for every pound of body weight. If you weigh 150 pounds, multiply this figure by 10 to get 1,500 calories. To keep dieting efforts from being sabotaged, a person who weighs 150 pounds should not drop below the 1,200 calorie level. Couple this not-so-severe calorie restriction with increased amounts of exercise, and weight should come off slowly but surely.

Savor a warm fall evening with a grilled meal featuring Glazed Salmon Steaks, Grilled Vegetable Medley, and Herbed Garlic Bread (page 86).

An Indian Summer Supper

Tossed Greens with Citrus Vinaigrette
Glazed Salmon Steaks
Grilled Vegetable Medley
Herbed Garlic Bread
Grilled Plums with Spiced Vanilla Cream
Sparkling Mineral Water

SERVES 6
TOTAL CALORIES PER SERVING: 555
(Calories from Fat: 29%)

Crisp, cool air and rustling yellow, red, and brown leaves are signs of autumn. But just when it seems that fall is here, Mother Nature tempts us with a burst of warm weather called Indian Summer. This spell of warm weather is the perfect opportunity to pull out the grill and the patio furniture and enjoy one more meal outdoors.

Recapture some flavors of summer with a crisp tossed salad and fresh herb bread. While the marinated salmon steaks sizzle on the grill alongside the vegetable medley and the fresh plums, sit on the patio and enjoy the last vestiges of summer. (Menu calories have been calculated for 1 wedge of bread per person.)

TOSSED GREENS WITH CITRUS VINAIGRETTE

2½ cups torn curly endive
2½ cups torn Boston lettuce
½ cup thinly sliced cucumber
½ cup sliced radishes
1 pink grapefruit, peeled and sectioned
3 tablespoons unsweetened orange juice
1 tablespoon lime juice
1½ teaspoons vegetable oil
½ teaspoon sugar
¼ teaspoon chili powder

Combine endive, lettuce, cucumber, radishes, and grapefruit sections in a large bowl; toss gently. Cover and chill.

Combine orange juice, lime juice, oil, sugar, and chili powder; stir well with a wire whisk. Pour over lettuce mixture, and toss gently. Yield: 6 servings (34 calories per 1-cup serving).

PROTEIN 0.7   FAT 1.3   (Saturated Fat 0.2)   CARBOHYDRATE 5.7
FIBER 0.5   CHOLESTEROL 0   IRON 0.2   SODIUM 6   CALCIUM 13

GLAZED SALMON STEAKS

¼ cup low-sodium soy sauce
10 cloves garlic, halved
6 (4-ounce) salmon steaks (½ inch thick)
3 tablespoons brown sugar
2 tablespoons honey
1 tablespoon water
2 teaspoons vegetable oil
Vegetable cooking spray
Fresh basil (optional)

Combine soy sauce and garlic in a large zip-top heavy-duty plastic bag; add salmon steaks. Seal bag, and marinate steaks in refrigerator up to 4 hours, turning occasionally.

Combine brown sugar and next 3 ingredients in a small saucepan; cook over medium heat, stirring until sugar dissolves.

Remove salmon steaks from marinade; discard marinade. Brush brown sugar mixture on both sides of each steak.

Coat grill rack with cooking spray; place on grill over medium-hot coals. Place salmon steaks on rack, and cook 5 to 6 minutes on each side or until fish flakes easily when tested with a fork. Garnish with fresh basil, if desired. Yield: 6 servings (230 calories per serving).

PROTEIN 22.4   FAT 10.6   (Saturated Fat 1.8)   CARBOHYDRATE 10.4
FIBER 0   CHOLESTEROL 71   IRON 0.7   SODIUM 139   CALCIUM 10

GRILLED VEGETABLE MEDLEY

1 tablespoon minced fresh parsley
½ teaspoon garlic powder
¼ teaspoon pepper
3 tablespoons balsamic vinegar
1 tablespoon olive oil
18 baby yellow squash (about ½ pound)
1 large sweet red pepper, cut into 1-inch pieces
3 small zucchini, cut lengthwise into quarters
Vegetable cooking spray

Combine first 5 ingredients; stir well. Add squash, red pepper, and zucchini; toss gently.

Arrange vegetables in a wire grilling basket coated with cooking spray. Place on grill over medium-hot coals. Cook 10 to 12 minutes or until tender, turning once. Yield: 6 servings (35 calories per serving).

PROTEIN 1.4   FAT 1.5   (Saturated Fat 0.2)   CARBOHYDRATE 5.2
FIBER 1.5   CHOLESTEROL 0   IRON 0.9   SODIUM 4   CALCIUM 19

HERBED GARLIC BREAD

1 package dry yeast
1 teaspoon sugar
1¼ cups warm water (105° to 115°)
¾ cup lite beer
2 tablespoons olive oil
2 teaspoons sugar
1 teaspoon salt
½ teaspoon garlic powder
4½ cups unbleached flour, divided
2 tablespoons unbleached flour
Vegetable cooking spray
¾ cup loosely packed fresh basil leaves, shredded
¼ cup minced fresh parsley
2 tablespoons grated Parmesan cheese

Dissolve yeast and 1 teaspoon sugar in water in a large bowl; let stand 5 minutes. Add beer (at room temperature), olive oil, 2 teaspoons sugar, salt, garlic powder, and 1½ cups flour; beat at medium speed of an electric mixer until blended. Gradually stir in enough of the remaining 3 cups flour to make a soft dough.

Sprinkle 2 tablespoons flour evenly over work surface. Turn dough out onto floured surface; knead until smooth and elastic (about 8 to 10 minutes). Place dough in a large bowl coated with cooking spray; turn to coat top. Cover and let rise in a warm place (85°), free from drafts, 1 hour or until doubled in bulk.

Punch dough down, and let rest 10 minutes. Turn dough out, and knead in shredded basil and minced parsley. Divide dough evenly into 3 portions. Shape each portion into a round, slightly flat loaf. Place loaves on baking sheets coated with cooking spray. Spray tops of loaves with cooking spray, and sprinkle loaves evenly with Parmesan cheese.

Cover and let rise in a warm place, free from drafts, 30 minutes. Bake at 400° for 15 minutes or until lightly browned. Remove from baking sheets, and let cool on wire racks. Cut each loaf into 8 wedges. Yield: 24 servings (114 calories per wedge).

PROTEIN 4.6   FAT 1.8   (Saturated Fat 0.3)   CARBOHYDRATE 20.8
FIBER 0.6   CHOLESTEROL 0   IRON 5.1   SODIUM 110   CALCIUM 124

GRILLED PLUMS WITH SPICED VANILLA CREAM

10 medium-size fresh plums, sliced
2 tablespoons sugar
2 teaspoons lemon juice
1½ tablespoons reduced-calorie margarine
¾ cup vanilla nonfat frozen yogurt, softened
1 (8-ounce) carton vanilla low-fat yogurt
½ teaspoon ground allspice
¼ teaspoon ground cinnamon
Lemon zest (optional)

Place plums on the bottom half of a large sheet of heavy-duty aluminum foil. Sprinkle evenly with sugar and lemon juice. Dot with margarine. Fold upper half of foil over plums, and seal. Place grill rack over medium-hot coals. Place plum packet on rack, and grill 5 to 8 minutes or until hot.

Combine frozen yogurt and next 3 ingredients in a small bowl; stir well.

Remove plums from foil, using a slotted spoon, and transfer to individual serving dishes. Top evenly with yogurt mixture. Garnish with lemon zest, if desired. Serve immediately. Yield: 6 servings (142 calories per serving).

PROTEIN 3.4   FAT 3.0   (Saturated Fat 0.6)   CARBOHYDRATE 27.8
FIBER 2.4   CHOLESTEROL 2   IRON 0.2   SODIUM 64   CALCIUM 95

Chilled Borscht (page 88) is a simple yet elegant first-course soup.

A Classic Affair

Chilled Borscht
Mustard-Crusted Rack of Lamb
Rosemary Potatoes
Steamed Asparagus
Commercial Hard Rolls
Brandied Pineapple à la Mode
Sparkling Mineral Water

SERVES 8
TOTAL CALORIES PER SERVING: 710
(Calories from Fat: 23%)

Simple and elegant, this menu upholds the traditions of a formal dinner party yet meets new healthy standards for fat and calories.

The meal begins with a colorful appetizer soup. For the entrée, racks of lamb are roasted with a savory breadcrumb coating. Accompany the lamb with potatoes that are tossed with fresh rosemary. Asparagus spears and warm dinner rolls complement the meal. (Menu calories allow for 4 ounces asparagus and 1 roll per person.) For dessert, guests can enjoy fresh pineapple marinated, broiled, and served with frozen yogurt.

A formal dinner party provides an opportunity to show off a grand meal and a beautifully appointed table. Silver, china, and flowers set the mood for the occasion and reflect the good taste of the host or hostess. Entertaining with style is never out of style.

CHILLED BORSCHT

2 cups canned low-sodium chicken broth,
   undiluted
½ cup water
¾ cup minced carrot
¼ cup minced onion
¼ cup minced celery
¼ cup Zinfandel or other sweet red wine
1 (16-ounce) can whole beets, undrained
1 teaspoon lemon juice
⅛ teaspoon salt
⅛ teaspoon ground white pepper
Fresh chive sprigs (optional)

Combine chicken broth, water, carrot, onion, and celery in a medium saucepan.

Bring mixture to a boil; reduce heat, and simmer 20 minutes or until vegetables are tender. Add wine, and cook 1 minute. Remove from heat, and let cool.

Combine vegetable mixture, beets, lemon juice, salt, and pepper in container of an electric blender or food processor. Top with cover, and process until smooth. Transfer mixture to a medium bowl; cover and chill thoroughly.

To serve, ladle soup into individual soup bowls. Garnish with fresh chive sprigs, if desired. Yield: 1½ quarts (35 calories per ¾-cup serving).

PROTEIN 0.9   FAT 0.1   (Saturated Fat 0)   CARBOHYDRATE 7.4
FIBER 1.0   CHOLESTEROL 0   IRON 0.5   SODIUM 179   CALCIUM 18

MUSTARD-CRUSTED RACK OF LAMB

2 (2-pound) racks of lamb (16 chops)
¼ cup frozen orange juice concentrate, thawed
1½ tablespoons Dijon mustard
1 tablespoon lemon juice
½ teaspoon pepper
4 large cloves garlic, minced
Vegetable cooking spray
⅓ cup Italian-seasoned breadcrumbs
Fresh watercress sprigs (optional)

Trim fat from racks, leaving only small eye of rib. Strip rib tips of all meat and fat. Combine orange juice concentrate, Dijon mustard, lemon juice, pepper, and garlic; stir well. Spread orange juice

mixture over meat portion of racks. Place racks, bone side down, on a rack in a roasting pan coated with cooking spray. Insert meat thermometer, making sure it does not touch bone.

Bake at 450° for 10 minutes. Remove from oven, and pat breadcrumbs on top of meat. Reduce heat to 400°, and bake an additional 45 minutes or until meat thermometer registers 160° (medium). Remove from oven, and let stand 10 minutes before slicing. Garnish with watercress sprigs, if desired. Yield: 8 servings (256 calories per serving).

PROTEIN 26.6   FAT 12.4   (Saturated Fat 4.3)   CARBOHYDRATE 7.8
FIBER 0.2   CHOLESTEROL 84   IRON 2.3   SODIUM 295   CALCIUM 26

ROSEMARY POTATOES

24 small new potatoes (about 2
   pounds)
1½ tablespoons reduced-calorie margarine,
   melted
1 tablespoon chopped fresh rosemary
¼ teaspoon pepper
⅛ teaspoon salt
Fresh rosemary sprigs (optional)

Peel a ½-inch strip around each potato. Cook, covered, in boiling water 20 minutes or until tender; drain. Combine margarine and next 3 ingredients. Add to potatoes; toss. Garnish with rosemary sprigs, if desired. Yield: 8 servings (88 calories per serving).

PROTEIN 2.2   FAT 1.5   (Saturated Fat 0.2)   CARBOHYDRATE 17.1
FIBER 1.9   CHOLESTEROL 0   IRON 1.5   SODIUM 65   CALCIUM 19

BRANDIED PINEAPPLE À LA MODE

1 large pineapple (about 4½-pounds)
½ cup brandy
3 tablespoons honey
3 tablespoons brown sugar
4 cups pineapple low-fat frozen yogurt
Pineapple leaves (optional)

Peel and core pineapple, reserving top. Cut pineapple into 8 (½-inch-thick) slices. Reserve remaining pineapple for other uses.

Combine pineapple slices and brandy in a zip-top heavy-duty plastic bag; seal bag, and shake until pineapple is well coated. Marinate in refrigerator 2 hours, turning occasionally.

Drain pineapple; discard brandy. Place pineapple on rack of a broiler pan. Drizzle honey over pineapple; sprinkle with brown sugar. Broil 3 inches from heat for 3 minutes or until bubbly. Transfer pineapple to individual dessert plates; top each with ½ cup frozen yogurt. Garnish with leaves from pineapple top, if desired. Yield: 8 servings (150 calories per serving).

PROTEIN 2.8 FAT 2.0 (Saturated Fat 1.2) CARBOHYDRATE 32.5
FIBER 0.9 CHOLESTEROL 9 IRON 0.4 SODIUM 33 CALCIUM 94

 WHY DO DIETS FAIL?

For many people, losing weight is a difficult proposition. In principle, cutting calories and increasing activity are all that's necessary to burn excess body fat. Yet the simplest of tasks often gets detoured by common mistakes. If you're trying to lose weight, avoid the following diet traps:
• Overestimating portion sizes. It's very easy to slice up an extra ounce of meat or pour on an overly generous helping of salad dressing without realizing it. Invest in measuring cups and spoons and a small food scale to accurately determine food portions.
• Stepping on the scale too often. Weight loss and weight gain happen slowly. Chances are the numbers won't change quickly enough for most people, and that in itself can be discouraging. If you must weigh, do so no more than once per week.
• Forgetting that exercise is part of the equation. Creating a big enough calorie deficit to lose weight takes more than dieting—activity is crucial. Moreover, new studies show that dieters who exercise are more likely to keep off weight than those who don't.

• Ignoring hidden fats. Fat is twice as dense in calories as are carbohydrate and protein. Convenience foods, whole milk dairy products, and luncheon meats are examples of foods with hidden fats. Be sure to select low-fat versions of these foods.
• Selecting the wrong diet. Fad diets that promote one food or nutrient can be not only expensive but also harmful. But even balanced weight-loss plans can backfire. It's important to consider your lifestyle, family situation, and work habits when planning a diet. Making changes you can live with is the key to losing weight and keeping it off.
• Putting a time limit on the weight-loss period. Telling yourself that you must lose 10 pounds before a party, the swimsuit season, or a special event is not a good approach to weight loss. Even if you do trim off the weight, chances are the loss will be temporary because you won't last on a starvation diet plan. A more long-lasting approach to weight loss focuses on changing the eating and exercise habits that caused the weight gain in the first place.

Light
Recipes

Vine-ripened fruits fresh from the
garden can enhance any meal. Try
these light recipes that taste as
delicious as they are nutritious:
Fresh Strawberry Pie (page 241) and
Poppy Seed Fruit Salad (page 182).

In "Light Recipes," you will discover recipes that capture the best flavors of fresh, wholesome foods. From entrées of beef, pork, fish, poultry, and meatless main dishes to accompaniments of pasta, grains, salads, fruits, and vegetables, your family is sure to enjoy the variety that *Cooking Light* offers. And there is no better way to top off a meal than by including a *Cooking Light* dessert.

With a little planning, you can turn healthy recipes into nutritionally balanced meals whose taste and appearance say "delicious." Planning healthy meals begins with recipes that include nutrient-dense foods.

It does take more than a healthy recipe to make a balanced meal, and the nutrient analysis that follows each recipe will help you create nutritionally sound meals. When putting together recipes to create a menu, remember that of the total calories provided, at least 50 percent should be from carbohydrate, about 20 percent from protein, and no more than 30 percent from fat. By keeping this 50-20-30 ratio in mind, you can create balanced meals for optimal health. Also, remember that the saturated fat content should be limited to no more than 10 percent of the total calories.

Each *Cooking Light* recipe has been kitchen-tested by a staff of home economists to ensure that it meets strict standards for sound nutrition, excellent flavor, and visual appeal. Each recipe has been analyzed for key nutrients including total fat, saturated fat, and fiber. The fat content of each recipe has been carefully evaluated to keep it at the lowest level possible while allowing the product to maintain good flavor and texture. The use of saturated fats has been limited, and unsaturated fats such as vegetable oil have been used in place of shortening in breads, cakes, pastries, and other baked products.

Whether you are having a backyard picnic, a neighborhood gathering, a holiday celebration, or a last-minute lunch, you will find many ideas in the following recipe sections to help you create exciting meals that meet today's high standards in nutrition.

Greet guests with a variety of interesting appetizers: (from front) Smoked Trout Canapés (page 97), Brussels Sprouts Cups (page 97), Chicken-Stuffed Endive (page 99), and Nacho Olive Dip (page 94).

Appetizers & Beverages

WHITE BEAN DIP WITH FRUIT SALSA

1½ cups seeded, diced watermelon
1 cup orange sections, diced
¾ cup diced jicama
1 jalapeño pepper, seeded and minced
2 tablespoons chopped fresh cilantro
1 tablespoon fresh mint
1 tablespoon fresh lime juice
2 teaspoons olive oil
1 cup chopped onion
2 (14-ounce) cans cannellini beans, drained and
    coarsely mashed
2 (4-ounce) cans chopped green chiles, drained
Fresh cilantro sprigs (optional)

Combine first 7 ingredients in a medium bowl; toss well. Cover and let stand 30 minutes.

Heat oil in a large nonstick skillet over medium heat. Add onion, and sauté until tender. Add beans and green chiles; cook 3 to 4 minutes or until thoroughly heated, stirring constantly.

Transfer bean mixture to a wide, shallow serving dish. Spoon watermelon mixture over beans. Garnish with fresh cilantro sprigs, if desired. Serve immediately. Serve with commercial baked tortilla chips or toasted pita wedges. Yield: 20 appetizer servings (43 calories per serving).

PROTEIN 1.7   FAT 0.7   (Saturated Fat 0.1)   CARBOHYDRATE 7.7
FIBER 1.4   CHOLESTEROL 0   IRON 0.7   SODIUM 122   CALCIUM 16

NACHO OLIVE DIP

1 cup nonfat sour cream
½ cup nonfat mayonnaise
1 (4½-ounce) can chopped ripe olives, drained
¾ cup minced green onions
¾ cup seeded, chopped tomato
⅔ cup minced fresh cilantro
2 tablespoons fresh lime juice
2 cloves garlic, minced
1 teaspoon hot sauce

Combine all ingredients in a medium bowl. Cover and chill at least 2 hours. Serve with fresh raw vegetables, commercial baked tortilla chips, pita wedges, commercial breadsticks, or Melba rounds. Yield: 3¼ cups (9 calories per tablespoon).

PROTEIN 0.4   FAT 0.3   (Saturated Fat 0.1)   CARBOHYDRATE 1.3
FIBER 0.2   CHOLESTEROL 0   IRON 0.1   SODIUM 55   CALCIUM 9

MUSHROOM PÂTÉ

½ ounce dried porcini mushrooms
½ cup water
½ cup tawny port
2 cups chopped fresh mushrooms
½ cup minced onion
3 ounces Neufchâtel cheese, softened
⅓ cup minced fresh parsley

Combine first 3 ingredients in a small saucepan. Bring to a boil; cover, reduce heat, and simmer 10 minutes. Remove from heat, and let stand 30 minutes. Drain, reserving liquid; finely chop porcini mushrooms. Set aside.

Pour reserved liquid through a cheesecloth-lined sieve or colander. Return liquid to saucepan. Bring to a boil; boil 5 to 7 minutes, uncovered, or until mixture reduces to ⅓ cup. Add fresh mushrooms and onion; reduce heat, and cook 8 to 10 minutes or until liquid evaporates. Remove from heat; stir in chopped porcini mushrooms. Let cool completely.

Beat Neufchâtel cheese at high speed of an electric mixer until light and fluffy; add parsley, and beat well. Stir in mushroom mixture. Transfer mixture to a small crock or bowl; cover and chill at least 1 hour. Serve with Melba rounds or unsalted crackers. Yield: 1½ cups (15 calories per tablespoon).

PROTEIN 0.6   FAT 0.9   (Saturated Fat 0.5)   CARBOHYDRATE 1.3
FIBER 0.3   CHOLESTEROL 3   IRON 0.2   SODIUM 15   CALCIUM 5

CARAMELIZED ONIONS

Vegetable cooking spray
1 tablespoon olive oil
3 large purple onions, thinly sliced and separated
 into rings
1 teaspoon sugar
2 (8-ounce) cartons plain nonfat yogurt
1 tablespoon balsamic vinegar
¼ teaspoon salt
Dash of freshly ground pepper

Coat a large nonstick skillet with cooking spray; add oil. Place over medium-high heat until hot. Add onion and sugar; sauté 10 to 15 minutes or until onion is tender, stirring mixture frequently. Reduce heat to medium-low, and cook 20 to 30 minutes or until onion is golden brown, stirring occasionally. Remove from heat, and let cool completely.

Spoon yogurt onto several layers of heavy-duty paper towels; spread to ½-inch thickness. Cover with additional paper towels; let stand 5 minutes. Scrape into a bowl, using a rubber spatula. Add vinegar and salt, stirring well. Stir in onion mixture. Transfer to a serving bowl, and sprinkle with pepper. Serve with Melba rounds or party pumpernickel bread. Yield: 2 cups (19 calories per tablespoon).

PROTEIN 1.0 FAT 0.5 (Saturated Fat 0.1) CARBOHYDRATE 2.8
FIBER 0.3 CHOLESTEROL 0 IRON 0.1 SODIUM 30 CALCIUM 32

SMOKED SALMON SPREAD

¾ pound smoked salmon, cut into 1-inch pieces
½ cup chopped green onions
1 tablespoon Dijon mustard
1 teaspoon lemon juice
½ teaspoon white pepper
1 cup plain nonfat yogurt
2 hard-cooked egg whites, diced
3 tablespoons minced fresh chives

Position knife blade in food processor bowl. Add first 5 ingredients. Pulse 8 times or until mixture is minced. Place mixture on a sheet of heavy-duty plastic wrap, and shape into a 2-inch-thick patty. Cover and chill at least 8 hours.

Spoon yogurt onto several layers of heavy-duty paper towels; spread to ½-inch thickness. Cover with additional paper towels; let stand 5 minutes. Scrape into a bowl, using a rubber spatula; cover and chill thoroughly.

Place salmon patty on a serving platter; spread yogurt over top and sides of patty. Sprinkle diced egg white and chives over yogurt. Serve with cucumber slices or Melba rounds. Yield: 1¾ cups (22 calories per tablespoon).

PROTEIN 3.0 FAT 0.6 (Saturated Fat 0.1) CARBOHYDRATE 0.9
FIBER 0.1 CHOLESTEROL 3 IRON 0.1 SODIUM 122 CALCIUM 19

STUFFED CHILE BITES

3 ounces Neufchâtel cheese, softened
2 tablespoons commercial spoonable nonfat
 salad dressing
1 (6⅛-ounce) can 60% less-salt tuna in water,
 drained
1 (2-ounce) can chopped green chiles,
 drained
2 tablespoons finely chopped green onions
2 tablespoons minced fresh cilantro
½ teaspoon ground cumin
4 mild poblano chiles (about 4 inches long), cored
 and seeded
Fresh cilantro sprigs (optional)

Combine Neufchâtel cheese and salad dressing in a medium bowl; beat at low speed of an electric mixer until smooth. Add tuna and next 4 ingredients, stirring well. Spoon tuna mixture evenly into chiles; cover and chill at least 2 hours.

To serve, cut chiles into 1-inch slices, and arrange on a serving platter. Garnish with fresh cilantro sprigs, if desired. Yield: 16 appetizers (37 calories each).

PROTEIN 4.1 FAT 1.3 (Saturated Fat 0.8) CARBOHYDRATE 2.3
FIBER 0.3 CHOLESTEROL 9 IRON 0.6 SODIUM 73 CALCIUM 10

CHEESY CRABMEAT WONTONS

½ (8-ounce) package Neufchâtel cheese, softened
½ cup lite ricotta cheese
½ teaspoon low-sodium soy sauce
1 cup minced fresh chives
½ pound fresh lump crabmeat, drained
2 egg whites
1 teaspoon water
1 (16-ounce) package fresh or frozen wonton skins, thawed
Olive oil-flavored vegetable cooking spray
½ cup balsamic vinegar
⅓ cup water
2 tablespoons finely shredded pickled gingerroot

Place Neufchâtel cheese in a medium bowl; beat well at medium speed of an electric mixer. Add ricotta cheese and soy sauce; beat until well blended. Stir in chives and crabmeat, stirring well.

Combine egg whites and 1 teaspoon water. Place 1 teaspoon cheese mixture in top corner of each wonton skin. Fold top point of wonton skin over filling; tuck point under filling. Roll once toward center, covering filling and leaving about 1 inch unrolled at bottom of skin. Moisten remaining corners with egg white mixture; bring corners together, and overlap, pressing ends together to seal securely. Place on a baking sheet coated with cooking spray. Cover filled wonton, and repeat procedure with remaining wonton skins, cheese mixture, and egg white mixture.

Cook wontons, in batches, in boiling water 3 minutes or until tender. Drain; coat wontons with cooking spray, and arrange on a serving platter. Combine vinegar, ⅓ cup water, and gingerroot; serve with wontons. Yield: 7 dozen appetizers (13 calories each).

PROTEIN 1.0   FAT 0.5   (Saturated Fat 0.2)   CARBOHYDRATE 0.9
FIBER 0   CHOLESTEROL 8.1   IRON 0.1   SODIUM 28   CALCIUM 6

WONTONS MADE EASY

Place 1 teaspoon cheese mixture in one corner of each wonton.

Fold top point of wonton over filling, tucking point under filling.

Roll toward center; moisten with egg white mixture.

Bring side corners of wonton skins together, and overlap.

Press ends together to seal wontons securely.

Cook, in batches, in boiling water 3 minutes or until wontons are tender.

SPICY PEPPER WEDGES

1 (7-ounce) jar roasted red peppers in water,
    drained
6 pimiento-stuffed olives
1 jalapeño pepper, seeded and coarsely chopped
2 tablespoons chopped fresh thyme
2 teaspoons olive oil
1½ teaspoons lemon juice
½ teaspoon freshly ground pepper
2 large sweet yellow peppers, seeded and cut into
    eighths

Position knife blade in food processor bowl; add
first 7 ingredients. Pulse 5 to 7 times or until peppers
are minced. Spoon mixture evenly onto pepper pieces.
Cover and chill. Yield: 16 appetizers (12 calories each).

PROTEIN 0.2   FAT 0.7   (Saturated Fat 0.1)   CARBOHYDRATE 1.4
FIBER 0.3   CHOLESTEROL 0   IRON 0.3   SODIUM 53   CALCIUM 3

BRUSSELS SPROUTS CUPS

48 large brussels sprout leaves
1 quart boiling water
1 (8-ounce) carton plain nonfat yogurt
1 teaspoon minced fresh dillweed
1 teaspoon grated onion
2 tablespoons red caviar, rinsed and drained

Place brussels sprout leaves in a colander. Pour
boiling water over leaves. Rinse under cold water until
cool. Drain on paper towels, and set aside.

Spoon yogurt onto several layers of heavy-duty
paper towels; spread to ½-inch thickness. Cover with
additional paper towels; let stand 5 minutes. Scrape
into a small bowl. Stir in dillweed and onion.

Place one brussels sprout leaf inside another leaf.
Spoon ½ teaspoon yogurt mixture onto leaf; top with
¼ teaspoon caviar. Repeat procedure with remaining leaves, yogurt mixture, and caviar. Yield: 2 dozen
(10 calories each).

PROTEIN 1.0   FAT 0.3   (Saturated Fat 0)   CARBOHYDRATE 1.1
FIBER 0.1   CHOLESTEROL 9   IRON 0.1   SODIUM 29   CALCIUM 22

SMOKED TROUT CANAPÉS

½ cup wild rice, uncooked
1½ cups water
1 cup part-skim ricotta cheese
1 egg yolk, lightly beaten
¼ cup reduced-calorie margarine, melted
¼ cup all-purpose flour
1½ teaspoons dried whole dillweed, divided
¼ teaspoon salt
4 egg whites
⅛ teaspoon cream of tartar
Vegetable cooking spray
½ cup nonfat sour cream
1 small cucumber, thinly sliced
4 ounces smoked freshwater trout, flaked
Fresh watercress sprigs (optional)

Rinse rice in 3 changes of hot water; drain. Place
1½ cups water in a medium saucepan; bring to a boil.
Add rice; cover, reduce heat, and simmer 50 minutes.
Drain; set aside, and let cool.

Combine ricotta cheese and egg yolk in a medium
bowl, stirring well. Add margarine, and stir well to
combine. Combine flour, 1 teaspoon dillweed, and salt;
add to cheese mixture, stirring just until dry ingredients are moistened.

Beat egg whites in a medium bowl at high speed
of an electric mixer until foamy. Add cream of tartar;
beat until stiff peaks form. Fold one-fourth of egg whites
into cheese mixture. Fold in rice. Gently fold in remaining egg whites.

For each canapé base, pour 1½ tablespoons batter onto a hot griddle coated with cooking spray,
spreading batter to a 2¼-inch circle. Turn when edges
look cooked.

Combine sour cream and remaining ½ teaspoon
dillweed; stir well.

To serve, place a cucumber slice on each canapé
base; top with 1 teaspoon sour cream mixture and
1 teaspoon smoked trout. Garnish canapés with fresh
watercress sprigs, if desired. Yield: 24 appetizers (57
calories each).

PROTEIN 4.1   FAT 2.5   (Saturated Fat 0.8)   CARBOHYDRATE 4.6
FIBER 0.3   CHOLESTEROL 16   IRON 0.4   SODIUM 110   CALCIUM 37

Sweet Red Pepper Terrine, accented with Watercress Vinaigrette, makes a colorful first-course presentation.

CHICKEN-STUFFED ENDIVE

½ cup thinly sliced green beans
4 ounces smoked chicken breast, cut into ¼-inch
    pieces
⅓ cup diced sweet red pepper
¼ cup minced shallot
2 tablespoons minced fresh basil
2 tablespoons grated Parmesan cheese
3 tablespoons lemon juice
1 tablespoon olive oil
2 teaspoons minced drained capers
½ teaspoon freshly ground pepper
25 endive spears (about 3 heads)
2 tablespoons pine nuts, toasted

Blanch beans in boiling water 30 seconds or until crisp-tender. Drain and rinse under cold water until cool. Drain well. Combine beans and next 9 ingredients in a bowl; cover and chill at least 1 hour.

Spoon mixture evenly into endive spears. Sprinkle with pine nuts. Yield: 25 appetizers (23 calories each).

PROTEIN 1.7 FAT 1.5 (Saturated Fat 0.3) CARBOHYDRATE 1.2
FIBER 0.2 CHOLESTEROL 3 IRON 0.3 SODIUM 79 CALCIUM 11

SWEET RED PEPPER TERRINE

6 large sweet red peppers (about 3 pounds)
4 large cloves garlic, unpeeled
¼ teaspoon salt
¼ teaspoon ground red pepper
1½ cups part-skim ricotta cheese
2 envelopes unflavored gelatin
½ cup canned low-sodium chicken broth, undiluted
10 thin fresh asparagus spears (about ¼ pound)
Watercress Vinaigrette

Cut peppers in half lengthwise; remove and discard seeds and membrane. Place peppers, skin side up, and garlic on a large baking sheet; flatten peppers with palm of hand. Broil 5½ inches from heat 15 to 20 minutes or until charred. Place peppers in ice water until cool. Remove from water; peel and discard skins.

Squeeze garlic pulp into container of an electric blender or food processor; add sweet red peppers, salt, and ground red pepper. Top with cover, and process until smooth. Transfer to a saucepan; cook over medium-low heat until mixture reduces to 1¾ cups. Remove from heat, and let cool. Return puree to container of blender; add ricotta cheese. Top with cover, and process until smooth. Transfer to a bowl.

Sprinkle gelatin over chicken broth in a small saucepan; let stand 1 minute. Cook over low heat, stirring until gelatin dissolves. Stir into pureed pepper mixture; cool to room temperature.

Snap off tough ends of asparagus. Remove scales from spears with a knife or vegetable peeler, if desired. Trim asparagus to 8½-inch lengths. Arrange asparagus in a vegetable steamer over boiling water. Cover and steam 4 to 5 minutes or until crisp-tender.

Line an 8½- x 4½- x 3-inch loafpan with heavy-duty plastic wrap. Pour half of pureed mixture into prepared loafpan; arrange asparagus spears lengthwise on mixture. Pour remaining pureed mixture over asparagus, spreading evenly. Cover with plastic wrap, and chill at least 4 hours or until set.

Remove top sheet of plastic wrap. Invert terrine onto a serving platter; remove remaining plastic wrap. Slice terrine with an electric knife. Transfer to individual serving plates. Spoon Watercress Vinaigrette in circles around slices of terrine. Draw a wooden pick through vinaigrette, creating a paisley design. Yield: 10 appetizer servings (89 calories per serving).

Watercress Vinaigrette

1½ cups trimmed fresh watercress
¾ cup commercial oil-free herb vinaigrette
    dressing
¼ teaspoon freshly ground pepper

Arrange watercress in a vegetable steamer over boiling water. Cover and steam 1 minute or until wilted but still bright green. Rinse under cold, running water; squeeze dry. Combine watercress, dressing, and pepper in container of an electric blender; top with cover, and process until smooth. Yield: ¾ cup.

PROTEIN 6.5 FAT 3.3 (Saturated Fat 1.9) CARBOHYDRATE 8.4
FIBER 1.5 CHOLESTEROL 11 IRON 1.3 SODIUM 316 CALCIUM 117

CABBAGE-WRAPPED THAI LAMB

1 pound lean ground lamb
½ cup chopped onion
2 cloves garlic, minced
1 (2-inch) piece fresh gingerroot, peeled and
  minced
1 teaspoon dried whole rosemary, crushed
½ teaspoon crushed red pepper flakes
½ cup minced fresh mint leaves
2 tablespoons lime juice
1 tablespoon low-sodium soy sauce
1 teaspoon sesame seeds
16 large Chinese cabbage leaves

Combine first 6 ingredients in a large nonstick skillet. Cook over medium-high heat until browned, stirring to crumble. Drain and pat dry with paper towels. Combine meat mixture, mint, lime juice, soy sauce, and sesame seeds in a medium bowl.

Blanch cabbage leaves in boiling water 30 seconds. Drain and rinse under cold water until cool; drain well.

Spoon 3 tablespoons lamb mixture in center of each cabbage leaf; fold ends over, and roll up. Serve warm. Yield: 16 appetizers (49 calories each.)

PROTEIN 6.1 FAT 2.0 (Saturated Fat 0.7) CARBOHYDRATE 1.6
FIBER 0.3 CHOLESTEROL 18 IRON 0.7 SODIUM 54 CALCIUM 32

STONE CRAB CLAWS WITH MUSTARD-FENNEL AIOLI

¾ pound fennel
Vegetable cooking spray
2 tablespoons Chablis or other dry white wine
4 large cloves garlic, sliced
1 cup 1% low-fat cottage cheese
½ cup plain nonfat yogurt
3 tablespoons Dijon mustard
1 teaspoon lemon juice
½ teaspoon ground red pepper
24 (3-ounce) precooked stone crab claws, chilled

Trim off leaves of fennel, reserving for other uses. Trim off tough outer stalks and discard. Cut bulb in half lengthwise; remove and discard core. Cut bulb crosswise into ⅛-inch slices.

Coat a medium nonstick skillet with cooking spray; place over medium-high heat until hot. Add fennel, wine, and garlic; sauté until tender. Remove from heat, and let cool.

Combine fennel mixture, cottage cheese, yogurt, mustard, lemon juice, and red pepper in container of an electric blender or food processor; top with cover, and process until smooth. Cover mixture, and chill at least 1 hour. Serve aioli with stone crab claws. Yield: 24 appetizer servings (37 calories per crab claw and 1½ tablespoons dip).

PROTEIN 6.0 FAT 0.7 (Saturated Fat 0.1) CARBOHYDRATE 1.4
FIBER 0.1 CHOLESTEROL 22 IRON 0.4 SODIUM 158 CALCIUM 46

TOMATILLO SALSA-SCALLOP APPETIZERS

⅔ cup husked, diced tomatillos
⅔ cup diced jicama
½ cup minced green onions
½ cup lime juice
⅓ cup minced fresh cilantro
¼ teaspoon salt
¼ teaspoon garlic powder
Vegetable cooking spray
1½ teaspoons olive oil
½ cup minced shallot
1 pound bay scallops
½ cup crushed ice
3 medium tomatoes, each cut into
  4 slices
6 large Bibb lettuce leaves

Combine first 7 ingredients in a medium bowl. Cover and chill 1 hour.

Coat a large nonstick skillet with cooking spray; add oil. Place over medium-high heat until hot. Add shallot, and sauté 2 minutes or until tender. Add scallops, and sauté 2 minutes or until scallops are opaque.

Add crushed ice to tomatillo mixture. Immediately add scallop mixture to tomatillo mixture; stir well. Cover and chill at least 2 hours.

To serve, arrange 2 tomato slices and a lettuce leaf on each individual serving plate. Spoon scallop mixture evenly onto lettuce leaves, using a slotted spoon. Yield: 6 appetizer servings (120 calories per serving).

PROTEIN 14.3 FAT 2.2 (Saturated Fat 0.3) CARBOHYDRATE 11.8
FIBER 1.7 CHOLESTEROL 25 IRON 1.2 SODIUM 233 CALCIUM 42

BAKED STUFFED SHRIMP

1 (8-ounce) package fresh, washed and
    trimmed spinach
Vegetable cooking spray
2 teaspoons olive oil
1 cup finely chopped fresh mushrooms
¼ cup minced shallot
¼ cup plus 2 tablespoons freshly grated
    Parmesan cheese, divided
2 tablespoons minced fresh basil
½ teaspoon hot sauce
16 jumbo unpeeled fresh shrimp (about 1 pound)
1 tablespoon fresh lemon juice

Cook spinach in a small amount of boiling water 1 minute. Drain well; chop spinach, and set aside.

Coat a large nonstick skillet with cooking spray; add olive oil. Place over medium-high heat until hot. Add chopped mushrooms and minced shallot; sauté 5 minutes or until tender. Add spinach, and cook over medium heat 5 minutes, stirring frequently. Remove from heat; stir in ¼ cup Parmesan cheese, basil, and hot sauce. Set aside.

Peel and devein shrimp, leaving tails intact. Butterfly shrimp. Brush shrimp with lemon juice. Top each shrimp with 1 tablespoon plus 1 teaspoon spinach mixture.

Place shrimp on a baking sheet coated with cooking spray. Sprinkle remaining 2 tablespoons Parmesan cheese over spinach mixture. Bake at 350° for 14 to 15 minutes or until shrimp turn pink. Transfer shrimp to a serving platter, and serve immediately. Yield: 16 appetizers (34 calories each).

PROTEIN 4.6 FAT 1.3 (Saturated Fat 0.4) CARBOHYDRATE 1.3
FIBER 0.6 CHOLESTEROL 32 IRON 1.0 SODIUM 77 CALCIUM 44

MARINATED SHRIMP KABOBS

¼ cup dry sherry
2 tablespoons low-sodium soy sauce
3 cloves garlic, crushed
1½ tablespoons peeled, grated gingerroot
2 bay leaves, crumbled
24 jumbo fresh shrimp (about 1½ pounds), peeled
    and deveined
24 small cherry tomatoes
24 large green onions tops, blanched and
    trimmed to 6-inch lengths
Vegetable cooking spray

Combine first 5 ingredients in a shallow dish. Add shrimp; toss gently. Cover and marinate in refrigerator at least 2 hours, stirring occasionally.

Soak 24 (6-inch) bamboo skewers in water 30 minutes; set aside.

Remove shrimp from marinade, discarding marinade. Thread 1 cherry tomato onto each skewer; thread 1 shrimp lengthwise onto end of each skewer, going not quite completely through shrimp. Tie a green onion strip around center of each shrimp.

Coat grill rack with cooking spray; place on grill over medium-hot coals. Place kabobs on rack, and cook 4 to 5 minutes on each side or until shrimp are done. Yield: 2 dozen (20 calories each).

PROTEIN 3.5 FAT 0.3 (Saturated Fat 0.1) CARBOHYDRATE 0.8
FIBER 0.2 CHOLESTEROL 31 IRON 0.6 SODIUM 53 CALCIUM 9

 BUTTERFLYING SHRIMP
To butterfly shrimp for recipes such as Baked Stuffed Shrimp, first peel and devein the shrimp. Then make a deeper slit down the back of the shrimp, cutting almost through it. Open the shrimp, and place cut side of shrimp down on a surface, pressing the flat side of knife across shrimp to flatten it.

BANANA-RUM COOLERS

1 large banana, peeled and sliced
1 cup skim milk, divided
1 cup ice cubes
¼ cup sparkling mineral water, chilled
1 tablespoon honey
⅛ to ¼ teaspoon rum flavoring

Place banana slices on a baking sheet. Cover and freeze until firm.

Combine banana and ¼ cup milk in container of an electric blender; top with cover, and process until smooth. Add remaining ¾ cup milk, ice cubes, and remaining ingredients; process until smooth. Pour into chilled glasses. Serve immediately. Yield: 4 cups (71 calories per 1-cup serving).

PROTEIN 2.5   FAT 0.3   (Saturated Fat 0.1)   CARBOHYDRATE 15.6
FIBER 1.0   CHOLESTEROL 1   IRON 0.2   SODIUM 35   CALCIUM 78

FUZZY NAVEL FREEZE

1½ cups skim milk
1½ cups frozen unsweetened sliced peaches
1 (6-ounce) can frozen orange juice concentrate,
    thawed and undiluted
12 ice cubes
2 tablespoons peach schnapps
1 (8-ounce) carton plain nonfat yogurt

Combine milk, peaches, orange juice concentrate, ice cubes, and schnapps in container of an electric blender; top with cover, and process until smooth. Add yogurt, and process just until blended. Pour into glasses, and serve immediately. Yield: 5 cups (136 calories per 1-cup serving).

PROTEIN 6.1   FAT 0.3   (Saturated Fat 0.2)   CARBOHYDRATE 25.1
FIBER 0.8   CHOLESTEROL 2   IRON 0.2   SODIUM 74   CALCIUM 193

PURPLE COW

⅔ cup unsweetened grape juice, chilled
½ cup skim milk
½ cup club soda, chilled
½ cup vanilla ice milk

Combine all ingredients in container of an electric blender; top with cover, and process until smooth. Pour into glasses, and serve immediately. Yield: 2 cups (123 calories per 1-cup serving).

PROTEIN 3.4   FAT 1.5   (Saturated Fat 1.0)   CARBOHYDRATE 24.5
FIBER 0   CHOLESTEROL 6   IRON 0.3   SODIUM 73   CALCIUM 133

SPICED FRUIT SLUSH

4½ cups cranberry-apple drink
½ teaspoon ground cinnamon
¼ teaspoon ground nutmeg
2 tea bags
½ cup sugar
½ cup vodka
3 cups lemon-lime-flavored sparkling
    mineral water, chilled

Combine first 3 ingredients in a medium saucepan; bring mixture to a boil. Add tea bags, and remove from heat. Cover and steep 5 minutes. Remove and discard tea bags. Add sugar, stirring until dissolved. Set aside to cool.

Combine tea mixture and vodka in a large freezer-proof container, stirring well. Cover and freeze 8 hours or until slushy, stirring occasionally.

To serve, spoon ½ cup juice mixture into each glass. Add ¼ cup mineral water to each; stir until slushy. Yield: 9 cups (116 calories per ¾-cup serving).

PROTEIN 0.1   FAT 0.0   (Saturated Fat 0)   CARBOHYDRATE 24.1
FIBER 0   CHOLESTEROL 0   IRON 0.1   SODIUM 14   CALCIUM 8

Fresh flavors of summer blend together in sparkling Melonade Punch.

MELONADE PUNCH

1 large watermelon (about 17 pounds)
2 cups fresh strawberries
1¼ cups sugar
1 cup unsweetened orange juice
5 cups lemon-flavored sparkling mineral water,
   chilled

Cut a thin slice from bottom of melon, if necessary, to prevent rolling; cut top third from other end. Scoop pulp from melon, and remove seeds. Use a U-shaped knife or paring knife to make decorative cuts around edge of melon shell. Set aside.

Combine pulp and strawberries in container of an electric blender in batches; top with cover, and process until pureed.

Combine sugar and orange juice in a saucepan. Bring to a boil; reduce heat, and simmer 5 minutes. Add to pureed watermelon mixture; cover and chill.

Just before serving, stir in mineral water. Serve in watermelon shell. Yield: 5½ quarts (100 calories per 1-cup serving).

PROTEIN 1.1   FAT 0.7   (Saturated Fat 0.3)   CARBOHYDRATE 24.1
FIBER 1.3   CHOLESTEROL 0   IRON 0.3   SODIUM 15   CALCIUM 15

CRANBERRY DAIQUIRI PUNCH

2 (12-ounce) cans frozen cranberry juice cocktail,
   undiluted
3 medium-size ripe bananas, peeled and sliced
½ cup rum
1 pint lime sherbet, softened
5 cups lemon-lime-flavored sparkling mineral
   water, chilled

Combine first 3 ingredients in container of an electric blender; top with cover, and process until smooth. Pour cranberry mixture into a punch bowl. Spoon small scoops of sherbet into punch bowl. Add mineral water; stir gently to blend. Serve immediately. Yield: 2½ quarts (144 calories per ½-cup serving).

PROTEIN 0.4 FAT 0.3 (Saturated Fat 0.2) CARBOHYDRATE 27.0
FIBER 0.6 CHOLESTEROL 0 IRON 0.1 SODIUM 34 CALCIUM 9

HARVEST COFFEE

¼ cup ground coffee
1½ teaspoons apple pie spice
3½ cups water
1 cup skim milk
2 tablespoons reduced-calorie maple-flavored
   syrup
4 (3-inch) sticks cinnamon (optional)

Combine coffee and apple pie spice in basket of a drip coffee maker or electric percolator. Fill pot to the 3½-cup mark with water. Prepare coffee according to manufacturer's instructions.

Combine milk and syrup in a small saucepan; cook over medium heat until thoroughly heated (do not boil). Pour ¾ cup coffee and ¼ cup milk mixture into each mug; stir well. Garnish each serving with a cinnamon stick, if desired. Yield: 4 cups (31 calories per 1-cup serving).

PROTEIN 2.3 FAT 0.3 (Saturated Fat 0.1) CARBOHYDRATE 5.3
FIBER 0.1 CHOLESTEROL 1 IRON 0.9 SODIUM 38 CALCIUM 86

ICED COFFEE BRACER

1 cup strong brewed coffee, chilled
1⅔ cups skim milk
2 tablespoons instant coffee granules
2 tablespoons brandy
1 tablespoon chocolate syrup
1 cup club soda, chilled

Pour coffee into an ice cube tray; freeze until firm. Combine milk and coffee granules; stir until granules dissolve. Add brandy and remaining ingredients; stir well. Pour over coffee ice cubes; serve immediately. Yield: 3 cups (93 calories per 1-cup serving).

PROTEIN 5.2 FAT 0.3 (Saturated Fat 0.2) CARBOHYDRATE 10.5
FIBER 0 CHOLESTEROL 3 IRON 0.6 SODIUM 93 CALCIUM 176

BLACK FOREST COCOA

¼ cup sugar
¼ cup unsweetened cocoa
4 cups skim milk, divided
1 cup pitted fresh or frozen sweet cherries
2 tablespoons kirsch or other cherry-flavored
   liqueur

Combine sugar and cocoa in a saucepan; stir well. Gradually add ½ cup milk; stir well. Add remaining 3½ cups milk, cherries, and kirsch; stir well. Place over medium heat; cook 5 minutes or until thoroughly heated, stirring frequently. Transfer mixture, in batches, to container of an electric blender; top with cover, and process until smooth. Serve immediately. Yield: 5 cups (154 calories per 1-cup serving).

PROTEIN 8.3 FAT 1.1 (Saturated Fat 0.6) CARBOHYDRATE 28.4
FIBER 0.1 CHOLESTEROL 4 IRON 1.0 SODIUM 105 CALCIUM 253

From left: Pepper-Topped Focaccia (page 112), Fennel-Onion Casserole Loaf (page 113), and Fresh Chive Buttermilk Biscuits (page 107) are flavorful ways to add carbohydrate to your meals.

Breads

CARAWAY-ONION CRACKERS

¾ cup all-purpose flour
½ cup whole wheat flour
2 tablespoons wheat germ
2 teaspoons sugar
¼ teaspoon salt
¼ teaspoon onion powder
⅓ cup margarine
¼ cup cold water
Vegetable cooking spray
1 egg white, lightly beaten
1 tablespoon caraway seeds

Combine first 6 ingredients in a large bowl; cut in margarine with a pastry blender until mixture resembles coarse meal. Sprinkle water, 1 tablespoon at a time, evenly over surface; stir with a fork just until dry ingredients are moistened. Shape into a ball.

Roll dough to ⅛-inch thickness between 2 sheets of heavy-duty plastic wrap. Remove top sheet of plastic wrap, and cut dough into 1½-inch diamonds. Remove diamonds from bottom sheet of plastic wrap, and place on baking sheets coated with cooking spray. Brush with egg white; sprinkle with caraway seeds. Bake at 375° for 12 to 14 minutes or until golden. Remove from baking sheets, and let cool on wire racks. Store in an airtight container. Yield: 3½ dozen (28 calories each).

PROTEIN 0.6   FAT 1.6   (Saturated Fat 0.3)   CARBOHYDRATE 3.1
FIBER 0.3   CHOLESTEROL 0   IRON 0.2   SODIUM 32   CALCIUM 3

WHOLE WHEAT BUTTERMILK PANCAKES

1½ cups all-purpose flour
½ cup whole wheat flour
1 teaspoon baking soda
¼ teaspoon salt
2 teaspoons sugar
2 cups nonfat buttermilk
2 eggs, lightly beaten
Vegetable cooking spray

Combine first 5 ingredients in a large bowl; make a well in center of mixture. Combine buttermilk and eggs; add to dry ingredients, stirring just until dry ingredients are moistened.

For each pancake, pour ¼ cup batter onto a hot griddle or skillet coated with cooking spray. Turn pancakes when tops are covered with bubbles and edges look cooked. Yield: 18 (4-inch) pancakes (67 calories each).

PROTEIN 3.1   FAT 0.9   (Saturated Fat 0.2)   CARBOHYDRATE 11.6
FIBER 0.7   CHOLESTEROL 24   IRON 0.7   SODIUM 114   CALCIUM 47

CARDAMOM YEAST WAFFLES

1 package dry yeast
1⅓ cups warm skim milk (105° to 115°)
3 tablespoons sugar
2 cups all-purpose flour
¼ teaspoon salt
¼ teaspoon ground cardamom
2 eggs, lightly beaten
2 tablespoons vegetable oil
2 teaspoons vanilla extract
Vegetable cooking spray
Powdered sugar (optional)
Fresh sliced strawberries (optional)

Dissolve yeast in warm milk in a bowl; add sugar, and let stand 5 minutes. Combine flour, salt, and cardamom; add to yeast mixture, beating at low speed of an electric mixer just until blended. Combine eggs, oil, and vanilla; add to flour mixture, and beat at low speed until blended. Cover and refrigerate 8 hours.

Coat a waffle iron with cooking spray; allow waffle iron to preheat. Gently stir batter to blend. For each waffle, spoon ¼ cup batter onto hot waffle iron, spreading batter to edges. Bake 4 to 5 minutes or until steaming stops. Repeat procedure with remaining batter. If desired, sift powdered sugar over waffles, and top with sliced strawberries. Yield: 12 (4-inch) waffles (130 calories each).

PROTEIN 4.2   FAT 3.6   (Saturated Fat 0.7)   CARBOHYDRATE 19.7
FIBER 0.7   CHOLESTEROL 36   IRON 1.1   SODIUM 74   CALCIUM 41

FRESH CHIVE BUTTERMILK BISCUITS

2 cups all-purpose flour
1 tablespoon baking powder
½ teaspoon sugar
¼ teaspoon baking soda
¼ teaspoon salt
3 tablespoons chopped fresh chives
3 tablespoons margarine
¾ cup plus 1 tablespoon nonfat buttermilk
1 tablespoon all-purpose flour
¼ teaspoon paprika

Combine first 6 ingredients in a medium bowl; cut in margarine with a pastry blender until mixture resembles coarse meal. Add buttermilk, stirring just until dry ingredients are moistened.

Sprinkle 1 tablespoon flour evenly over work surface. Turn dough out onto floured surface, and knead 10 to 12 times. Roll dough to ½-inch thickness; cut into rounds with a 2-inch biscuit cutter. Place rounds on an ungreased baking sheet, and sprinkle evenly with paprika. Bake at 425° for 10 to 12 minutes or until biscuits are golden. Yield: 21 biscuits (60 calories each).

PROTEIN 1.6   FAT 1.8   (Saturated Fat 0.3)   CARBOHYDRATE 9.4
FIBER 0.3   CHOLESTEROL 0   IRON 0.5   SODIUM 110   CALCIUM 43

CARROT AND PINEAPPLE MUFFINS

1¾ cups all-purpose flour
1 teaspoon baking soda
1 teaspoon ground cinnamon
¼ teaspoon salt
¼ teaspoon ground allspice
⅓ cup sugar
1 (8-ounce) can crushed pineapple in juice, undrained
1 cup shredded carrot
¼ cup vegetable oil
3 tablespoons skim milk
1 egg, lightly beaten
Vegetable cooking spray

Combine first 6 ingredients in a medium bowl; make a well in center of mixture. Combine pineapple, carrot, oil, milk, and egg; add to dry ingredients, stirring just until dry ingredients are moistened.

Spoon batter into muffin pans coated with cooking spray, filling two-thirds full. Bake at 400° for 20 to 25 minutes or until golden. Remove from pans immediately. Yield: 14 muffins (127 calories each).

PROTEIN 2.2   FAT 4.7   (Saturated Fat 0.8)   CARBOHYDRATE 19.4
FIBER 0.7   CHOLESTEROL 15   IRON 0.9   SODIUM 110   CALCIUM 28

WHOLE GRAIN-PUMPKIN MUFFINS

¾ cup shreds of wheat bran cereal
¾ cup nonfat buttermilk
½ cup cooked, mashed pumpkin
¼ cup vegetable oil
1 egg, lightly beaten
1 teaspoon grated orange rind
¾ cup all-purpose flour
¾ cup whole wheat flour
½ teaspoon baking powder
½ teaspoon baking soda
⅛ tcaspoon salt
⅓ cup sugar
1 teaspoon ground cinnamon
Vegetable cooking spray
1 tablespoon sugar
¼ teaspoon ground cinnamon

Combine cereal and buttermilk in a bowl; let stand 5 minutes. Add pumpkin, oil, egg, and orange rind; stir well. Combine all-purpose flour and next 6 ingredients in a bowl; make a well in center of mixture. Add buttermilk mixture, stirring just until dry ingredients are moistened (batter will be thick).

Spoon batter into muffin pans coated with cooking spray, filling two-thirds full. Combine 1 tablespoon sugar and ¼ teaspoon cinnamon; sprinkle evenly over muffins. Bake at 400° for 15 to 20 minutes or until golden. Yield: 1 dozen (142 calories each).

PROTEIN 3.4   FAT 5.5   (Saturated Fat 1.0)   CARBOHYDRATE 21.8
FIBER 2.5   CHOLESTEROL 18   IRON 1.4   SODIUM 125   CALCIUM 46

Weekend guests will be delighted when you serve Lemon-Apricot Soda Bread. Spread low-sugar orange marmalade on each slice for a low-fat condiment.

LEMON-APRICOT SODA BREAD

2¾ cups all-purpose flour
1 teaspoon baking powder
1 teaspoon baking soda
¼ teaspoon salt
¼ cup sugar
¼ teaspoon ground nutmeg
1⅓ cups nonfat buttermilk
½ cup chopped dried apricots
¼ cup margarine, melted
1 egg, lightly beaten
1 teaspoon grated lemon rind
Vegetable cooking spray

Combine first 6 ingredients; make a well in center of mixture. Combine buttermilk, apricots, margarine, egg, and lemon rind. Add to dry ingredients, stirring just until dry ingredients are moistened.

Spoon batter into an 8½- x 4½- x 3-inch loafpan coated with cooking spray. Bake at 350° for 45 minutes or until a wooden pick inserted in center comes out clean. Let cool in pan 10 minutes; remove from pan. Yield: 16 servings (135 calories per ½-inch slice).

PROTEIN 3.4   FAT 3.6   (Saturated Fat 0.6)   CARBOHYDRATE 22.5
FIBER 0.7   CHOLESTEROL 13   IRON 1.2   SODIUM 170   CALCIUM 55

MINIATURE BROWN BREAD LOAVES

1½ cups whole wheat flour
½ cup yellow cornmeal
1 teaspoon baking soda
¼ teaspoon salt
½ cup raisins
⅓ cup firmly packed brown sugar
¼ teaspoon ground ginger
1¼ cups nonfat buttermilk
¼ cup molasses
Vegetable cooking spray

Combine first 7 ingredients in a medium bowl; make a well in center of mixture. Combine buttermilk and molasses; add to dry ingredients, stirring just until dry ingredients are moistened.

Spoon batter into two 5¾- x 3- x 2⅛-inch miniature loafpans coated with cooking spray. Bake at 350° for 35 minutes or until golden. Let cool in pans 10 minutes; remove from pans, and let cool completely on a wire rack. Yield: 20 servings (84 calories per ½-inch slice).

PROTEIN 2.2 FAT 0.4 (Saturated Fat 0.1) CARBOHYDRATE 19.0
FIBER 1.5 CHOLESTEROL 0 IRON 0.9 SODIUM 89 CALCIUM 42

BANANA-DATE LOAF

1¼ cups whole wheat flour
1 cup all-purpose flour
2 teaspoons baking powder
½ teaspoon baking soda
½ teaspoon ground nutmeg
¼ teaspoon salt
½ cup sugar
1 cup mashed ripe banana
⅓ cup skim milk
¼ cup vegetable oil
1 egg, lightly beaten
½ cup finely chopped dates
Vegetable cooking spray

Combine first 7 ingredients in a medium bowl; make a well in center of mixture. Combine mashed banana, milk, vegetable oil, and egg; add to dry ingredients, stirring just until dry ingredients are moistened. Stir in chopped dates.

Spoon batter into a 9- x 5- x 3-inch loafpan coated with cooking spray. Bake at 350° for 45 to 55 minutes or until a wooden pick inserted in center comes out clean. Let cool in pan 10 minutes; remove from pan, and let cool on a wire rack. Yield: 18 servings (134 calories per ½-inch slice).

PROTEIN 2.5 FAT 3.7 (Saturated Fat 0.7) CARBOHYDRATE 24.0
FIBER 2.1 CHOLESTEROL 12 IRON 0.8 SODIUM 96 CALCIUM 40

HEARTY OAT AND GRAIN LOAF

1 cup all-purpose flour
1 cup whole wheat flour
1 cup medium rye flour
1 tablespoon baking powder
½ teaspoon salt
½ cup quick-cooking oats, uncooked
⅓ cup firmly packed brown sugar
1½ cups plus 2 tablespoons skim milk
¼ cup vegetable oil
1 egg, lightly beaten
Vegetable cooking spray

Combine first 7 ingredients in a large bowl; make a well in center of mixture. Combine milk, oil, and egg; add to dry ingredients, stirring just until dry ingredients are moistened.

Spoon batter into a 9- x 5- x 3-inch loafpan coated with cooking spray. Bake at 350° for 50 to 55 minutes or until a wooden pick inserted in center comes out clean.

Let cool in pan 10 minutes; remove loaf from pan, and let cool completely on a wire rack. Yield: 18 servings (127 calories per ½-inch slice).

PROTEIN 3.4 FAT 3.8 (Saturated Fat 0.7) CARBOHYDRATE 20.3
FIBER 2.0 CHOLESTEROL 12 IRON 0.9 SODIUM 132 CALCIUM 70

GARLIC-MUSTARD SOFT PRETZELS

1½ cups all-purpose flour, divided
1 cup whole wheat flour
1 package dry yeast
1 tablespoon sugar
½ teaspoon salt
½ teaspoon garlic powder
½ teaspoon dry mustard
1 cup water
1 tablespoon margarine
2 tablespoons all-purpose flour
Vegetable cooking spray
1 egg white, lightly beaten
2 teaspoons water
2 teaspoons wheat germ

Combine ½ cup all-purpose flour and next 6 ingredients in a large bowl; stir well. Set aside.

Combine 1 cup water and margarine in a small saucepan; cook over medium heat until very warm (120° to 130°). Gradually add to flour mixture, beating at low speed of an electric mixer until blended. Beat an additional 3 minutes at medium speed. Stir in enough of the remaining 1 cup all-purpose flour to make a soft dough.

Sprinkle 2 tablespoons all-purpose flour evenly over work surface. Turn dough out onto floured surface, and knead until smooth and elastic (about 8 to 10 minutes). Place dough in a large bowl coated with cooking spray, turning to coat top. Cover and let rise in a warm place (85°), free from drafts, 45 minutes or until doubled in bulk.

Punch dough down; cover and let rest 15 minutes. Divide dough in half. Working with 1 portion at a time, divide each portion into 8 pieces; roll each into a 14-inch rope. Twist each rope into a pretzel shape. Place pretzels on baking sheets coated with cooking spray.

Cover and let rise in a warm place, free from drafts, 20 minutes or until doubled in bulk. Combine egg white and 2 teaspoons water; brush over pretzels. Sprinkle with wheat germ. Bake at 400° for 10 minutes or until golden. Yield: 16 pretzels (83 calories each).

PROTEIN 2.8 FAT 1.1 (Saturated Fat 0.8) CARBOHYDRATE 15.6
FIBER 1.5 CHOLESTEROL 0 IRON 0.9 SODIUM 86 CALCIUM 6

ADD SPICE FOR HEALTH

Stirring ground ginger into a batch of cookies or sprinkling cinnamon on baked fruit adds flavor, but that's not all. Scientists are discovering health benefits of these and other spices.

In a study of college students sensitive to motion sickness, ground ginger proved to be a more successful treatment than a commonly used motion sickness medication.

Cinnamon, apple pie spice, cloves, and turmeric are beneficial in another way. USDA scientists found that these spices helped improve blood sugar levels. In laboratory tests, the spices appeared to help insulin, the hormone that controls blood sugar levels, work more effectively.

But more research is needed to understand how this works and just how much of these spices would be needed to help regulate blood sugar. The current findings, although preliminary, are good news for many people with diabetes. And for all of us, the benefits of these spices are just another reason to enjoy a touch of flavor.

SWEET POTATO BUBBLE ROLLS

3 cups all-purpose flour, divided
1 cup whole wheat flour
2 tablespoons sugar
1 teaspoon grated orange rind
1 teaspoon ground cinnamon
¼ teaspoon salt
¼ teaspoon ground nutmeg
¼ teaspoon ground cloves
1 package dry yeast
1 cup skim milk
1 cup canned mashed, unsweetened sweet potato
2 tablespoons margarine
1 egg, lightly beaten
1 tablespoon all-purpose flour
Vegetable cooking spray
1 egg white, lightly beaten
1 tablespoon water
2 tablespoons sugar
½ teaspoon ground cinnamon

For hearty breads that are also healthful, try (from left) Sweet Potato Bubble Rolls and Cinnamon-Raisin Batter Bread (page 115).

Combine 1 cup all-purpose flour and next 8 ingredients in a large bowl; stir well. Set aside.

Combine milk, mashed sweet potato, and margarine in a small saucepan; cook over medium heat until margarine melts, stirring occasionally. Cool mixture to 120° to 130°.

Gradually add sweet potato mixture and egg to flour mixture, beating at low speed of an electric mixer until blended. Beat an additional 2 minutes at medium speed. Gradually add ¾ cup all-purpose flour, beating 2 minutes at medium speed. Gradually stir in enough of the remaining 1¼ cups all-purpose flour to make a soft dough.

Sprinkle 1 tablespoon all-purpose flour evenly over work surface. Turn dough out onto floured surface, and knead until smooth and elastic (about 8 to 10 minutes). Place dough in a large bowl coated with cooking spray, turning to coat top. Cover and let rise in a warm place (85°), free from drafts, 1 hour or until doubled in bulk.

Punch dough down, and divide into 4 equal portions; shape each portion into 6 balls. Place dough in a 13- x 9- x 2-inch baking pan coated with cooking spray. Cover and let rise in a warm place, free from drafts, 30 minutes or until doubled in bulk.

Combine egg white and water in a small bowl; brush over rolls. Combine 2 tablespoons sugar and ½ teaspoon cinnamon; sprinkle evenly over rolls. Bake at 350° for 20 minutes. Remove from pan immediately; let cool slightly on wire racks. Serve warm. Yield: 2 dozen (107 calories each).

PROTEIN 3.3 FAT 1.5 (Saturated Fat 0.3) CARBOHYDRATE 20.3
FIBER 1.5 CHOLESTEROL 9 IRON 1.1 SODIUM 48 CALCIUM 23

POTATO-WHOLE WHEAT CLOVERLEAF ROLLS

1¾ cups all-purpose flour, divided
1 cup whole wheat flour
¾ cup instant potato flakes
2 tablespoons sugar
¼ teaspoon salt
1 package dry yeast
1½ cups skim milk
3 tablespoons margarine
1 tablespoon all-purpose flour
Vegetable cooking spray

Combine ½ cup all-purpose flour and next 5 ingredients in a large bowl; stir well. Set aside.

Combine milk and margarine in a small saucepan; cook over medium heat until margarine melts, stirring occasionally. Cool to 120° to 130°.

Gradually add milk mixture to flour mixture, beating at low speed of an electric mixer until well blended.

Beat an additional 2 minutes at medium speed. Gradually stir in enough of the remaining 1¼ cups all-purpose flour to make a soft dough.

Sprinkle 1 tablespoon all-purpose flour over work surface. Turn dough out onto floured surface; knead until smooth and elastic (about 8 to 10 minutes). Place dough in a bowl coated with cooking spray; turn to coat top. Cover and let rise in a warm place (85°), free from drafts, 1 hour or until doubled in bulk.

Coat muffin pans with cooking spray. Punch dough down. Divide into 48 equal portions; shape portions into balls. Place 3 balls in each muffin cup. Cover and let rise in a warm place, free from drafts, 45 minutes or until doubled in bulk. Bake at 350° for 15 minutes or until golden. Yield: 16 rolls (116 calories each).

PROTEIN 3.5   FAT 2.6   (Saturated Fat 0.5)   CARBOHYDRATE 20.0
FIBER 1.5   CHOLESTEROL 0   IRON 1.0   SODIUM 77   CALCIUM 35

PEPPER-TOPPED FOCACCIA

2 cups plus 2 tablespoons all-purpose flour, divided
½ cup whole wheat flour
1 teaspoon dried whole oregano
½ teaspoon salt
⅛ teaspoon pepper
1 package dry yeast
1 cup warm water (120° to 130° F)
3 tablespoons olive oil
2 tablespoons all-purpose flour
Vegetable cooking spray
2 teaspoons olive oil
½ cup chopped green pepper
½ cup chopped sweet red pepper
1½ tablespoons grated Parmesan cheese

Combine 1 cup all-purpose flour and next 5 ingredients in a large bowl. Gradually add water and 3 tablespoons oil to flour mixture, beating at low speed of an electric mixer until blended. Beat an additional 2 minutes at medium speed. Gradually stir in enough of the remaining 1 cup plus 2 tablespoons all-purpose flour to make a soft dough.

Sprinkle 2 tablespoons all-purpose flour evenly over work surface. Turn dough out onto floured surface, and knead until smooth and elastic (about 8 to 10 minutes). Place dough in a large bowl coated with cooking spray, turning to coat top. Cover and let rise in a warm place (85°), free from drafts, 45 to 55 minutes or until doubled in bulk.

Coat a large nonstick skillet with cooking spray; add 2 teaspoons oil. Place over medium-high heat until hot. Add peppers, and sauté until crisp-tender. Remove from heat, and let cool slightly.

Punch dough down. Press onto a 12-inch round pizza pan coated with cooking spray. Poke holes in dough at 1-inch intervals with handle of a wooden spoon. Spread pepper mixture over dough; press lightly. Sprinkle with cheese. Let rise, uncovered, in a warm place, free from drafts, 30 minutes. Bake at 375° for 25 minutes or until golden. Cut into wedges. Serve warm. Yield: 16 servings (106 calories per wedge).

PROTEIN 2.6   FAT 3.6   (Saturated Fat 0.6)   CARBOHYDRATE 15.8
FIBER 1.2   CHOLESTEROL 0   IRON 1.1   SODIUM 83   CALCIUM 13

FENNEL-ONION CASSEROLE LOAF

2 cups all-purpose flour, divided
⅔ cup whole wheat flour
2 tablespoons sugar
2 tablespoons finely chopped green onions
½ teaspoon fennel seeds, crushed
¼ teaspoon baking soda
¼ teaspoon salt
1 package dry yeast
1 cup 1% low-fat cottage cheese
¼ cup skim milk
1 tablespoon margarine
1 egg, lightly beaten
Vegetable cooking spray

Combine ½ cup all-purpose flour and next 7 ingredients in a large bowl; stir well. Set aside.

Combine cottage cheese, milk, and margarine in a small saucepan; cook over medium heat until margarine melts, stirring occasionally. Cool to 120° to 130°.

Gradually add cottage cheese mixture to flour mixture, beating at low speed of an electric mixer until blended. Beat an additional 2 minutes at medium speed. Add egg; beat an additional 2 minutes. Gradually stir in enough of the remaining 1½ cups all-purpose flour to make a soft dough.

Place dough in a large bowl coated with cooking spray, turning to coat top. Cover and let rise in a warm place (85°), free from drafts, 1 hour or until doubled in bulk.

Punch dough down, and shape into a ball, gently smoothing surface of dough. Place dough in a 2-quart casserole coated with cooking spray. Cover and let rise in a warm place, free from drafts, 30 to 40 minutes or until doubled in bulk. Bake at 350° for 25 minutes or until loaf sounds hollow when tapped. Remove from casserole immediately, and let cool on a wire rack. Cut into wedges. Yield: 18 servings (89 calories per wedge).

PROTEIN 4.1 FAT 1.3 (Saturated Fat 0.3) CARBOHYDRATE 15.2
FIBER 1.1 CHOLESTEROL 12 IRON 0.9 SODIUM 109 CALCIUM 21

HONEY-MUSTARD RYE ROUNDS

2¼ cups all-purpose flour, divided
1½ cups rye flour
¼ teaspoon salt
1 package dry yeast
1 cup skim milk
2 tablespoons honey
2 tablespoons Dijon mustard
2 tablespoons margarine
1 egg, lightly beaten
1½ tablespoons all-purpose flour
Vegetable cooking spray

Combine ½ cup all-purpose flour, rye flour, salt, and yeast in a large bowl; stir well. Set aside.

Combine milk, honey, mustard, and margarine in a saucepan; cook over medium heat until margarine melts, stirring occasionally. Cool to 120° to 130°.

Gradually add milk mixture to flour mixture, beating at low speed of an electric mixer until blended. Add egg; beat an additional 2 minutes at medium speed. Stir in enough of the remaining 1¾ cups all-purpose flour to make a soft dough.

Sprinkle 1½ tablespoons all-purpose flour evenly over work surface. Turn dough out onto floured surface, and knead until smooth and elastic (about 8 to 10 minutes). Place dough in a large bowl coated with cooking spray, turning to coat top. Cover and let rise in a warm place (85°), free from drafts, 1 hour or until doubled in bulk.

Punch dough down; divide in half. Shape each portion into a round loaf. Place loaves on a baking sheet coated with cooking spray.

Cover and let rise in a warm place, free from drafts, 45 minutes or until doubled in bulk. Using a sharp knife, make ¼-inch-deep slits 1 inch apart to form a lattice design across top of each loaf. Bake at 350° for 30 minutes or until loaves sound hollow when tapped. Cut into wedges. Yield: 24 servings (84 calories per wedge).

PROTEIN 2.4 FAT 1.5 (Saturated Fat 0.3) CARBOHYDRATE 15.2
FIBER 1.2 CHOLESTEROL 9 IRON 0.7 SODIUM 81 CALCIUM 17

TOASTED OAT-WHEAT BREAD

1 cup plus 2 tablespoons regular oats,
  uncooked
3 cups all-purpose flour, divided
2½ cups whole wheat flour
⅓ cup firmly packed brown sugar
½ teaspoon salt
2 packages dry yeast
1 cup skim milk
1 cup water
3 tablespoons margarine
2 tablespoons molasses
1 egg, lightly beaten
2 tablespoons all-purpose flour, divided
Vegetable cooking spray
1 egg white, lightly beaten
2 teaspoons water

Spread oats in a shallow baking pan. Bake at 375° for 8 to 10 minutes or until lightly toasted, stirring frequently. Let cool slightly. Reserve 2 tablespoons toasted oats for topping.

Combine remaining 1 cup toasted oats, 1 cup all-purpose flour, whole wheat flour, brown sugar, salt, and yeast in a large bowl. Stir well.

Combine milk, 1 cup water, margarine, and molasses in a saucepan; cook over medium heat until margarine melts, stirring occasionally. Cool to 120° to 130°.

Gradually add milk mixture and egg to flour mixture, beating at low speed of an electric mixer until blended. Beat an additional 2 minutes at medium speed. Gradually stir in enough of the remaining 2 cups all-purpose flour to make a soft dough.

Sprinkle 1 tablespoon all-purpose flour evenly over work surface. Turn dough out onto floured surface, and knead until smooth and elastic (about 8 to 10 minutes). Place dough in a large bowl coated with cooking spray, turning to coat top. Cover and let rise in a warm place (85°), free from drafts, 45 minutes or until doubled in bulk.

Punch dough down; divide dough in half. Sprinkle 1½ teaspoons all-purpose flour evenly over work surface. Roll 1 portion of dough into a 10- x 6-inch rectangle. Roll up, starting at short side, pressing firmly to eliminate air pockets; pinch ends to seal. Place seam side down in an 8½- x 4½- x 3-inch loafpan coated with cooking spray. Repeat procedure with remaining dough and 1½ teaspoons all-purpose flour.

Cover and let rise in a warm place, free from drafts, 45 minutes or until doubled in bulk. Combine egg white and 2 teaspoons water; brush over loaves, and sprinkle with reserved 2 tablespoons toasted oats. Bake at 350° for 25 minutes or until loaves sound hollow when tapped. Remove from pans immediately; cool on wire racks. Yield: 34 servings (71 calories per ½-inch slice).

PROTEIN 2.3   FAT 1.5   (Saturated Fat 0.3)   CARBOHYDRATE 12.7
FIBER 1.4   CHOLESTEROL 6   IRON 0.7   SODIUM 55   CALCIUM 18

 ## FLOUR POWER

Supermarkets now stock a larger variety of flours made from grains such as corn, wheat, oats, rye, and barley. For the most part, whole grain flours behave differently in baking than refined flours, and this should be taken into account before making substitutions.

Whole grain flour is much heavier and produces less gluten than refined flour. Because high levels of gluten lend a delicate texture to baked goods, refined flour normally needs to be mixed with whole grain flour to produce moist, crumbly baked goods. Even refined flours can vary in their uses.

Keep in mind that because whole grain flours contain some fat, they need to be stored in the refrigerator. Here are some popular flours and their performance ability:
• All-purpose flour—mixture of hard (high-gluten) wheat and soft wheat; used for breads, pastries, and general baking.
• Bread flour—made from hard wheat; high gluten levels make bread dough strong and elastic.
• Cake flour—made from soft wheat; used for light-textured cakes and pastries.
• Self-rising flour—all-purpose flour to which baking powder and salt are added; used in many traditional Southern recipes.
• Whole wheat flour—made from whole grain wheat (includes the bran, germ, and starchy endosperm); available in coarsely or finely ground varieties.

CINNAMON-RAISIN BATTER BREAD

3 cups all-purpose flour, divided
2 tablespoons sugar
1 teaspoon ground cinnamon
¼ teaspoon salt
¼ teaspoon ground allspice
1 package dry yeast
1 cup skim milk
¼ cup molasses
2 tablespoons margarine
1 egg, lightly beaten
½ cup raisins
Vegetable cooking spray

Combine 1½ cups flour, sugar, cinnamon, salt, allspice, and yeast in a large bowl; stir well. Set flour mixture aside.

Combine milk, molasses, and margarine in a small saucepan; cook over medium heat until very warm (120° to 130°). Gradually add to flour mixture, beating at low speed of an electric mixer until smooth. Add egg, and beat at low speed of electric mixer until blended. Beat an additional 3 minutes at medium speed. Stir in remaining 1½ cups flour and raisins.

Spoon batter into a 9- x 5- x 3-inch loafpan coated with cooking spray. Cover and let rise in a warm place (85°), free from drafts, 40 minutes or until doubled in bulk. Bake at 350° for 35 to 40 minutes or until golden. Remove from pan, and let cool on a wire rack. Yield: 18 servings (126 calories per ½-inch slice).

PROTEIN 3.1   FAT 1.8   (Saturated Fat 0.4)   CARBOHYDRATE 24.4
FIBER 1.0   CHOLESTEROL 12   IRON 1.4   SODIUM 60   CALCIUM 34

LEMON-RASPBERRY SWEET ROLLS

2 cups all-purpose flour, divided
3 tablespoons sugar
1 teaspoon grated lemon rind
⅛ teaspoon salt
1 package dry yeast
½ cup skim milk
2 tablespoons margarine
1 egg, lightly beaten
2 tablespoons all-purpose flour
Vegetable cooking spray
¼ cup no-sugar-added raspberry spread
¼ cup sifted powdered sugar
1¼ teaspoons lemon juice

Combine ¾ cup flour and next 4 ingredients in a large bowl; stir well. Set aside.

Combine milk and margarine in a saucepan; cook over medium heat until margarine melts, stirring occasionally. Cool to 120° to 130°.

Gradually add milk mixture to flour mixture, beating at low speed of an electric mixer until blended. Beat 2 minutes at medium speed. Add egg, and beat well. Gradually stir in enough of the remaining 1¼ cups flour to make a soft dough.

Sprinkle 2 tablespoons flour evenly over work surface. Turn dough out onto floured surface, and knead until smooth and elastic (about 8 to 10 minutes). Place dough in a large bowl coated with cooking spray, turning to coat top. Cover dough and let rise in a warm place (85°), free from drafts, 1 hour or until dough is doubled in bulk.

Punch dough down, and divide into 12 equal portions. Roll each portion into a 12-inch rope. Shape each rope into a loose coil on a large baking sheet coated with cooking spray, leaving a ½-inch hole in center (center will close up during rising and leave an indentation). Cover dough and let rise in a warm place, free from drafts, 40 minutes or until dough is doubled in bulk.

Fill each indentation with 1 teaspoon raspberry spread. Bake at 350° for 12 minutes or until golden. Remove from baking sheet immediately. Combine powdered sugar and lemon juice, stirring well. Drizzle over warm rolls. Serve warm. Yield: 1 dozen (147 calories each.)

PROTEIN 3.2   FAT 2.7   (Saturated Fat 0.5)   CARBOHYDRATE 27.3
FIBER 0.7   CHOLESTEROL 18   IRON 1.1   SODIUM 57   CALCIUM 19

CITRUS-CRANBERRY TWISTS

2¾ cups all-purpose flour, divided
2 tablespoons instant nonfat dry milk powder
½ teaspoon salt
½ teaspoon ground cardamom
1 package dry yeast
¾ cup unsweetened orange juice
3 tablespoons brown sugar
2 tablespoons unsalted margarine
1 egg, lightly beaten
¼ cup all-purpose flour, divided
Vegetable cooking spray
¼ cup sugar
3 tablespoons grated orange rind
½ cup chopped fresh cranberries
½ cup cranberry juice cocktail
2 teaspoons cornstarch

Combine 2 cups flour and next 4 ingredients in a large bowl; stir well. Set aside.

Combine orange juice, brown sugar, and margarine in a saucepan; cook over medium heat until margarine melts, stirring occasionally. Cool to 120° to 130°.

Add orange juice mixture to flour mixture, beating at low speed of an electric mixer until blended. Beat 2 minutes at medium speed. Add egg; beat 3 minutes at medium speed. Gradually stir in enough of the remaining ¾ cup flour to make a soft dough.

Sprinkle 3 tablespoons flour evenly over work surface. Turn dough out onto floured surface, and knead until smooth and elastic (about 8 to 10 minutes). Place dough in a large bowl coated with cooking spray, turning to coat top. Cover and let rise in a warm place (85°), free from drafts, 1½ hours or until dough is doubled in bulk.

Punch dough down; sprinkle remaining 1 tablespoon all-purpose flour evenly over work surface. Turn dough out onto floured surface, and roll to an 18- x 15-inch rectangle.

Combine ¼ cup sugar and orange rind in a small bowl, stirring well; sprinkle over dough. Sprinkle chopped cranberries over dough. Fold dough in thirds lengthwise; cut into 22 (¾-inch) strips. Twist each strip twice, and place 2 inches apart on baking sheets coated with cooking spray.

Cover dough, and let rise in a warm place, free from drafts, 1 hour or until dough is doubled in bulk. Bake at 350° for 10 to 12 minutes or until twists are golden. Remove twists from baking sheets; place on wire racks.

Combine cranberry juice and cornstarch in a small saucepan; stir well. Cook over medium heat, stirring constantly, until thickened. Drizzle over warm twists. Yield: 22 twists (99 calories each).

PROTEIN 2.4   FAT 1.5   (Saturated Fat 0.3)   CARBOHYDRATE 19.2
FIBER 0.6   CHOLESTEROL 10   IRON 0.9   SODIUM 61   CALCIUM 17

Chilled Lobster Tails with Mustard Vinaigrette (page 126) adorned with cucumber and lemon is the perfect dinner attraction for a warm summer evening.

Fish & Shellfish

COLD POACHED STRIPED BASS WITH AVOCADO SAUCE

9 cups water
½ teaspoon dried whole thyme, crushed
½ teaspoon dried whole oregano, crushed
1 tablespoon white wine vinegar
4 (4-ounce) striped bass fillets
1 cup cubed ripe avocado
1½ tablespoons minced onion
2 tablespoons water
1½ tablespoons lime juice
1 teaspoon olive oil
16 asparagus spears
4 large Boston lettuce leaves
2 cups thinly sliced cucumber
1½ cups cherry tomatoes, halved

Bring 9 cups water to a boil in a large nonstick skillet. Add thyme and oregano; cover, reduce heat, and simmer 10 minutes. Stir in vinegar.

Add fillets; bring to a boil. Cover, reduce heat, and simmer 8 minutes or until fish flakes easily when tested with a fork. Remove fish from liquid; discard liquid. Cover fish, and chill thoroughly.

Combine avocado and next 4 ingredients in container of an electric blender; top with cover, and process until smooth. Cover and chill.

Snap off tough ends of asparagus. Remove scales from stalks with a knife or vegetable peeler, if desired. Blanch asparagus in boiling water 4 minutes or until crisp-tender; drain. Rinse under cold water until cool; drain and chill.

To serve, place fillets on individual lettuce-lined serving plates. Top each fillet evenly with avocado mixture, and arrange asparagus, cucumber, and tomato around fillets. Yield: 4 servings (226 calories per serving).

PROTEIN 26.7 FAT 9.1 (Saturated Fat 1.4) CARBOHYDRATE 11.0
FIBER 2.6 CHOLESTEROL 36 IRON 2.4 SODIUM 77 CALCIUM 90

CREOLE CATFISH

¼ cup clam juice
¼ cup water
1 cup chopped onion
1 cup chopped celery
½ cup chopped green pepper
2 teaspoons minced garlic
1 (14½-ounce) can no-salt-added whole
    tomatoes, undrained and pureed
¼ pound chopped fresh mushrooms
¼ cup Chablis or other dry white wine
2 tablespoons lemon juice
1 tablespoon low-sodium Worcestershire
    sauce
½ teaspoon sugar
¼ teaspoon pepper
⅛ teaspoon ground red pepper
4 drops of hot sauce
2 bay leaves
1 pound farm-raised catfish fillets
3 cups cooked long-grain rice (cooked without
    salt or fat)

Combine clam juice and water in a medium saucepan; bring to a boil. Add onion, celery, green pepper, and garlic; cover, reduce heat, and simmer 10 minutes or until vegetables are tender. Add tomato and next 9 ingredients; stir well. Bring to a boil; cover, reduce heat, and simmer 20 minutes.

Cut fillets into 1½-inch pieces; add to tomato mixture. Cook, uncovered, 10 minutes or until fish flakes easily when tested with a fork, stirring occasionally. Remove and discard bay leaves.

Place ½ cup long-grain rice in each of 6 individual serving bowls; spoon 1 cup catfish mixture over each serving. Yield: 6 servings (252 calories per serving).

PROTEIN 18.0 FAT 3.7 (Saturated Fat 0.9) CARBOHYDRATE 36.1
FIBER 1.8 CHOLESTEROL 44 IRON 2.8 SODIUM 112 CALCIUM 86

FLOUNDER EN PAPILLOTE

Butter-flavored vegetable cooking spray
1 tablespoon reduced-calorie margarine
¾ cup sliced fresh mushrooms
1 tablespoon chopped green onions
1 tablespoon all-purpose flour
¾ cup skim milk
2¼ teaspoons lemon juice
½ teaspoon dried whole dillweed
⅛ teaspoon salt
⅛ teaspoon pepper
1 (10-ounce) package frozen baby carrots, thawed
4 (4-ounce) flounder fillets
Lemon wedges (optional)

Coat a large nonstick skillet with cooking spray; add margarine. Place over medium-high heat until margarine melts. Add mushrooms and green onions; sauté until tender. Sprinkle flour over mushrooms, stirring until well blended. Gradually add milk, and cook until mushroom mixture is thickened, stirring constantly. Stir in lemon juice and next 3 ingredients; cook 1 minute or until thoroughly heated. Remove from heat; set aside, and keep warm.

Arrange carrots in a vegetable steamer over boiling water. Cover and steam 8 to 10 minutes or until almost tender.

Cut 4 (12-inch) squares of parchment paper; fold each square in half, and trim each into a large heart shape. Place parchment hearts on a baking sheet, and open out flat. Coat open side of parchment paper with cooking spray.

Place 1 fillet on half of each parchment heart near the crease. Spoon carrots evenly over fillets; top evenly with mushroom mixture.

Fold paper edges over to seal securely. Starting with rounded edges of hearts, pleat and crimp edges of parchment to make an airtight seal. Bake at 375° for 20 to 25 minutes or until packets are puffed and lightly browned.

Place packets on individual serving plates; cut an opening in the top of each packet, and fold paper back. Garnish with lemon wedges, if desired. Serve immediately. Yield: 4 servings (178 calories per serving).

PROTEIN 24.3 FAT 3.9 (Saturated Fat 0.7) CARBOHYDRATE 11.2
FIBER 1.3 CHOLESTEROL 55 IRON 1.2 SODIUM 260 CALCIUM 105

HALIBUT WITH MANGO SAUCE

6 (4-ounce) halibut steaks (¾ inch thick)
¼ cup lemon juice
1 tablespoon minced garlic
1 tablespoon olive oil
1½ cups peeled, chopped mango
¼ cup chopped sweet red pepper
3 tablespoons chopped green onions
1 teaspoon brown sugar
½ teaspoon minced garlic
Vegetable cooking spray
Fresh parsley sprigs (optional)

Place halibut steaks in a shallow dish. Combine lemon juice, 1 tablespoon garlic, and olive oil; pour over steaks. Cover and marinate in refrigerator 1 hour, turning occasionally.

Combine mango, sweet red pepper, green onions, brown sugar, and ½ teaspoon garlic in a small saucepan. Cook over medium heat 6 minutes or until thoroughly heated, stirring frequently.

Remove steaks from marinade; discard marinade. Coat grill rack with cooking spray; place on grill over medium-hot coals. Place steaks on rack, and cook 6 minutes on each side or until fish flakes easily when tested with a fork.

Transfer steaks to a large serving platter, and spoon mango sauce evenly over steaks. Garnish with fresh parsley sprigs, if desired. Yield: 6 servings (166 calories per serving).

PROTEIN 24.0 FAT 3.7 (Saturated Fat 0.5) CARBOHYDRATE 8.7
FIBER 0.8 CHOLESTEROL 36 IRON 1.1 SODIUM 63 CALCIUM 62

Catch the flavor of fresh fish in Mahimahi with Papaya and Roasted Red Pepper.

MAHIMAHI WITH PAPAYA AND ROASTED RED PEPPER

1 teaspoon cornstarch
1 tablespoon water
2 teaspoons reduced-calorie margarine
1 tablespoon finely chopped shallot
1 (7-ounce) jar roasted red peppers in water,
   drained and cut into julienne strips
1 cup peeled, chopped ripe papaya
1 teaspoon minced jalapeño pepper
3 tablespoons fresh lime juice, divided
1 teaspoon reduced-calorie margarine, melted
4 (4-ounce) mahimahi fillets
Butter-flavored vegetable cooking spray
3 tablespoons chopped pistachios

Combine cornstarch and water in a small bowl, stirring well; set aside.

Melt 2 teaspoons margarine in a large skillet over medium heat. Add shallot, and sauté 2 minutes. Add red pepper, papaya, and jalapeño pepper; sauté 2 minutes. Add cornstarch mixture and 2 tablespoons lime juice; cook until thickened, stirring constantly. Remove from heat, and keep warm.

Combine remaining 1 tablespoon lime juice and 1 teaspoon melted margarine; stir well. Place fillets on rack of a broiler pan coated with cooking spray, and brush with lime mixture. Broil 5½ inches from heat 4 minutes on each side. Sprinkle fillets with pistachios, pressing nuts into flesh of fish. Broil an additional 3 minutes or until fish flakes easily when tested with a fork.

Transfer fillets to a large serving platter. Serve with roasted red pepper sauce. Yield: 4 servings (172 calories per serving).

PROTEIN 22.0   FAT 5.7   (Saturated Fat 0.7)   CARBOHYDRATE 8.9
FIBER 1.6   CHOLESTEROL 49   IRON 1.1   SODIUM 102   CALCIUM 35

SEAFOOD AT THE TOP

Americans are eating about 16 pounds of seafood per person a year, according to the National Fisheries Institute. The six favorites are, in order, tuna (primarily due to the canned form), shrimp, cod, Alaskan Pollock (mainly as surimi for imitation crabmeat, lobster, and shrimp), salmon, and catfish.

SESAME ORANGE ROUGHY

2 tablespoons low-sodium soy sauce
1 teaspoon dry mustard
2 teaspoons honey
1 teaspoon light sesame oil
½ teaspoon peeled, minced gingerroot
¼ teaspoon minced garlic
4 (4-ounce) orange roughy fillets
2 tablespoons fresh lime juice
2 tablespoons sesame seeds, toasted
Butter-flavored vegetable cooking spray
1 tablespoon reduced-calorie margarine
3 tablespoons chopped green onions

Combine first 6 ingredients in a small bowl; stir well, and set aside.

Brush both sides of each fillet with lime juice, and sprinkle with sesame seeds. Coat a large nonstick skillet with cooking spray; add margarine. Place skillet over medium-low heat until margarine melts. Add fillets, and cook 3 to 4 minutes on each side or until fish flakes

easily when tested with a fork. Transfer to a serving platter; drizzle with soy sauce mixture, and sprinkle with green onions. Serve immediately. Yield: 4 servings (225 calories per serving).

PROTEIN 23.1   FAT 12.5   (Saturated Fat 2.1)   CARBOHYDRATE 4.5
FIBER 0.3   CHOLESTEROL 68   IRON 0.9   SODIUM 283   CALCIUM 12

HERBED SALMON FILLETS

2 tablespoons lemon juice
1 tablespoon low-sodium Worcestershire sauce
6 (4-ounce) salmon fillets
2 tablespoons soft French bread crumbs
2 tablespoons grated Romano cheese
2 teaspoons minced garlic
1 teaspoon dried whole oregano
½ teaspoon dried whole tarragon
½ teaspoon dried whole marjoram
Butter-flavored vegetable cooking spray
1 tablespoon reduced-calorie margarine
Fresh oregano sprigs (optional)

Combine lemon juice and Worcestershire sauce in a small bowl. Place fillets in an 11- x 7- x 2-inch baking dish; pour lemon juice mixture over fillets. Cover and marinate in refrigerator 1 hour.

Combine bread crumbs and next 5 ingredients in a small bowl; set aside.

Remove fillets from marinade; discard marinade. Coat a large nonstick skillet with cooking spray; add margarine. Place over medium-high heat until margarine melts. Add fillets, and cook 1 to 2 minutes on each side or until lightly browned.

Transfer fillets to an 11- x 7- x 2-inch baking dish coated with cooking spray. Sprinkle bread crumb mixture evenly over fillets. Bake, uncovered, at 400° for 15 minutes or until fish flakes easily when tested with a fork. Transfer to a serving platter. Garnish with fresh oregano sprigs, if desired. Yield: 6 servings (171 calories per serving).

PROTEIN 24.4   FAT 6.6   (Saturated Fat 1.6)   CARBOHYDRATE 2.4
FIBER 0.1   CHOLESTEROL 64   IRON 1.1   SODIUM 169   CALCIUM 58

Oven-crisp Sole Fillet Phyllo Packets come with a surprise. The flavors of goat cheese and chives melt throughout each packet.

SOLE FILLET PHYLLO PACKETS

½ (8-ounce) package Neufchâtel cheese, softened
2 ounces goat cheese, softened
1 tablespoon chopped fresh chives
2 teaspoons fresh lemon juice
4 sheets commercial frozen phyllo pastry, thawed
Butter-flavored vegetable cooking spray
4 (3-ounce) sole fillets
Fresh chives (optional)
Lemon slices (optional)

Combine first 4 ingredients in a small bowl. Stir well, and set aside.

Place 1 sheet of phyllo on a damp towel (keep remaining phyllo covered). Lightly coat phyllo with cooking spray; fold in half crosswise. Spread one-fourth of cheese mixture across bottom 2 inches of phyllo; place 1 fillet on phyllo above cheese mixture. Fold cheese-covered phyllo over fish; fold lengthwise edges in about 1 inch, and roll up, jellyroll fashion.

Lightly coat phyllo packet with cooking spray; place on a baking sheet coated with cooking spray. Repeat procedure with remaining phyllo, cheese mixture, and fillets.

Bake at 375° for 20 minutes. Transfer to a serving platter. If desired, garnish with fresh chives and lemon slices. Serve immediately. Yield: 4 servings (268 calories per serving).

PROTEIN 21.7   FAT 13.2   (Saturated Fat 6.9)   CARBOHYDRATE 14.9
FIBER 0   CHOLESTEROL 87   IRON 1.8   SODIUM 326   CALCIUM 154

SWORDFISH WITH MUSHROOM AND TOMATO SAUCE

Butter-flavored vegetable cooking spray
2 teaspoons reduced-calorie margarine
4 (4-ounce) swordfish steaks (¾ inch thick)
2 cups coarsely chopped fresh shiitake mushrooms
½ cup seeded, chopped tomato
¼ cup chopped green onions
¼ cup Chablis or other dry white wine
¼ cup clam juice
2 tablespoons no-salt-added tomato paste
2 teaspoons minced garlic
1 teaspoon minced fresh thyme
¼ teaspoon ground cumin
1 tablespoon lemon juice

Coat a large nonstick skillet with cooking spray; add margarine. Place over medium heat until hot. Add swordfish, and cook 3 minutes on each side; set aside, and keep warm. Wipe skillet dry with a paper towel.

Coat skillet with cooking spray. Add mushrooms, and sauté 1 minute. Add tomato and next 7 ingredients, stirring well. Top with fish; cover and cook over medium heat 5 minutes or until fish flakes easily when tested with a fork. Transfer fish to a serving platter. Stir lemon juice into tomato mixture, and spoon over fish. Serve immediately. Yield: 4 servings (186 calories per serving).

PROTEIN 23.9 FAT 6.1 (Saturated Fat 1.4) CARBOHYDRATE 9.1
FIBER 1.1 CHOLESTEROL 44 IRON 1.4 SODIUM 161 CALCIUM 22

TROUT DIJON

4 (4-ounce) trout fillets
Vegetable cooking spray
¼ cup Chablis or other dry white wine
2½ tablespoons Dijon mustard
½ teaspoon grated lemon rind
1 tablespoon lemon juice
1½ tablespoons minced shallot
1 clove garlic, minced
1 teaspoon dried whole dillweed
⅛ teaspoon pepper

Place fillets in an 11- x 7- x 2-inch baking dish coated with cooking spray; set aside.

Combine wine and remaining ingredients in a small bowl; stir well. Pour mixture evenly over fillets. Bake, uncovered, at 350° for 25 minutes or until fish flakes easily when tested with a fork. Transfer fillets to a serving platter. Yield: 4 servings (187 calories per serving).

PROTEIN 23.8 FAT 8.3 (Saturated Fat 1.3) CARBOHYDRATE 2.2
FIBER 0.1 CHOLESTEROL 66 IRON 2.0 SODIUM 340 CALCIUM 58

TUNA STEAKS SICILIAN

Olive oil-flavored vegetable cooking spray
3 cloves garlic, minced
1 (8-ounce) can no-salt-added tomato sauce
2 cups chopped plum tomatoes (about 4 medium)
¼ cup chopped fresh parsley
½ teaspoon dried whole oregano
¼ teaspoon crushed red pepper flakes
2 (12-ounce) tuna steaks (1 inch thick)
¼ cup sliced pimiento-stuffed olives
2 tablespoons capers
Fresh parsley sprigs (optional)

Coat a large nonstick skillet with cooking spray; place over medium-high heat until hot. Add garlic, and sauté until lightly browned. Add tomato sauce and next 4 ingredients; stir well. Reduce heat, and simmer, uncovered, 5 minutes.

Spoon half of tomato mixture into an 11- x 7- x 2-inch baking dish; place tuna steaks on tomato mixture. Spoon remaining tomato mixture evenly over steaks. Sprinkle evenly with olives and capers. Cover and bake at 350° for 40 minutes or until fish flakes easily when tested with a fork. Transfer to a serving platter. Garnish with fresh parsley sprigs, if desired. Yield: 6 servings (197 calories per serving).

PROTEIN 27.6 FAT 6.3 (Saturated Fat 1.5) CARBOHYDRATE 6.5
FIBER 0.9 CHOLESTEROL 43 IRON 1.8 SODIUM 250 CALCIUM 15

GRILLED TUNA WITH TOMATO-SHALLOT SALSA

6 (4-ounce) tuna steaks (¾ inch thick)
1 tablespoon olive oil
2 teaspoons white wine vinegar
2 teaspoons minced garlic
2 teaspoons fresh oregano leaves
1½ cups peeled, seeded, and chopped tomato
¼ cup finely chopped shallot
2 tablespoons chopped fresh basil
3 tablespoons red wine vinegar
1 tablespoon water
2 teaspoons minced jalapeño pepper
1 teaspoon minced garlic
1 teaspoon chopped fresh thyme
Vegetable cooking spray

Place tuna in a shallow dish. Combine olive oil, white wine vinegar, 2 teaspoons garlic, and oregano; pour over tuna. Cover and marinate in refrigerator 1 hour, turning once.

Combine tomato and next 7 ingredients in a small bowl; stir well, and set aside.

Coat grill rack with cooking spray; place on grill over medium-hot coals. Place tuna on rack, and cook 3 to 5 minutes on each side or until fish flakes easily when tested with a fork. Transfer steaks to a serving platter. Spoon tomato mixture evenly over tuna. Yield: 6 servings (205 calories per serving).

PROTEIN 27.3 FAT 8.2 (Saturated Fat 1.8) CARBOHYDRATE 4.4
FIBER 0.7 CHOLESTEROL 43 IRON 1.7 SODIUM 51 CALCIUM 15

MIXED GRILL KABOBS

½ pound medium-size unpeeled fresh shrimp
½ pound amberjack fillets
1 (8-ounce) tuna steak (1 inch thick)
½ pound sea scallops
2 tablespoons white wine vinegar
2 tablespoons water
1 tablespoon vegetable oil
1 tablespoon plus 1 teaspoon honey
2 teaspoons prepared horseradish
2 teaspoons minced garlic
2 teaspoons dry mustard
2 teaspoons dried whole thyme
Vegetable cooking spray

Peel and devein shrimp, leaving tails intact. Cut amberjack and tuna into 8 pieces each. Place fish, shrimp, and scallops in a shallow dish. Combine vinegar and next 7 ingredients; pour over shrimp mixture. Cover and marinate in refrigerator 1 hour, stirring occasionally.

Remove shrimp mixture from marinade, discarding marinade. Alternate fish, shrimp, and scallops on 8 (10-inch) skewers. Coat grill rack with cooking spray, and place on grill over medium-hot coals. Place kabobs on rack, and cook 4 to 5 minutes on each side or until fish flakes easily when tested with a fork and scallops are opaque. Yield: 8 servings (137 calories per serving).

PROTEIN 20.4 FAT 4.4 (Saturated Fat 1.0) CARBOHYDRATE 2.8
FIBER 0.1 CHOLESTEROL 53 IRON 1.5 SODIUM 83 CALCIUM 24

WALK, DON'T RUN

Looking for something a little less pounding than running but a bit more intense than brisk walking? Consider racewalking. Experts say that a racewalker (traveling at a pace of 5 miles per hour or a 12-minute mile) burns just as many—if not more—calories as a runner. The reason: Racewalkers actually have to take more steps than do runners to cover the same distance, thereby building the intensity of the workout.

Racewalking involves pumping the arms and rotating the pelvis in an exaggerated walking motion. The trick is to keep your lead foot on the ground while your trailing foot and leg push off. It's also important that the knee remains straight on the lead leg until your body passes over that leg. Once you master the long "rocking-like" strides of racewalking, expect to reach about the same level of fitness as do runners and joggers.

The flavors of garlic and saffron blend together in Easy Coastal Paella, a quick-to-prepare version of the traditional dish.

EASY COASTAL PAELLA

12 fresh mussels
Olive oil-flavored vegetable cooking spray
2 teaspoons olive oil
1 cup chopped onion
1 cup chopped leeks
⅔ cup chopped celery
1 tablespoon minced garlic
1 teaspoon saffron threads
2 cups peeled, seeded, and chopped tomato
½ cup Chablis or other dry white wine
½ cup canned low-sodium chicken broth, undiluted
2 (4-ounce) red snapper fillets, skinned
1 (4-ounce) monkfish fillet, cut into 8 pieces
2 cups cooked long-grain rice (cooked without salt or fat)
1 tablespoon plus 1 teaspoon chopped fresh parsley

Remove beards on mussels, and scrub shells with a brush. Discard opened, cracked, or heavy mussels (they're filled with sand).

Coat a large nonstick skillet with cooking spray; add olive oil. Place over medium-high heat until hot. Add onion and next 4 ingredients; sauté 3 minutes or until vegetables are tender. Add tomato, wine, and chicken broth; cook, uncovered, 10 minutes, stirring occasionally. Add fish and mussels to tomato mixture; cover and cook 5 minutes or until mussels are open and fish flakes easily when tested with a fork.

Place ½ cup rice in each individual serving bowl; spoon 1 cup fish mixture over each serving. Sprinkle with parsley. Serve immediately. Yield: 4 servings (305 calories per serving).

PROTEIN 22.9 FAT 4.8 (Saturated Fat 0.8) CARBOHYDRATE 41.5
FIBER 3.1 CHOLESTEROL 34 IRON 3.5 SODIUM 141 CALCIUM 79

CHILLED LOBSTER TAILS WITH MUSTARD VINAIGRETTE

4 (8-ounce) frozen lobster tails, thawed
¼ cup plus 1 tablespoon Chablis or other dry
  white wine
1½ tablespoons white wine vinegar
1 tablespoon finely chopped fresh parsley
1 tablespoon Dijon mustard
1 teaspoon chopped fresh dillweed
1 teaspoon olive oil
½ teaspoon sugar
½ teaspoon minced garlic
1 medium cucumber, scored and
  thinly sliced
Lemon wedges (optional)

Cook lobster tails in boiling water 6 to 8 minutes or until done; drain. Rinse with cold water. Split lobster tails lengthwise, cutting through upper hard shell with an electric knife. Remove lobster meat through split shell, leaving meat intact. Set shells aside.

Score lobster meat at 1-inch intervals. Place lobster in a zip-top heavy-duty plastic bag. Combine wine and next 7 ingredients; pour over lobster. Seal bag securely; place bag in a medium bowl. Marinate in refrigerator 4 hours, turning occasionally.

Remove lobster from marinade, reserving marinade. Place reserved shells on individual serving plates. Place lobster meat on shells. Dip cucumber slices in reserved marinade. Place a cucumber slice in each score on lobster. Arrange remaining cucumber slices around tails. Garnish with lemon wedges, if desired. Yield: 4 servings (145 calories per serving).

PROTEIN 25.2 FAT 1.5 (Saturated Fat 0.2) CARBOHYDRATE 4.7
FIBER 0.5 CHOLESTEROL 87 IRON 0.8 SODIUM 516 CALCIUM 90

INDIVIDUAL LOBSTER CASSEROLES

3 (8-ounce) fresh or frozen lobster
  tails, thawed
1 (10-ounce) package frozen artichoke hearts,
  thawed and quartered
Vegetable cooking spray
2 teaspoons reduced-calorie margarine
2 cups sliced fresh mushrooms
¼ cup chopped green onions
¼ cup dry vermouth
¼ cup canned low-sodium chicken broth,
  undiluted
2 teaspoons lemon juice
1 teaspoon Dijon mustard
3 ounces Neufchâtel cheese, cubed
½ cup (2 ounces) shredded reduced-fat Jarlsberg
  cheese
Lemon twists (optional)

Cook lobster tails in boiling water 6 to 8 minutes or until done; drain. Rinse tails thoroughly with cold water. Split and clean tails. Coarsely chop lobster meat, and set aside.

Cook artichoke hearts according to package directions, omitting salt. Drain well, and set aside.

Coat a large nonstick skillet with cooking spray; add margarine. Place over medium-high heat until margarine melts. Add mushrooms and green onions; sauté until tender.

Combine vermouth and next 3 ingredients; add to mushroom mixture, and stir well. Add Neufchâtel cheese, stirring constantly, until cheese melts. Add artichoke hearts and lobster meat; stir well. Cook over medium heat 2 minutes or until thoroughly heated, stirring constantly.

Spoon lobster mixture evenly into 4 individual gratin dishes coated with cooking spray. Broil 5½ inches from heat 2 minutes. Sprinkle Jarlsberg cheese evenly over lobster mixture. Broil an additional 2 minutes or until cheese melts. Garnish with lemon twists, if desired. Serve immediately. Yield: 4 servings (238 calories per serving).

PROTEIN 27.4 FAT 9.4 (Saturated Fat 4.2) CARBOHYDRATE 10.4
FIBER 1.1 CHOLESTEROL 89 IRON 1.3 SODIUM 571 CALCIUM 90

STIR FRY OF SCALLOPS

1 tablespoon cornstarch, divided
1 tablespoon water
¾ pound bay scallops
Vegetable cooking spray
2 teaspoons peanut oil, divided
1 tablespoon minced garlic, divided
¼ cup canned low-sodium chicken broth,
    undiluted
1 tablespoon dry vermouth
½ teaspoon sugar
4 ounces fresh snow pea pods
¾ cup sliced leek
½ cup thinly sliced sweet red pepper
2 cups sliced fresh mushrooms
4 cups cooked long-grain rice (cooked without
    salt or fat)

Combine 1½ teaspoons cornstarch and water in a small bowl; stir well. Add scallops, tossing gently. Set aside.

Coat a large nonstick skillet with cooking spray; add 1 teaspoon oil. Place over medium-high heat until hot. Add 1½ teaspoons garlic; sauté 10 seconds. Add scallop mixture, and sauté 2 minutes. Remove scallop mixture from skillet; set aside. Wipe drippings from skillet with a paper towel.

Combine chicken broth, vermouth, remaining 1½ teaspoons cornstarch, and sugar in a small bowl; stir well. Set aside.

Wash snow peas; trim ends, and remove strings. Place remaining 1 teaspoon oil in skillet; place over medium-high heat until hot. Add remaining 1½ teaspoons garlic, snow peas, leek, and sweet red pepper; sauté 2 minutes. Add mushrooms; sauté 2 minutes. Add scallop mixture and chicken broth mixture; cook until mixture is thickened and thoroughly heated, stirring constantly. Serve over rice. Yield: 4 servings (389 calories per serving).

PROTEIN 18.6 FAT 3.8 (Saturated Fat 0.6) CARBOHYDRATE 68.1
FIBER 2.7 CHOLESTEROL 22 IRON 4.1 SODIUM 120 CALCIUM 69

SHRIMP AND ASPARAGUS MEDLEY

1 pound fresh asparagus
6 ounces linguine, uncooked
6 cups water
1¾ pounds medium-size fresh shrimp,
    peeled and deveined
Vegetable cooking spray
1 teaspoon margarine
⅔ cup chopped onion
½ cup diced green pepper
½ pound sliced fresh mushrooms
1 teaspoon dried thyme
¼ teaspoon pepper
⅛ teaspoon salt
⅛ teaspoon celery seeds
2 tablespoons lemon juice

Snap off tough ends of asparagus. Remove scales from stalks with a knife or vegetable peeler, if desired. Cut asparagus into 1-inch pieces.

Cook pasta according to package directions, omitting salt and fat. Drain pasta well. Set pasta aside, and keep warm.

Bring water to a boil in a large saucepan; add shrimp, and cook 3 to 5 minutes or until done. Drain well, and set aside.

Coat a large nonstick skillet with cooking spray; add margarine. Place over medium-high heat until margarine melts. Add asparagus, onion, and green pepper; sauté until vegetables are crisp-tender.

Add sliced mushrooms, thyme, pepper, salt, and celery seeds; stir well. Cook, uncovered, over medium heat 3 to 4 minutes or until mushrooms are tender, stirring frequently. Stir in shrimp and lemon juice; cook until thoroughly heated, stirring frequently.

Place pasta on a large serving platter; spoon shrimp mixture over pasta. Serve immediately. Yield: 6 servings (224 calories per serving).

PROTEIN 22.9 FAT 2.3 (Saturated Fat 0.4) CARBOHYDRATE 28.6
FIBER 3.3 CHOLESTEROL 147 IRON 4.9 SODIUM 232 CALCIUM 63

SHRIMP SATÉ

2½ tablespoons rice wine vinegar
2½ tablespoons water
1 tablespoon plus 1 teaspoon minced garlic,
    divided
2 teaspoons peanut oil, divided
1½ teaspoons hot sauce, divided
1½ pounds medium-size fresh shrimp, peeled and
    deveined
¼ cup minced shallot
¾ cup canned low-sodium chicken broth,
    undiluted
2 tablespoons peanut butter
1 teaspoon honey
1 tablespoon lemon juice
Vegetable cooking spray

Combine vinegar, water, 1 teaspoon garlic, 1 teaspoon oil, and ½ teaspoon hot sauce; stir well. Place
shrimp in a shallow dish; add vinegar mixture, and
toss gently. Cover and marinate in refrigerator 1 hour,
stirring occasionally.

Heat remaining 1 teaspoon oil in a small nonstick
skillet over medium heat until hot. Add shallot and
remaining 1 tablespoon garlic; sauté 3 minutes or until
tender. Add chicken broth, peanut butter, honey, and
remaining 1 teaspoon hot sauce; stir well with a wire
whisk. Reduce heat to low, and cook 10 minutes,
stirring frequently. Stir in lemon juice. Remove from
heat; set aside, and keep warm.

Remove shrimp from marinade. Place marinade
in a small saucepan; bring to a boil. Reduce heat, and
simmer 5 minutes.

Thread shrimp onto 4 (10-inch) skewers. Coat grill
rack with cooking spray; place on grill over medium-
hot coals. Place kabobs on rack, and cook 4 minutes
on each side or until shrimp are done, basting frequently with marinade. Serve with peanut butter
sauce. Yield: 4 servings (188 calories per serving).

PROTEIN 22.9 FAT 7.6 (Saturated Fat 1.4) CARBOHYDRATE 6.2
FIBER 0.6 CHOLESTEROL 187 IRON 3.3 SODIUM 271 CALCIUM 50

SHRIMP CURRY

6 cups water
1¼ pounds medium-size fresh shrimp, peeled and
    deveined
Vegetable cooking spray
2 teaspoons reduced-calorie margarine
½ cup chopped onion
2 tablespoons plus 1 teaspoon all-purpose flour
1 tablespoon curry powder
2 cups skim milk
2 teaspoons lemon juice
¼ teaspoon salt
2 cups cooked long-grain rice (cooked without salt
    or fat)
¼ cup chopped green onions
¼ cup cubed banana
¼ cup raisins
1 tablespoon plus 1 teaspoon unsweetened coconut
2 tablespoons chopped fresh parsley

Bring 6 cups water to a boil in a large saucepan.
Add shrimp; cook 3 minutes or until done. Drain well.

Coat a large nonstick skillet with cooking spray; add
margarine. Place over medium-high heat until margarine melts. Add ½ cup onion; sauté until tender.
Combine flour and curry powder; sprinkle over onion, stirring until blended. Gradually add milk, stirring constantly. Cook 10 minutes or until thickened,
stirring constantly. Add lemon juice and salt; stir well.
Add shrimp, and cook until thoroughly heated.

Place rice on a large serving platter. Spoon shrimp
mixture over rice; top evenly with green onions and
remaining ingredients. Serve immediately. Yield: 4
servings (345 calories per serving).

PROTEIN 25.1 FAT 4.2 (Saturated Fat 1.6) CARBOHYDRATE 51.4
FIBER 2.7 CHOLESTEROL 158 IRON 4.8 SODIUM 414 CALCIUM 219

*Clockwise from left: Offer your family
Fruited Wild Rice (page 133) as a
carbohydrate-rich side dish. Try
Tortellini with Zucchini and Sun-
Dried Tomatoes (page 139) or
Capellini with Clam Sauce (page 137)
for a hearty entrée.*

Grains & Pastas

PESTO BARLEY

2 cups water
1 cup pearl barley, uncooked
1 cup chopped fresh parsley
½ cup chopped fresh basil
¼ cup chopped walnuts
1 tablespoon olive oil
1 tablespoon water
½ teaspoon salt
½ teaspoon garlic powder

Combine 2 cups water and barley in a medium saucepan; bring to a boil. Cover, reduce heat, and simmer 30 minutes or until barley is tender. Drain.

Combine parsley and remaining ingredients in container of an electric blender or food processor; top with cover, and process until smooth.

Combine barley and parsley mixture in a medium bowl; stir well. Serve immediately. Yield: 8 servings (130 calories per ½-cup serving).

PROTEIN 3.6   FAT 4.2   (Saturated Fat 0.4)   CARBOHYDRATE 20.6
FIBER 4.5   CHOLESTEROL 0   IRON 1.3   SODIUM 152   CALCIUM 22

MOROCCAN COUSCOUS

1 tablespoon olive oil
¾ cup diced purple onion
½ cup diced carrot
½ cup diced turnip
½ cup diced zucchini
¾ cup diced tomato
1 to 2 tablespoons ground cumin
1 teaspoon curry powder
1 teaspoon paprika
1½ cups canned low-sodium chicken broth, undiluted
1 cup couscous, uncooked
¼ teaspoon salt
½ teaspoon pepper

Heat olive oil in a large saucepan over medium-high heat; add onion, and sauté until tender. Stir in carrot, turnip, and zucchini; cook 5 minutes, stirring occasionally. Add tomato, cumin, curry powder, and paprika; cook 2 minutes, stirring constantly.

Add chicken broth; bring to a boil. Remove from heat. Add couscous; cover and let stand 5 minutes or until couscous is tender and liquid is absorbed. Stir in salt and pepper. Fluff couscous with a fork, and transfer to a serving bowl. Yield: 9 servings (57 calories per ½-cup serving).

PROTEIN 1.6   FAT 1.8   (Saturated Fat 0.2)   CARBOHYDRATE 8.8
FIBER 1.4   CHOLESTEROL 0   IRON 0.9   SODIUM 77   CALCIUM 20

CHEESE GRITS SOUFFLÉ

¼ cup quick-cooking grits, uncooked
2 eggs, separated
⅔ cup evaporated skimmed milk
½ cup (2 ounces) shredded reduced-fat Cheddar cheese, divided
¼ teaspoon salt
¼ teaspoon ground white pepper
4 egg whites
Vegetable cooking spray

Cook grits according to package directions, omitting salt and fat. Remove from heat, and let cool slightly.

Lightly beat egg yolks in a large bowl. Add grits, milk, ¼ cup cheese, salt, and pepper; stir well.

Beat 6 egg whites at high speed of an electric mixer until stiff peaks form. Fold one-third of egg whites into grits mixture; fold in remaining egg whites. Pour into a 2-quart soufflé dish coated with cooking spray. Sprinkle with remaining ¼ cup cheese. Bake at 375° for 25 to 30 minutes or until puffed and golden. Serve immediately. Yield: 8 servings (79 calories per serving).

PROTEIN 6.6   FAT 2.4   (Saturated Fat 1.0)   CARBOHYDRATE 8.0
FIBER 0.3   CHOLESTEROL 58   IRON 0.5   SODIUM 178   CALCIUM 118

Grated cheese and fresh oregano showcase Polenta with Chunky Tomato Sauce.

POLENTA WITH CHUNKY TOMATO SAUCE

3 cups water
¼ teaspoon salt
2 cloves garlic, minced
1 cup instant polenta, uncooked
Chunky Tomato Sauce
2 tablespoons freshly grated Parmesan cheese
Fresh oregano sprigs (optional)

Combine first 3 ingredients in a saucepan; bring to a boil. Add polenta in a slow, steady stream; stir constantly. Reduce heat; cook over medium-low heat 10 minutes or until mixture pulls away from sides of pan, stirring constantly. Press polenta evenly into individual gratin dishes. Top with Chunky Tomato Sauce; sprinkle with cheese. Garnish with oregano, if desired. Yield: 6 servings (116 calories per serving).

Chunky Tomato Sauce

2½ cups chopped fresh tomato
2 tablespoons chopped onion
1 clove garlic, minced
½ teaspoon dried whole basil
½ teaspoon dried whole oregano
½ teaspoon dried whole thyme
¼ teaspoon salt
¼ teaspoon pepper

Combine all ingredients in a medium bowl; stir well. Cover mixture, and let stand 1 hour at room temperature. Yield: 2 cups.

PROTEIN 3.6   FAT 1.5   (Saturated Fat 0.5)   CARBOHYDRATE 22.5
FIBER 2.4   CHOLESTEROL 2   IRON 1.6   SODIUM 241   CALCIUM 44

FOUR GRAIN PILAF

1 tablespoon reduced-calorie margarine
½ cup chopped shallots
¼ cup quinoa, uncooked
1 cup long-grain rice, uncooked
½ cup bulgur wheat, uncooked
¼ cup barley, uncooked
3 cups canned no-salt-added beef broth, undiluted
½ teaspoon salt
½ teaspoon pepper
¼ cup chopped fresh parsley

Heat margarine in a large saucepan over medium-high heat until margarine melts. Add shallot, and sauté 2 to 3 minutes or until tender.

Rinse quinoa in 3 changes of water; drain. Add quinoa, rice, bulgur, and barley to saucepan; stir well. Cook 5 minutes, stirring constantly. Add beef broth, salt, and pepper. Bring to a boil; cover, reduce heat, and simmer 25 minutes or until grains are tender and broth is absorbed. Fluff with a fork, and stir in parsley. Serve immediately. Yield: 10 servings (147 calories per ½-cup serving).

PROTEIN 3.8   FAT 1.2   (Saturated Fat 0.2)   CARBOHYDRATE 29.3
FIBER 1.7   CHOLESTEROL 0   IRON 1.3   SODIUM 134   CALCIUM 14

GREEN RICE WITH PINE NUTS

1 tablespoon reduced-calorie margarine
¾ cup finely chopped green onions
1½ cups chopped fresh spinach
½ cup finely chopped fresh parsley
¼ cup chopped celery leaves
1 cup long-grain rice, uncooked
2 cups canned no-salt-added chicken broth, undiluted
2 tablespoons pine nuts, toasted
½ teaspoon pepper
¼ teaspoon salt

Heat margarine in a large nonstick skillet over medium-high heat until margarine melts. Add green onions, and sauté until tender. Add spinach, parsley, and celery leaves; sauté 1 to 2 minutes or until spinach wilts. Add rice, stirring gently.

Add chicken broth to rice mixture; bring to a boil. Cover, reduce heat, and simmer 20 minutes or until rice is tender and liquid is absorbed. Stir in pine nuts, pepper, and salt. Yield: 6 servings (151 calories per ½-cup serving).

PROTEIN 3.8   FAT 3.3   (Saturated Fat 0.7)   CARBOHYDRATE 26.2
FIBER 1.0   CHOLESTEROL 0   IRON 2.1   SODIUM 172   CALCIUM 28

 ## GLOSSARY OF UNUSUAL GRAINS

Expand your knowledge of whole grains and enjoy the merits—both taste and nutritional—of ancient grain and grainlike foods.

Barley—Studies show that this grain is high in soluble fiber, the type that can help lower blood cholesterol. A good source of B vitamins and protein, barley lends a distinctly nutty flavor to soups and salads.

Buckwheat—Buckwheat is a common ingredient in Asian foods while Americans use it primarily in the ground form to make flour for pancakes. The hulled, crushed buckwheat kernels, also known as kasha, are used in side dishes and meatless entrées. Studies show that buckwheat, because it is digested slowly, may help control blood sugar. Rich in protein, buckwheat is also a good source of several B vitamins.

Bulgur—Middle Eastern dishes favor this dried form of whole wheat berries (whole, unprocessed wheat kernels) that is traditionally served pilaf-style. The wheat is steamed, dried, and then coarsely ground. It is rich in B vitamins, iron, and protein.

Quinoa—When cooked, this high-protein seed is similar to a mild brown rice; it is soft with a delicate crunch. Quinoa is rich in B vitamins, vitamin E, calcium, iron, and phosphorus.

From left: barley, buckwheat, bulgur, and quinoa.

FRIED RICE AND VEGETABLES

1¾ cups water
¾ cup long-grain brown rice, uncooked
¾ cup diced carrot
¼ pound fresh snow peas
1 tablespoon vegetable oil
1 cup frozen English peas, thawed
1 cup frozen whole kernel corn, thawed
¼ cup sliced green onions
2 tablespoons low-sodium soy sauce

Bring 1¾ cups water to a boil in a medium sauce-pan; stir in rice. Cover, reduce heat, and simmer 35 minutes. Stir in carrot; cover and cook an additional 10 minutes or until rice is tender and liquid is absorbed. Chill rice mixture thoroughly.

Wash snow peas; trim ends, and remove strings. Cut into 1-inch pieces; set aside.

Heat oil in a wok over medium-high heat (375°) until hot. Add chilled rice mixture, and stir-fry 2 minutes. Add English peas and corn; stir-fry 3 minutes. Stir in snow peas, green onions, and soy sauce. Cover and cook 2 to 3 minutes or until thoroughly heated. Yield: 6 servings (156 calories per ¾-cup serving).

PROTEIN 4.3 FAT 3.0 (Saturated Fat 0.6) CARBOHYDRATE 27.7
FIBER 3.4 CHOLESTEROL 0 IRON 1.2 SODIUM 162 CALCIUM 25

FRUITED WILD RICE

½ cup wild rice, uncooked
1 tablespoon vegetable oil
⅔ cup long-grain brown rice, uncooked
1 cup chopped onion
½ cup chopped celery
1 clove garlic, minced
⅓ cup raisins
1 teaspoon lemon juice
1 teaspoon grated orange rind
½ teaspoon salt
2 cups canned no-salt-added chicken broth,
    undiluted
2 tablespoons chopped walnuts

Rinse wild rice in 3 changes of hot water; drain. Cover with hot water, and let stand 1 hour; drain.

Heat oil in a large skillet over medium-high heat; add brown rice, and cook 2 to 3 minutes or until lightly browned, stirring constantly. Add onion, celery, and garlic; sauté until tender. Stir in raisins, lemon juice, orange rind, and salt. Add chicken broth; bring to a boil. Add wild rice; cover, reduce heat, and simmer 45 minutes. Uncover and simmer an additional 10 minutes or until liquid is absorbed. Stir in walnuts. Yield: 8 servings (149 calories per ½-cup serving).

PROTEIN 4.0 FAT 3.8 (Saturated Fat 0.6) CARBOHYDRATE 25.3
FIBER 1.8 CHOLESTEROL 0 IRON 0.7 SODIUM 191 CALCIUM 18

WHEAT BERRIES PRIMAVERA

2 quarts water
1¼ cups whole grain wheat berries
1 tablespoon reduced-calorie margarine
½ pound sliced fresh mushrooms
½ cup chopped green onions
¼ cup diced sweet red pepper
1 clove garlic, minced
1 small zucchini, sliced
4 asparagus spears, cut into 1-inch pieces
¼ teaspoon salt

Combine water and wheat berries in a large sauce-pan; bring to a boil. Partially cover; reduce heat and simmer 1 hour or until wheat berries are tender. Drain and set aside.

Melt margarine in a large skillet over medium-high heat. Add mushrooms and next 3 ingredients; sauté until vegetables are tender and liquid is absorbed.

Arrange zucchini and asparagus in a vegetable steamer over boiling water. Cover and steam 3 to 5 minutes or until crisp-tender.

Combine wheat berries, vegetables, and salt in a serving bowl; toss gently. Yield: 10 servings (93 calories per ½-cup serving).

PROTEIN 4.0 FAT 1.3 (Saturated Fat 0.1) CARBOHYDRATE 18.5
FIBER 3.9 CHOLESTEROL 0 IRON 0.5 SODIUM 73 CALCIUM 8

BASIC SPINACH PASTA

3½ cups fresh torn spinach
1 egg
¼ teaspoon salt
1½ cups plus 1 tablespoon all-purpose flour
2 teaspoons water
3 quarts boiling water

Place spinach in a large saucepan; cover and cook over medium heat, stirring frequently, until spinach wilts. Drain and press dry between paper towels. Chop spinach.

Position knife blade in food processor bowl; add spinach, egg, and salt. Process 30 seconds or until blended. Add flour, and process 30 seconds to 1 minute or until mixture forms pea-size balls. Slowly add 2 teaspoons water through food chute with processor running; blend just until mixture forms a ball.

Continue to process 2 minutes or until dough is smooth and elastic. Wrap dough in plastic wrap, and let stand 10 minutes.

Divide dough in half. Working with 1 portion at a time, pass dough through smooth rollers of pasta machine on widest setting. Continue moving width gauge to narrower settings; pass dough through rollers once at each setting. Roll to desired thinness (about ¹⁄₁₆ inch). Pass each dough sheet through fettuccine cutting rollers of machine. Hang pasta on a wooden drying rack (dry no longer than 30 minutes).

Cook pasta in boiling water 2 minutes; drain. Serve immediately. Yield: 3½ cups (108 calories per ½-cup serving).

PROTEIN 4.0   FAT 1.0   (Saturated Fat 0.3)   CARBOHYDRATE 20.3
FIBER 1.1   CHOLESTEROL 30   IRON 1.9   SODIUM 105   CALCIUM 30

SPINACH FETTUCCINE WITH SUN-DRIED TOMATO SAUCE

1 (7-ounce) jar sun-dried tomatoes in olive oil, undrained
Olive oil-flavored vegetable cooking spray
½ cup chopped purple onion
1 tablespoon minced garlic
½ cup Chablis or other dry white wine
½ teaspoon crushed red pepper
Basic Spinach Pasta (recipe above)
1½ cups peeled, seeded, and finely chopped ripe tomato
1 cup shredded fresh spinach leaves
½ cup coarsely chopped fresh basil
1 cup crumbled feta cheese

Drain sun-dried tomatoes, reserving 1 tablespoon olive oil. Coarsely chop ¼ cup tomatoes. Reserve remaining olive oil and sun-dried tomatoes for other uses. Coat a large nonstick skillet with cooking spray; add reserved 1 tablespoon olive oil. Place skillet over medium-high heat until hot. Add onion and garlic; sauté 4 minutes or until tender. Add wine and red pepper; reduce heat to low, and cook, uncovered, 10 minutes. Stir in chopped sun-dried tomatoes; cook 1 minute or until thoroughly heated.

Cook pasta in boiling water 2 minutes; drain. Combine pasta, sun-dried tomato mixture, chopped tomato, spinach, and basil; toss gently. Add feta cheese; toss just until combined. Serve immediately. Yield: 11 servings (126 calories per ½-cup serving).

PROTEIN 4.9   FAT 4.3   (Saturated Fat 1.9)   CARBOHYDRATE 17.3
FIBER 1.4   CHOLESTEROL 28   IRON 1.6   SODIUM 242   CALCIUM 83

It takes only minutes to prepare Spaghetti with Vegetables and Pine Nuts. This colorful side dish complements any meat or poultry entrée.

SPAGHETTI WITH VEGETABLES AND PINE NUTS

Vegetable cooking spray
2 teaspoons olive oil
1 cup fresh broccoli flowerets
1 cup fresh cauliflower flowerets
1 cup julienned carrots
1 cup julienned zucchini
1 tablespoon plus 1 teaspoon minced garlic
1 cup snow pea pods, trimmed
¼ cup canned no-salt-added chicken broth, undiluted
1 cup cherry tomatoes, halved
8 ounces spaghetti, uncooked
2 tablespoons pine nuts, toasted
2 tablespoons chopped fresh parsley

Coat a large nonstick skillet with cooking spray; add oil. Place over medium-high heat until hot. Add broccoli, cauliflower, carrot, zucchini, and garlic; sauté 4 minutes. Stir in snow peas and chicken broth. Cover, reduce heat, and cook 6 minutes. Stir in tomato halves, and cook an additional 3 minutes.

Cook pasta according to package directions, omitting salt and fat; drain. Add pasta to vegetable mixture; toss well. Sprinkle with pine nuts and parsley. Serve immediately. Yield: 8 servings (161 calories per 1-cup serving).

PROTEIN 6.0   FAT 3.7   (Saturated Fat 0.5)   CARBOHYDRATE 27.1
FIBER 2.4   CHOLESTEROL 0   IRON 2.1   SODIUM 18   CALCIUM 31

TOMATO AND HERB RIGATONI

2 cups peeled, seeded, and chopped tomato
¼ cup chopped fresh parsley
2 tablespoons shredded fresh basil
1½ teaspoons minced garlic
1½ tablespoons fresh lemon juice
1½ teaspoons olive oil
½ teaspoon chopped fresh mint
½ teaspoon pepper
¼ teaspoon crushed red pepper
⅛ teaspoon salt
8 ounces rigatoni pasta, uncooked
Fresh basil sprigs (optional)

Combine first 10 ingredients in a large bowl. Let stand at room temperature 1 hour.

Cook pasta according to package directions, omitting salt and fat; drain. Add pasta to tomato mixture, and toss well. Garnish with fresh basil sprigs, if desired. Serve immediately. Yield: 10 servings (99 calories per ½-cup serving).

PROTEIN 3.3   FAT 1.2   (Saturated Fat 0.2)   CARBOHYDRATE 19.0
FIBER 1.1   CHOLESTEROL 0   IRON 1.2   SODIUM 35   CALCIUM 10

ROTELLE WITH BROCCOLI

3 cups fresh broccoli flowerets
Vegetable cooking spray
1 tablespoon olive oil
1 tablespoon finely chopped onion
1½ teaspoons drained, chopped anchovy
    fillets
1 teaspoon minced garlic
8 ounces rotelle pasta, uncooked
½ cup grated Romano cheese
¼ cup sliced ripe olives
2 tablespoons chopped fresh basil

Arrange broccoli in a vegetable steamer over boiling water. Cover and steam 5 minutes or until crisp-tender. Set aside.

Coat a large nonstick skillet with cooking spray; add olive oil. Place over medium-high heat until hot. Add onion, anchovies, and garlic; sauté 2 minutes. Add broccoli, and cook until thoroughly heated.

Cook pasta according to package directions, omitting salt and fat; drain well.

Place pasta in a serving bowl. Add broccoli mixture, Romano cheese, olives, and basil; toss gently. Serve immediately. Yield: 8 servings (168 calories per 1-cup serving).

PROTEIN 7.4   FAT 4.9   (Saturated Fat 1.6)   CARBOHYDRATE 23.8
FIBER 1.7   CHOLESTEROL 7   IRON 1.7   SODIUM 199   CALCIUM 108

MUSHROOM-PASTA TOSS

Butter-flavored vegetable cooking spray
1 tablespoon reduced-calorie margarine
1¼ cups sliced fresh mushrooms
3 ounces fresh shiitake mushrooms, sliced
3 ounces fresh cremini mushrooms, sliced
2 teaspoons minced garlic
½ cup chopped fresh parsley
½ cup canned no-salt-added beef broth,
    undiluted
1 tablespoon no-salt-added tomato paste
2 teaspoons chopped fresh marjoram
¼ teaspoon salt
8 ounces rotini pasta, uncooked
1 ounce prosciutto, chopped
Fresh parsley sprigs (optional)

Coat a large nonstick skillet with cooking spray; add margarine. Place over medium-high heat until margarine melts. Add mushrooms and garlic; sauté 3 minutes or until mushrooms are tender. Stir in chopped parsley and next 4 ingredients; cook an additional 1 to 2 minutes or until thoroughly heated. Remove from heat, and keep warm.

Cook pasta according to package directions, omitting salt and fat; drain. Place pasta in a serving bowl. Add mushroom mixture and prosciutto; toss gently. Garnish with parsley, if desired. Serve immediately. Yield: 10 servings (108 calories per ½-cup serving).

PROTEIN 4.4   FAT 1.6   (Saturated Fat 0.3)   CARBOHYDRATE 19.3
FIBER 1.1   CHOLESTEROL 2   IRON 2.0   SODIUM 117   CALCIUM 24

CAPELLINI WITH CLAM SAUCE

Vegetable cooking spray
1 teaspoon olive oil
⅓ cup chopped onion
2 tablespoons chopped green pepper
2 cloves garlic, minced
3 cups unpeeled, seeded, and chopped tomato
1 (8-ounce) can no-salt-added tomato sauce
½ teaspoon crushed red pepper
¼ teaspoon salt
1 (6½-ounce) can minced clams
¼ cup chopped fresh flat-leaf parsley
8 ounces capellini (angel hair pasta), uncooked

Coat a large nonstick skillet with cooking spray; add oil. Place over medium-high heat until hot. Add onion, green pepper, and garlic; sauté until tender. Stir in tomato and next 3 ingredients. Cover, reduce heat, and simmer 20 minutes.

Drain clams; reserve juice. Add juice to tomato mixture, and simmer an additional 5 minutes. Stir in clams and parsley; cook 5 minutes or until thoroughly heated. Remove from heat; keep warm.

Cook pasta according to package directions, omitting salt and fat; drain. Place pasta in a large bowl. Add clam mixture, and toss gently. Serve immediately. Yield: 5 servings (242 calories per 1-cup serving).

PROTEIN 10.3 FAT 2.4 (Saturated Fat 0.4) CARBOHYDRATE 45.0
FIBER 2.9 CHOLESTEROL 12 IRON 4.0 SODIUM 352 CALCIUM 43

CHICKEN MARSALA FETTUCCINE

3 (6-ounce) skinned chicken breast halves
2 cups water
2½ cups sliced fresh mushrooms
1¼ cups Marsala
¼ cup chopped green onions
½ teaspoon pepper
¼ teaspoon salt
2½ teaspoons cornstarch
1 tablespoon water
8 ounces fettuccine, uncooked
2 tablespoons chopped fresh parsley

Combine chicken and 2 cups water in a large saucepan. Bring to a boil; cover, reduce heat, and simmer 15 to 20 minutes or until chicken is tender. Remove chicken from broth, and let cool slightly. Shred chicken, and set aside. Skim and discard fat from broth; reserve broth for another use.

Combine mushrooms and next 4 ingredients in a large skillet; bring to a boil. Reduce heat, and cook, uncovered, 5 minutes. Combine cornstarch and 1 tablespoon water; stir well. Add to mushroom mixture; cook until thickened, stirring constantly. Add chicken, and cook 2 minutes or until thoroughly heated, stirring constantly.

Cook pasta according to package directions, omitting salt and fat; drain. Place pasta in a large bowl; add chicken mixture, tossing well. Sprinkle with parsley. Serve immediately. Yield: 6 servings (238 calories per 1-cup serving).

PROTEIN 21.9 FAT 2.4 (Saturated Fat 0.6) CARBOHYDRATE 33.5
FIBER 5.1 CHOLESTEROL 42 IRON 2.6 SODIUM 144 CALCIUM 34

 SAY GOOD-BYE TO BACK PAIN

Once the back is injured, the pain and frustration of recuperation often prove agonizing. Although many factors contribute to back pain, prevention seems the best cure. Taking a few simple measures now can help reduce the chance of a future back injury. If you already suffer from back pain, the following precautions may help reduce that pain and speed recovery:
• Sleep on a firm mattress. If your mattress is soft, insert a sheet of plywood between the mattress and the box springs.
• Shed any excess pounds. Extra weight puts strain on the spine, back muscles, and ligaments.
• Work to tone the muscles that support the back—abdominal, buttock, leg, and hip.
• Wear flat-soled or low-heeled shoes. High heels may throw the back out of proper alignment.
• Lift objects bending your legs, not your back. Squat in front of the article to be lifted; then rise gently from the squatting position.

VEAL AND CHICKEN CANNELLONI

Basic Spinach Pasta (recipe on page 134)
Olive oil-flavored vegetable cooking spray
1 teaspoon olive oil
6 ounces veal cutlets
1 (4-ounce) skinned, boned chicken breast half
½ cup chopped onion
¾ cup nonfat ricotta cheese
¼ cup grated Romano cheese
3 tablespoons Neufchâtel cheese
2 tablespoons minced fresh basil
¼ cup plus 1 tablespoon Chablis or other dry
    white wine, divided
3 cups chopped fresh tomato
⅓ cup water
½ teaspoon sugar
¼ teaspoon salt
1 clove garlic, minced
1 tablespoon minced fresh rosemary
¼ cup (1 ounce) shredded part-skim mozzarella
    cheese

Follow Basic Spinach Pasta recipe until dough is rolled to desired thickness (about ¹⁄₁₆ inch). Roll to 24- x 6-inch rectangle; cut into 6 (6- x 4-inch) rectangles.

Cook pasta in boiling water 10 minutes. Drain and rinse under cold water. Spread flat on wax paper, and set aside.

Coat a large nonstick skillet with cooking spray; add oil. Place over medium-high heat until hot. Add veal and chicken; cook 15 minutes or until done, turning frequently. Remove from skillet; drain and pat dry with paper towels. Shred veal and chicken; set aside. Wipe drippings from skillet with a paper towel.

Coat skillet with cooking spray; place over medium-high heat until hot. Add onion, and sauté 4 minutes or until tender.

Position knife blade in food processor bowl. Add ricotta cheese, Romano cheese, and Neufchâtel cheese; process until smooth. Add veal, chicken, onion, basil, and 1 tablespoon wine; stir well. Spoon cheese mixture evenly onto each pasta rectangle just below the center; roll pasta around cheese mixture. Place pasta rolls, seam side down, in a 13- x 9- x 2-inch baking dish coated with cooking spray. Set aside.

Coat skillet with cooking spray. Add remaining ¼ cup wine, tomato, and next 4 ingredients; bring to a boil. Cover, reduce heat, and simmer 20 minutes. Add rosemary, and simmer an additional 5 minutes. Remove from heat, and cool slightly.

Position knife blade in food processor bowl; add tomato mixture, and process until smooth. Spoon evenly over pasta rolls. Sprinkle with mozzarella cheese. Bake at 400° for 15 minutes or until mixture is bubbly and cheese melts. Yield: 6 servings (266 calories per serving).

PROTEIN 20.2　FAT 7.1　(Saturated Fat 2.5)　CARBOHYDRATE 30.6
FIBER 2.6　CHOLESTEROL 80　IRON 3.1　SODIUM 326　CALCIUM 141

FILLING CANNELLONI

To fill cannelloni for recipes such as Veal and Chicken Cannelloni, place the cooked pasta rectangles on wax paper. Spoon the cheese mixture along the length of the rectangle, just below the center of each rectangle. Beginning at the bottom edge of each rectangle, roll the pasta around the cheese mixture.

KOREAN VERMICELLI WITH BEEF AND VEGETABLES

8 ounces Korean vermicelli, uncooked
½ cup plus 2 tablespoons canned low-sodium
    chicken broth, undiluted
1½ tablespoons low-sodium soy sauce
1 tablespoon hoisin sauce
½ teaspoon chili paste
Vegetable cooking spray
2 teaspoons vegetable oil, divided
1 large sweet red pepper, cut into julienne strips
1 large green pepper, cut into julienne strips
1 cup chopped green onions, divided
1 tablespoon minced garlic
1 (¾-pound) lean flank steak
1½ cups sliced fresh mushrooms

Place vermicelli in a large bowl; add warm water to cover. Let stand 20 minutes. Drain.

Combine chicken broth and next 3 ingredients in a small bowl; stir well, and set aside.

Coat a wok or large nonstick skillet with cooking spray; add 1 teaspoon oil. Heat at medium-high heat (375°) until hot. Add peppers, and stir-fry 1 minute. Add ¾ cup green onions and garlic; stir-fry 1 minute. Remove vegetables from wok, and keep warm.

Partially freeze steak; trim fat from steak. Slice steak diagonally across grain into ⅛-inch-thick slices. Add remaining 1 teaspoon oil to wok; heat at medium-high heat until hot. Add steak and mushrooms; stir-fry 2 minutes. Add vermicelli, and toss well. Add chicken broth mixture and vegetable mixture; stir well. Cook, stirring constantly, 2 to 3 minutes or until mixture is thoroughly heated. Sprinkle with remaining ¼ cup chopped green onions. Serve immediately. Yield: 7 cups (229 calories per 1-cup serving).

PROTEIN 11.6 FAT 6.9 (Saturated Fat 2.2) CARBOHYDRATE 29.7
FIBER 1.2 CHOLESTEROL 24 IRON 2.7 SODIUM 246 CALCIUM 46

PASTA E FAGIOLI

1¼ cups dried Great Northern beans
2 quarts water
Olive oil-flavored vegetable cooking spray
1 teaspoon olive oil
½ cup finely chopped red onion
¼ cup finely chopped celery
1 tablespoon minced garlic
2 teaspoons chopped fresh rosemary
2 teaspoons chopped fresh sage
1 cup peeled, seeded, and finely chopped tomato
¼ teaspoon salt
1 teaspoon pepper
8 ounces ditalini pasta, uncooked
3 cups coarsely chopped fresh spinach

Sort and wash beans; place in a Dutch oven. Cover with water to a depth of 2 inches above beans; let soak 8 hours. Drain and rinse beans.

Combine beans and 2 quarts water in pan. Bring to a boil; cover, reduce heat, and simmer 1 hour.

Transfer 2 cups beans, without liquid, to container of an electric blender or food processor; top with cover, and process until smooth. Return to pan.

Coat a large nonstick skillet with cooking spray; add oil. Place over medium heat until hot; add onion and next 4 ingredients, and sauté 5 minutes. Add onion mixture, tomato, salt, and pepper to bean mixture. Cook over medium-low heat 15 minutes. Add pasta, and cook an additional 20 minutes, stirring frequently. Add spinach, and cook 2 minutes or until spinach wilts. Yield: 8 servings (261 calories per 1-cup serving).

PROTEIN 13.2 FAT 1.8 (Saturated Fat 0.3) CARBOHYDRATE 49.2
FIBER 17.9 CHOLESTEROL 0 IRON 4.0 SODIUM 98 CALCIUM 103

TORTELLINI WITH ZUCCHINI AND SUN-DRIED TOMATOES

¼ cup sun-dried tomatoes (without salt or oil)
½ cup hot water
Olive oil-flavored vegetable cooking spray
1 tablespoon olive oil
1 cup chopped zucchini
3 cloves garlic, minced
2 green onions, cut into 1-inch pieces
¼ cup chopped sweet red pepper
1 teaspoon dried whole oregano
1 (9-ounce) package fresh cheese tortellini

Combine tomatoes and water in a small bowl; cover and let stand 15 minutes. Drain tomatoes, and slice thinly; set aside.

Coat a large nonstick skillet with cooking spray; add olive oil. Place over medium-high heat until hot. Add zucchini and garlic; sauté 2 minutes. Add green onions, sweet red pepper, and oregano; sauté 1 minute. Stir in tomato. Remove from heat, and keep warm.

Cook tortellini according to package directions, omitting salt and fat; drain well. Place tortellini in a serving bowl. Add zucchini mixture; toss gently. Serve immediately. Yield: 4 servings (249 calories per 1-cup serving).

PROTEIN 12.1 FAT 6.9 (Saturated Fat 2.0) CARBOHYDRATE 47.7
FIBER 0.4 CHOLESTEROL 30 IRON 2.3 SODIUM 384 CALCIUM 167

RAVIOLI WITH CILANTRO-TOMATO SAUCE

1½ cups nonfat ricotta cheese
¼ cup chopped onion
¼ cup canned chopped roasted red pepper in
   water, drained
1 cup (4 ounces) shredded reduced-fat
   Monterey Jack cheese
½ teaspoon ground cumin
60 fresh or frozen wonton skins, thawed
3 quarts water
Cilantro-Tomato Sauce
Fresh cilantro sprigs (optional)

Combine first 5 ingredients in a medium bowl; stir well. Place 1 tablespoon cheese mixture in center of each of 30 wonton skins. Brush edges of wonton skins with water; top with remaining 30 wonton skins.

Press wonton edges together to seal, pushing out air. Trim wonton edges with a fluted pastry wheel, if desired.

Bring 3 quarts water to a boil in a Dutch oven. Add one-third of ravioli, and return water to a boil; reduce heat, and simmer 5 minutes or until ravioli are tender. Remove ravioli with a slotted spoon. Repeat procedure with remaining ravioli.

Spoon Cilantro-Tomato Sauce evenly onto each of 6 individual serving plates. Place 5 ravioli on each plate. Garnish with cilantro sprigs, if desired. Serve immediately. Yield: 6 servings (181 calories per serving).

Cilantro-Tomato Sauce

Vegetable cooking spray
½ cup minced onion
1 clove garlic, minced
2 (8-ounce) cans no-salt-added tomato sauce
1 (4-ounce) can chopped green chiles, drained
⅓ cup minced fresh cilantro
1 teaspoon sugar
¼ teaspoon salt

Coat a medium saucepan with cooking spray; place over medium-high heat until hot. Add onion and garlic; sauté 3 minutes or until tender. Add tomato sauce and remaining ingredients; stir well. Reduce heat, and cook, uncovered, 20 minutes, stirring occasionally. Serve warm. Yield: 2½ cups.

PROTEIN 13.3 FAT 5.0 (Saturated Fat 2.5) CARBOHYDRATE 22.1
FIBER 1.2 CHOLESTEROL 67 IRON 1.1 SODIUM 392 CALCIUM 222

Compose the entrée for your guests. Cumin, yogurt, and sour cream blend to add accent lines for embellishing Stuffed Green Chiles with Yellow Pepper Sauce (page 143).

Meatless Main

Summer's harvest goes straight from the garden into the kitchen for Farmer's Market Vegetable Bowl.

FARMER'S MARKET VEGETABLE BOWL

2 small sweet red peppers
Vegetable cooking spray
2 teaspoons olive oil, divided
2 cups sliced zucchini
1 small onion, sliced
½ cup thinly sliced carrot
2 cloves garlic, crushed
12 cherry tomatoes, halved
1½ tablespoons minced fresh basil
1 cup frozen egg substitute, thawed
⅔ cup all-purpose flour
½ cup skim milk
¼ teaspoon salt
2 ounces feta cheese, crumbled

Cut sweet red peppers in half lengthwise; remove and discard seeds and membranes. Place peppers, skin side up, on a large baking sheet; flatten with palm of hand.

Broil 5½ inches from heat 12 minutes or until charred. Place peppers in ice water; chill 5 minutes. Remove from water; peel and discard skins. Cut into thin strips, and set aside.

Coat a large nonstick skillet with cooking spray; add 1 teaspoon olive oil. Place over medium-high heat until hot. Add zucchini, onion, carrot, and garlic; sauté 10 to 12 minutes or until vegetables are tender. Stir in peppers, tomatoes, and basil. Remove from heat, and keep warm.

Combine egg substitute, flour, milk, and salt in a medium bowl; beat with a wire whisk until smooth.

Coat a 9-inch cast-iron skillet with cooking spray; brush with remaining 1 teaspoon olive oil. Place skillet in a 450° oven 4 minutes or until hot. Pour batter into skillet. Bake at 450° for 15 minutes. Reduce heat to 375°, and bake 15 minutes or until puffed and browned.

Spoon vegetable mixture into shell; sprinkle with feta cheese. Serve immediately. Yield: 4 servings (224 calories per serving).

PROTEIN 13.4 FAT 6.3 (Saturated Fat 2.6) CARBOHYDRATE 29.5
FIBER 3.4 CHOLESTEROL 13 IRON 3.6 SODIUM 426 CALCIUM 166

STUFFED GREEN CHILES WITH YELLOW PEPPER SAUCE

12 whole fresh green chiles (about 2 pounds)
¼ cup plus 2 tablespoons nonfat sour cream
¼ cup plus 2 tablespoons plain nonfat yogurt
¼ teaspoon ground cumin
¼ teaspoon salt
Vegetable cooking spray
2 teaspoons vegetable oil
½ cup minced green onions
2 cloves garlic, minced
1 (15-ounce) can pinto beans, drained
½ teaspoon ground oregano
½ teaspoon ground cumin
½ cup minced fresh cilantro
Yellow Pepper Sauce
1½ cups diced, seeded tomato
Fresh cilantro (optional)

Make a lengthwise slit down each chile, and carefully remove seeds. Place chiles on a baking sheet. Broil 5½ inches from heat 15 to 20 minutes or until charred, turning occasionally. Place in ice water; chill 5 minutes. Remove from water; peel chiles, and discard skins. Set aside.

Combine sour cream and next 3 ingredients in a small bowl; stir well. Cover and chill.

Coat a large nonstick skillet with cooking spray; add oil. Place over medium-high heat until hot. Add green onions and garlic; sauté 2 minutes. Add pinto beans, oregano, and ½ teaspoon cumin; stir well. Reduce heat to low; cook until mixture is thoroughly heated, mashing beans slightly with a potato masher or wooden spoon. Remove from heat; stir in minced cilantro.

Carefully stuff bean mixture evenly in chiles; gently reshape chiles. Arrange chiles in a single layer in a 13- x 9- x 2-inch baking dish coated with cooking spray. Bake at 325° for 15 minutes or until thoroughly heated.

Spoon ¼ cup Yellow Pepper Sauce onto each individual serving plate. Spoon sour cream mixture into a zip-top plastic bag or a decorating bag fitted with a No. 2 round tip; seal plastic bag. Snip a tiny hole in one corner of zip-top bag, using scissors. Pipe mixture in thin parallel lines ½ inch apart across Yellow Pepper Sauce. Pull the point of a wooden pick back and forth perpendicular to the lines to create a webbed pattern. Arrange 3 chiles over sauce on each plate; top evenly with tomato. Garnish with fresh cilantro, if desired. Serve immediately. Yield: 4 servings (235 calories per serving).

Yellow Pepper Sauce

⅓ cup Chablis or other dry white wine
⅓ cup canned low-sodium chicken broth, undiluted
1 cup chopped sweet yellow pepper
⅔ cup peeled, diced potato

Combine all ingredients in a small saucepan; stir well. Bring to a boil; cover, reduce heat, and simmer 20 minutes or until pepper and potato are tender. Transfer mixture to container of an electric blender; top with cover, and process until smooth. Strain through a sieve. Serve warm. Yield: 1 cup.

PROTEIN 11.2 FAT 4.1 (Saturated Fat 0.6) CARBOHYDRATE 42.2
FIBER 5.7 CHOLESTEROL 0 IRON 4.7 SODIUM 207 CALCIUM 159

CURRIED VEGETABLE-POTATO BAKE

2 pounds baking potatoes, peeled
1 cup diced carrot
1 cup diced parsnip
Vegetable cooking spray
1 teaspoon olive oil
2 cups chopped onion
¼ teaspoon salt
¼ teaspoon ground turmeric
¼ teaspoon curry powder
¼ teaspoon ground nutmeg
¼ teaspoon ground red pepper
1½ cups frozen egg substitute, thawed
1 cup frozen English peas, thawed
½ cup minced fresh parsley
¼ cup plus 2 tablespoons grated Parmesan cheese,
    divided

Cook potatoes in a large saucepan in boiling water to cover 25 to 30 minutes or until tender. Remove potatoes with a slotted spoon, and transfer to a large bowl. Add carrot and parsnip to boiling water; cook 5 to 10 minutes or until tender. Drain vegetables, and set aside.

Coat a large saucepan with cooking spray; add olive oil, and place over medium-low heat until hot. Add onion, and sauté 20 minutes or until golden, stirring frequently. Add salt and next 4 ingredients, stirring well; cook 1 minute. Remove from heat, and set aside.

Mash potatoes. Add egg substitute, ¼ cup at a time, stirring well after each addition. Stir in carrot mixture, onion mixture, peas, parsley, and 3 tablespoons Parmesan cheese.

Coat a 2-quart casserole with cooking spray. Spoon potato mixture into casserole. Sprinkle with remaining 3 tablespoons Parmesan cheese. Bake at 350° for 50 to 60 minutes or until a knife inserted in center comes out clean. Yield: 6 servings (207 calories per serving).

PROTEIN 14.0   FAT 2.9   (Saturated Fat 1.1)   CARBOHYDRATE 32.7
FIBER 5.8   CHOLESTEROL 4   IRON 6.5   SODIUM 335   CALCIUM 164

POTATO LASAGNA

1 (10-ounce) package frozen chopped
    broccoli, thawed
1 (15-ounce) carton nonfat ricotta
    cheese
1 cup shredded carrot
½ cup minced green onions
1 teaspoon dried whole marjoram
½ teaspoon freshly ground pepper
Vegetable cooking spray
5 large red potatoes, peeled and thinly sliced
    (about 2¼ pounds)
1½ cups (6 ounces) shredded part-skim
    mozzarella cheese
½ cup freshly grated Parmesan
    cheese

Press broccoli between paper towels until barely moist. Combine broccoli, ricotta cheese, and next 4 ingredients in a medium bowl; stir well. Set aside.

Coat an 11- x 7- x 2-inch baking dish with cooking spray. Place one-third of potato slices in bottom of dish. Spread with half of broccoli mixture; sprinkle with half of mozzarella cheese. Repeat layers. Top with remaining potato slices, and sprinkle with Parmesan cheese. Cover and bake at 375° for 30 minutes; uncover and bake an additional 55 minutes or until potato is tender and top is golden. Let stand 10 minutes before serving. Yield: 8 servings (194 calories per serving).

PROTEIN 18.8   FAT 5.6   (Saturated Fat 3.4)   CARBOHYDRATE 28.5
FIBER 3.3   CHOLESTEROL 23   IRON 1.5   SODIUM 262   CALCIUM 349

Three types of cheese add protein, calcium, and flavor to rich-tasting Potato Lasagna.

POTATO PANCAKE WITH CORN CHILI

Vegetable cooking spray
½ cup chopped onion
1¼ pounds red potatoes, peeled and shredded
½ cup grated Parmesan cheese
2 eggs, separated
¼ teaspoon garlic powder
¼ teaspoon pepper
2 teaspoons olive oil, divided
Corn Chili

Coat a nonstick skillet with cooking spray; place over medium-high heat until hot. Add onion; sauté until tender. Place onion in a bowl. Add potato, cheese, egg yolks, garlic powder, and pepper; stir well.

Beat egg whites at high speed of an electric mixer until stiff peaks form. Fold into potato mixture.

Coat a 10-inch nonstick skillet with cooking spray; brush with 1 teaspoon olive oil. Place over medium heat until hot. Spoon potato mixture into skillet, smoothing top. Cook 10 minutes or until browned on bottom. Slide potato pancake onto a plate. Brush skillet with remaining 1 teaspoon olive oil. Place over medium heat until hot. Invert pancake, and place in skillet; cook 10 minutes or until browned. Cut pancake into 6 wedges, and place on individual serving plates. Spoon Corn Chili evenly over each wedge. Yield: 6 servings (243 calories per serving).

Corn Chili

3¼ cups fresh corn cut from cob (about 5 ears)
1 (14½-ounce) can no-salt-added whole tomatoes, undrained and coarsely chopped
¾ cup diced sweet red pepper
½ cup minced green onions
¼ cup canned no-salt-added chicken broth, undiluted
¼ cup water
1 tablespoon seeded, minced jalapeño pepper
1 teaspoon chili powder
¼ teaspoon salt
¼ teaspoon ground cumin
¼ teaspoon ground oregano
½ cup chopped fresh cilantro

Combine first 11 ingredients in a large saucepan; bring mixture to a boil. Cook, uncovered, 20 minutes, stirring occasionally. Remove from heat, and stir in cilantro. Yield: 3½ cups.

PROTEIN 10.8 FAT 6.8 (Saturated Fat 2.2) CARBOHYDRATE 39.1
FIBER 5.5 CHOLESTEROL 76 IRON 2.6 SODIUM 285 CALCIUM 152

CURRIED GARBANZOS AND POTATOES

Vegetable cooking spray
4 cloves garlic, minced
1 cup chopped green pepper
6 green onions, cut into 1-inch pieces
3½ cups canned low-sodium chicken broth, undiluted
1⅓ pounds round red potatoes, peeled and cut into 1-inch chunks
2 (15-ounce) cans garbanzo beans, drained
1 (6-ounce) can no-salt-added tomato paste
1 tablespoon curry powder
½ teaspoon ground red pepper
¼ teaspoon salt
4 cups cooked long-grain rice (cooked without salt or fat)
¼ cup raisins
¼ cup chopped unsalted dry roasted peanuts
¼ cup minced green onions

Coat a large saucepan with cooking spray; place over medium-high heat until hot. Add garlic; sauté 1 minute. Add green pepper and green onion pieces; sauté 2 minutes. Add chicken broth and next 6 ingredients, stirring well to combine. Bring to a boil; cover, reduce heat, and simmer 40 to 45 minutes or until potato is tender.

Place ½ cup rice in each individual serving bowl; spoon potato mixture evenly over each serving. Top each serving evenly with raisins, dry roasted peanuts, and minced green onions. Yield: 8 servings (342 calories per serving).

PROTEIN 11.7 FAT 3.9 (Saturated Fat 0.5) CARBOHYDRATE 65.3
FIBER 4.7 CHOLESTEROL 0 IRON 4.3 SODIUM 303 CALCIUM 69

SPINACH-FILLED TORTILLA ROLLS WITH BASIL-TOMATO SAUCE

2 (14½-ounce) cans no-salt-added whole tomatoes, undrained
1 cup minced fresh basil
1 (10-ounce) package frozen chopped spinach, thawed and drained
1 (15-ounce) carton lite ricotta cheese
2 eggs, lightly beaten
¼ teaspoon salt
6 (8-inch) flour tortillas
Vegetable cooking spray
¼ cup freshly grated Parmesan cheese

Position knife blade in food processor bowl; add tomato. Pulse 6 to 8 times or until tomato is coarsely pureed.

Transfer tomato to a medium saucepan; add basil. Bring to a boil; reduce heat, and simmer 25 minutes, stirring frequently.

Combine spinach, ricotta cheese, eggs, and salt; stir well. Spoon spinach mixture evenly down centers of tortillas. Roll up tortillas; place seam side down in a 13- x 9- x 2-inch baking dish coated with cooking spray. Spoon tomato mixture over tortillas, and sprinkle with Parmesan cheese. Bake at 375° for 30 minutes or until thoroughly heated. Yield: 6 servings (234 calories per serving).

PROTEIN 16.0 FAT 7.5 (Saturated Fat 1.8) CARBOHYDRATE 29.0
FIBER 2.2 CHOLESTEROL 87 IRON 3.1 SODIUM 298 CALCIUM 289

VEGETABLE RISOTTO IN A BAG

1 tablespoon all-purpose flour
3 cups shredded fresh spinach
1 cup diced sweet red pepper
1 cup sliced fresh mushrooms
1 cup sliced green onions
⅔ cup Arborio or other short-grain rice, uncooked
2 cloves garlic, minced
1 (10½-ounce) can low-sodium chicken broth, undiluted
¾ cup Chablis or other dry white wine
½ teaspoon dried whole basil
1 (14-ounce) can cannellini beans, drained
1 cup freshly grated Parmesan cheese
¼ teaspoon freshly ground pepper

Add flour to a large oven cooking bag; twist end to close, and shake to coat inside. Add spinach and next 5 ingredients; squeeze bag to blend ingredients. Add chicken broth, wine, basil, and beans; squeeze bag gently to distribute ingredients evenly in a single layer. Secure bag with an oven-proof tie or string.

Place bag in a 13- x 9- x 2-inch baking pan. Cut six ½-inch slits in top of bag. Bake at 350° for 1 hour or until rice is tender and mixture is creamy. Transfer rice mixture to a serving dish; stir in cheese and ground pepper. Serve immediately. Yield: 6 servings (216 calories per serving).

PROTEIN 11.8 FAT 5.4 (Saturated Fat 3.2) CARBOHYDRATE 29.1
FIBER 2.9 CHOLESTEROL 13 IRON 3.1 SODIUM 469 CALCIUM 268

FIBER HIGH FIVE

The soluble fiber found in dried beans and oats is beneficial in helping control blood sugar levels and lowering blood cholesterol levels. That's why health experts now recommend that people aim for at least 5 grams of this type of fiber each day.

To reach this recommendation, start the day with 1 ounce of oatmeal or oat bran cereal (2 grams soluble fiber). Then include just ½ cup of any kind of dried beans such as pinto beans, black beans, or red kidney beans; each of these contains at least 2 grams of soluble fiber. To round out the daily total to 5 grams, reach for an apple (1 gram soluble fiber).

Although most whole grains, fruits, and vegetables contain small amounts of both soluble and insoluble fiber, the suggested choices are particularly good sources. Keep in mind that if you are already mixing and matching high-fiber foods on a regular basis, you probably are getting an adequate amount of soluble fiber without even counting grams.

STUFFED TOMATOES EN PAPILLOTE

12 small ripe plum tomatoes (about 2 pounds)
1 pound yellow squash, grated
1 pound zucchini, grated
2 cups cooked long-grain rice (cooked without salt or fat)
¾ cup minced fresh basil, divided
⅛ teaspoon salt
6 ounces Montrachet goat cheese, crumbled
¼ teaspoon freshly ground pepper
Vegetable cooking spray

Cut tomatoes in half lengthwise, and scoop out pulp, reserving for other uses. Invert tomato halves in pairs, cut side down, on paper towels; let stand 30 minutes.

Spread squash and zucchini in a single layer on paper towels. Cover with additional paper towels; let stand 15 minutes. Press gently to remove excess water. Combine squash, zucchini, rice, ¼ cup minced basil, and salt; stir well. Set aside.

Combine remaining ½ cup basil, goat cheese, and pepper in a small bowl; stir well. Shape into a log, 1-inch in diameter; cut log into 12 equal portions. Place 1 portion in each of 12 tomato halves; cover with remaining tomato halves.

Cut 4 (15-inch) squares of parchment paper; fold each square in half, and trim each into a heart shape. Place parchment hearts on 2 large baking sheets, and open out flat. Coat open side of parchment paper with cooking spray.

Spoon rice mixture evenly on half of each parchment heart near the crease. Arrange 3 tomatoes on rice mixture on each heart.

Fold paper edges over to seal securely. Starting with rounded edges of hearts, pleat and crimp edges together to seal securely. Bake at 350° for 20 minutes. Transfer to individual serving plates; cut an opening in the top of each packet, and fold paper back. Serve immediately. Yield: 4 servings (313 calories per serving).

PROTEIN 12.7 FAT 10.4 (Saturated Fat 6.6) CARBOHYDRATE 44.6
FIBER 4.9 CHOLESTEROL 38 IRON 3.5 SODIUM 569 CALCIUM 282

GRILLED VEGETABLES WITH SPANISH WILD RICE

½ cup commercial oil-free Italian dressing
¼ cup water
¼ cup vinegar
1 teaspoon dried whole oregano
24 medium-size fresh mushrooms (about ¾ pound)
18 yellow pear-shaped cherry tomatoes
3 medium-size sweet onions, cut into 1-inch cubes
2 medium-size sweet red peppers, cut into 1½-inch pieces
2 medium zucchini, cut into 1½-inch slices
Vegetable cooking spray
Spanish Wild Rice

Combine first 4 ingredients in a large zip-top heavy-duty plastic bag; seal bag, and shake well. Add mushrooms, cherry tomatoes, onion, red pepper, and zucchini to bag; seal bag, and shake until vegetables are well coated. Marinate in refrigerator 2 hours, turning occasionally.

Drain vegetables; discard marinade. Arrange vegetables on 8 (12-inch) skewers. Coat grill rack with cooking spray, and place on grill over hot coals. Place kabobs on rack, and cook 12 to 15 minutes or until vegetables are tender.

Place ⅔ cup Spanish Wild Rice on each individual serving plate. Remove vegetables from skewers, and arrange over rice. Yield 6 servings (283 calories per serving).

Spanish Wild Rice

½ cup wild rice, uncooked
Vegetable cooking spray
1 cup chopped sweet onion
1 cup finely chopped green pepper
2 cloves garlic, minced
⅔ cup long-grain brown rice, uncooked
1½ cups canned low-sodium chicken broth, undiluted
2 cups no-salt-added vegetable juice cocktail
1 cup (4 ounces) shredded 40% less-fat Cheddar cheese

Rinse wild rice in 3 changes of hot water; drain well, and set aside.

Coat a medium saucepan with cooking spray; place over medium-high heat until hot. Add onion, green pepper, and garlic; sauté until tender. Stir in wild rice, brown rice, chicken broth, and vegetable juice cocktail; bring to a boil. Cover, reduce heat, and simmer 50 minutes or until rice is tender and liquid is absorbed; remove from heat. Add cheese; stir until cheese melts. Yield: 4 cups.

PROTEIN 11.7   FAT 4.6   (Saturated Fat 1.9)   CARBOHYDRATE 52.9
FIBER 5.6   CHOLESTEROL 10   IRON 3.4   SODIUM 238   CALCIUM 189

JICAMA BURRITOS

Vegetable cooking spray
2 teaspoons vegetable oil
1 cup peeled, diced jicama
1 cup chopped onion
1 teaspoon cumin seeds
1½ cups cooked brown rice (cooked without salt or fat)
1¼ cups (5 ounces) shredded 40% less-fat Cheddar cheese
1 cup shredded carrot
½ cup seeded, diced tomato
6 (8-inch) flour tortillas
½ cup commercial no-salt-added salsa
¾ cup nonfat sour cream

Coat a medium nonstick skillet with cooking spray; add oil. Place over medium heat until hot. Add jicama, and sauté 3 minutes. Add onion and cumin seeds; sauté 5 minutes or until vegetables are tender. Remove from heat; stir in brown rice, cheese, carrot, and tomato.

Spoon jicama mixture evenly down center of each tortilla. Roll up tortillas, and place seam side down in a 13- x 9- x 2-inch baking pan coated with cooking spray. Cover and bake at 425° for 15 minutes or until thoroughly heated.

Transfer to individual serving plates. Top each with 1 tablespoon plus 1 teaspoon salsa and 2 tablespoons sour cream. Serve immediately. Yield: 6 servings (273 calories per serving).

PROTEIN 10.6   FAT 7.5   (Saturated Fat 2.9)   CARBOHYDRATE 44.2
FIBER 3.2   CHOLESTEROL 13   IRON 1.6   SODIUM 159   CALCIUM 239

ROASTED HERBED BROWN RICE WITH BEANS

1 cup long-grain brown rice, uncooked
3 cups sliced fresh mushrooms
1½ cups chopped onion
1 teaspoon dried whole basil
1 teaspoon dried whole oregano
1 teaspoon dried whole marjoram
2 cloves garlic, minced
2 bay leaves
½ cup water
2 (10½-ounce) cans low-sodium chicken broth, undiluted
¼ teaspoon salt
2 cups canned cannellini beans, drained
¾ cup seeded, diced tomato
¼ cup plus 2 tablespoons sliced green onions
¾ cup nonfat sour cream

Place rice in a 9-inch square baking pan. Bake at 350° for 30 minutes or until rice is browned, stirring occasionally. Set aside.

Combine mushrooms and next 7 ingredients in a large skillet. Bring to a boil; cover, reduce heat, and simmer 12 minutes or until vegetables are tender. Stir in reserved rice, chicken broth, and salt. Bring to a boil; cover, reduce heat, and simmer 25 minutes or until rice is tender and liquid is absorbed. Remove and discard bay leaves.

Stir in beans; cook over medium heat 2 to 3 minutes or until thoroughly heated. Spoon mixture evenly onto individual serving plates. Top each serving with 2 tablespoons diced tomato, 1 tablespoon green onions, and 2 tablespoons sour cream. Serve immediately. Yield: 6 servings (242 calories per serving).

PROTEIN 10.0   FAT 1.6   (Saturated Fat 0.2)   CARBOHYDRATE 44.8
FIBER 4.6   CHOLESTEROL 0   IRON 2.7   SODIUM 378   CALCIUM 80

Serve steaming bowls of Southwest Hopping John with Toasted Cornbread Triangles.

SOUTHWEST HOPPING JOHN

Vegetable cooking spray
1½ cups chopped onion
1½ cups chopped green pepper
1 teaspoon ground cumin
2 cloves garlic, minced
1 (16-ounce) package frozen black-eyed peas
2 cups canned low-sodium chicken broth,
   undiluted
1 cup light beer
¾ cup long-grain brown rice, uncooked
¼ pound reduced-fat, low-salt ham, diced
2 teaspoons minced jalapeño pepper
¼ teaspoon salt
2 cups diced, seeded tomato
Toasted Cornbread Triangles

Coat a Dutch oven with cooking spray; place over medium-high heat until hot. Add onion, green pepper, cumin, and garlic; sauté until vegetables are tender. Add black-eyed peas and next 6 ingredients,

stirring well. Bring to a boil; cover, reduce heat, and simmer 45 to 50 minutes or until peas and rice are tender. Stir in tomato.

Spoon mixture evenly into individual serving bowls; top each serving with 4 Toasted Cornbread Triangles. Serve immediately. Yield: 8 servings (280 calories per serving).

Toasted Cornbread Triangles

½ cup all-purpose flour
½ cup yellow cornmeal
½ teaspoon baking powder
⅛ teaspoon salt
1 tablespoon sugar
¾ cup nonfat buttermilk
2 egg whites, lightly beaten
Butter-flavored vegetable cooking spray

Combine first 5 ingredients in a bowl. Combine buttermilk and egg whites; add to dry ingredients, stirring just until dry ingredients are moistened. Pour batter into a 9-inch square baking pan coated with cooking spray. Bake at 350° for 15 minutes; remove from oven, and let cool completely on a wire rack.

Cut into 16 squares; cut each square into 2 triangles. Place triangles on a baking sheet; spray with cooking spray. Broil 3 inches from heat 1 to 2 minutes or until lightly browned. Turn cornbread triangles; spray with cooking spray. Broil an additional 1 to 2 minutes or until lightly browned. Yield: 32 triangles.

PROTEIN 13.5 FAT 2.5 (Saturated Fat 0.6) CARBOHYDRATE 51.1
FIBER 3.8 CHOLESTEROL 7 IRON 3.1 SODIUM 291 CALCIUM 75

 SPILLING THE BEANS
Presoaking dried beans before cooking usually removes most of the indigestible starches and helps keep the beans from causing gas and indigestion. An exception to this rule is legumes, such as lentils and split peas.

Soak dried beans for 4 hours or overnight. When in a hurry, the soaking time can be shortened by first bringing the beans to a boil and cooking for 2 minutes. Then remove the pan from the heat, and let the beans soak for 1 hour.

The standard cooking time for pinto, navy, lima, black, and Great Northern beans ranges from 1 to 2 hours. To cook the beans, add 3 cups of water per cup of beans, and bring to a boil. It's important to simmer the beans over low heat; if you allow beans to boil rapidly, the skins will break. The result will be mushy beans that are more like a soup than a main dish.

Since beans are somewhat bland, you can create an endless variety of flavors by adding herbs, celery, carrot, or onion during the simmering process. But be sure to wait until the beans are tender before adding salt or acidic juices such as tomato juice, tomatoes, vinegar, or lemon juice. These ingredients tend to toughen bean skins and prevent the beans from softening.

When preparing beans, remember the nutritional benefits. Beans are an excellent source of soluble fiber, the type that helps lower blood cholesterol, and a notable source of iron, protein, and other key nutrients. These nutritional pluses put beans near the top of the healthy foods list.

ITALIAN WHITE BEAN-POLENTA PIE

½ pound fennel
2 cups water
¼ teaspoon salt
⅔ cup instant polenta
Vegetable cooking spray
1 teaspoon olive oil
¾ cup finely chopped carrot
¾ cup finely chopped onion
2 cloves garlic, crushed
2 (14-ounce) cans cannellini beans, drained
½ teaspoon rubbed sage
¼ teaspoon ground red pepper
1 cup (4 ounces) shredded provolone cheese

Wash fennel; trim off leaves and mince, reserving 2 tablespoons. Trim off tough outer stalks and discard. Cut bulb in half lengthwise; remove and discard core. Cut bulb crosswise into ¼-inch slices, reserving ¾ cup. Reserve remaining fennel leaves and bulb for other uses.

Combine water and salt in a 10-inch cast-iron skillet; bring to a boil. Add polenta in a slow, steady stream, stirring constantly. Reduce heat; cook, uncovered, 5 minutes or until mixture pulls away from sides of skillet, stirring constantly. Remove from heat, and spread evenly in skillet. Let stand 5 minutes.

Coat a large nonstick skillet with cooking spray; add olive oil. Place over medium heat until hot. Add ¾ cup fennel, carrot, onion, and garlic; sauté until tender. Stir in beans, 2 tablespoons fennel leaves, sage, and red pepper.

Spoon bean mixture evenly over polenta; sprinkle with cheese. Bake at 400° for 12 to 15 minutes or until thoroughly heated and cheese melts. Let stand 15 minutes before serving. Yield: 6 servings (217 calories per serving).

PROTEIN 10.8 FAT 6.6 (Saturated Fat 3.4) CARBOHYDRATE 27.9
FIBER 3.6 CHOLESTEROL 13 IRON 2.6 SODIUM 472 CALCIUM 184

EGGS NAVAHO

1 (15-ounce) can black beans, drained and mashed
⅓ cup minced green onions
⅓ cup minced sweet red pepper
2 tablespoons minced cilantro
¾ teaspoon creole seasoning
¼ cup yellow cornmeal
Vegetable cooking spray
1 tablespoon reduced-calorie margarine
4 eggs
2 cups finely shredded romaine lettuce
Avocado-Tomato Salsa
¼ cup plain nonfat yogurt

Combine first 5 ingredients in a medium bowl. Shape mixture into 4 (½-inch-thick) patties. Sprinkle cornmeal on wax paper, and dredge each patty in cornmeal. Set aside.

Coat a large cast-iron skillet with cooking spray; add margarine. Place over medium-high heat until hot. Place patties in skillet, and cook 3 minutes on each side or until thoroughly heated and lightly browned. Set aside, and keep warm.

Add water to a large saucepan to a depth of 2 inches. Bring to a boil; reduce heat, and maintain at a light simmer. Break eggs, 1 at a time, into water. Simmer 7 to 9 minutes or until internal temperature of egg reaches 160°. Remove eggs with a slotted spoon.

Place ½ cup romaine lettuce on each individual serving plate; top each with 1 bean patty. Place 1 egg on each bean patty; top each evenly with Avocado-Tomato Salsa and 1 tablespoon yogurt. Serve immediately. Yield: 4 servings (260 calories per serving).

Avocado-Tomato Salsa

1 clove garlic
1 small onion, quartered
1 jalapeño pepper, seeded and quartered
2 small tomatoes, peeled and seeded
⅓ cup finely chopped ripe avocado
¼ cup minced fresh cilantro
1½ teaspoons fresh lime juice
¼ teaspoon creole seasoning

Position knife blade in food processor; top with cover. Drop garlic through food chute with processor running; process 3 seconds or until chopped. Add onion and jalapeño pepper; process 3 to 5 seconds or until minced. Add tomato; process 2 to 3 seconds or until finely chopped. Transfer mixture to a medium bowl. Stir in chopped avocado and remaining ingredients. Yield: 1½ cups.

PROTEIN 15.2 FAT 9.3 (Saturated Fat 1.9) CARBOHYDRATE 31.4
FIBER 5.5 CHOLESTEROL 213 IRON 3.7 SODIUM 580 CALCIUM 106

An unusual blend of peppers, pear, tarragon, and chives transforms Veal Roast with Salsa (page 161) into a flavorful entrée.

Meats

ITALIAN BEEF PIE

1 pound ground chuck
½ cup chopped onion
1 clove garlic, minced
1 (10-ounce) package frozen chopped spinach,
    thawed and well drained
½ cup lite ricotta cheese
½ cup (2 ounces) shredded part-skim mozzarella
    cheese
⅓ cup fine, dry breadcrumbs
⅓ cup reduced-calorie catsup
¼ cup plain nonfat yogurt
1 teaspoon dried Italian seasoning
Butter-flavored vegetable cooking spray
8 sheets commercial frozen phyllo pastry,
    thawed
Fresh oregano sprigs (optional)

Combine ground chuck, onion, and garlic in a large
nonstick skillet; cook over medium heat until browned,
stirring to crumble. Drain and pat dry with paper
towels.

Combine meat mixture, spinach, and next 6 ingredients in a medium bowl; stir well, and set aside.

Coat a 9-inch pieplate with cooking spray. Place
1 sheet phyllo pastry on a damp towel (keep remaining
phyllo covered). Lightly coat phyllo with cooking spray.
Fold in half lengthwise, and spray again. Place, coated
side down, in prepared pieplate, allowing 1 end to
extend over edge of pieplate. Repeat with remaining
phyllo, fanning each folded sheet to the right. (The
overhanging sheets of phyllo will form a circle around
the pieplate.)

Spoon beef mixture into prepared pieplate. Bring
overhanging sheets of phyllo toward center of pieplate; gently twist ends together, and coat with cooking spray. Bake at 375° for 30 minutes or until phyllo
is crisp and golden. Let stand 5 minutes before serving.
Garnish with fresh oregano sprigs, if desired. Yield:
8 servings (246 calories per serving).

PROTEIN 16.9   FAT 10.4   (Saturated Fat 3.9)   CARBOHYDRATE 20.5
FIBER 1.5   CHOLESTEROL 39   IRON 2.5   SODIUM 127   CALCIUM 124

CHEESE-STUFFED BURGERS

1½ pounds ground round
2 tablespoons minced fresh basil
2 tablespoons grated Parmesan cheese
½ teaspoon garlic powder
⅛ teaspoon pepper
4 ounces part-skim mozzarella cheese, cut into
    6 pieces
Vegetable cooking spray

Combine first 5 ingredients in a medium bowl; stir
well. Divide mixture into 12 thin patties. Top 6 patties with cheese. Top with remaining 6 patties, and
seal edges.

Coat rack of a broiler pan with cooking spray. Place
patties on rack; broil 5½ inches from heat 5 minutes
on each side or to desired degree of doneness. Drain
well on paper towels. Transfer to a serving platter.
Yield: 6 servings (213 calories per serving).

PROTEIN 28.2   FAT 10.0   (Saturated Fat 4.6)   CARBOHYDRATE 0.8
FIBER 0   CHOLESTEROL 78   IRON 2.3   SODIUM 171   CALCIUM 152

BEEF STROGANOFF MEAT LOAF

1 pound ground round
¾ cup soft whole wheat breadcrumbs
½ cup finely chopped onion
¼ cup frozen egg substitute, thawed
1 (4-ounce) can mushrooms, drained and chopped
3 tablespoons plain nonfat yogurt
2 tablespoons Burgundy or other dry red wine
½ teaspoon coarsely ground pepper
Vegetable cooking spray
1 teaspoon beef-flavored bouillon granules
2 teaspoons all-purpose flour
¼ cup hot water
⅔ cup nonfat sour cream
2 tablespoons sliced green onions
⅛ teaspoon ground white pepper

Combine first 8 ingredients in a medium bowl; stir
well. Shape mixture into an 8- x 4-inch loaf; place on
a rack in a roasting pan coated with cooking spray.

Bake at 350° for 1 hour. Transfer meat loaf to a serving platter, and keep warm.

Combine bouillon granules, flour, and water in a small saucepan; stir well. Cook over medium heat until thickened, stirring constantly. Combine sour cream, green onions, and white pepper; add to bouillon mixture, stirring well. Cook over low heat until thoroughly heated, stirring constantly (do not boil). Spoon evenly over meat loaf. Serve warm. Yield: 6 servings (196 calories per serving).

PROTEIN 24.8 FAT 8.2 (Saturated Fat 3.2) CARBOHYDRATE 8.9
FIBER 0.6 CHOLESTEROL 49 IRON 2.9 SODIUM 284 CALCIUM 66

ARTICHOKE-BEEF ROLL

2 pounds ground round
2 cups soft whole wheat breadcrumbs
¼ cup frozen egg substitute, thawed
¼ cup low-sodium Worcestershire sauce
1 teaspoon garlic powder
1 teaspoon curry powder
1 (9-ounce) package frozen artichoke hearts, thawed, drained, and chopped
1½ cups finely chopped mushrooms
¾ cup (3 ounces) shredded reduced-fat Monterey Jack cheese
Vegetable cooking spray

Combine first 6 ingredients in a large bowl; stir well. Shape mixture into a 12- x 10-inch rectangle on wax paper. Combine artichokes and mushrooms; spread evenly over beef mixture, leaving a 1-inch margin on all sides. Sprinkle evenly with cheese. Carefully roll up meat, jellyroll fashion, starting at narrow end, using wax paper to support meat. Pinch ends and seam to seal. Remove from wax paper.

Place roll, seam side down, on a rack in a roasting pan coated with cooking spray. Bake at 350° for 1 hour or until done. Transfer to a serving platter. Let stand 10 minutes before slicing. Yield: 10 servings (241 calories per serving).

PROTEIN 29.6 FAT 11.3 (Saturated Fat 4.7) CARBOHYDRATE 10.4
FIBER 0.9 CHOLESTEROL 65 IRON 3.5 SODIUM 225 CALCIUM 100

THAI MARINATED BEEF RIBBONS

1 (1-pound) lean flank steak
½ cup chopped fresh basil
¼ cup low-sodium soy sauce
2 tablespoons minced jalapeño pepper
2 teaspoons sugar
2 teaspoons minced fresh mint
2 teaspoons vinegar
Vegetable cooking spray
3 cups water
1 cup no-salt-added beef broth
2 tablespoons low-sodium soy sauce
1 (3¾-ounce) package cellophane noodles, uncooked
Fresh mint sprigs (optional)

Partially freeze steak; trim fat from steak. Slice steak diagonally across grain into ¼-inch-wide strips.

Combine basil and next 5 ingredients in a large zip-top heavy-duty plastic bag; seal bag, and shake well. Add steak to bag; seal bag, and shake until steak is well coated. Marinate in refrigerator 8 hours, turning bag occasionally.

Remove steak from marinade, and discard marinade. Thread steak onto 4 (12-inch) skewers. Coat grill rack with cooking spray, and place on grill over medium-hot coals. Place skewers on rack, and cook 5 minutes or to desired degree of doneness, turning skewers frequently.

Combine water, beef broth, and 2 tablespoons soy sauce in a large saucepan; bring to a boil. Add cellophane noodles. Reduce heat, and simmer 12 minutes; drain. Place noodles on a large serving platter, and top with steak. Garnish with fresh mint sprigs, if desired. Serve immediately. Yield: 4 servings (328 calories per serving).

PROTEIN 23.2 FAT 13.8 (Saturated Fat 5.6) CARBOHYDRATE 23.8
FIBER 0.1 CHOLESTEROL 61 IRON 3.3 SODIUM 562 CALCIUM 42

Fan glazed papaya slices around individual servings of Gingered Beef Stir-Fry.

GINGERED BEEF STIR-FRY

1 (1-pound) lean flank steak
1 teaspoon cornstarch
½ teaspoon grated lime rind
¼ cup Chablis or other dry white wine
Vegetable cooking spray
1½ teaspoons vegetable oil, divided
1 tablespoon peeled, minced gingerroot
½ cup sliced green onions
1 medium-size green pepper, cut into julienne
    strips
1 medium-size sweet red pepper, cut into
    julienne strips
2 teaspoons sugar
2 teaspoons ground ginger
1 large papaya, peeled, seeded and cut into
    ½-inch-thick slices
2 tablespoons lime juice

Partially freeze steak; trim fat from steak. Slice steak diagonally across grain into ¼-inch-wide strips.

Combine cornstarch, lime rind, and wine in a small bowl; stir well, and set aside.

Coat a wok or large nonstick skillet with cooking spray; add 1 teaspoon oil. Heat at medium-high (375°) until hot. Add steak strips and gingerroot; stir-fry 5 minutes. Remove steak strips and gingerroot from wok; set aside. Wipe wok dry with a paper towel.

Add sliced green onions, green pepper, and red pepper to wok; stir-fry 3 minutes. Add steak strips and wine mixture; cook, stirring constantly, 1 to 2 minutes or until mixture is slightly thickened. Remove mixture from wok, and keep warm.

Add remaining ½ teaspoon oil, sugar, and ground ginger to wok; stir well. Add papaya slices, and drizzle with lime juice. Gently stir-fry until papaya is glazed and thoroughly heated. Arrange papaya slices in a spoke-pattern on a serving platter. Spoon beef mixture in center. Serve immediately. Yield: 6 servings (223 calories per serving).

PROTEIN 15.8 FAT 12.6 (Saturated Fat 4.4) CARBOHYDRATE 12.2 FIBER 2.1 CHOLESTEROL 41 IRON 2.2 SODIUM 54 CALCIUM 30

BLUE CHEESE-STUFFED SIRLOIN STEAK

1 (1-pound) lean boneless beef sirloin steak
⅔ cup light beer
¼ cup lemon juice
2 cloves garlic, minced
¾ teaspoon hot sauce
4 ounces crumbled blue cheese
1 tablespoon salt-free lemon-pepper seasoning
Vegetable cooking spray

Trim fat from steak. Cut a large pocket in steak, cutting to, but not through, remaining 3 sides. Place steak in a large shallow dish. Combine beer, lemon juice, garlic, and hot sauce; pour over steak. Cover and marinate in refrigerator 8 hours, turning steak occasionally.

Remove steak from marinade; discard marinade. Place cheese in steak pocket, spreading evenly throughout pocket. Secure opening with wooden picks. Press lemon-pepper seasoning onto both sides of steak.

Coat grill rack with cooking spray; place on grill over medium-hot coals. Place steak on rack, and cook 6 to 7 minutes on each side or to desired degree of doneness. Transfer to a serving platter, and remove wooden picks. Yield: 4 servings (294 calories per serving).

PROTEIN 33.5 FAT 16.2 (Saturated Fat 8.5) CARBOHYDRATE 2.3 FIBER 0.4 CHOLESTEROL 101 IRON 3.6 SODIUM 456 CALCIUM 167

POT ROAST WITH RHUBARB SAUCE

1 (4-pound) lean boneless rump roast
1 teaspoon dried whole rosemary, crushed
½ teaspoon garlic powder
Vegetable cooking spray
1 small onion, sliced
1 teaspoon beef-flavored bouillon granules
1 cup hot water
Rhubarb Sauce

Trim fat from roast. Combine rosemary and garlic powder; rub over entire surface of roast. Coat an ovenproof Dutch oven with cooking spray; place over medium-high heat until hot. Add roast; cook until browned on all sides. Place onion slices over roast.

Combine bouillon granules and water; pour over roast. Cover and bake at 350° for 2½ hours or until roast is tender. Transfer roast and onions to a serving platter, using a slotted spoon. Serve with Rhubarb Sauce. Yield: 16 servings (168 calories per serving).

Rhubarb Sauce

2 cups sliced rhubarb
¼ cup sugar
¼ cup raspberry vinegar
½ teaspoon dried whole rosemary, crushed
½ teaspoon dry mustard
⅛ teaspoon salt

Combine all ingredients in a saucepan; bring to a boil. Cover, reduce heat, and simmer 10 minutes or until rhubarb is tender. Transfer mixture to container of an electric blender or food processor; top with cover, and process until mixture is smooth. Yield: 1¼ cups plus 2 tablespoons.

PROTEIN 25.3 FAT 4.6 (Saturated Fat 1.6) CARBOHYDRATE 4.9 FIBER 0.3 CHOLESTEROL 63 IRON 2.4 SODIUM 136 CALCIUM 20

VEAL PATTIES MARSALA

1½ pounds ground veal
½ teaspoon pepper
Vegetable cooking spray
1 (8-ounce) package presliced fresh mushrooms
½ cup sliced green onions
1½ cups peeled, seeded, and chopped tomato
⅓ cup Marsala
2 tablespoons chopped fresh parsley

Combine veal and pepper in a medium bowl; stir well. Shape mixture into 6 (¾-inch-thick) patties.

Coat a large nonstick skillet with cooking spray; place over medium-high heat until hot. Add veal patties, and cook 5 minutes on each side or to desired degree of doneness. Remove patties from skillet; drain and pat dry with paper towels. Wipe drippings from skillet with a paper towel.

Coat skillet with cooking spray; place over medium-high heat until hot. Add mushrooms, and sauté until tender. Transfer to a bowl, and set aside.

Coat skillet with cooking spray; place over medium-high heat until hot. Add green onions, and sauté 2 minutes. Stir in tomato and Marsala. Bring to a boil; reduce heat, and simmer, uncovered, 5 minutes. Stir in sautéed mushrooms. Return veal patties to skillet, and spoon mushroom mixture over patties. Cover and cook over low heat until thoroughly heated. Transfer patties and mushroom mixture to a serving platter, and sprinkle with parsley. Serve immediately. Yield: 6 servings (173 calories per serving).

PROTEIN 25.2 FAT 5.5 (Saturated Fat 1.4) CARBOHYDRATE 5.0
FIBER 1.3 CHOLESTEROL 88 IRON 1.8 SODIUM 75 CALCIUM 30

 PROFILE ON VEAL
The lack of familiarity keeps many shoppers from selecting veal. Veal can be as lean as the white meat of chicken. A 3-ounce cooked veal loin contains just 149 calories, 90 milligrams cholesterol, and less than 6 grams of fat. The cholesterol content doesn't seem so bad when you realize that the American Heart Association allows 300 milligrams of cholesterol per day on a heart-healthy diet.

VEAL PAPRIKASH

1 pound veal cutlets (¼ inch thick)
Vegetable cooking spray
1 large onion, thinly sliced
½ cup thinly sliced celery
1 clove garlic, minced
½ cup no-salt-added tomato sauce
½ cup water
2 teaspoons paprika
¼ teaspoon salt
¼ teaspoon ground red pepper
3 cups cooked medium egg noodles (cooked without salt or fat)
2 tablespoons chopped fresh parsley

Trim fat from cutlets; cut cutlets into 1-inch-wide strips. Coat a large nonstick skillet with cooking spray; place over medium-high heat until hot. Add veal; cook 3 minutes on each side or until browned. Remove veal from skillet. Drain and pat dry with paper towels. Wipe drippings from skillet with a paper towel.

Coat skillet with cooking spray. Add onion, celery, and garlic; sauté until tender. Add tomato sauce and next 4 ingredients; stir well. Return veal to skillet. Bring to a boil; cover, reduce heat, and simmer 20 minutes or until veal is tender. Remove from heat; let stand 2 minutes.

Combine veal mixture and cooked noodles in a medium bowl; toss gently. Sprinkle with chopped parsley. Serve immediately. Yield: 6 servings (270 calories per serving).

PROTEIN 25.1 FAT 7.1 (Saturated Fat 1.8) CARBOHYDRATE 25.6
FIBER 3.0 CHOLESTEROL 102 IRON 2.8 SODIUM 168 CALCIUM 52

Veal's slightly higher cholesterol content is due to the fact that young calves have a much higher amount of muscle versus fat tissue than older animals. Since the bulk of cholesterol is located in lean (muscle) tissues, veal is higher in cholesterol than mature meats such as beef or chicken. On the other hand, the low fat content makes this meat worth including in your menus.

MEXICAN VEAL KIEV

½ (8-ounce) package Neufchâtel cheese
1 tablespoon minced fresh cilantro
1½ pounds veal cutlets
¾ teaspoon chili powder
½ teaspoon garlic powder
¼ teaspoon ground cumin
¼ teaspoon pepper
2 (4-ounce) cans whole green chiles, seeded and
  sliced lengthwise into strips
3 tablespoons frozen egg substitute, thawed
1½ teaspoons skim milk
¼ cup plus 2 tablespoons fine, dry breadcrumbs
1½ teaspoons reduced-calorie margarine
1½ teaspoons vegetable oil
Vegetable cooking spray
Fresh cilantro sprigs (optional)

Cut cheese into 8 equal portions; sprinkle with minced cilantro. Cover and freeze 30 minutes or until firm.

Trim fat from cutlets; cut cutlets into 8 equal portions. Place cutlets between 2 sheets of heavy-duty plastic wrap; flatten to ⅛-inch thickness, using a meat mallet or rolling pin.

Combine chili powder and next 3 ingredients; stir well. Sprinkle evenly on both sides of each cutlet. Divide green chile strips into 8 equal portions; wrap chile strips around each portion of cheese. Place 1 cheese portion in center of each cutlet. Roll up cutlets, jellyroll fashion, starting at short side; tuck ends under, and secure with wooden picks.

Combine egg substitute and milk in a shallow dish; dip veal rolls in egg mixture, and dredge in breadcrumbs. Heat margarine and oil in a large nonstick skillet over medium heat until margarine melts. Add veal rolls; cook 3 minutes on each side or until browned. Remove from skillet, and place in an 11- x 7- x 2-inch baking dish coated with cooking spray. Bake at 375° for 25 minutes. Remove wooden picks. Garnish with fresh cilantro sprigs, if desired. Serve immediately. Yield: 8 servings (172 calories per serving).

PROTEIN 19.9 FAT 7.4 (Saturated Fat 3.1) CARBOHYDRATE 5.2
FIBER 0.6 CHOLESTEROL 82 IRON 1.2 SODIUM 207 CALCIUM 34

BLUE CHEESE-TOPPED VEAL CHOPS

4 (6-ounce) lean veal loin chops (¾ inch thick)
½ teaspoon dried whole thyme
½ teaspoon dry mustard
¼ teaspoon pepper
Vegetable cooking spray
1 teaspoon vegetable oil
½ cup Chablis or other dry white wine
2 cups sliced leeks
2 tablespoons crumbled blue cheese
¼ cup chopped tomato
Fresh thyme sprigs (optional)

Trim fat from veal chops. Combine thyme, mustard, and pepper in a small bowl; sprinkle mixture over veal chops.

Coat a large nonstick skillet with cooking spray; add oil. Place over medium-high heat until hot. Add chops, and cook 3 to 4 minutes on each side or until browned. Remove chops from skillet. Drain chops, and pat dry with paper towels. Wipe drippings from skillet with a paper towel.

Return chops to skillet; add wine. Bring to a boil; cover, reduce heat, and simmer 20 to 25 minutes or until veal is tender. Transfer veal to a serving platter, and keep warm. Drain skillet, reserving liquid. Wipe drippings from skillet with a paper towel.

Coat skillet with cooking spray; place over medium-high heat until hot. Add leeks, and sauté until tender. Combine reserved liquid and cheese in a small saucepan; cook over medium heat, stirring constantly, until cheese melts and mixture is smooth. Spoon evenly over chops, and top with tomato. Garnish with fresh thyme sprigs, if desired. Serve immediately. Yield: 4 servings (255 calories per serving).

PROTEIN 23.5 FAT 13.9 (Saturated Fat 5.8) CARBOHYDRATE 8.3
FIBER 0.8 CHOLESTEROL 93 IRON 2.2 SODIUM 168 CALCIUM 81

Veal Chops Italiano is a simple recipe that makes an impressive entrée.

VEAL CHOPS ITALIANO

¾ cup tightly packed fresh basil leaves
1 tablespoon grated Parmesan cheese
1 tablespoon pine nuts, toasted
1 clove garlic, minced
¼ cup plain nonfat yogurt
4 (6-ounce) lean veal loin chops (¾ inch thick)
Vegetable cooking spray
4 thin slices tomato
4 (½-ounce) slices Fontina cheese
Fresh basil sprigs (optional)

Position knife blade in food processor bowl; add first 4 ingredients. Process 1 minute or until smooth.

Transfer basil mixture to a small bowl; add yogurt, and stir well. Cover and chill 30 minutes.

Trim fat from chops. Place chops on rack of a boiler pan coated with cooking spray. Broil 5½ inches from heat 5 minutes on each side. Spread 2 tablespoons basil mixture over each chop; broil an additional 5 minutes. Top each with 1 tomato slice and 1 cheese slice; broil 2 to 3 minutes or until cheese melts. Garnish with fresh basil sprigs, if desired. Serve immediately. Yield: 4 servings (282 calories per serving).

PROTEIN 27.5   FAT 17.4   (Saturated Fat 7.8)   CARBOHYDRATE 3.3
FIBER 0.3   CHOLESTEROL 106   IRON 1.7   SODIUM 216   CALCIUM 155

VEAL ROAST WITH SALSA

1½ cups finely chopped pear
1 cup finely chopped sweet red pepper
1 cup finely chopped green pepper
½ cup minced fresh parsley
¼ cup chopped purple onion
1 tablespoon minced fresh tarragon
1 tablespoon fresh chives
2 tablespoons lemon juice
1 tablespoon red wine vinegar
2 jalapeño peppers, seeded and finely minced
1 (3½-pound) boneless rolled veal rump roast
1 clove garlic, halved
1 teaspoon cracked pepper
Vegetable cooking spray
1 teaspoon vegetable oil
¾ cup Chablis or other dry white wine
½ teaspoon beef-flavored bouillon granules
Flat-leaf parsley (optional)

Combine first 10 ingredients in a medium bowl; stir well. Cover and refrigerate at least 8 hours.

Unroll roast; trim fat from roast. Rub roast with cut sides of garlic; roll roast, and tie securely at 2-inch intervals with string. Sprinkle pepper over entire surface of roast.

Coat a large ovenproof Dutch oven with cooking spray; add oil, and place over medium-high heat until hot. Add roast, and cook until browned on all sides, turning occasionally. Add wine and bouillon granules.

Cover and bake at 325° for 1½ hours, basting frequently with pan juices. Remove string before slicing. Garnish with flat-leaf parsley, if desired. Serve with chilled pepper mixture. Yield: 14 servings (121 calories per serving).

PROTEIN 19.5 FAT 2.2 (Saturated Fat 0.6) CARBOHYDRATE 5.2
FIBER 1.0 CHOLESTEROL 70 IRON 1.3 SODIUM 94 CALCIUM 14

LAMB DIANE

1 pound lean boneless lamb
½ teaspoon cracked pepper
¼ cup plus 2 tablespoons Burgundy or other
  dry red wine
2 tablespoons lemon juice
1½ tablespoons low-sodium Worcestershire sauce
1½ teaspoons cornstarch
Vegetable cooking spray
1 teaspoon vegetable oil
¼ cup finely chopped shallots
2 cloves garlic, minced
2 tablespoons minced fresh parsley
2 tablespoons minced fresh chives
2 cups cooked long-grain rice (cooked without
  salt or fat)
Fresh chives (optional)

Trim fat from lamb; cut lamb into thin strips, and sprinkle with pepper. Set aside.

Combine wine and next 3 ingredients in a small bowl; stir well. Set aside.

Coat a wok or large nonstick skillet with cooking spray; add oil. Place over medium-high heat (375°) until hot. Add lamb, and stir-fry 5 minutes. Remove lamb from wok. Drain and pat dry with paper towels. Wipe drippings from wok with a paper towel.

Coat wok with cooking spray; place over medium-high heat until hot. Add shallots and garlic; stir-fry 1 minute. Return lamb to wok. Add reserved wine mixture. Cook until mixture is thickened and thoroughly heated, stirring constantly. Stir in parsley and minced chives. Serve over cooked rice. Garnish with fresh chives, if desired. Yield: 4 servings (332 calories per serving).

PROTEIN 26.6 FAT 9.4 (Saturated Fat 3.0) CARBOHYDRATE 33.3
FIBER 0.8 CHOLESTEROL 74 IRON 3.1 SODIUM 93 CALCIUM 40

Serve Grilled Lamb Chops hot off the grill for an easy, no-fuss entrée.

GRILLED LAMB CHOPS

4 (5-ounce) lean lamb loin chops (1 inch thick)
½ cup frozen apple juice concentrate,
   thawed and undiluted
½ teaspoon curry powder
½ teaspoon ground cumin
¼ teaspoon garlic powder
Vegetable cooking spray

Trim fat from chops. Place chops in a zip-top heavy-duty plastic bag. Combine apple juice concentrate and next 3 ingredients; stir well. Pour over chops; seal bag, and shake until chops are well coated. Marinate in refrigerator 8 hours, turning bag occasionally. Remove lamb from marinade. Place marinade in a small saucepan. Bring to a boil; reduce heat, and simmer 5 minutes.

Coat grill rack with cooking spray; place on grill over medium-hot coals. Place chops on rack, and cook 7 to 9 minutes on each side or to desired degree of doneness, basting chops frequently with marinade. Yield: 4 servings (253 calories per serving).

PROTEIN 26.8 FAT 9.0 (Saturated Fat 3.1) CARBOHYDRATE 14.8
FIBER 0.1 CHOLESTEROL 84 IRON 2.3 SODIUM 84 CALCIUM 28

TERIYAKI LAMB CHOPS

4 (5-ounce) lean lamb loin chops (1 inch thick)
½ cup dry sherry
¼ cup firmly packed brown sugar
¼ cup low-sodium soy sauce
2 tablespoons water
1 tablespoon peeled, minced gingerroot
Vegetable cooking spray

Trim fat from chops. Place chops in a large zip-top heavy-duty plastic bag. Combine sherry and next 4 ingredients; stir well. Pour over chops; seal bag, and shake until chops are well coated. Marinate in refrigerator 8 hours, turning bag occasionally.

Remove chops from marinade. Place marinade in a small saucepan. Bring to a boil; reduce heat, and simmer 2 minutes.

Coat grill rack with cooking spray; place on grill over medium-hot coals. Place chops on rack, and cook 7 to 9 minutes on each side or to desired degree of doneness, basting occasionally with marinade. Yield: 4 servings (257 calories per serving).

PROTEIN 26.6 FAT 8.8 (Saturated Fat 3.1) CARBOHYDRATE 14.6
FIBER 0 CHOLESTEROL 84 IRON 2.3 SODIUM 471 CALCIUM 31

HEARTY LAMB STEAKS

4 (6-ounce) lean lamb sirloin steaks (¾ inch thick)
Vegetable cooking spray
¼ teaspoon salt
¼ teaspoon pepper
2 cups sliced fresh oyster mushrooms
½ cup thinly sliced onion
1 clove garlic, minced
6 cups shredded escarole
1 cup halved cherry tomatoes
½ teaspoon liquid smoke seasoning

Trim fat from lamb. Coat a nonstick skillet with cooking spray; place over medium heat until hot. Add lamb; cook until browned on each side. Sprinkle with salt and pepper. Reduce heat; cook 6 to 7 minutes or to desired degree of doneness. Remove lamb from skillet. Drain and pat dry with paper towels. Set aside; keep warm. Wipe drippings from skillet with a paper towel.

Coat skillet with cooking spray; place over medium-high heat until hot. Add mushrooms, onion, and garlic; sauté until tender. Add escarole, and cook 1 minute, stirring frequently. Add cherry tomatoes and liquid smoke seasoning; stir gently. Cook until thoroughly heated. Transfer to a serving platter; top with lamb steaks. Yield: 4 servings (246 calories per serving).

PROTEIN 31.2 FAT 10.0 (Saturated Fat 3.5) CARBOHYDRATE 7.1
FIBER 1.8 CHOLESTEROL 95 IRON 3.3 SODIUM 236 CALCIUM 45

COFFEE-GLAZED LEG OF LAMB

1 (3½-pound) lean boneless leg of lamb
¾ cup hot water
1 tablespoon instant espresso powder
3 tablespoons brown sugar
2 tablespoons lemon juice
¾ teaspoon dry mustard
½ teaspoon freshly ground pepper
¼ teaspoon garlic powder
¼ teaspoon hot sauce
Vegetable cooking spray

Trim fat from lamb. Place lamb in a large zip-top heavy-duty plastic bag. Combine water and espresso powder; stir until espresso dissolves. Add brown sugar and next 5 ingredients. Pour over lamb; seal bag, and shake until lamb is well coated. Marinate in refrigerator 8 hours, turning bag occasionally.

Remove lamb from marinade. Place marinade in a small saucepan. Bring to a boil; reduce heat, and simmer 2 minutes.

Place lamb on a rack in a roasting pan coated with cooking spray. Insert meat thermometer into thickest part of roast, if desired. Bake, uncovered, at 325° for 2 hours or until meat thermometer registers 140° (rare) to 160° (medium), basting frequently with marinade. Transfer lamb to a serving platter. Let stand 15 minutes. Yield: 14 servings (141 calories per serving).

PROTEIN 19.5 FAT 5.4 (Saturated Fat 2.0) CARBOHYDRATE 2.2
FIBER 0 CHOLESTEROL 61 IRON 1.6 SODIUM 48 CALCIUM 8

QUICK HARVEST PORK SKILLET

Vegetable cooking spray
1 pound lean ground pork
1 cup thinly sliced onion
½ cup thinly sliced celery
¾ cup canned low-sodium chicken broth,
    undiluted
¼ cup Chablis or other dry white wine
1 cup peeled, seeded, and chopped tomato
3 ounces dried fruit bits
½ teaspoon pumpkin pie spice
¼ teaspoon dried whole thyme
3 cups cooked medium egg noodles (cooked
    without salt or fat)

Coat a large nonstick skillet with cooking spray;
place over medium-high heat until hot. Add ground
pork, onion, and celery; cook until pork is browned,
stirring to crumble. Drain and pat pork mixture dry
with paper towels. Wipe drippings from skillet with
a paper towel.

Return pork mixture to skillet; add chicken broth
and next 5 ingredients. Bring to a boil; reduce heat,
and simmer 25 minutes or until almost all liquid
evaporates and mixture is thoroughly heated, stirring
occasionally. Serve over noodles. Yield: 6 servings (308
calories per serving).

PROTEIN 19.9 FAT 9.8 (Saturated Fat 3.1) CARBOHYDRATE 34.4
FIBER 2.9 CHOLESTEROL 78 IRON 2.6 SODIUM 64 CALCIUM 32

MUSTARD-TARRAGON BAKED
PORK CHOPS

4 (6-ounce) lean center-cut loin pork chops
    (½ inch thick)
3 tablespoons plain nonfat yogurt
½ teaspoon low-sodium Worcestershire sauce
½ cup wheat germ, toasted
1 tablespoon minced fresh tarragon
1 teaspoon dry mustard
¼ teaspoon pepper
Vegetable cooking spray

Trim fat from chops. Combine yogurt and Worcestershire sauce; brush on both sides of each chop.
Combine wheat germ and next 3 ingredients; dredge
chops in wheat germ mixture.

Place chops on rack of a broiler pan coated with
cooking spray. Broil 5½ inches from heat 10 minutes
on each side or until done. Yield: 4 servings (226
calories per serving).

PROTEIN 27.6 FAT 9.3 (Saturated Fat 3.1) CARBOHYDRATE 6.8
FIBER 1.7 CHOLESTEROL 70 IRON 1.8 SODIUM 85 CALCIUM 37

PORK WITH BALSAMIC VINEGAR

¼ cup all-purpose flour
1 teaspoon salt-free lemon-herb seasoning
1 pound pork tenderloin medaillons
Vegetable cooking spray
1 teaspoon vegetable oil
½ pound fresh arugula
1 teaspoon reduced-calorie margarine
3 tablespoons balsamic vinegar
2 tablespoons canned no-salt-added chicken broth,
    undiluted
1 tablespoon minced fresh chives

Combine flour and lemon-herb seasoning in a small
bowl; stir well. Dredge pork in flour mixture.

Coat a large nonstick skillet with cooking spray; add
oil. Place over medium-high heat until hot. Add
medaillons, and cook 4 to 5 minutes on each side or
until browned. Remove from skillet, and keep warm.
Wipe drippings from skillet with a paper towel.

Remove stems from arugula. Coat skillet with cooking spray; add margarine. Place over medium heat
until margarine melts. Add arugula, and cook 40
seconds or until wilted, stirring constantly. Arrange
arugula on a serving platter. Place pork on arugula.

Combine vinegar and broth in a small saucepan;
cook over medium heat until thoroughly heated.
Spoon over pork; sprinkle with chives. Serve immediately. Yield: 4 servings (204 calories per serving).

PROTEIN 27.5 FAT 6.7 (Saturated Fat 1.8) CARBOHYDRATE 7.4
FIBER 0.4 CHOLESTEROL 83 IRON 2.0 SODIUM 80 CALCIUM 69

Classic winter flavors bring warmth to Brandy-Pear Pork Tenderloins.

BRANDY-PEAR PORK TENDERLOINS

2 (¾-pound) pork tenderloins
½ cup brandy
⅔ cup finely chopped fresh pear
2 tablespoons finely chopped almonds, toasted
2 tablespoons raisins, chopped
1 tablespoon cider vinegar
2 teaspoons chopped crystallized ginger
Vegetable cooking spray
Fresh pear slices (optional)

Trim fat from pork. Cut pork lengthwise to within ½ inch of outer edge of each tenderloin, leaving 1 long side connected; flip cut piece over to enlarge tenderloin. Place in a shallow dish; pour brandy over tenderloins, and turn to coat. Cover tenderloins, and marinate in refrigerator at least 2 hours, turning occasionally.

Remove tenderloins from marinade. Place marinade in a small saucepan; bring to a boil. Reduce heat, and simmer 5 minutes.

Combine chopped pear and next 4 ingredients; stir well. Spread half of mixture in center of each tenderloin to within ½ inch of sides. Bring sides of meat together and secure at 2-inch intervals with string.

Place tenderloins on a rack in a roasting pan coated with cooking spray. Bake, uncovered, at 375° for 45 to 50 minutes or until meat thermometer registers 160°, basting frequently with marinade. Let stand 10 minutes; slice into 18 slices, and arrange on a large serving platter. Garnish with fresh pear slices, if desired. Yield: 6 servings (179 calories per serving).

PROTEIN 24.0   FAT 5.3   (Saturated Fat 1.2)   CARBOHYDRATE 8.4
FIBER 1.3   CHOLESTEROL 71   IRON 1.9   SODIUM 55   CALCIUM 26

CINNAMON-ORANGE PORK TENDERLOIN

½ cup corn flakes cereal
1 tablespoon brown sugar
2 teaspoons grated orange rind
2 teaspoons ground cinnamon
2 (½-pound) pork tenderloins
1½ tablespoons plain nonfat yogurt
1½ tablespoons orange juice
Vegetable cooking spray

Position knife blade in food processor bowl; add corn flakes cereal, brown sugar, grated orange rind, and ground cinnamon. Process mixture until cereal is crushed, and set cereal mixture aside.

Trim fat from tenderloins. Combine yogurt and orange juice in a small bowl; brush over tenderloins. Dredge tenderloins in cereal mixture. Place tenderloins on a rack in a roasting pan coated with cooking spray. Insert meat thermometer into thickest part of tenderloin, if desired. Bake at 350° for 45 to 50 minutes or until meat thermometer registers 160°.

Transfer tenderloins to a serving platter. Let stand 10 minutes; slice diagonally across grain into thin slices. Yield: 4 servings (157 calories per serving.)

PROTEIN 24.4   FAT 3.0   (Saturated Fat 1.0)   CARBOHYDRATE 6.8
FIBER 0.3   CHOLESTEROL 74   IRON 2.2   SODIUM 96   CALCIUM 37

GLAZED PORK ROAST WITH RAISIN SAUCE

1 (2½-pound) lean boneless double pork loin
   roast, tied
½ teaspoon ginger
½ teaspoon dry mustard
Vegetable cooking spray
2 tablespoons honey
1 tablespoon fine, dry breadcrumbs
½ cup unsweetened pineapple juice
½ cup vinegar
½ cup raisins
¼ cup firmly packed brown sugar
1 tablespoon cornstarch
1 tablespoon water

Untie roast, and trim fat. Retie roast. Combine ginger and dry mustard; rub mixture over surface of roast. Place roast on a rack in a roasting pan coated with cooking spray. Insert meat thermometer into thickest part of roast, if desired. Place roast in a 450° oven.

Reduce heat to 350°, and bake roast 1 hour and 15 minutes.

Brush roast with honey; sprinkle with breadcrumbs. Combine pineapple juice and vinegar; pour over roast. Bake an additional 30 minutes or until meat thermometer registers 160°.

Remove roast from pan, reserving drippings. Let roast stand 10 minutes. Skim fat from drippings, and place drippings in a small saucepan. Bring to a boil; add raisins, and simmer 5 minutes. Combine brown sugar, cornstarch, and water; stir well. Add to raisin mixture. Cook, stirring constantly, until thickened.

Remove string from roast; slice diagonally across grain into ¼-inch slices, and arrange on a large serving platter. Serve with raisin sauce. Yield: 10 servings (243 calories per serving).

PROTEIN 22.7   FAT 8.3   (Saturated Fat 2.8)   CARBOHYDRATE 19.2
FIBER 0.5   CHOLESTEROL 65   IRON 1.4   SODIUM 77   CALCIUM 20

Serve Poppy Seed Roasted Cornish Hens (page 175) with steamed baby vegetables for a mellow-tasting, family-pleasing meal.

Poultry

CHICKEN CHILES RELLENOS

3 (4-ounce) cans whole green chiles,
    drained
1 (4-ounce) can chopped green chiles,
    drained
2 cups seeded, chopped tomato
2 tablespoons minced green onions
1 tablespoon chopped fresh cilantro
1 tablespoon white wine vinegar
Vegetable cooking spray
½ cup chopped onion
2 cloves garlic, minced
1½ cups chopped cooked chicken breast (skinned
    before cooking and cooked without salt)
½ cup (2 ounces) shredded reduced-fat
    Monterey Jack cheese
¼ teaspoon salt
¼ teaspoon pepper
2 tablespoons reduced-calorie mayonnaise
1 teaspoon water
1⅓ cups soft French bread crumbs, toasted
Fresh cilantro sprigs (optional)

Reserve 8 whole chiles; chop remaining whole chiles. Combine chopped whole chiles, drained chopped chiles, and next 4 ingredients; stir well. Cover and chill thoroughly.

Coat a large nonstick skillet with cooking spray; place over medium-high heat until hot. Add onion and garlic; sauté until tender. Remove from heat, and let cool slightly. Stir in chicken, cheese, salt, and pepper. Spoon ¼ cup chicken mixture into each whole chile.

Combine mayonnaise and water in a small bowl; stir well. Dip stuffed chiles in mayonnaise mixture, and dredge in bread crumbs. Place on a baking sheet coated with cooking spray. Bake at 450° for 10 to 12 minutes or until golden brown. Serve with chilled tomato mixture. Garnish with fresh cilantro sprigs, if desired. Yield: 4 servings (251 calories per serving).

PROTEIN 21.8   FAT 7.4   (Saturated Fat 2.5)   CARBOHYDRATE 22.5
FIBER 3.2   CHOLESTEROL 52   IRON 2.0   SODIUM 564   CALCIUM 151

CHICKEN SATÉ KABOBS

¾ cup chopped onion
1 tablespoon brown sugar
1 tablespoon creamy peanut butter
2 tablespoons lemon juice
1 tablespoon low-sodium soy sauce
2 cloves garlic, peeled
¼ teaspoon hot sauce
4 (4-ounce) skinned, boned chicken breast halves,
    cut into ½-inch-wide strips
1 medium-size sweet red pepper, cut into
    1-inch pieces
Vegetable cooking spray
2 cups cooked long-grain rice (cooked without salt
    or fat)

Combine first 7 ingredients in container of an electric blender; top with cover, and process until smooth, scraping sides of container occasionally.

Place chicken in a zip-top heavy-duty plastic bag; add onion mixture. Seal and marinate in refrigerator 15 minutes, turning once.

Drain chicken; discard marinade. Thread chicken and pepper pieces alternately on 8 (10-inch) skewers.

Coat grill rack with cooking spray; place on grill over medium-hot coals. Place kabobs on rack, and cook 10 to 12 minutes or until chicken is done, turning occasionally. Serve over cooked rice. Yield: 4 servings (324 calories per serving).

PROTEIN 30.3   FAT 5.7   (Saturated Fat 1.3)   CARBOHYDRATE 36.1
FIBER 1.9   CHOLESTEROL 70   IRON 2.7   SODIUM 186   CALCIUM 37

BUFFALO CHICKEN

4 (4-ounce) skinned, boned chicken breast halves
¼ cup light beer
¼ cup hot sauce
2 tablespoons white wine vinegar
¼ teaspoon cracked pepper
Vegetable cooking spray
¼ cup commercial nonfat blue cheese dressing

Place chicken between 2 sheets of heavy-duty plastic wrap, and flatten to ¼-inch thickness, using a meat mallet or rolling pin. Place chicken in a zip-top heavy-duty plastic bag. Combine beer, hot sauce, vinegar, and pepper; pour over chicken. Seal bag securely; marinate in refrigerator 10 minutes.

Drain chicken, discarding marinade. Coat grill rack with cooking spray; place on grill over medium-hot coals. Place chicken on rack, and cook 5 minutes on each side or until done. Serve with blue cheese dressing. Yield: 4 servings (160 calories per serving).

PROTEIN 27.6 FAT 3.3 (Saturated Fat 0.9) CARBOHYDRATE 2.4
FIBER 0 CHOLESTEROL 75 IRON 1.0 SODIUM 258 CALCIUM 15

JALAPEÑO CHICKEN BREASTS

6 (4-ounce) skinned, boned chicken breast halves
2 tablespoons all-purpose flour
Vegetable cooking spray
2 cloves garlic, minced
½ cup hot jalapeño jelly
1 tablespoon low-sodium soy sauce
1½ tablespoons chopped ripe olives

Place chicken between 2 sheets of heavy-duty plastic wrap, and flatten to ¼-inch thickness, using a meat mallet or rolling pin. Sprinkle chicken with flour. Coat a large nonstick skillet with cooking spray; place over medium-high heat until hot. Add chicken, and cook 4 minutes on each side or until browned.

Coat a small saucepan with cooking spray; place over medium-high heat until hot. Add garlic, and sauté until tender. Add jelly and soy sauce; reduce heat, and cook until jelly melts, stirring constantly.

Spoon jelly mixture over chicken; simmer, uncovered, 5 minutes or until chicken is tender. Transfer chicken to a serving platter; spoon sauce over chicken. Sprinkle with olives. Yield: 6 servings (208 calories per serving).

PROTEIN 26.5 FAT 1.8 (Saturated Fat 0.4) CARBOHYDRATE 19.9
FIBER 0.1 CHOLESTEROL 66 IRON 1.4 SODIUM 162 CALCIUM 22

JAMAICAN CHICKEN

4 (4-ounce) skinned, boned chicken breast halves
2½ tablespoons all-purpose flour
1 tablespoon flaked coconut, minced
1 teaspoon curry powder, divided
¼ teaspoon salt
¼ teaspoon pepper
1 egg white, lightly beaten
Vegetable cooking spray
2 teaspoons reduced-calorie margarine, divided
1 medium banana, cut into ½-inch slices
¾ cup unsweetened pineapple juice
3 green onions, cut diagonally into ¼-inch pieces
2 cups cooked long-grain rice (cooked without salt or fat)
Green onion fans (optional)

Place chicken between 2 sheets of heavy-duty plastic wrap, and flatten to ¼-inch thickness, using a meat mallet or rolling pin.

Combine flour, coconut, ½ teaspoon curry powder, salt, and pepper; stir well. Brush both sides of each chicken breast with egg white; dredge in flour mixture. Set aside.

Coat a large nonstick skillet with cooking spray; add 1 teaspoon margarine. Place over medium-high heat until margarine melts. Stir in remaining ½ teaspoon curry powder. Add banana, and sauté 2 minutes or until banana is lightly browned. Remove banana from skillet, and set aside. Wipe drippings from skillet with a paper towel.

Coat skillet with cooking spray; add remaining 1 teaspoon margarine. Place over medium-high heat until margarine melts. Add chicken, and cook 2 minutes on each side or until browned. Add pineapple juice and green onions. Cover, reduce heat, and simmer 10 minutes or until chicken is tender. Serve over rice. Garnish with green onion fans, if desired. Yield: 4 servings (350 calories per serving).

PROTEIN 30.8 FAT 4.1 (Saturated Fat 1.2) CARBOHYDRATE 46.2
FIBER 2.4 CHOLESTEROL 66 IRON 2.7 SODIUM 261 CALCIUM 48

CHICKEN MONTE CRISTO

6 (4-ounce) skinned, boned chicken breast halves
¼ teaspoon pepper
3 (1-ounce) slices reduced-fat, low-salt ham
3 (⅔-ounce) slices low-fat process Swiss cheese
2 egg whites, lightly beaten
½ cup Italian-seasoned breadcrumbs
Vegetable cooking spray

Place chicken between 2 sheets of heavy-duty plastic wrap, and flatten to ¼-inch thickness, using a meat mallet or rolling pin. Sprinkle chicken with pepper. Cut each ham slice and cheese slice in half. Place 1 piece of ham and 1 piece of cheese on each chicken breast. Roll up chicken lengthwise, tucking ends under; secure with wooden picks.

Dip chicken rolls in egg white, and dredge in breadcrumbs. Place on a baking sheet coated with cooking spray. Bake at 375° for 25 minutes or until chicken is done. Transfer to a serving platter, and remove wooden picks. Serve immediately. Yield: 6 servings (200 calories per serving).

PROTEIN 33.6   FAT 3.1   (Saturated Fat 1.1)   CARBOHYDRATE 7.7
FIBER 0.1   CHOLESTEROL 75   IRON 1.1   SODIUM 575   CALCIUM 89

VERACRUZ-STYLE POACHED CHICKEN

4 (4-ounce) skinned, boned chicken breast halves
Vegetable cooking spray
1 teaspoon olive oil
1 small onion, thinly sliced and separated
  into rings
2 cloves garlic, minced
1 (14½-ounce) can no-salt-added whole tomatoes,
  undrained
3 tablespoons fresh lime juice
2 jalapeño peppers, seeded and thinly sliced
⅛ teaspoon pepper
¼ cup ripe olives, thinly sliced
Fresh lime wedges (optional)

Place chicken between 2 sheets of heavy-duty plastic wrap, and flatten to ½-inch thickness, using a meat mallet or rolling pin. Set aside.

Coat a large nonstick skillet with cooking spray; add oil. Place over medium-high heat until hot. Add onion and garlic; sauté until tender. Drain tomatoes, reserving ½ cup juice; chop tomatoes. Add chopped tomato, reserved tomato juice, lime juice, and jalapeño pepper to skillet; stir well.

Bring mixture to a boil; reduce heat. Arrange chicken over tomato mixture; sprinkle with pepper. Cover and simmer 12 minutes or until chicken is done. Transfer chicken to a serving platter, and keep warm. Bring tomato mixture to a boil; cook 3 minutes or until slightly reduced. Spoon around chicken, and top with olives. Garnish with lime wedges, if desired. Yield: 4 servings (179 calories per serving).

PROTEIN 27.6   FAT 3.5   (Saturated Fat 0.7)   CARBOHYDRATE 9.0
FIBER 0.8   CHOLESTEROL 66   IRON 1.6   SODIUM 150   CALCIUM 62

TOMATILLO CHICKEN BAKE

4 (6-ounce) skinned chicken breast halves
6 fresh tomatillos
Vegetable cooking spray
¾ cup chopped onion
½ cup water
4 cloves garlic, halved
½ teaspoon chicken-flavored bouillon
  granules
1 cup loosely packed fresh cilantro
2 cups sliced fresh mushrooms
¾ cup nonfat sour cream
¾ teaspoon chili powder
½ teaspoon ground cumin
½ teaspoon pepper
¼ teaspoon salt
1 cup (4 ounces) shredded reduced-fat sharp
  Cheddar cheese
6 (6-inch) corn tortillas, cut into 8 wedges
Tomato wedges (optional)
Fresh cilantro sprigs (optional)

Fill individual baking dishes with generous portions of Tomatillo Chicken Bake.

Place chicken in a large Dutch oven; add water to cover. Bring to a boil; cover, reduce heat, and simmer 35 minutes or until chicken is tender. Remove chicken from broth, and let cool slightly. Bone and shred chicken; set aside. Skim and discard fat from broth; reserve broth for another use.

Remove and discard husks from tomatillos; thinly slice tomatillos. Coat a large skillet with cooking spray; place over medium-high heat until hot. Add tomatillos, and sauté until tender. Remove from skillet, and let cool slightly. Set aside.

Combine onion, ½ cup water, garlic, and bouillon granules in skillet; cook over high heat until liquid evaporates (about 5 minutes).

Combine sautéed tomatillos, onion mixture, and 1 cup fresh cilantro in container of an electric blender or food processor; top with cover, and process until mixture is smooth.

Coat skillet with cooking spray; place over medium-high heat until hot. Add mushrooms; sauté until tender. Remove from heat; stir in shredded chicken, sour cream, and next 4 ingredients. Set aside; keep warm.

Spoon half of tomatillo mixture evenly into 6 individual oven-proof dishes coated with cooking spray. Sprinkle evenly with ⅓ cup cheese; top each with ¼ cup chicken mixture. Repeat procedure with remaining tomatillo mixture, ⅓ cup cheese, and chicken mixture. Sprinkle with remaining ⅓ cup cheese. Arrange 8 tortilla wedges around edges of each dish. Cover and bake at 350° for 15 minutes. Uncover and bake 10 minutes or until thoroughly heated. If desired, garnish with tomato wedges and cilantro sprigs. Yield: 6 servings (261 calories per serving).

PROTEIN 27.6   FAT 7.4   (Saturated Fat 0.7)   CARBOHYDRATE 20.4
FIBER 2.9   CHOLESTEROL 59   IRON 3.1   SODIUM 425   CALCIUM 272

ROASTED HERBED CHICKEN WITH MUSHROOM PESTO

1 cup loosely packed fresh basil leaves
¾ cup sliced fresh mushrooms
4 cloves garlic
2 tablespoons nonfat buttermilk
6 (6-ounce) skinned chicken breast halves
Vegetable cooking spray
3 tablespoons low-sodium soy sauce
2 tablespoon honey
½ teaspoon dark sesame oil

Position knife blade in food processor bowl; add first 3 ingredients. Process 3 seconds or until blended. Slowly add buttermilk through food chute with processor running, blending until mixture forms a paste.

Place 1 chicken breast, bone side down, on a cutting board; cut lengthwise into side of breast, forming a pocket. Stuff pocket with one-sixth of mushroom mixture. Place chicken, breast side up, on a rack in a roasting pan coated with cooking spray. Repeat procedure with remaining chicken breasts and mushroom mixture.

Combine soy sauce, honey, and sesame oil; brush over chicken. Bake at 400° for 30 minutes or until chicken is tender and golden, basting occasionally. Yield: 6 servings (162 calories per serving).

PROTEIN 26.8 FAT 2.0 (Saturated Fat 0.5) CARBOHYDRATE 8.3
FIBER 0.1 CHOLESTEROL 64 IRON 1.3 SODIUM 384 CALCIUM 34

 ## SUPERMARKET SALT MINES
Avoiding the salt shaker is not the way to dramatically reduce sodium intake, according to a study conducted by researchers at Monell Chemical Senses Center in Philadelphia.

Specifically, 77 percent of the daily sodium intake for study participants came from processed foods; salt added during cooking or at the table accounted for only about 12 percent. So to reduce sodium intake, reduce the amount of frequently eaten high-sodium foods such as luncheon meats and cheese.

CRISPY CHICKEN DRUMSTICKS

½ cup regular oats, uncooked
2 tablespoons grated Parmesan cheese
⅛ teaspoon salt
¼ teaspoon paprika
¼ teaspoon pepper
Dash of garlic powder
8 chicken drumsticks, skinned (about 1¾ pounds)
2 tablespoons honey
Fresh parsley sprigs (optional)

Combine first 6 ingredients in container of an electric blender or food processor; top with cover, and process until mixture resembles coarse meal.

Brush chicken drumsticks lightly with honey; dredge in oat mixture. Place drumsticks on a rack in a roasting pan. Bake at 400° for 15 minutes. Turn drumsticks, and bake an additional 20 minutes or until chicken is tender and golden. Transfer drumsticks to a large serving platter. Garnish with fresh parsley sprigs, if desired. Yield: 4 servings (240 calories per serving).

PROTEIN 27.9 FAT 6.8 (Saturated Fat 2.0) CARBOHYDRATE 15.7
FIBER 1.1 CHOLESTEROL 103 IRON 1.8 SODIUM 228 CALCIUM 56

MADEIRA-GLAZED CHICKEN THIGHS

8 pitted prunes, halved
1 cup Madeira
2 teaspoons coriander seeds
¼ teaspoon freshly ground pepper
1½ pounds chicken thighs, skinned
Vegetable cooking spray
½ cup water
½ teaspoon beef-flavored bouillon granules
Fresh sage leaves (optional)

Combine prunes and Madeira in a small bowl; cover and let stand 8 hours.

Place a small nonstick skillet over medium-high heat until hot. Add coriander seeds; cook 1 minute or until golden, stirring constantly. Remove from heat, and let cool. Crush seeds until pulverized, using a mortar and pestle. Set aside.

Sprinkle pepper evenly over chicken. Coat a large nonstick skillet with cooking spray, and place over medium-high heat until hot. Add chicken, and cook 2 minutes on each side or until browned. Remove from skillet. Drain and pat dry with paper towels. Wipe drippings from skillet with a paper towel.

Add prune mixture, coriander seeds, water, and bouillon granules to skillet; bring to a boil. Return chicken to skillet; cover, reduce heat, and simmer 30 minutes or until chicken is tender.

Transfer chicken and prunes to a serving platter, using a slotted spoon. Cook Madeira mixture 5 minutes or until reduced to ½ cup. Spoon over chicken. Garnish with fresh sage leaves, if desired. Yield: 4 servings (243 calories per serving).

PROTEIN 24.2   FAT 8.9   (Saturated Fat 2.3)   CARBOHYDRATE 16.2
FIBER 1.8   CHOLESTEROL 79   IRON 2.0   SODIUM 204   CALCIUM 35

THAI CHICKEN BARBECUE

½ cup firmly packed brown sugar
½ cup low-sodium soy sauce
2 tablespoons fresh lime juice
6 cloves garlic, minced
1 teaspoon crushed red pepper
¾ teaspoon curry powder
2 (3-pound) broiler-fryers, cut up and skinned
Vegetable cooking spray
Green onion fans (optional)

Combine first 6 ingredients in an extra-large zip-top heavy-duty plastic bag; add chicken. Seal bag, and marinate in refrigerator at least 4 hours, turning occasionally.

Remove chicken from marinade, reserving marinade. Transfer marinade to a small saucepan; bring to a boil. Reduce heat, and simmer 3 minutes.

Coat grill rack with cooking spray; place on grill over medium-hot coals. Place chicken on rack, and cook 20 to 25 minutes or until chicken is done, turning and basting frequently with marinade. Transfer to a large

serving platter. Garnish with green onion fans, if desired. Yield: 12 servings (197 calories per serving).

PROTEIN 23.7   FAT 6.1   (Saturated Fat 1.7)   CARBOHYDRATE 9.7
FIBER 0.1   CHOLESTEROL 73   IRON 1.4   SODIUM 333   CALCIUM 24

SHERRIED ROAST CHICKEN

1 (3-pound) broiler-fryer, skinned
1 cup dry sherry
1 cup unsweetened apple juice
½ cup reduced-sodium soy sauce
¼ cup white wine vinegar
Vegetable cooking spray
1 small apple, cored and quartered
1 small onion, quartered
¼ cup reduced-calorie apple spread
1 tablespoon hot water
¼ to ½ teaspoon freshly ground pepper
Apple wedges (optional)
Fresh parsley sprigs (optional)

Trim excess fat from chicken. Remove giblets and neck from chicken; reserve for other uses. Rinse chicken under cold, running water; pat dry. Combine sherry and next 3 ingredients in a large zip-top heavy-duty plastic bag; seal bag and shake. Place chicken in bag; seal and shake until chicken is well coated. Marinate in refrigerator 8 hours, turning bag occasionally.

Remove chicken from marinade; discard marinade. Place chicken, breast side up, on a rack in a roasting pan coated with cooking spray. Stuff with quartered apple and onion. Truss chicken.

Combine apple spread and hot water; stir until smooth. Sprinkle chicken evenly with pepper, and brush with apple spread mixture. Insert meat thermometer in meaty part of thigh, making sure it does not touch bone. Bake, uncovered, at 375° for 1½ hours or until meat thermometer registers 185°. Transfer to a serving platter. If desired, garnish with apple wedges and fresh parsley sprigs. Yield: 6 servings (193 calories per serving).

PROTEIN 24.1   FAT 6.3   (Saturated Fat 1.7)   CARBOHYDRATE 8.8
FIBER 1.0   CHOLESTEROL 73   IRON 1.2   SODIUM 240   CALCIUM 20

Healthy cooking is easy when you prepare Harvest Cornbread Chicken Pie for the main course.

HARVEST CORNBREAD CHICKEN PIE

1 (3-pound) broiler-fryer, skinned
3 quarts water
2 cups peeled, cubed sweet potato
1 tablespoon cornstarch
1 tablespoon water
Vegetable cooking spray
1 cup chopped onion
1 cup frozen whole kernel corn, thawed
2 cloves garlic, minced
¾ cup self-rising flour
¾ cup self-rising cornmeal
1 teaspoon sugar
¾ teaspoon chili powder
¾ cup nonfat buttermilk
1 egg, lightly beaten

Place broiler-fryer and 3 quarts water in a Dutch oven. Bring to a boil; cover, reduce heat, and simmer 45 minutes or until chicken is tender. Remove chicken from broth, reserving broth. Let chicken cool to touch. Bone and chop chicken. Return chopped chicken to broth; cover and chill 8 hours.

Skim and discard fat from broth. Remove chicken with a slotted spoon; set aside. Bring broth to a boil; cook 50 minutes or until reduced by half. Add sweet potato, and cook 13 minutes or until tender; remove with a slotted spoon. Set sweet potato aside. Cook broth 20 minutes or until reduced to 1 cup.

Combine cornstarch and 1 tablespoon water; stir well. Add to broth; cook, stirring constantly, until thickened and bubbly.

Coat a large nonstick skillet with cooking spray; place over medium-high heat until hot. Add onion, corn, and garlic; sauté until tender. Add chicken, sweet potato, and broth mixture; stir well. Spoon mixture into an 11- x 7- x 2-inch baking dish coated with cooking spray. Set aside.

Combine flour, cornmeal, sugar, and chili powder in a bowl; make a well in center of mixture. Combine buttermilk and egg; add to dry ingredients, stirring just until dry ingredients are moistened. Spoon over chicken mixture. Bake at 425° for 15 minutes or until golden. Yield: 8 servings (318 calories per serving).

PROTEIN 23.6 FAT 6.0 (Saturated Fat 1.6) CARBOHYDRATE 37.9
FIBER 2.0 CHOLESTEROL 81 IRON 2.4 SODIUM 422 CALCIUM 138

POPPY SEED ROASTED CORNISH HENS

2 (1-pound) Cornish hens, skinned
¼ teaspoon pepper
Vegetable cooking spray
⅓ cup honey
2 tablespoons poppy seeds
2 teaspoons dry mustard
½ teaspoon ground ginger
½ teaspoon pepper
¼ teaspoon salt
Fresh basil sprigs (optional)

Remove giblets from hens; reserve for another use. Rinse hens under cold, running water, and pat dry. Split each hen in half lengthwise, using an electric knife. Sprinkle evenly with ¼ teaspoon pepper. Place hens, cut side down, on rack of a broiler pan coated with cooking spray.

Combine honey and next 5 ingredients in a small bowl, stirring well. Brush hens with honey mixture. Bake at 350° for 40 to 45 minutes or until hens are done, turning occasionally. Transfer hens to a serving platter. Garnish with fresh basil sprigs, if desired. Yield: 4 servings (289 calories per serving).

PROTEIN 27.1 FAT 9.3 (Saturated Fat 2.0) CARBOHYDRATE 24.9
FIBER 0.4 CHOLESTEROL 80 IRON 1.8 SODIUM 226 CALCIUM 84

TURKEY LASAGNA

Vegetable cooking spray
1 pound freshly ground raw turkey
1 cup chopped sweet red pepper
½ cup chopped onion
1 clove garlic, minced
1 (8-ounce) can no-salt-added tomato sauce
1 (6-ounce) can no-salt-added tomato paste
¾ cup water
¼ teaspoon salt
¼ teaspoon dried whole thyme
¼ teaspoon dried whole oregano
1½ cups part-skim ricotta cheese
1 cup (4 ounces) shredded part-skim mozzarella cheese, divided
6 lasagna noodles (cooked without salt or fat)
1 (10-ounce) package frozen chopped spinach, thawed and well drained
2 tablespoons chopped fresh parsley
1 tablespoon grated Romano cheese

Coat a large nonstick skillet with cooking spray; place over medium-high heat until hot. Add turkey, sweet red pepper, onion, and garlic; cook until turkey is browned, stirring to crumble. Drain turkey mixture, and pat dry with paper towels. Wipe drippings from skillet with a paper towel.

Return turkey mixture to skillet. Add tomato sauce and next 5 ingredients; bring to a boil. Cover, reduce heat, and simmer 25 minutes, stirring occasionally. Set aside. Combine ricotta cheese and ½ cup mozzarella cheese in a small bowl; stir well.

Coat an 11- x 7- x 2-inch baking dish with cooking spray. Spoon ½ cup turkey mixture into dish. Layer one-third each of lasagna noodles, ricotta cheese mixture, spinach, and one-third of remaining turkey mixture; repeat layers twice. Cover and bake at 350° for 25 minutes. Uncover and sprinkle with remaining ½ cup mozzarella cheese, parsley, and Romano cheese. Bake, uncovered, an additional 10 minutes. Let stand 10 minutes before serving. Yield: 8 servings (294 calories per serving).

PROTEIN 26.5 FAT 9.2 (Saturated Fat 4.8) CARBOHYDRATE 26.5
FIBER 2.2 CHOLESTEROL 57 IRON 3.2 SODIUM 293 CALCIUM 303

TURKEY-VEGETABLE SPIRAL

Vegetable cooking spray
1 teaspoon olive oil
1 cup chopped sweet red pepper
¾ cup frozen whole kernel corn, thawed
½ cup chopped carrot
2 pounds freshly ground raw turkey
1 cup soft whole wheat breadcrumbs
¾ cup chopped onion
1 egg, lightly beaten
½ teaspoon chili powder
½ teaspoon paprika
¼ teaspoon salt
¼ teaspoon garlic powder
¼ teaspoon pepper

Coat a large nonstick skillet with cooking spray; add olive oil. Place over medium-high heat until hot. Add sweet pepper, corn, and carrot; sauté until tender.

Combine turkey and remaining ingredients. Shape into a 15- x 10-inch rectangle on wax paper. Spread corn mixture evenly over turkey mixture, leaving a 1-inch margin on all sides. Roll up turkey mixture, jellyroll fashion, starting at narrow end, using wax paper to support turkey mixture. Pinch ends and seam to seal. Remove from wax paper, using 2 wide spatulas. Place roll, seam side down, in a 13- x 9- x 2-inch baking dish coated with cooking spray. Bake at 350° for 1 hour and 15 minutes; let stand 10 minutes before slicing. Yield: 10 servings (156 calories per serving).

PROTEIN 21.7 FAT 4.0 (Saturated Fat 1.1) CARBOHYDRATE 7.8
FIBER 1.2 CHOLESTEROL 80 IRON 1.9 SODIUM 163 CALCIUM 27

SAUTÉED TURKEY IN MEXICAN BROWN SAUCE

Vegetable cooking spray
1 tablespoon vegetable oil
1 tablespoon plus 2 teaspoons all-purpose flour
1 pound turkey tenderloins, cut into 1-inch cubes
1 medium-size green pepper, cut into julienne strips
4 green onions, cut into 1-inch pieces
½ cup canned no-salt-added chicken broth, undiluted
⅓ cup no-salt-added chunky-style salsa
1 teaspoon lemon juice
½ teaspoon minced fresh cilantro
¼ teaspoon salt
2 cups cooked long-grain rice (cooked without salt or fat)
Fresh cilantro sprigs (optional)

Coat a large nonstick skillet with cooking spray; add oil. Place over medium heat until hot. Add flour, stirring well; cook, stirring constantly, 5 minutes or until flour mixture is dark brown. Add turkey; sauté 3 to 4 minutes or until lightly browned.

Add green pepper and green onions; sauté until crisp-tender. Add chicken broth, salsa, lemon juice, minced cilantro, and salt, stirring well; cook 10 minutes or until turkey is tender, stirring occasionally. Serve over rice. Garnish with fresh cilantro sprigs, if desired. Yield: 4 servings (309 calories per serving).

PROTEIN 29.6 FAT 5.0 (Saturated Fat 0.7) CARBOHYDRATE 34.3
FIBER 1.8 CHOLESTEROL 71 IRON 3.3 SODIUM 215 CALCIUM 41

 ## WHAT'S SPECIAL ABOUT CANOLA?

Although long popular in Canada, canola oil only recently arrived stateside. It is extracted from the rapeseed plant, a relative of the mustard plant. A nutritional plus, canola oil contains only 6 percent saturated fat, which is less saturated fat than olive (16 percent), corn (13 percent), or any other vegetable oil. The oil is also high in mono-unsaturated fat, another heart-healthy advantage.

Regardless of these features, getting people to substitute canola oil for every vegetable oil is not the primary objective for most nutritionists. The differences between canola and other vegetable oils may not make a large impact healthwise, especially when only a teaspoon or two is used. It's the saturated fats such as lard, animal fat, and coconut or palm kernel oil that create more health problems.

Holiday Turkey Cutlets, topped with a tasty cranberry sauce, puts bright colors and festive flavors on your dinner table in a hurry.

HOLIDAY TURKEY CUTLETS

1 pound turkey breast cutlets, cut into 8 pieces
3 tablespoons all-purpose flour
2 teaspoons vegetable oil
¾ cup chopped onion
¾ cup fresh cranberries
½ cup canned low-sodium chicken broth,
  undiluted
2 tablespoons sugar
2 tablespoons red wine vinegar
2 tablespoons commercial fat-free Catalina dressing
¼ teaspoon salt
Fresh sage sprigs (optional)
Orange slices (optional)

Place turkey breast cutlets between 2 sheets of heavy-duty plastic wrap, and flatten to ⅛-inch thickness, using a meat mallet or rolling pin. Dredge turkey cutlets in flour.

Heat oil in a large nonstick skillet over medium heat until hot. Add cutlets, and cook 2 minutes on each side or until browned. Transfer to a platter, and keep warm. Wipe drippings from skillet with a paper towel.

Place skillet over medium-high heat until hot. Add onion, and sauté until tender. Add cranberries and next 5 ingredients; bring to a boil. Reduce heat, and simmer 3 to 4 minutes or until cranberries pop. Spoon over cutlets, and serve immediately. If desired, garnish with fresh sage sprigs and orange slices. Yield: 4 servings (218 calories per serving).

PROTEIN 27.5   FAT 4.1   (Saturated Fat 1.0)   CARBOHYDRATE 15.7
FIBER 0.5   CHOLESTEROL 68   IRON 1.6   SODIUM 295   CALCIUM 19

POACHED TURKEY BREAST WITH PESTO

1 pound boneless turkey breast, skinned
1 small onion, cut into ½-inch slices
3 tablespoons lemon juice
¼ teaspoon salt
1 bay leaf
4 peppercorns
Pesto
Roasted red pepper strips (optional)

Cut a piece of parchment paper long enough to cover a large saucepan, allowing 2 to 3 inches to extend over sides. Fold parchment into fourths; beginning at folded center, roll into a cone. Hold tip of cone over center of saucepan, allowing outer edge to extend beyond edge of saucepan. Trim parchment that extends from edge of saucepan. Cut ⅛ inch from tip of cone to form a vent. Unroll parchment, and set aside.

Place turkey in saucepan. Add onion and next 4 ingredients. Add enough water to cover turkey breast. Bring to a boil; immediately reduce heat to medium-low. Place prepared parchment paper over water (the circle should be just the area of the saucepan). Simmer 25 to 30 minutes or until done.

Remove and discard parchment paper. Remove turkey with a slotted spoon, and place on a serving platter. Reserve broth for another use. Spoon Pesto over turkey breast. Garnish with roasted red pepper strips, if desired. Yield: 4 servings (182 calories per serving).

Pesto

½ cup tightly packed fresh basil leaves
½ cup tightly packed fresh parsley leaves
¼ cup minced celery
1 tablespoon olive oil
1½ teaspoons capers, drained
1½ teaspoons red wine vinegar
1 clove garlic, minced
2 tablespoons turkey broth
1 tablespoon fresh lemon juice
⅛ teaspoon salt
Dash of freshly ground pepper

Position knife blade in food processor bowl; add first 7 ingredients. Process until finely chopped. Add turkey broth and lemon juice; process 10 minutes or until smooth. Stir in salt and pepper. Yield: ½ cup.

PROTEIN 27.5 FAT 5.2 (Saturated Fat 1.0) CARBOHYDRATE 5.2
FIBER 0.8 CHOLESTEROL 68 IRON 1.9 SODIUM 382 CALCIUM 39

Showcase the flavor of blackened tuna in Harbor Salad (page 190). Sugared walnuts add additional flavor to this main-dish salad.

Salads & Salad Dressings

GLAZED WALDORF SALAD

3 tablespoons lemon juice
3 tablespoons reduced-calorie apple spread
2 cups chopped Red Delicious apple
⅓ cup raisins
⅓ cup chopped celery
3 tablespoons finely chopped dry roasted cashews

Combine lemon juice and apple spread in a small saucepan; bring to a boil, stirring constantly. Remove from heat, and cool completely.

Combine apple and remaining ingredients in a small bowl. Pour apple spread mixture over apple mixture; toss gently to coat. Yield: 5 servings (103 calories per ½-cup serving).

PROTEIN 1.4   FAT 2.9   (Saturated Fat 0.6)   CARBOHYDRATE 20.4
FIBER 2.6   CHOLESTEROL 0   IRON 0.7   SODIUM 45   CALCIUM 15

FESTIVE CRANBERRY-PEAR SALAD

1¼ cups fresh cranberries
⅓ cup sugar
⅓ cup water
2 cups cubed fresh pear
½ cup diced celery
2 tablespoons minced walnuts
¼ teaspoon ground nutmeg
Dash of ground allspice
Lettuce leaves (optional)

Combine cranberries, sugar, and water in a small saucepan; bring to a boil. Cook over medium-high heat 6 minutes or until cranberries pop, stirring frequently. Remove from heat, and cool completely.

Combine cranberry mixture, pear, and next 4 ingredients in a medium bowl; stir gently. Serve on lettuce leaves, if desired. Yield: 6 servings (99 calories per ½-cup serving).

PROTEIN 0.9   FAT 1.6   (Saturated Fat 0.1)   CARBOHYDRATE 22.0
FIBER 1.9   CHOLESTEROL 0   IRON 0.3   SODIUM 11   CALCIUM 13

MAKE-AHEAD BERRY SALAD

2 envelopes unflavored gelatin
1 cup cold water
3 cups fresh raspberries
¼ cup plus 2 tablespoons frozen orange juice
    concentrate, thawed and undiluted
¼ cup honey
Vegetable cooking spray
Orange Cream Dressing
Additional fresh raspberries (optional)
Orange rind curls (optional)

Sprinkle gelatin over cold water in a small saucepan; let stand 1 minute. Cook over low heat, stirring constantly, until gelatin dissolves. Remove from heat. Combine gelatin mixture, 3 cups raspberries, orange juice concentrate, and honey in container of an electric blender; top with cover, and process until smooth.

Coat 8 (½-cup) molds with cooking spray. Spoon raspberry mixture evenly into molds. Cover and chill until firm. Unmold salads onto individual salad plates, and top each with 1 tablespoon Orange Cream Dressing. If desired, garnish with fresh raspberries and orange rind curls. Yield: 8 servings (122 calories per serving).

Orange Cream Dressing

2 tablespoons light process cream cheese product
½ cup marshmallow cream
1 tablespoon frozen orange juice concentrate,
    thawed and undiluted
¼ teaspoon grated orange rind

Beat cream cheese in a small bowl at medium speed of an electric mixer 2 to 3 minutes or until smooth. Add marshmallow cream, orange juice concentrate, and orange rind; stir well. Yield: ½ cup.

PROTEIN 2.9   FAT 1.2   (Saturated Fat 0.4)   CARBOHYDRATE 26.7
FIBER 4.1   CHOLESTEROL 2   IRON 0.4   SODIUM 25   CALCIUM 22

Sliced fresh fruits comprise refreshing Strawberry-Plum Salad Cups, a summertime salad.

STRAWBERRY-PLUM SALAD CUPS

1 (3-inch) vanilla bean, split lengthwise
2 tablespoons sugar
2 cups sliced fresh strawberries
2 medium-size fresh plums, pitted and
 thinly sliced
Crisp Salad Shells
Fresh mint sprigs (optional)

Crisp Salad Shells
1 tablespoon hot water
½ teaspoon vanilla extract
4 (6-inch) flour tortillas
1 tablespoon sugar
1 teaspoon ground cinnamon
Vegetable cooking spray

Scrape seeds from vanilla bean into a small bowl. Add sugar, stirring until combined. Place strawberries in a medium bowl; sprinkle sugar mixture over strawberries, and toss gently. Cover and chill strawberry mixture until sugar dissolves and mixture is thick. Stir in plum slices.

Place Crisp Salad Shells on individual salad plates; spoon strawberry mixture evenly into cups, using a slotted spoon. Garnish with fresh mint sprigs, if desired. Serve immediately. Yield: 4 servings (198 calories per serving).

Combine water and vanilla; set aside. Coat both sides of each tortilla with cooking spray, and brush with water mixture. Combine sugar and cinnamon; sprinkle over both sides of each tortilla. Place each in a 6-ounce custard cup, pressing gently in center to form a cup. Bake at 400° for 5 minutes or until lightly browned. Cool completely in custard cups. Yield: 4 salad shells.

PROTEIN 3.1 FAT 3.2 (Saturated Fat 0.6) CARBOHYDRATE 42.7
FIBER 3.8 CHOLESTEROL 0 IRON 1.2 SODIUM 1 CALCIUM 43

ICY HOT WATERMELON SALAD

2 cups seeded watermelon balls
2 tablespoons diced jicama
2 tablespoons canned chopped green chiles
2 tablespoons balsamic vinegar
1 teaspoon vegetable oil
¼ teaspoon crushed red pepper
⅛ teaspoon garlic powder
Green leaf lettuce (optional)

Combine watermelon, jicama, and green chiles in a medium bowl; toss gently.

Combine vinegar and next 3 ingredients; stir well. Pour over watermelon mixture; toss gently. Cover and chill 4 hours.

Line individual salad plates with leaf lettuce, if desired. Spoon watermelon mixture onto plates, using a slotted spoon. Yield: 4 servings (45 calories per ½-cup serving).

PROTEIN 0.8   FAT 1.6   (Saturated Fat 0.4)   CARBOHYDRATE 8.0
FIBER 0.7   CHOLESTEROL 0   IRON 0.3   SODIUM 16   CALCIUM 9

POPPY SEED FRUIT SALAD

1 banana, peeled and cut into
   ¼-inch-thick slices
¼ cup unsweetened orange juice
1 tablespoon sugar
2 tablespoons frozen apple juice concentrate,
   thawed and undiluted
2 tablespoons lemon juice
1 teaspoon poppy seeds
¼ teaspoon almond extract
2 cups seeded, cubed watermelon
2 cups cubed cantaloupe
2 cups strawberries, sliced
6 green leaf lettuce leaves
¼ cup sliced almonds, toasted

Combine first 7 ingredients in a large bowl, and toss gently. Add cubed watermelon, cubed cantaloupe, and sliced strawberries; toss gently. Cover mixture and chill at least 2 hours.

To serve, toss fruit mixture gently, and spoon onto individual lettuce-lined salad plates, using a slotted spoon. Sprinkle with almonds, and serve immediately. Yield: 6 servings (109 calories per 1-cup serving).

PROTEIN 2.1   FAT 2.1   (Saturated Fat 0.4)   CARBOHYDRATE 22.8
FIBER 3.1   CHOLESTEROL 0   IRON 0.7   SODIUM 10   CALCIUM 36

ORIENTAL VEGETABLE SALAD

¾ pound fresh asparagus
1 ounce cellophane noodles, uncooked
6 dried porcini mushrooms
2 medium carrots, cut into julienne strips
1 cup fresh bean sprouts
2 tablespoons chopped water chestnuts
1 tablespoon sugar
1 teaspoon dry mustard
¼ teaspoon salt
3 tablespoons white wine vinegar
1½ tablespoons low-sodium soy sauce
2 teaspoons dark sesame oil
8 romaine lettuce leaves

Snap off tough ends of asparagus. Remove scales from spears with a knife or vegetable peeler, if desired. Cut asparagus into 1-inch pieces. Blanch asparagus in boiling water 30 seconds. Drain; rinse under cold water until cool. Set aside.

Combine noodles and mushrooms in boiling water to cover; let stand 15 minutes or until soft. Drain well. Slice mushrooms into thin strips. Combine noodles, mushrooms, asparagus, carrot, bean sprouts, and water chestnuts; toss well. Cover vegetable mixture, and chill thoroughly.

Combine sugar and next 5 ingredients in a small bowl, stirring well. Pour over vegetable mixture; toss gently to combine. Spoon onto individual lettuce-lined salad plates. Serve immediately. Yield: 8 servings (79 calories per ½-cup serving).

PROTEIN 2.8   FAT 1.5   (Saturated Fat 0.2)   CARBOHYDRATE 13.8
FIBER 2.4   CHOLESTEROL 0   IRON 1.0   SODIUM 197   CALCIUM 28

SIMPLE SESAME-BEAN SALAD

1 pound fresh green beans
1 teaspoon vegetable oil
2 cloves garlic, minced
½ teaspoon crushed red pepper
3 tablespoons lemon juice
¼ teaspoon salt
¼ teaspoon pepper
1 tablespoon sesame seeds, toasted

Wash beans; trim ends, and remove strings. Cook, covered, in boiling water 5 minutes or until crisp-tender. Drain; rinse under cold water, and drain.

Heat oil in a small nonstick skillet over medium-high heat. Add minced garlic and red pepper; sauté until garlic is browned. Remove mixture from heat, and let cool.

Combine garlic mixture, lemon juice, salt, and pepper; stir well. Combine beans, lemon juice mixture, and sesame seeds in a medium bowl, tossing well. Cover and chill at least 1 hour. Yield: 6 servings (42 calories per ½-cup serving).

PROTEIN 1.9 FAT 1.7 (Saturated Fat 0.3) CARBOHYDRATE 6.5
FIBER 1.6 CHOLESTEROL 0 IRON 0.9 SODIUM 103 CALCIUM 32

MARINATED GARDEN SALAD

2 cups fresh cut green beans
2 cups cauliflower flowerets
2 cups sliced carrot
1 cup chopped sweet red pepper
1 medium onion, thinly sliced
2 banana peppers, cut lengthwise in ¼-inch-wide strips
3 cloves garlic, sliced
2 cups water
1½ cups tarragon vinegar
¼ cup sugar
2 teaspoons mixed pickling spice
½ teaspoon salt
½ teaspoon dried whole thyme
½ teaspoon crushed red pepper

Arrange green beans in a vegetable steamer over boiling water; cover and steam 10 minutes. Add cauliflower, carrot, sweet red pepper, onion, banana pepper, and garlic; cover and steam an additional 5 to 7 minutes or until vegetables are crisp-tender. Plunge vegetables immediately into cold water until cool; drain.

Combine 2 cups water and remaining ingredients in a large bowl. Add vegetables, and toss well. Cover and marinate in refrigerator 8 hours, stirring occasionally. Serve with a slotted spoon. Yield: 16 servings (37 calories per ½-cup serving).

PROTEIN 1.1 FAT 0.2 (Saturated Fat 0) CARBOHYDRATE 8.9
FIBER 1.6 CHOLESTEROL 0 IRON 0.8 SODIUM 84 CALCIUM 21

MINTED CARROT SALAD

4 medium carrots, cut in julienne strips
1 cup red seedless grapes, halved
3 tablespoons fresh lime juice
2 tablespoons sugar
1 tablespoon minced fresh mint
¼ teaspoon vanilla extract

Arrange carrot strips in a vegetable steamer over boiling water. Cover and steam 5 minutes or until crisp-tender. Rinse under cold water until cool; drain well.

Combine carrot strips and grapes in a medium bowl. Combine lime juice and remaining ingredients, stirring gently until sugar dissolves. Pour over carrot mixture, and toss gently. Cover and chill mixture at least 2 hours, stirring occasionally. Serve salad with a slotted spoon. Yield: 6 servings (56 calories per ½-cup serving).

PROTEIN 0.7 FAT 0.2 (Saturated Fat 0.1) CARBOHYDRATE 14.4
FIBER 1.7 CHOLESTEROL 0 IRON 0.3 SODIUM 16 CALCIUM 18

FESTIVAL SLAW

3 cups shredded cabbage
1 cup shredded red cabbage
1 cup shredded carrot
¼ cup finely chopped onion
¼ cup chopped dry roasted cashews
¼ cup white wine vinegar
¼ cup unsweetened pineapple juice
1 tablespoon Dijon mustard
⅛ teaspoon salt
⅛ teaspoon pepper

Combine cabbage, red cabbage, carrot, onion, and cashews in a medium bowl, toss gently.

Combine vinegar and remaining ingredients; stir well. Add to cabbage mixture, and toss gently. Cover and chill thoroughly. Yield: 8 servings (43 calories per ½-cup serving).

PROTEIN 1.1   FAT 1.9   (Saturated Fat 0.3)   CARBOHYDRATE 5.8
FIBER 1.4   CHOLESTEROL 0   IRON 0.5   SODIUM 124   CALCIUM 22

ROASTED GARLIC POTATO SALAD

3 whole heads garlic
Butter-flavored vegetable cooking spray
4 cups cooked, cubed potato
½ cup chopped sweet red pepper
2 tablespoons white wine vinegar
2 tablespoons lemon juice
1 tablespoon low-sodium soy sauce
2 teaspoons vegetable oil
1½ teaspoons water
¼ teaspoon salt
⅛ teaspoon pepper
Dash of ground red pepper

Cut stem end off each head of garlic, exposing individual cloves. Place each garlic head on a square of aluminum foil to make individual bundles. Spray each head thoroughly with cooking spray. Fold foil edges over, and wrap securely; place bundles on a baking sheet. Bake at 350° for 25 minutes. Loosen foil, and bake an additional 8 to 10 minutes or until garlic is soft. Remove from oven, and let garlic cool completely. Remove and discard papery skin from garlic. Scoop out soft garlic with a small spoon, and set aside.

Place potato and sweet red pepper in a large bowl. Combine garlic, vinegar, and remaining ingredients, stirring well with a wire whisk. Pour over potato mixture; toss gently. Cover and chill mixture thoroughly. Yield: 8 servings (109 calories per ½-cup serving).

PROTEIN 2.6   FAT 1.5   (Saturated Fat 0.3)   CARBOHYDRATE 22.1
FIBER 1.6   CHOLESTEROL 0   IRON 0.7   SODIUM 129   CALCIUM 34

MIXED GREEN SALAD WITH RASPBERRY VINAIGRETTE

2 cups torn romaine lettuce
2 cups torn Boston lettuce
1 cup torn arugula
1 cup torn watercress
1 cup torn red leaf lettuce
1 cup fresh raspberries
⅔ cup canned low-sodium chicken broth, undiluted
3 tablespoons raspberry vinegar
1 teaspoon Dijon mustard
½ teaspoon sugar
⅛ teaspoon pepper

Combine first 6 ingredients in a large bowl; toss gently. Cover and chill.

Combine chicken broth, vinegar, mustard, sugar, and pepper in a jar. Cover tightly, and shake vigorously; chill thoroughly.

Pour vinegar mixture over lettuce mixture, and toss gently. Serve immediately. Yield: 8 servings (18 calories per 1-cup serving).

PROTEIN 0.8   FAT 0.2   (Saturated Fat 0)   CARBOHYDRATE 3.4
FIBER 1.7   CHOLESTEROL 0   IRON 0.4   SODIUM 24   CALCIUM 25

CAESAR SALAD

4 (½-inch-thick) slices French bread
Butter-flavored vegetable cooking spray
½ teaspoon garlic powder
6 cups torn romaine lettuce
2 tablespoons freshly grated Parmesan cheese
3½ tablespoons fresh lemon juice
1½ tablespoons water
1 tablespoon low-sodium Worcestershire sauce
2 teaspoons olive oil
¼ teaspoon garlic powder
6 anchovies, cut in half crosswise
Dash of freshly ground pepper

Cut bread into ½-inch cubes; place cubes on a baking sheet. Coat cubes on all sides with cooking spray; sprinkle with ½ teaspoon garlic powder. Broil 3 inches from heat until browned on all sides, turning frequently.

Combine lettuce and cheese in a large bowl. Combine lemon juice, water, Worcestershire, olive oil, and ¼ teaspoon garlic powder; stir with a wire whisk until blended. Pour over salad; toss gently to coat.

Arrange 1½ cups lettuce mixture on each individual salad plate, and top each with 3 anchovy halves. Sprinkle with toasted bread cubes and freshly ground pepper. Serve immediately. Yield: 4 servings (114 calories per serving).

PROTEIN 5.2 FAT 4.4 (Saturated Fat 1.1) CARBOHYDRATE 13.4
FIBER 1.3 CHOLESTEROL 3 IRON 1.2 SODIUM 347 CALCIUM 80

WILTED SPINACH-CHEESE SALAD

½ pound fresh spinach
1 cup sliced fresh strawberries
2 ounces reduced-fat Cheddar cheese, cut into
　　½-inch cubes
Sweet-Hot Dressing

Remove and discard stems from spinach; wash leaves thoroughly, and pat dry. Tear spinach into bite-size pieces. Combine spinach, strawberries, and cheese in a large bowl. Pour Sweet-Hot Dressing over salad, and toss gently. Serve immediately. Yield: 8 servings (45 calories per 1-cup serving).

Sweet-Hot Dressing

2 teaspoons cornstarch
¼ cup water
⅔ cup unsweetened apple juice
⅓ cup cider vinegar
1 tablespoon brown sugar
1 teaspoon poppy seeds
1 teaspoon Dijon mustard

Combine cornstarch and water in a small non-aluminum saucepan, stirring until smooth. Stir in apple juice and remaining ingredients. Bring to a boil, and cook 1 minute, stirring constantly. Yield: 1⅓ cups.

PROTEIN 2.7 FAT 0.9 (Saturated Fat 0.3) CARBOHYDRATE 7.4
FIBER 1.7 CHOLESTEROL 4 IRON 1.1 SODIUM 153 CALCIUM 89

LEMON-SAFFRON RICE MOLDS

2 tablespoons chopped fresh parsley
2 tablespoons diced pimiento
3 tablespoons fresh lemon juice
2 tablespoons nonfat mayonnaise
½ teaspoon grated lemon rind
¼ teaspoon salt
⅛ teaspoon ground white pepper
⅛ teaspoon saffron
3 cups cooked long-grain rice (cooked without
　　salt or fat)
Vegetable cooking spray
6 Boston lettuce leaves

Combine first 8 ingredients in a medium bowl; stir well. Add rice, and stir well.

Coat 6 (½-cup) molds with cooking spray. Spoon mixture into molds, packing gently with the back of a spoon. Cover and chill at least 2 hours. Unmold salads onto individual lettuce-lined salad plates. Yield: 6 serving (140 calories per serving).

PROTEIN 3.0 FAT 0.5 (Saturated Fat 0.1) CARBOHYDRATE 30.3
FIBER 0.7 CHOLESTEROL 0 IRON 1.4 SODIUM 166 CALCIUM 15

Arrange Cold Couscous and Cucumber Salad on individual salad plates. Dillweed enhances the creamy yogurt-based dressing.

COLD COUSCOUS AND CUCUMBER SALAD

¼ cup sugar
¼ cup white wine vinegar
¼ teaspoon salt
1 cup seeded, diced cucumber
1 cup water
1 cup couscous, uncooked
1 teaspoon dried whole dillweed
40 Belgian endive leaves (about 4 heads)
16 tomato slices (¼ inch thick)
Yogurt Dressing
Fresh dillweed sprigs (optional)

Combine sugar, vinegar, and salt in a small bowl; stir well. Add cucumber, and toss well. Cover and chill.

Bring water to a boil in a medium saucepan; remove from heat. Add couscous; cover and let stand 5 minutes or until couscous is tender and liquid is absorbed.

Fluff couscous with a fork, and transfer to a medium bowl. Stir in cucumber mixture and dillweed. Cover and chill thoroughly.

Place 5 endive leaves and 2 tomato slices on each individual salad plate. Spoon chilled couscous mixture evenly over tomato and endive. Drizzle 2 tablespoons Yogurt Dressing evenly over each salad. Garnish salads with fresh dillweed sprigs, if desired. Serve salads immediately. Yield: 8 servings (142 calories per serving).

Yogurt Dressing

½ cup plain nonfat yogurt
½ cup nonfat sour cream
¼ teaspoon dried whole dillweed
⅛ teaspoon salt

Combine yogurt, sour cream, dillweed, and salt in a small bowl, stirring well. Yield: 1 cup.

PROTEIN 5.5 FAT 0.2 (Saturated Fat 0.1) CARBOHYDRATE 29.3
FIBER 1.3 CHOLESTEROL 0 IRON 0.9 SODIUM 138 CALCIUM 62

DILLED PASTA SALAD

6½ ounces corkscrew macaroni (about 2 cups),
   uncooked
¼ pound fresh snow pea pods, trimmed
1 cup broccoli flowerets
1 cup cherry tomato halves
½ cup sweet yellow pepper strips
½ cup evaporated skimmed milk
2 tablespoons grated onion
1 tablespoon chopped fresh dillweed
3 tablespoons white wine vinegar
2 teaspoons vegetable oil
½ teaspoon dry mustard
¼ teaspoon salt
⅛ teaspoon ground white pepper

Cook pasta according to package directions, omitting salt and fat. Drain; rinse under cold water, and drain. Place in a large bowl.

Blanch snow peas and broccoli in boiling water 30 seconds or until crisp-tender. Drain and rinse under cold water until cool. Drain. Add snow peas, broccoli, tomato halves, and yellow pepper to pasta, and toss gently.

Combine milk and remaining ingredients in a jar; cover tightly, and shake vigorously. Pour over pasta mixture; toss gently. Cover and chill thoroughly. Yield: 6 servings (166 calories per 1-cup serving).

PROTEIN 6.8 FAT 2.3 (Saturated Fat 0.4) CARBOHYDRATE 29.4
FIBER 1.9 CHOLESTEROL 1 IRON 2.0 SODIUM 131 CALCIUM 88

TEXAS CAVIAR SALAD

1 (10-ounce) package frozen black-eyed peas
2 cups cooked rice (cooked without salt or fat)
2 cups seeded, coarsely chopped tomato
¼ cup chopped celery
2 tablespoons chopped fresh parsley
2½ tablespoons white wine vinegar
2 teaspoons vegetable oil
2 teaspoons water
½ teaspoon curry powder
½ teaspoon chili powder
¼ teaspoon salt
¼ teaspoon pepper
¼ teaspoon hot sauce
⅛ teaspoon ground cumin

Cook black-eyed peas according to package directions, omitting salt and fat. Drain; rinse under cold water, and drain. Combine peas, rice, tomato, celery, and parsley in a large bowl.

Combine vinegar and remaining ingredients in a small bowl; stir with a wire whisk until blended. Pour over vegetable mixture; toss gently. Cover and chill at least 2 hours. Yield: 12 servings (88 calories per ½-cup serving).

PROTEIN 3.3 FAT 1.1 (Saturated Fat 0.2) CARBOHYDRATE 16.4
FIBER 1.0 CHOLESTEROL 0 IRON 1.1 SODIUM 57 CALCIUM 14

 HEARTENING FITNESS CHECK
It's been weeks since you started exercising. Brisk walking, aerobic dancing, or whatever activity you've chosen has done a lot to tone your muscles. You feel better, too. But how much is the heart benefiting from all this effort?

By taking your pulse 5 minutes into your exercise routine and then again 1 minute after you stop exercising, you can find out. Pulse rate is proportional to the heart's fitness level. The stronger the heart, the slower it beats and the more quickly it recovers from bursts of activity. Make sure to count the pulse for only 6 seconds each time; multiply that number by 10. If the difference is more than 30 beats, you're out of shape.

South-of-the-border flavors unite in Layered Nacho Salad, a main-dish salad.

LAYERED NACHO SALAD

6 (8-inch) corn tortillas
Vegetable cooking spray
⅓ cup chopped onion
2 (16-ounce) cans red kidney beans, drained
2 pickled jalapeño peppers, seeded and chopped
¼ cup water
1 small ripe avocado (about ½ pound), peeled and
   cut into chunks
½ cup seeded, chopped tomato
2 tablespoons chopped onion
2 tablespoons lime juice
¼ teaspoon salt
3 cups finely shredded romaine lettuce
¼ cup (1 ounce) finely shredded reduced-fat
   Cheddar cheese
3 radishes, thinly sliced
Southwestern Vinaigrette

Place tortillas on a baking sheet coated with cooking spray. Bake at 350° for 6 minutes; turn tortillas over, and bake an additional 6 minutes or until crisp. Cool completely.

Coat a medium saucepan with cooking spray; place over medium-high heat until hot. Add ⅓ cup chopped onion; sauté until tender. Stir in kidney beans, jalapeño pepper, and water. Reduce heat; cook, uncovered, 15 minutes or until mixture becomes a thick paste, stirring occasionally and mashing beans with a wooden spoon. Set aside.

Place avocado in container of an electric blender; top with cover, and process until smooth. Stir in tomato and next 3 ingredients. Set aside.

Place 1 tortilla on each individual serving plate; top each with ½ cup lettuce. Spoon bean mixture evenly over lettuce; top evenly with avocado mixture. Sprinkle

2 teaspoons cheese over each; top with radish. Serve with Southwestern Vinaigrette. Yield: 6 servings (188 calories per serving).

Southwestern Vinaigrette

½ cup no-salt-added mild salsa
2 tablespoons minced fresh cilantro
3 tablespoons lime juice
1 tablespoon white wine vinegar
1 tablespoon Dijon mustard
¼ teaspoon chili powder
¼ teaspoon pepper

Combine all ingredients in a small bowl, stirring well with a wire whisk. Cover and chill at least 2 hours. Yield: ¾ cup plus 2 tablespoons.

PROTEIN 12.6 FAT 6.2 (Saturated Fat 1.2) CARBOHYDRATE 38.1
FIBER 6.4 CHOLESTEROL 3 IRON 4.8 SODIUM 300 CALCIUM 122

MAKING FRESH HERBS LAST

The shelf life of fresh herbs can be prolonged by using special storage, freezing, and drying techniques. Cold storage: Clean parsley, sage, or cilantro, and place the herb in a glass jar with a small amount of water. Cover tightly and refrigerate, changing the water every five days. This can extend the shelf life from just days to three to four weeks.

Freezer storage: Freeze herbs whole or chopped. For whole stems, blanch for 5 to 10 seconds in boiling water. Place herbs on paper towels, and allow them to dry thoroughly. Wrap tightly in heavy-duty aluminum foil and freeze. For chopped herbs, clean and dry thoroughly and place in plastic freezer bags.

Dry storage: Wash herbs, leaving stems intact. Shake dry. Bundle the stems together with string. Place bundles in a paper sack that has small slits cut into the sides. Tie the sack shut, and hang it in an area that has good circulation. The herbs will air dry in about a week. Before removing the herbs from the sack, carefully roll the sack on a counter to separate the leaves from the stems. Bottle the crumbled leaves in an airtight container and use within 6 to 12 months.

FAST FIRE STEAK SALAD

1 (1-pound) lean flank steak
1 tablespoon brown sugar
3 tablespoons lemon juice
3 tablespoons reduced-sodium soy sauce
½ teaspoon garlic powder
1 tablespoon cracked pepper
Vegetable cooking spray
6 romaine lettuce leaves
1 (10¼-ounce) can mandarin oranges in water, drained
2 cups fresh bean sprouts
18 thin cucumber slices
Tangy Horseradish Dressing

Trim fat from steak. Place steak in a large zip-top heavy-duty plastic bag. Combine brown sugar, lemon juice, soy sauce, and garlic powder; pour over steak. Seal bag securely. Place bag in a large bowl; marinate steak in refrigerator 1 hour.

Remove steak from marinade; discard marinade. Press cracked pepper onto one side of steak. Coat grill rack with cooking spray; place on grill over medium-hot coals. Place steak on rack, and cook 5 to 6 minutes on each side or to desired degree of doneness. Remove steak from grill, and let stand 5 minutes. Slice steak diagonally across grain into ¼-inch-thick slices.

Place 1 lettuce leaf on each of 6 individual salad plates. Arrange steak, orange sections, bean sprouts, and cucumber on lettuce leaves. Drizzle Tangy Horseradish Dressing evenly over salads. Serve immediately. Yield: 6 servings (217 calories per serving).

Tangy Horseradish Dressing

¾ cup commercial nonfat Catalina dressing
3 tablespoons prepared horseradish
2 tablespoons lemon juice
¼ teaspoon ground red pepper

Combine all ingredients in a small bowl; stir with a wire whisk until well blended. Cover and chill thoroughly. Yield: 1 cup plus 1 tablespoon.

PROTEIN 16.9 FAT 9.0 (Saturated Fat 3.8) CARBOHYDRATE 18.4
FIBER 1.3 CHOLESTEROL 41 IRON 3.5 SODIUM 465 CALCIUM 34

SHRIMP AND ARTICHOKE SALAD

4 medium artichokes (about 2 pounds)
1 lemon wedge
1¼ pounds medium-size unpeeled fresh shrimp
4 cups water
1 ancho chile
1 cup boiling water
½ cup nonfat mayonnaise
⅓ cup soft tofu
1½ teaspoons lime juice
¼ teaspoon olive oil
1 clove garlic, minced
Lemon slices (optional)

Wash artichokes by plunging up and down in cold water. Cut off stem ends; trim about ½ inch from top of each artichoke. Remove any loose bottom leaves. Rub top of each artichoke with lemon wedge to prevent discoloration.

Arrange artichokes in a vegetable steamer over boiling water. Cover and steam 25 minutes or until almost tender. Drain; let cool. Spread leaves apart; scrape out the fuzzy thistle center (choke) with a spoon and discard. Chill artichokes thoroughly.

Peel and devein shrimp, leaving tails intact. Bring 4 cups water to a boil; add shrimp, and cook 3 to 5 minutes or until done. Drain well; rinse with cold water. Chill.

Place ancho chile in boiling water. Cover and let stand 1 hour or until softened. Drain; remove and discard stem and seeds. Chop chile, and place in container of an electric blender or food processor. Add mayonnaise and next 4 ingredients; top with cover, and process until mixture is smooth, scraping sides of container occasionally. Cover and chill at least 30 minutes.

Place an artichoke on each of 4 individual serving plates. Spoon chilled chile mixture evenly into artichoke cavities. Arrange shrimp around top of each artichoke. Garnish with lemon slices, if desired. Serve immediately. Yield: 4 servings (163 calories per serving).

PROTEIN 20.3 FAT 1.9 (Saturated Fat 0.3) CARBOHYDRATE 17.9
FIBER 4.5 CHOLESTEROL 155 IRON 4.2 SODIUM 428 CALCIUM 95

HARBOR SALAD

2 tablespoons sugar
2 tablespoons finely chopped walnuts
Vegetable cooking spray
1 teaspoon paprika
½ teaspoon ground cumin
½ teaspoon chili powder
¼ teaspoon salt
¼ teaspoon ground red pepper
3 (4-ounce) tuna steaks
1 cup torn romaine lettuce
1 cup torn leaf lettuce
1 cup torn iceberg lettuce
¼ cup sliced green onions
8 cherry tomatoes, quartered
Creamy Dressing

Sprinkle sugar in an even layer in a small saucepan; place over medium heat. Cook, stirring constantly, until sugar melts and syrup is light brown. Stir in walnuts; cook until syrup becomes caramel colored. Immediately pour mixture out onto a piece of aluminum foil coated with cooking spray. Let cool completely; crush into small pieces. Set aside.

Combine paprika and next 4 ingredients. Rub mixture on both sides of each steak. Place a cast-iron skillet over medium-high heat until hot. Add steaks; and cook 3 minutes on each side or until fish flakes easily when tested with a fork. Remove from heat, and flake fish into bite-size pieces.

Place greens in a bowl. Add fish, green onions, and tomatoes; toss gently. Sprinkle with sugared walnuts. Drizzle with Creamy Dressing, and serve immediately. Yield: 4 servings (227 calories per serving).

Creamy Dressing

½ cup nonfat sour cream
¼ cup plain nonfat yogurt
1 tablespoon lemon juice

Combine all ingredients in a small bowl, stirring well. Yield: ¾ cup.

PROTEIN 25.0 FAT 7.7 (Saturated Fat 1.3) CARBOHYDRATE 14.0
FIBER 1.7 CHOLESTEROL 33 IRON 2.0 SODIUM 222 CALCIUM 86

FRENCH GARLIC VINAIGRETTE

½ cup no-salt-added tomato sauce
⅓ cup no-salt-added tomato juice
2 tablespoons chopped fresh parsley
2 tablespoons red wine vinegar
2 tablespoons lemon juice
1 tablespoon olive oil
1 tablespoon Dijon mustard
3 cloves garlic, minced

Combine all ingredients in a small jar; cover tightly, and shake vigorously to blend. Cover and refrigerate at least 8 hours. Serve with salad greens. Yield: 1¼ cups (11 calories per tablespoon).

PROTEIN 0.1   FAT 0.7   (Saturated Fat 0.1)   CARBOHYDRATE 1.0
FIBER 0   CHOLESTEROL 0   IRON 0   SODIUM 24   CALCIUM 1

CREAMY BUTTERMILK DRESSING

½ cup plus 1 tablespoon nonfat buttermilk
¼ cup plus 1 tablespoon nonfat mayonnaise
1 tablespoon grated onion
¼ to ½ teaspoon pepper
¼ teaspoon salt
¼ teaspoon garlic powder
¼ teaspoon dried whole thyme
Dash of curry powder

Combine all ingredients in a small bowl, stirring well with a wire whisk. Cover and chill thoroughly. Serve with salad greens or fresh raw vegetables. Yield: 1 cup (8 calories per tablespoon).

PROTEIN 0.4   FAT 0   (Saturated Fat 0)   CARBOHYDRATE 1.6
FIBER 0   CHOLESTEROL 0   IRON 0   SODIUM 106   CALCIUM 12

TART MUSTARD DRESSING

1 egg
1 egg white
3 tablespoons sugar
1 teaspoon dry mustard
¼ teaspoon salt
⅛ teaspoon ground red pepper
⅓ cup white wine vinegar
1 tablespoon reduced-calorie margarine
2 teaspoons coarse-grained mustard

Combine first 6 ingredients in a small saucepan; beat at high speed of an electric mixer 3 minutes. Add vinegar, and beat just until blended. Bring to a boil; cook 1 minute, stirring constantly with a wire whisk.
Remove from heat; stir in margarine and mustard. Cover and chill thoroughly. Serve with salad greens or steamed fresh vegetables. Yield: ¾ cup (27 calories per tablespoon).

PROTEIN 0.9   FAT 1.1   (Saturated Fat 0.2)   CARBOHYDRATE 3.3
FIBER 0   CHOLESTEROL 18   IRON 0.1   SODIUM 80   CALCIUM 4

CHEESE-HERB DRESSING

3 tablespoons light process cream cheese
    product, softened
2 tablespoons cider vinegar
½ cup plus 1 tablespoon plain nonfat
    yogurt
1 tablespoon chopped fresh
    parsley
1 teaspoon chopped fresh chives
¼ teaspoon celery seeds
¼ teaspoon salt
1 (2-ounce) jar diced pimiento,
    drained

Combine cream cheese and vinegar in a small bowl, stirring until smooth. Add yogurt, parsley, chives, celery seeds, and salt; stir well. Stir in pimiento. Serve with salad greens. Yield: 1 cup (11 calories per tablespoon).

PROTEIN 0.8   FAT 0.5   (Saturated Fat 0.3)   CARBOHYDRATE 1.0
FIBER 0   CHOLESTEROL 2   IRON 0.1   SODIUM 58   CALCIUM 21

GREEN GODDESS DRESSING

½ cup light process cream cheese product,
    softened
⅔ cup plain nonfat yogurt
¼ cup tarragon vinegar
2 teaspoons anchovy paste
2 cloves garlic, minced
¼ teaspoon pepper
2 tablespoons minced green onions

    Beat cream cheese in a bowl at medium speed of
an electric mixer until smooth. Add yogurt and next
4 ingredients, beating until smooth. Stir in green
onions. Cover and chill thoroughly. Serve with salad
greens. Yield: 1½ cups plus 2 tablespoons (14 calories per tablespoon).

PROTEIN 0.9 FAT 0.8 (Saturated Fat 0.4) CARBOHYDRATE 0.9
FIBER 0 CHOLESTEROL 3 IRON 0 SODIUM 82 CALCIUM 18

CITRUS DRESSING

1 tablespoon cornstarch
⅔ cup orange juice, divided
1 tablespoon lime juice
2 tablespoons honey
⅛ teaspoon ground cinnamon
¾ cup vanilla low-fat frozen yogurt, softened

    Combine cornstarch and 2 tablespoons orange juice
in a small saucepan; stir until smooth. Add remaining orange juice, lime juice, honey, and cinnamon;
stir well. Cook over medium heat, stirring frequently,
until thickened and bubbly. Remove from heat; transfer
mixture to a small bowl. Cover and chill thoroughly.
    To serve, stir in softened yogurt. Serve with fresh
fruit salad. Yield: 1½ cups (15 calories per serving).

PROTEIN 0.2 FAT 0.1 (Saturated Fat 0.1) CARBOHYDRATE 3.5
FIBER 0 CHOLESTEROL 1 IRON 0 SODIUM 2 CALCIUM 6

PEANUT BUTTER FRUIT DRESSING

1 small banana, peeled and sliced
1 tablespoon lemon juice
2 tablespoons honey
2 tablespoons creamy peanut butter
½ cup vanilla low-fat yogurt

    Combine banana and lemon juice in container of
an electric blender; top with cover, and process until smooth. Add honey and peanut butter; process until
blended. Transfer to a small bowl; stir in yogurt. Cover
and chill thoroughly. Serve with fresh fruit salad. Yield:
1 cup (33 calories per tablespoon).

PROTEIN 1.0 FAT 1.2 (Saturated Fat 0.2) CARBOHYDRATE 5.2
FIBER 0.3 CHOLESTEROL 0 IRON 0.1 SODIUM 15 CALCIUM 13

COOL PINEAPPLE DRESSING

½ cup pineapple low-fat yogurt
3 tablespoons frozen pineapple juice concentrate,
    thawed and undiluted
1 tablespoon nonfat mayonnaise
Dash of ground nutmeg

    Combine all ingredients in a small bowl, stirring
well with a wire whisk. Cover and chill thoroughly.
Serve with fresh fruit salad. Yield: ¾ cup (19 calories
per tablespoon).

PROTEIN 0.4 FAT 0.1 (Saturated Fat 0.1) CARBOHYDRATE 4.0
FIBER 0 CHOLESTEROL 0 IRON 0 SODIUM 21 CALCIUM 15

---

*Caesar Steak Sandwiches (page 198)
are intriguing sandwiches made with
lavash or Armenian cracker bread.*

Sandwiches & Snacks

APPLE BREAKFAST SANDWICHES

⅓ cup grated apple
½ cup light process cream cheese product
2 tablespoons crunchy peanut butter
1½ tablespoons apple butter
⅛ teaspoon ground cinnamon
12 (1-ounce) slices raisin bread, toasted

Press apple dry between layers of paper towels; set apple aside.

Beat cream cheese in a medium bowl at medium speed of an electric mixer until light and fluffy. Add peanut butter, apple butter, and cinnamon; beat well. Stir in apple.

Spread apple mixture evenly over each of 6 bread slices; top with remaining bread slices. Cut sandwiches in half. Yield: 6 servings (236 calories per serving).

PROTEIN 7.2 FAT 7.4 (Saturated Fat 2.7) CARBOHYDRATE 36.2
FIBER 2.6 CHOLESTEROL 13 IRON 0.9 SODIUM 338 CALCIUM 69

PEAR AND BRIE SANDWICHES

1 tablespoon country-style Dijon mustard
1 teaspoon honey
4 (½-ounce) slices pumpernickel bread, toasted
6 ounces Brie cheese, sliced
1 medium pear, thinly sliced
½ cup alfalfa sprouts

Combine mustard and honey; spread 1 teaspoon mustard mixture on each bread slice. Top evenly with cheese. Broil 5½ inches from heat 2 minutes or until cheese melts.

Top evenly with pear slices and alfalfa sprouts, and serve immediately. Yield: 4 servings (214 calories per serving).

PROTEIN 11.0 FAT 12.4 (Saturated Fat 7.4) CARBOHYDRATE 16.2
FIBER 2.2 CHOLESTEROL 43 IRON 0.8 SODIUM 385 CALCIUM 98

DOES SPOT REDUCING WORK?

Would you like to trim weight off just your hips, your thighs, or around your middle? Forget about spot reducing schemes. They may be advertised as a way to melt away fat from a particular area, but that's a biologically impossible feat. In a study of college students, exercises geared toward trimming thighs, hips, and stomachs were no more effective at reducing fat in these areas than just general exercise.

It's true that exercise can tone the muscles of the mid-section, thighs, and hips. But that doesn't mean fat stores will disappear or shift to a new location. The only way to get rid of excess fat is to eat less and exercise more. Fat typically "melts" away from all over the body no matter what strenuous exercise you choose. Fortunately, the areas of greatest fat concentration (hips, thighs, midriffs) are often the first place to show that loss.

TOASTED MOZZARELLA SANDWICHES WITH MARINARA SAUCE

Vegetable cooking spray
¼ cup chopped onion
1 clove garlic, minced
2 teaspoons minced fresh parsley
¼ teaspoon dried whole oregano
¼ teaspoon dried whole thyme
⅛ teaspoon salt
Dash of freshly ground pepper
½ (14½-ounce) can no-salt-added whole tomatoes, undrained and chopped
¼ cup Burgundy or other dry red wine
¼ cup water
1½ tablespoons no-salt-added tomato paste
1 bay leaf
½ cup frozen egg substitute, thawed
½ cup skim milk
8 (1-ounce) slices part-skim mozzarella cheese
16 (½-ounce) slices French bread
¾ cup finely crushed shredded whole wheat cereal biscuits

Toasted Mozzarella Sandwiches with Marinara Sauce oozes with exceptional flavor.

Coat a small saucepan with cooking spray; place over medium-high heat until hot. Add onion and garlic; sauté until tender. Add parsley and next 4 ingredients; cook 30 seconds, stirring constantly. Add tomato, wine, water, tomato paste, and bay leaf, stirring to combine. Reduce heat, and simmer, uncovered, 20 to 30 minutes or until slightly thickened, stirring frequently. Remove and discard bay leaf. Set aside.

Combine egg substitute and milk in a shallow bowl, beating well. Set aside.

Place 1 cheese slice on each of 8 bread slices; top with remaining 8 bread slices.

Carefully dip sandwiches into egg substitute mixture, allowing excess to drip off. Sprinkle each sandwich with crushed cereal.

Place sandwiches on a large baking sheet coated with cooking spray. Bake at 400° for 3 minutes; turn sandwiches, and bake an additional 4 to 6 minutes or until crisp and golden. Serve immediately with warm marinara sauce. Yield: 8 servings (213 calories per serving).

PROTEIN 12.9   FAT 5.5   (Saturated Fat 3.1)   CARBOHYDRATE 27.5
FIBER 1.7   CHOLESTEROL 18   IRON 1.7   SODIUM 370   CALCIUM 236

EGGPLANT TURNOVERS

Vegetable cooking spray
1 (1-pound) eggplant, peeled and cut into
   ½-inch slices
½ cup finely chopped plum tomato
3 tablespoons chopped green pepper
3 tablespoons chopped purple onion
2 tablespoons minced fresh parsley
1 tablespoon minced fresh basil
1 tablespoon lemon juice
1 clove garlic, minced
1 tablespoon olive oil
12 sheets commercial frozen phyllo pastry, thawed
¼ cup plus 2 tablespoons (1½ ounces) shredded
   part-skim mozzarella cheese
1 teaspoon reduced-calorie margarine, melted

Coat grill rack with cooking spray; place on grill over medium-hot coals.

Coat eggplant slices with cooking spray. Place eggplant slices on rack, and cook 7 minutes on each side or until tender. Chop eggplant, and place in a medium bowl. Add tomato and next 6 ingredients; toss gently. Add olive oil, and toss gently.

Place 1 sheet of phyllo on wax paper (keep remaining phyllo covered). Coat phyllo with cooking spray. Top with another sheet of phyllo, and coat with cooking spray. Cut phyllo in half lengthwise; place 1 half on top of the other, forming 4 layers.

Place one-sixth of eggplant mixture at base of phyllo stack; sprinkle 1 tablespoon mozzarella cheese over eggplant mixture. Fold right bottom corner of phyllo over filling, making a triangle. Continue folding back and forth into a triangle to end of sheet. Place triangle, seam side down, on a baking sheet coated with cooking spray. (Keep triangles covered before baking.) Repeat process with remaining phyllo, eggplant mixture, and mozzarella cheese. Brush triangles with melted margarine.

Bake at 425° for 15 to 18 minutes or until golden. Let cool 5 minutes on wire racks; serve warm. Yield: 6 servings (201 calories per serving).

PROTEIN 6.9　FAT 5.4　(Saturated Fat 1.1)　CARBOHYDRATE 32.5
FIBER 1.4　CHOLESTEROL 4　IRON 1.6　SODIUM 44　CALCIUM 72

BRUNCH POPOVER SANDWICHES

Vegetable cooking spray
¼ cup minced onion
3 tablespoons minced sweet red pepper
⅓ cup peeled, chopped tomato
1½ cups frozen egg substitute, thawed
3 tablespoons skim milk
2 tablespoons crumbled blue cheese
1 tablespoon minced fresh chives
¼ teaspoon ground white pepper
Herbed Popovers

Coat a medium nonstick skillet with cooking spray; place over medium-high heat until hot. Add minced onion and sweet red pepper; sauté until tender. Stir in chopped tomato.

Combine egg substitute and next 4 ingredients; beat well with a wire whisk. Pour over onion mixture in skillet; cook over medium heat, stirring often, until egg mixture is firm but still moist.

Cut slits in tops of Herbed Popovers; spoon ¼ cup egg mixture into each popover. Serve immediately. Yield: 6 servings (175 calories per serving).

Herbed Popovers

1 cup bread flour
1 cup skim milk
2 eggs, lightly beaten
2 egg whites
2 teaspoons reduced-calorie margarine,
   melted
½ teaspoon Italian seasoning
⅛ teaspoon salt
Vegetable cooking spray

Combine first 7 ingredients in a medium bowl; stir with a wire whisk until smooth. Pour batter evenly into 6 (6-ounce) custard cups coated with cooking spray. Place in a cold oven. Turn oven on 450°, and bake 15 minutes. Reduce heat to 350°, and bake an additional 35 to 40 minutes or until popovers are crusty and brown. Serve immediately. Yield: 6 popovers.

PROTEIN 14.2　FAT 4.3　(Saturated Fat 1.4)　CARBOHYDRATE 19.1
FIBER 0.8　CHOLESTEROL 74　IRON 2.5　SODIUM 267　CALCIUM 116

For a family fun meal, team Unsloppy Joes with Festival Slaw (page 184).

UNSLOPPY JOES

Vegetable cooking spray
½ cup chopped onion
½ cup chopped celery
½ cup diced carrot
½ cup diced green pepper
1 clove garlic, minced
1 (14½-ounce) can no-salt-added whole tomatoes,
   undrained and crushed
1½ tablespoons chili powder
1 tablespoon no-salt-added tomato paste
1 tablespoon vinegar
1 teaspoon pepper
1 (15½-ounce) can red kidney beans,
   drained
8 (2½-ounce) kaiser rolls

Coat a large nonstick skillet with cooking spray; place over medium-high heat until hot. Add onion, celery, carrot, green pepper, and garlic; sauté until tender. Stir in tomato and next 4 ingredients. Cover, reduce heat, and simmer 10 minutes. Add kidney beans, and cook an additional 5 minutes or until thoroughly heated.

Cut a ¼-inch slice off top of each kaiser roll; set aside. Hollow out center of rolls, leaving ½-inch-thick shells; reserve inside of rolls for other uses. Spoon bean mixture evenly into rolls; top with slices. Serve immediately. Yield: 8 servings (135 calories per serving).

PROTEIN 5.9   FAT 1.8   (Saturated Fat 0.4)   CARBOHYDRATE 25.0
FIBER 2.5   CHOLESTEROL 0   IRON 2.6   SODIUM 279   CALCIUM 46

CHICKEN SALAD SANDWICHES SUPREME

1 (8-ounce) carton plain nonfat yogurt
3 cups shredded, cooked chicken breast (skinned before cooking and cooked without salt)
1 (14-ounce) can artichoke hearts, drained and chopped
¼ cup sliced green onions
3 tablespoons grated Parmesan cheese
4 drops of hot sauce
1 clove garlic, minced
6 curly leaf lettuce leaves
6 reduced-calorie hamburger buns, split and toasted

Spoon yogurt onto several layers of heavy-duty paper towels; spread to ½-inch thickness. Cover with additional paper towels; let stand 5 minutes. Scrape yogurt into a bowl, using a rubber spatula. Add chicken and next 5 ingredients; toss gently to combine. Cover and chill thoroughly.

Place lettuce leaves on bottom halves of buns. Spoon chicken mixture evenly onto lettuce. Top with remaining bun halves. Yield: 6 servings (235 calories per serving).

PROTEIN 23.7   FAT 3.9   (Saturated Fat 1.1)   CARBOHYDRATE 25.6
FIBER 2.3   CHOLESTEROL 49   IRON 1.6   SODIUM 384   CALCIUM 150

SPICY CHICKEN SANDWICHES

½ cup chopped fresh tomatillo (about 3 medium)
2 tablespoons finely chopped onion
1 jalapeño pepper, seeded and finely chopped
1 tablespoon minced fresh basil
1 tablespoon lime juice
2 teaspoons red wine vinegar
4 (4-ounce) skinned, boned chicken breast halves
½ teaspoon ground cumin
½ teaspoon cracked pepper
Vegetable cooking spray
2 ounces goat cheese, softened
4 (2-ounce) kaiser rolls, split
4 red leaf lettuce leaves

Combine first 6 ingredients in a small bowl; let stand 30 minutes.

Place chicken between 2 sheets of heavy-duty plastic wrap; flatten chicken to ¼-inch thickness, using a meat mallet or rolling pin. Sprinkle evenly with cumin and pepper.

Coat grill rack with cooking spray; place on grill over medium-hot coals. Place chicken on rack, and cook 5 to 6 minutes on each side or until done.

Spread cheese evenly over bottom halves of rolls. Top each with 1 lettuce leaf and 1 grilled chicken breast. Spoon tomatillo mixture evenly over chicken, using a slotted spoon. Top with remaining roll halves. Serve immediately. Yield: 4 servings (270 calories per serving).

PROTEIN 30.4   FAT 7.4   (Saturated Fat 3.0)   CARBOHYDRATE 18.7
FIBER 2.3   CHOLESTEROL 83   IRON 1.6   SODIUM 445   CALCIUM 106

CAESAR STEAK SANDWICHES

1 (14-inch-diameter) round lavash (Armenian cracker bread)
½ (8-ounce) package light process cream cheese product
2 tablespoons grated Parmesan cheese
1 tablespoon lemon juice
1 tablespoon skim milk
1 teaspoon low-sodium Worcestershire sauce
½ teaspoon salt-free lemon-pepper seasoning
¼ teaspoon garlic powder
½ pound thinly sliced cooked roast beef
12 romaine lettuce leaves
Fresh watercress sprigs (optional)

Hold bread under a gentle spray of cold water for 10 seconds on each side or until moistened. Place between damp towels. Let stand 1 hour or until bread is soft and pliable. (If bread seems crisp in spots, sprinkle with more water.)

Beat cream cheese in a small bowl at medium speed of an electric mixer until smooth. Add Parmesan cheese and next 5 ingredients; stir well. Spread cream cheese mixture on softened bread. Top with roast beef and lettuce leaves.

Roll up bread jellyroll fashion. Cover tightly with plastic wrap, and chill 2 hours. Cut roll into 6 slices. Garnish with fresh watercress, if desired. Yield: 6 servings (186 calories per serving).

PROTEIN 13.7 FAT 7.9 (Saturated Fat 3.4) CARBOHYDRATE 15.3
FIBER 0.3 CHOLESTEROL 12 IRON 1.8 SODIUM 541 CALCIUM 68

HARVEST PORK SANDWICHES

2 (½-pound) pork tenderloins
2 egg whites, lightly beaten
½ cup toasted wheat germ
Vegetable cooking spray
1 teaspoon vegetable oil
2 (7-ounce) French bread baguettes
¼ cup chutney
¼ cup nonfat mayonnaise
1 apple, cored and thinly sliced
1 small purple onion, thinly sliced

Trim fat from pork. Slice pork diagonally across grain into ½-inch-thick slices. Place pork between 2 sheets of heavy-duty plastic wrap, and flatten to ¼-inch thickness, using a meat mallet or rolling pin.

Dip pork slices in egg whites, and sprinkle both sides of each slice with wheat germ.

Coat a large nonstick skillet with cooking spray; add oil. Place over medium-high heat until hot. Add pork, and cook 4 minutes on each side or until browned. Drain on paper towels.

Cut each baguette crosswise into quarters to make 8 sandwich rolls. Split each roll in half lengthwise. Divide pork evenly among bottom halves of rolls. Combine chutney and mayonnaise; spread chutney mixture evenly over pork.

Coat a large nonstick skillet with cooking spray; place over medium-high heat until hot. Add apple and onion; sauté until tender. Arrange apple and onion slices evenly over chutney mixture; place tops of rolls on sandwiches. Serve immediately. Yield: 8 servings (282 calories per serving).

PROTEIN 18.4 FAT 3.8 (Saturated Fat 1.0) CARBOHYDRATE 42.1
FIBER 3.0 CHOLESTEROL 36 IRON 2.4 SODIUM 441 CALCIUM 34

GRILLED TURKEY AND CHEESE SANDWICHES

2 tablespoons Dijon mustard
2 tablespoons finely chopped green onions
8 (¾-ounce) slices reduced-calorie whole wheat bread
1 cup (4 ounces) shredded reduced-fat Jarlsberg cheese, divided
2 ripe plum tomatoes, each cut into 4 slices
8 (1-ounce) slices skinned turkey breast
Vegetable cooking spray

Combine mustard and green onions; spread mustard mixture evenly over 4 bread slices. Top each with 2 tablespoons cheese, 2 tomato slices, and 2 turkey slices. Sprinkle an additional 2 tablespoons cheese over each; top with remaining 4 bread slices.

Transfer sandwiches to a sandwich press or hot griddle coated with cooking spray. Cook until bread is lightly browned and cheese melts. Yield: 4 servings (252 calories per serving).

PROTEIN 29.2 FAT 7.1 (Saturated Fat 2.8) CARBOHYDRATE 17.0
FIBER 5.8 CHOLESTEROL 62 IRON 2.4 SODIUM 551 CALCIUM 197

 GALLBLADDER TROUBLE
Two to three times as many women develop gallbladder disease as men. Usually the problems occur around middle age. Perhaps the biggest step to avoid gallbladder disease is to keep your weight in a healthy range since obesity puts a person at risk for gallbladder problems. Conversely, fasting or following a very low calorie diet for long periods of time may encourage the development of gallstones.

Normally, bile—the substance stored in the gallbladder that helps digest fat—is released from the gallbladder following a meal. During a starvation diet, however, the bile can stagnate in the gallbladder, possibly contributing to gallbladder problems. Other risk factors include eating a high-fat diet, bearing many children, and taking birth control pills.

Italian Tuna Submarine Sandwiches, accompanied by Dilled Pasta Salad (page 187), makes a mouthwatering meal.

ITALIAN TUNA SUBMARINE SANDWICHES

2 medium-size sweet red peppers
2 tablespoons sun-dried tomatoes (without salt
   or oil)
2 (6⅛-ounce) cans 60% less-salt tuna packed in
   spring water, drained
¼ cup plain nonfat yogurt
2 tablespoons thinly sliced green onions
1 tablespoon plus 1 teaspoon minced fresh basil
½ teaspoon cracked pepper
½ teaspoon hot sauce
4 romaine lettuce leaves
4 (2½-ounce) submarine rolls, split

Cut peppers in half lengthwise; remove and discard seeds and membrane. Place peppers, skin side up, on a baking sheet; flatten with palm of hand. Broil 5½ inches from heat 15 to 20 minutes or until charred. Place peppers in ice water, and chill 5 minutes. Remove from water; peel and discard skins. Cut peppers into julienne strips; set aside.

Place tomatoes in a small bowl; cover with hot water, and let stand 15 minutes. Drain well; mince tomatoes.

Combine minced tomato and next 6 ingredients in a medium bowl. Arrange lettuce leaves and red pepper strips over bottom halves of rolls. Spread tuna mixture evenly over peppers. Place roll tops over tuna mixture, and serve immediately. Yield: 4 servings (299 calories per serving).

PROTEIN 18.2 FAT 2.9 (Saturated Fat 0.6) CARBOHYDRATE 49.6
FIBER 1.3 CHOLESTEROL 20 IRON 3.5 SODIUM 588 CALCIUM 85

CHEESE-STUFFED CELERY

½ (8-ounce) package Neufchâtel cheese, softened
½ cup (2 ounces) shredded 40% less-fat Cheddar
  cheese
¼ cup plain nonfat yogurt
2 tablespoons chopped pecans
2 tablespoons diced pimiento
½ teaspoon dry mustard
¼ teaspoon hot sauce
⅛ teaspoon pepper
30 (3-inch) celery sticks
2 tablespoons minced fresh parsley

Combine Neufchâtel cheese, Cheddar cheese, and yogurt in a small bowl; stir well. Add chopped pecans, diced pimiento, mustard, hot sauce, and pepper; stir gently to combine.

Spoon cheese mixture evenly into celery sticks, and sprinkle evenly with chopped parsley. Cover and refrigerate at least 30 minutes. Yield: 2½ dozen (22 calories each).

PROTEIN 1.0   FAT 1.5   (Saturated Fat 0.8)   CARBOHYDRATE 1.5
FIBER 0.3   CHOLESTEROL 4   IRON 0.1   SODIUM 44   CALCIUM 28

NUTTY CEREAL SNACK

3 cups bite-size crispy corn cereal squares
⅓ cup unsalted dry roasted peanuts
1½ tablespoons reduced-calorie margarine
1 tablespoon creamy peanut butter
Vegetable cooking spray

Combine cereal and peanuts in a large bowl; set mixture aside.

Combine margarine and peanut butter in a small saucepan. Cook over low heat until mixture melts, stirring frequently. Pour peanut butter mixture over cereal mixture; tossing gently to coat. Spread cereal mixture in a single layer in a 15- x 10- x 1-inch jelly-roll pan coated with cooking spray. Bake at 200° for 20 minutes, stirring once. Turn oven off, and leave cereal mixture in oven 1 hour. Remove from oven, and spread on wax paper. Cool completely. Store in an airtight container. Yield: 3½ cups (110 calories per ½-cup serving).

PROTEIN 3.1   FAT 5.9   (Saturated Fat 0.8)   CARBOHYDRATE 12.1
FIBER 0.9   CHOLESTEROL 0   IRON 0.9   SODIUM 152   CALCIUM 7

SPICY PITA CHIPS

3 (6-inch) pita bread rounds
Butter-flavored vegetable cooking spray
1½ teaspoons garlic powder
1½ teaspoons onion powder
1½ teaspoons sugar
1 teaspoon ground red pepper
1 teaspoon paprika
½ teaspoon pepper

Split each pita round in half crosswise; cut each half into 4 wedges. Coat each wedge with cooking spray.

Combine garlic powder, onion powder, sugar, red pepper, paprika, and pepper in a large zip-top plastic bag; shake well.

Add pita wedges, a few at a time; secure bag, and shake to coat wedges. Place wedges on a baking sheet coated with cooking spray. Bake at 300° for 20 minutes or until lightly browned and crisp. Yield: 2 dozen (29 calories each).

PROTEIN 0.6   FAT 0.4   (Saturated Fat 0.1)   CARBOHYDRATE 5.3
FIBER 0.9   CHOLESTEROL 0   IRON 0.3   SODIUM 50   CALCIUM 9

SWEET WONTON SNACKS

1 (8-ounce) package dried apples
1 cup water
3 tablespoons sugar
¼ teaspoon apple pie spice
24 fresh or frozen wonton skins, thawed
Vegetable cooking spray
¼ cup sifted powdered sugar
¼ teaspoon ground cinnamon

Combine apples and 1 cup water in a saucepan; bring to a boil. Cover, reduce heat, and simmer 30 minutes or until tender. Mash apple until smooth. Stir in sugar and apple pie spice.

Spoon 2 teaspoons apple mixture in center of each wonton. Brush edges of wontons with water; fold each wonton in half diagonally, and press edges to seal.

Coat each wonton with cooking spray. Place on a baking sheet coated with cooking spray. Bake at 450° for 4 minutes on each side or until lightly browned and crisp. Remove from baking sheet, and drain wontons on paper towels.

Combine powdered sugar and cinnamon. Sift over warm wontons. Serve immediately. Yield: 2 dozen (43 calories each).

PROTEIN 0.4   FAT 0.4   (Saturated Fat 0.1)   CARBOHYDRATE 20.3
FIBER 0.3   CHOLESTEROL 6   IRON 0.2   SODIUM 24   CALCIUM 3

SALSA DEVILED EGGS

6 hard-cooked eggs
¼ cup commercial no-salt-added mild salsa
2 tablespoons nonfat mayonnaise
Fresh parsley sprigs (optional)

Slice eggs in half lengthwise, and carefully remove yolks. Mash yolks; add salsa and mayonnaise, stirring well. Pipe or spoon yolk mixture evenly into egg whites. Garnish with fresh parsley sprigs, if desired. Yield: 12 servings (40 calories each).

PROTEIN 3.2   FAT 2.5   (Saturated Fat 0.8)   CARBOHYDRATE 1.1
FIBER 0.1   CHOLESTEROL 106   IRON 0.4   SODIUM 63   CALCIUM 13

PEANUT BUTTER-BANANA POPS

1 (8-ounce) carton vanilla low-fat yogurt
1 cup pineapple-orange juice
2 small bananas, peeled and cut into 1-inch pieces
2 tablespoons creamy peanut butter
Dash of ground cinnamon
8 (3-ounce) paper cups
8 wooden sticks

Combine first 5 ingredients in container of an electric blender or food processor; top with cover, and process until smooth. Pour evenly into paper cups. Cover tops of cups with aluminum foil, and insert a wooden stick through aluminum foil into center of each cup. Freeze until firm.

To serve, remove foil, and peel paper cup away from pop. Yield: 8 servings (90 calories per serving).

PROTEIN 2.9   FAT 2.6   (Saturated Fat 0.6)   CARBOHYDRATE 15.2
FIBER 1.1   CHOLESTEROL 1   IRON 0.2   SODIUM 39   CALCIUM 53

Savory Currant-Mustard Sauce (page 207) accents pork tenderloin with a hint of orange and allspice.

Sauces & Condiments

BANANA SPLIT SAUCE

2 cups sliced fresh strawberries
1 medium banana, peeled and sliced
½ cup diced fresh pineapple
3 tablespoons chopped pecans
½ teaspoon vanilla extract
¼ teaspoon coconut extract

Combine strawberries, banana, and pineapple in container of an electric blender or food processor; top with cover, and process until smooth. Stir in pecans and flavorings. Serve over ice milk or angel food cake. Yield: 2¼ cups (12 calories per tablespoon).

PROTEIN 0.2 FAT 0.6 (Saturated Fat 0.1) CARBOHYDRATE 1.9
FIBER 0.4 CHOLESTEROL 0 IRON 0.1 SODIUM 0 CALCIUM 2

CHOCOLATE RUM-RAISIN SAUCE

2 tablespoons sugar
2 tablespoons unsweetened cocoa
1 tablespoon cornstarch
1 cup skim milk
2 tablespoons light-colored corn syrup
1 tablespoon dark rum
2 tablespoons raisins
½ teaspoon vanilla extract

Combine first 3 ingredients in a saucepan. Gradually stir in milk, corn syrup, and rum. Cook over medium heat, stirring constantly, until thickened. Remove from heat. Stir in raisins and vanilla. Serve warm or at room temperature over vanilla ice milk. Yield: 1¼ cups (22 calories per tablespoon).

PROTEIN 0.6 FAT 0.1 (Saturated Fat 0.1) CARBOHYDRATE 4.7
FIBER 0.1 CHOLESTEROL 0 IRON 0.1 SODIUM 9 CALCIUM 16

CUSTARD-PEAR SAUCE

¼ cup frozen egg substitute, thawed
2 teaspoons cornstarch
½ cup skim milk
½ cup pear nectar
2 tablespoons apricot brandy
⅛ teaspoon salt
⅛ teaspoon ground ginger
⅛ teaspoon ground mace

Combine egg substitute and cornstarch in a small saucepan, stirring until smooth.

Add milk and remaining ingredients; stir well with a wire whisk. Cook over medium heat, stirring constantly, until milk mixture is thickened (do not boil). Cover sauce, and chill thoroughly. Serve sauce over angel food cake or fresh fruit. Yield: 1¼ cups (13 calories per tablespoon).

PROTEIN 0.5 FAT 0.0 (Saturated Fat 0) CARBOHYDRATE 1.8
FIBER 0 CHOLESTEROL 0 IRON 0.1 SODIUM 22 CALCIUM 9

RASPBERRY-CHAMBORD SAUCE

2 cups fresh or frozen raspberries
¼ cup sugar
¼ cup red currant jelly
2 tablespoons Chambord or other raspberry-flavored liqueur

Position knife blade in food processor bowl; add raspberries and sugar, and process raspberry mixture until smooth. Strain raspberry puree, and discard seeds. Set aside.

Combine red currant jelly and liqueur in a small heavy saucepan. Bring mixture to a boil, stirring frequently until jelly melts.

Combine jelly mixture and raspberry puree, stirring well. Cover and chill thoroughly. Serve sauce over ice milk, angel food cake, or fruit desserts. Yield: 1½ cups (25 calories per tablespoon).

PROTEIN 0.1 FAT 0.1 (Saturated Fat 0) CARBOHYDRATE 6.0
FIBER 0.8 CHOLESTEROL 0 IRON 0.1 SODIUM 0 CALCIUM 2

RASPBERRY BARBECUE SAUCE

1 (8-ounce) can no-salt-added tomato sauce
¾ cup chopped purple onion
½ cup plus 2 tablespoons no-salt-added chili sauce
½ cup raspberry vinegar
1 tablespoon honey
1 teaspoon low-sodium Worcestershire sauce
1 clove garlic, minced
½ teaspoon dry mustard
½ teaspoon ground cinnamon
¼ teaspoon ground cloves
⅛ teaspoon ground ginger

Combine first 6 ingredients in a saucepan. Add garlic, mustard, cinnamon, cloves, and ginger. Bring to a boil, stirring frequently; reduce heat, and simmer 10 minutes. Use for basting beef, pork, or chicken while cooking. Yield: 2½ cups (6 calories per tablespoon).

PROTEIN 0.1 FAT 0.0 (Saturated Fat 0) CARBOHYDRATE 1.5
FIBER 0.1 CHOLESTEROL 0 IRON 0.1 SODIUM 3 CALCIUM 1

GINGERED TOMATO SAUCE

1 teaspoon reduced-calorie margarine
¼ cup plus 1 tablespoon chopped onion
1 clove garlic, minced
1 (8-ounce) can no-salt-added tomato sauce
1 teaspoon sugar
2 teaspoons Dijon mustard
1 teaspoon reduced-sodium soy sauce
1 teaspoon grated orange rind
½ teaspoon ground ginger

Heat margarine in a small saucepan. Place over medium-high heat until margarine melts. Add onion and garlic; sauté until tender. Stir in tomato sauce and remaining ingredients. Reduce heat, and cook until thoroughly heated, stirring frequently. Use for basting beef, pork, or chicken while cooking. Yield: 1¼ cups (8 calories per tablespoon).

PROTEIN 0.2 FAT 0.2 (Saturated Fat 0) CARBOHYDRATE 1.5
FIBER 0 CHOLESTEROL 0 IRON 0 SODIUM 29 CALCIUM 1

WEST INDIES MARINADE

½ cup finely chopped onion
¼ cup plus 3 tablespoons lemon juice
¼ cup lime juice
1 tablespoon chopped fresh parsley
1 tablespoon seeded, minced jalapeño pepper
2 tablespoons cider vinegar
1 tablespoon Dijon mustard
1 teaspoon dried whole basil
2 teaspoons vegetable oil
½ teaspoon dried whole thyme
¼ teaspoon salt
¼ teaspoon garlic powder
¼ teaspoon pepper

Combine all ingredients in a jar. Cover tightly, and shake vigorously.
Use to marinate beef, lamb, or fish before cooking. Remove meat from marinade, and bring marinade to a boil in a saucepan. Reduce heat; simmer 5 minutes. Remove from heat, and use marinade for basting meat while cooking. Yield: 1¼ cups (9 calories per tablespoon).

PROTEIN 0.1 FAT 0.5 (Saturated Fat 0.1) CARBOHYDRATE 1.3
FIBER 0.1 CHOLESTEROL 0 IRON 0.1 SODIUM 52 CALCIUM 4

FOUR-SPICE APRICOT SAUCE

½ cup nonfat mayonnaise
½ cup plain nonfat yogurt
½ cup no-sugar-added apricot spread
¼ teaspoon ground ginger
¼ teaspoon ground coriander
⅛ teaspoon ground cardamom
Dash of ground cumin

Combine all ingredients in a small bowl; stir mixture well. Cover and chill at least 2 hours. Serve sauce with chicken or pork. Yield: 1¼ cups (20 calories per tablespoon).

PROTEIN 0.4 FAT 0.0 (Saturated Fat 0) CARBOHYDRATE 4.6
FIBER 0 CHOLESTEROL 0 IRON 0 SODIUM 87 CALCIUM 13

Spicy Eggplant Sauce, accented by an unusual blend of herbs and spices, teams well with rice.

SPICY EGGPLANT SAUCE

Olive oil-flavored vegetable cooking spray
1 teaspoon olive oil
3 cups peeled, diced eggplant
½ cup chopped onion
2 cloves garlic, minced
1¾ cups peeled, seeded, and chopped tomato
1 (6-ounce) can no-salt-added tomato paste
½ cup water
1 small serrano chile, seeded and chopped
2 teaspoons peeled, grated gingerroot
1 teaspoon chopped fresh basil
¼ teaspoon salt
¼ teaspoon ground cumin
¼ cup chopped fresh cilantro
Fresh cilantro sprigs (optional)

Coat a large saucepan with cooking spray; add oil. Place over medium-high heat until hot. Add diced eggplant, chopped onion, and minced garlic; sauté 5 minutes or until tender.

Add chopped tomato, tomato paste, water, and serrano chile, stirring well to combine. Add grated gingerroot, fresh basil, salt, and cumin; stir well.

Bring mixture to a boil; cover, reduce heat, and simmer 25 minutes, stirring occasionally. Stir in chopped fresh cilantro. Serve warm over cooked rice or pasta. Garnish with fresh cilantro sprigs, if desired. Yield: 3½ cups (6 calories per tablespoon).

PROTEIN 0.2   FAT 0.1   (Saturated Fat 0)   CARBOHYDRATE 1.3
FIBER 0.2   CHOLESTEROL 0   IRON 0.1   SODIUM 13   CALCIUM 4

CURRANT-MUSTARD SAUCE

1 cup reduced-calorie apple spread
½ cup frozen orange juice concentrate, thawed
   and undiluted
2 tablespoons Dijon mustard
1 teaspoon grated orange rind
¼ teaspoon ground allspice
¼ cup currants

Combine first 5 ingredients in a small bowl; stir with a wire whisk until well blended. Stir in currants. Let stand at room temperature 30 minutes. Serve with lean baked ham or pork. Yield: 1½ cups (20 calories per tablespoon).

PROTEIN 0.2 FAT 0.1 (Saturated Fat 0) CARBOHYDRATE 4.5
FIBER 0.1 CHOLESTEROL 0 IRON 0 SODIUM 37 CALCIUM 3

ROQUEFORT SAUCE

¼ cup reduced-calorie margarine
¼ cup sliced green onions
¼ cup all-purpose flour
½ teaspoon dry mustard
¼ teaspoon ground white pepper
1½ cups skim milk
½ cup Chablis or other dry white wine
1 (4-ounce) jar diced pimientos, drained
¼ cup crumbled Roquefort cheese

Melt margarine in a saucepan over medium heat. Add green onions, and sauté until tender.

Stir in flour, dry mustard, and pepper; cook 1 minute. Gradually add milk, stirring until smooth. Cook over medium heat until thickened and bubbly, stirring constantly.

Gradually add wine, stirring constantly. Cook an additional minute, stirring constantly. Stir in pimiento and Roquefort cheese. Serve sauce immediately over steamed vegetables. Yield: 2¼ cups (17 calories per tablespoon).

PROTEIN 0.7 FAT 1.1 (Saturated Fat 0.3) CARBOHYDRATE 1.3
FIBER 0 CHOLESTEROL 1 IRON 0.1 SODIUM 32 CALCIUM 19

FRESH AND CREAMY PESTO SAUCE

1 cup firmly packed fresh basil leaves
1 cup 1% low-fat cottage cheese
½ cup firmly packed fresh parsley leaves
2 tablespoons chopped fresh thyme
2 tablespoons chopped blanched almonds
2 tablespoons freshly grated Parmesan
   cheese
2 cloves garlic, minced
2 teaspoons olive oil

Combine all ingredients in container of an electric blender or food processor; top with cover, and process 1 minute or until smooth, scraping sides of container occasionally. Serve sauce immediately over cooked pasta or fish. Yield: 1½ cups (17 calories per tablespoon).

PROTEIN 1.6 FAT 0.9 (Saturated Fat 0.2) CARBOHYDRATE 0.6
FIBER 0.1 CHOLESTEROL 1 IRON 0.1 SODIUM 48 CALCIUM 17

SOUTHWEST MELON SALSA

1½ cups diced cantaloupe
1½ cups diced honeydew
½ cup chopped green pepper
½ cup chopped purple onion
2 serrano chiles, seeded and chopped
2 tablespoons fresh cilantro
1 clove garlic, minced
3 tablespoons lime juice
1 tablespoon white wine vinegar
1 teaspoon vegetable oil
¼ teaspoon ground cumin

Combine first 7 ingredients in a large bowl; toss well. Combine lime juice, vinegar, oil, and cumin; stir well with a wire whisk. Pour over melon mixture; toss gently. Serve with chicken or fish. Yield: 4 cups (4 calories per tablespoon).

PROTEIN 0.1 FAT 0.1 (Saturated Fat 0) CARBOHYDRATE 0.9
FIBER 0.1 CHOLESTEROL 0 IRON 0 SODIUM 1 CALCIUM 1

ORIENTAL-STYLE SALSA

2 cups peeled, seeded, and chopped tomato
1 cup coarsely chopped fresh mushrooms
½ cup thinly sliced celery
½ cup sliced green onions
¼ cup chopped fresh parsley
2 cloves garlic, minced
1 teaspoon peeled, minced gingerroot
¼ teaspoon crushed red pepper
2 tablespoons white wine vinegar
2 teaspoons dark sesame oil
1 teaspoon reduced-sodium soy sauce

Combine first 8 ingredients in a medium bowl; toss well. Combine vinegar, sesame oil, and soy sauce; pour over tomato mixture, tossing gently to coat. Serve salsa with fish, chicken, or pork. Yield: 4 cups (4 calories per tablespoon).

PROTEIN 0.1   FAT 0.2   (Saturated Fat 0)   CARBOHYDRATE 0.5
FIBER 0.1   CHOLESTEROL 0   IRON 0.1   SODIUM 5   CALCIUM 2

CRUNCHY CELERY RELISH

3 cups chopped celery
1 cup chopped green pepper
1 cup chopped sweet red pepper
½ cup chopped onion
1 clove garlic, minced
½ cup cider vinegar
2 tablespoons brown sugar
2 tablespoons prepared mustard
½ teaspoon celery seeds
½ teaspoon mustard seeds
¼ teaspoon ground white pepper
¼ teaspoon ground allspice

Combine chopped celery, green pepper, sweet red pepper, onion, and garlic in a medium bowl; toss gently. Set aside.

Combine vinegar and remaining ingredients in a small saucepan; stir well. Cook over medium heat 2 to 3 minutes or until thoroughly heated. Pour over vegetable mixture, and toss gently to coat. Cover relish, and refrigerate 8 hours. Serve relish with beef, pork, or poultry. Yield: 5½ cups (3 calories per tablespoon).

PROTEIN 0.1   FAT 0.0   (Saturated Fat 0)   CARBOHYDRATE 0.8
FIBER 0.1   CHOLESTEROL 0   IRON 0.1   SODIUM 8   CALCIUM 3

GARDEN RELISH

2 cups coarsely chopped cauliflower
2 cups coarsely chopped cabbage
2 cups coarsely chopped red cabbage
1 cup coarsely chopped onion
1 cup chopped sweet red pepper
1 cup coarsely chopped cucumber
½ cup sliced celery
½ cup sugar
3 tablespoons all-purpose flour
2 teaspoons dry mustard
1 teaspoon ground ginger
½ teaspoon ground turmeric
¼ teaspoon salt
2½ cups vinegar
½ cup water

Combine first 7 ingredients in a large bowl, and toss well.

Combine sugar, flour, mustard, ginger, turmeric, and salt in a small saucepan; stir with a wire whisk until well blended. Stir in vinegar and water. Cook over medium heat until thickened, stirring constantly. Remove from heat. Pour over vegetable mixture, and toss well to coat. Let stand at room temperature 20 minutes.

Spoon into hot sterilized jars, leaving ½-inch headspace. Cover at once with metal lids, and screw on bands. Refrigerate 24 hours before serving. Store relish in the refrigerator. Yield: 4 pints (6 calories per tablespoon).

PROTEIN 0.1   FAT 0.0   (Saturated Fat 0)   CARBOHYDRATE 1.6
FIBER 0.2   CHOLESTEROL 0   IRON 0.1   SODIUM 6   CALCIUM 3

Tempt your tastebuds with Peach-Raspberry Butter, made with red raspberries and orchard-fresh peaches.

PEACH-RASPBERRY BUTTER

1 cup fresh raspberries
¼ cup peach nectar
3 medium-size fresh peaches (about 1¼ pounds),
   peeled and quartered
¼ cup sugar
1 teaspoon grated orange rind
½ teaspoon almond extract
¼ teaspoon ground mace
¼ teaspoon vanilla extract

Combine raspberries and peach nectar in a medium saucepan; bring to a boil. Reduce heat, and simmer 5 minutes. Strain raspberries through a sieve, and discard seeds.

Return raspberry mixture to saucepan; add peaches and remaining ingredients. Bring to a boil; cover, reduce heat, and simmer 12 to 14 minutes or until peaches are tender, stirring occasionally.

Pour mixture into container of an electric blender; top with cover, and process until mixture is smooth. Return pureed mixture to saucepan; cook over medium heat 10 to 12 minutes or until thickened, stirring constantly. Cover and chill thoroughly. Serve butter with toast or muffins. Yield: 1½ cups (18 calories per tablespoon).

PROTEIN 0.1 FAT 0.0 (Saturated Fat 0) CARBOHYDRATE 4.5
FIBER 0.6 CHOLESTEROL 0 IRON 0.1 SODIUM 0 CALCIUM 2

PLUM CHUTNEY

3 cups coarsely chopped fresh plums
⅓ cup raisins
3 tablespoons dark brown sugar
¼ cup cider vinegar
1 tablespoon grated orange rind
1 teaspoon diced crystallized ginger
½ teaspoon ground cinnamon
¼ teaspoon ground allspice
¼ teaspoon crushed red pepper

Combine all ingredients in a saucepan. Bring to a boil; reduce heat, and simmer, uncovered, 20 to 25 minutes or until thickened, stirring frequently. Serve chutney with beef, pork, or poultry. Yield: 1¾ cups (18 calories per tablespoon).

PROTEIN 0.2   FAT 0.1   (Saturated Fat 0)   CARBOHYDRATE 4.7
FIBER 0.5   CHOLESTEROL 0   IRON 0.1   SODIUM 1   CALCIUM 4

 SATISFYING SUMMER CUISINE
Ever wonder why watermelon, grapes, and iceberg lettuce are so appealing in the summer? Part of the reason is fluid. These foods are practically all water. And water is what the body craves in warm summer months. When the internal thermostat registers "hot," that's a signal for the body to seek out water-rich foods and beverages. Diluted fruit juices (1 part juice to 3 parts water) and sparkling seltzers are almost as good as plain water when it comes to thirst-quenching ability. But watch out for beverages such as coffee, cola, or iced tea that contain caffeine.

The caffeine acts like a diuretic and causes the body to lose fluid, not gain it. Initially, caffeine-rich drinks seem to quench thirst. But in the long-term they rob the body of needed fluid. In addition, caffeine also can cause blood vessels to constrict near the skin, which interferes with the body's mechanism for cooling itself.

Other advantages of water-rich foods are their healthy nutritional profiles. A source of fiber and low in fat, summer produce is true lean cuisine.

MINTED FRUIT CHUTNEY

1 cup chopped fresh pineapple
1 cup chopped fresh nectarines
¾ cup peeled, seeded, and chopped papaya
¾ cup chopped ripe mango
½ cup finely chopped sweet red pepper
½ cup thinly sliced green onions
¼ cup plus 2 tablespoons raspberry vinegar
2 tablespoons water
2 tablespoons honey
1 tablespoon grated lemon rind
½ teaspoon ground cardamom
¼ teaspoon ground ginger
¼ teaspoon crushed red pepper
2 tablespoons finely chopped fresh mint

Combine first 13 ingredients in a saucepan; stir well. Bring to a boil; reduce heat, and simmer 20 to 25 minutes or until thickened, stirring occasionally. Transfer to a bowl; let cool 20 minutes. Stir in mint. Cover and refrigerate. Serve with lamb, pork, or poultry. Yield: 3½ cups (9 calories per tablespoon).

PROTEIN 0.1   FAT 0.1   (Saturated Fat 0)   CARBOHYDRATE 2.4
FIBER 0.3   CHOLESTEROL 0   IRON 0.1   SODIUM 0   CALCIUM 2

Fresh herbs impart a savory flavor to (from left) Grilled Vegetable Kabobs (page 217) and Italian Stuffed Squash (page 217).

Side Dishes

ASPARAGUS DIJON

1½ pounds fresh asparagus spears
1 tablespoon cornstarch
1 cup nonfat buttermilk
2 teaspoons Dijon mustard
¾ teaspoon lemon juice
½ teaspoon dried whole tarragon
¼ teaspoon ground white pepper

Snap off tough ends of asparagus. Remove scales from spears with a knife or vegetable peeler, if desired. Arrange asparagus in a vegetable steamer over boiling water. Cover and steam 7 minutes or until crisp-tender. Set aside, and keep warm.

Combine cornstarch and buttermilk in a small saucepan; stir well. Cook over medium heat until thickened and bubbly, stirring constantly. Remove from heat; stir in mustard, lemon juice, tarragon, and white pepper.

Arrange asparagus on a serving platter. Spoon sauce over asparagus. Serve immediately. Yield: 6 servings (42 calories per serving).

PROTEIN 4.1 FAT 0.5 (Saturated Fat 0.1) CARBOHYDRATE 6.5
FIBER 1.8 CHOLESTEROL 0 IRON 0.6 SODIUM 94 CALCIUM 11

BLACK BEAN MEDLEY

Vegetable cooking spray
1 cup chopped onion
½ cup chopped green pepper
2 teaspoons minced garlic
2 (15-ounce) cans black beans, undrained
2 cups chopped tomato
1 cup cooked long-grain rice (cooked without
    salt or fat)
¼ cup chopped fresh cilantro
¼ teaspoon ground white pepper
¼ teaspoon ground red pepper
¼ teaspoon pepper
Fresh cilantro (optional)

Coat a large nonstick skillet with cooking spray; place over medium-high heat until hot. Add onion, green pepper, and garlic; sauté until tender. Add black beans, tomato, and rice; stir well. Stir in chopped cilantro and next 3 ingredients. Cook over medium heat 20 minutes, stirring occasionally. Transfer to a serving bowl; garnish with fresh cilantro, if desired. Yield: 10 servings (108 calories per ½-cup serving).

PROTEIN 5.7 FAT 0.7 (Saturated Fat 0.1) CARBOHYDRATE 21.0
FIBER 3.3 CHOLESTEROL 0 IRON 1.7 SODIUM 144 CALCIUM 25

SESAME BROCCOLI STIR-FRY

Vegetable cooking spray
2 teaspoons dark sesame oil
8 cups chopped fresh broccoli
1 large sweet red pepper, seeded and cut into
    thin strips
1 medium onion, cut into wedges
2 cloves garlic, minced
1 tablespoon brown sugar
3 tablespoons low-sodium soy sauce
3 tablespoons canned no-salt-added beef broth,
    undiluted
1½ tablespoons red wine vinegar
1½ teaspoons cornstarch
1 teaspoon peeled, minced gingerroot
4 drops hot sauce
¼ cup sliced water chestnuts
1 tablespoon sesame seeds, toasted

Coat a wok or large nonstick skillet with cooking spray; add oil. Place over medium-high heat (375°) until hot. Add broccoli, sweet red pepper, onion, and garlic; stir-fry 4 to 5 minutes or until vegetables are crisp-tender.

Combine brown sugar and next 6 ingredients in a small bowl, stirring well; add to vegetable mixture. Cook, stirring constantly, until mixture is thickened. Add water chestnuts and sesame seeds. Cook, stirring constantly, until thoroughly heated. Serve immediately. Yield: 12 servings (47 calories per ½-cup serving).

PROTEIN 2.4 FAT 1.5 (Saturated Fat 0.2) CARBOHYDRATE 7.1
FIBER 2.5 CHOLESTEROL 0 IRON 0.8 SODIUM 119 CALCIUM 37

CABBAGE AND BEET BAKE

1 pound medium-size fresh beets
6 cups coarsely shredded red cabbage
1 medium-size purple onion, thinly sliced and
  separated into rings
1 cup Burgundy or other dry red wine
1 cup unsweetened apple juice
2 tablespoons red wine vinegar
2 teaspoons sugar
¼ teaspoon salt

Trim stems and roots from beets. Peel beets; cut into julienne strips. Layer cabbage, onion, and beets alternately in a 3-quart baking dish. Combine wine and remaining ingredients, stirring well. Pour over cabbage mixture.

Cover and bake at 325° for 1 hour and 45 minutes or until vegetables are tender, stirring every 30 minutes. Yield: 7 servings (64 calories per 1-cup serving).

PROTEIN 1.7 FAT 0.3 (Saturated Fat 0) CARBOHYDRATE 14.8
FIBER 2.2 CHOLESTEROL 0 IRON 0.9 SODIUM 118 CALCIUM 51

MINTED PINEAPPLE CARROTS

4 cups chopped fresh pineapple
3 cups sliced carrot
1 cup unsweetened pineapple juice
1 cup water
2 tablespoons rum
½ teaspoon sugar
¼ teaspoon salt
¼ teaspoon ground white pepper
2 tablespoons chopped fresh mint

Combine first 8 ingredients in a medium saucepan, stirring well. Bring mixture to a boil; cover, reduce heat, and simmer 30 minutes. Add mint, and cook an additional 5 minutes or until carrot is tender. Serve with a slotted spoon. Yield: 12 servings (58 calories per ½-cup serving).

PROTEIN 0.7 FAT 0.3 (Saturated Fat 0.1) CARBOHYDRATE 14.3
FIBER 1.6 CHOLESTEROL 0 IRON 0.5 SODIUM 73 CALCIUM 19

CAULIFLOWER MORNAY

4 cups cauliflower flowerets
1 cup skim milk
1 tablespoon cornstarch
¼ cup plus 2 tablespoons (1½ ounces) shredded
  reduced-fat Swiss cheese
¼ teaspoon ground white pepper
⅛ teaspoon freshly grated nutmeg
⅛ teaspoon hot sauce

Arrange cauliflower in a vegetable steamer over boiling water. Cover and steam 12 minutes. Drain; transfer to a serving platter, and keep warm.

Combine milk and cornstarch in a small heavy saucepan; stir until smooth. Cook over medium heat until thickened, stirring constantly. Add cheese and remaining ingredients; stir until cheese melts. Spoon over cauliflower. Serve immediately. Yield: 4 servings (102 calories per 1-cup serving).

PROTEIN 9.0 FAT 2.3 (Saturated Fat 1.2) CARBOHYDRATE 13.3
FIBER 4.0 CHOLESTEROL 8 IRON 1.0 SODIUM 75 CALCIUM 249

MEXICAN ROASTED CORN

4 ears fresh corn
2 tablespoons chopped green chiles
1 tablespoon chopped fresh cilantro
1 tablespoon reduced-calorie margarine,
  melted
1 teaspoon minced garlic
½ teaspoon cumin seeds, crushed

Remove husks and silks from corn; set aside.

Combine chopped green chiles and remaining ingredients in a small bowl; stir well. Brush green chile mixture evenly over corn.

Wrap each ear in a 12-inch sheet of heavy-duty aluminum foil, twisting ends to seal. Bake at 400° for 30 minutes, turning after 15 minutes. Yield: 4 servings (84 calories per serving).

PROTEIN 2.1 FAT 2.6 (Saturated Fat 0.4) CARBOHYDRATE 16.0
FIBER 2.4 CHOLESTEROL 0 IRON 0.6 SODIUM 49 CALCIUM 7

Green onions, green pepper, and fresh basil provide additional flavor to the corn in Summer Sweet Corn.

SUMMER SWEET CORN

6 cups fresh corn cut from cob (about 12 ears)
1½ cups water
½ cup chopped green onions
¼ cup chopped green pepper
2 tablespoons chopped fresh basil
2 tablespoons white wine vinegar
½ teaspoon sugar
¼ teaspoon salt
¼ teaspoon ground white pepper
¼ teaspoon hot sauce
Fresh basil sprigs (optional)

Combine corn, water, green onions, and green pepper in a medium saucepan. Bring to a boil; reduce heat, and simmer, uncovered, 20 minutes. Add chopped basil and next 5 ingredients; cook 10 minutes or until corn is tender. Transfer to a serving bowl; serve with a slotted spoon. Garnish with fresh basil sprigs, if desired. Yield: 10 servings (84 calories per ½-cup serving).

PROTEIN 3.1 FAT 1.1 (Saturated Fat 0.2) CARBOHYDRATE 18.5
FIBER 3.1 CHOLESTEROL 0 IRON 0.6 SODIUM 75 CALCIUM 6

ORANGE-GLAZED MIXED VEGETABLES

2 (16-ounce) packages frozen mixed vegetables
¾ cup water
½ cup unsweetened orange juice
1 tablespoon cornstarch
2 teaspoons honey
2 teaspoons grated orange rind
1 teaspoon ground ginger
¼ teaspoon pepper

Arrange vegetables in a vegetable steamer over boiling water. Cover and steam 10 minutes; drain.

Combine water, orange juice, and cornstarch in a small saucepan; stir well. Cook over medium heat until thickened and bubbly, stirring constantly. Stir in honey and remaining ingredients; reduce heat, and simmer 5 minutes. Pour over vegetables, and toss well. Yield: 11 servings (71 calories per ½-cup serving).

PROTEIN 2.8   FAT 0.4   (Saturated Fat 0.1)   CARBOHYDRATE 14.3
FIBER 3.2   CHOLESTEROL 0   IRON 0.8   SODIUM 39   CALCIUM 23

VEGETABLE-STUFFED PEPPERS

6 small green peppers (about 1½ pounds)
1 cup fresh broccoli flowerets
½ cup chopped onion
½ cup chopped carrot
½ cup chopped fresh mushrooms
½ cup chopped fresh broccoli
½ cup chopped zucchini
1 cup no-salt-added tomato sauce
2 tablespoons chopped green chiles
½ teaspoon dried Italian seasoning
¼ teaspoon salt
¼ teaspoon ground red pepper
1½ cups cooked brown rice (cooked without
    salt or fat)
¼ cup (1 ounce) shredded reduced-fat Swiss
    cheese

Cut tops off green peppers, and remove seeds. Arrange peppers in a vegetable steamer over boiling water. Cover and steam 5 minutes. Drain peppers and set aside.

Arrange broccoli flowerets and next 5 ingredients in vegetable steamer. Cover and steam 5 minutes; drain and set aside.

Combine tomato sauce, chiles, Italian seasoning, salt, and red pepper in a bowl; stir in broccoli mixture and rice. Spoon evenly into peppers; place peppers in an 11- x 7- x 2-inch baking dish. Top evenly with cheese. Bake at 325° for 25 minutes or until thoroughly heated. Yield: 6 servings (125 calories per serving).

PROTEIN 5.2   FAT 1.9   (Saturated Fat 0.6)   CARBOHYDRATE 23.5
FIBER 3.7   CHOLESTEROL 3   IRON 1.8   SODIUM 131   CALCIUM 88

PUMPKIN SOUFFLÉ

Vegetable cooking spray
2 cups cooked, mashed pumpkin
¾ cup evaporated skimmed milk
½ cup frozen egg substitute, thawed
¼ cup firmly packed brown sugar
1½ teaspoons ground cinnamon
½ teaspoon ground allspice
¼ teaspoon salt
¼ teaspoon ground nutmeg
3 egg whites

Cut a piece of aluminum foil long enough to fit around a 2-quart soufflé dish, allowing a 1-inch overlap; fold lengthwise into thirds. Coat one side of foil with cooking spray; wrap foil around outside of dish, coated side against dish, allowing it to extend 3 inches above rim. Secure with string.

Combine pumpkin and next 7 ingredients in a large bowl; mix well, using a wire whisk.

Beat egg whites at high speed of an electric mixer until stiff peaks form. Fold one-third of egg whites into pumpkin mixture; fold in remaining egg whites. Spoon into prepared dish. Bake at 325° for 55 minutes or until golden. Serve immediately. Yield: 6 servings (109 calories per serving).

PROTEIN 7.1   FAT 0.5   (Saturated Fat 0.2)   CARBOHYDRATE 20.3
FIBER 1.5   CHOLESTEROL 1   IRON 2.1   SODIUM 199   CALCIUM 139

Stir up excitement with exotic Snow Pea-Carambola Stir-Fry.

SNOW PEA-CARAMBOLA STIR-FRY

¼ pound fresh snow pea pods
1 tablespoon reduced-calorie margarine
1 teaspoon peeled, minced gingerroot
1 medium carambola (starfruit), thinly
    sliced
1 medium-size red pear, cored and thinly
    sliced
3 tablespoons unsweetened apple juice
¼ teaspoon sugar
⅛ teaspoon salt

Wash snow peas; trim ends, and remove strings.
Cut snow peas in half diagonally; set aside.

Heat margarine in a large nonstick skillet over medium-high heat until margarine melts. Add gingerroot, and stir-fry 1 minute.

Add sliced carambola, and stir-fry 3 minutes. Add snow peas, sliced pear, apple juice, sugar, and salt; stir-fry an additional 3 to 5 minutes or until snow peas are crisp-tender.

Transfer mixture to a small serving bowl, and serve immediately. Yield: 4 servings (60 calories per ½-cup serving).

PROTEIN 1.0   FAT 2.1   (Saturated Fat 0.3)   CARBOHYDRATE 10.5
FIBER 1.9   CHOLESTEROL 0   IRON 0.7   SODIUM 103   CALCIUM 17

GRILLED VEGETABLE KABOBS

6 small round red potatoes (about ¾ pound)
12 medium-size fresh mushrooms
12 cherry tomatoes
1 large sweet red pepper, cut into 1½-inch pieces
1 large green pepper, cut into 1½-inch pieces
¼ cup commercial oil-free Italian dressing
2 tablespoons chopped fresh oregano
1 tablespoon chopped fresh basil
1 tablespoon Dijon mustard
½ teaspoon coarsely ground pepper
Vegetable cooking spray

Place potatoes in medium saucepan; add water to cover. Bring to a boil; cover, reduce heat, and simmer 12 minutes. Drain well. Cut each potato in half.

Clean mushrooms with damp paper towels. Remove stems, reserving stems for another use.

Thread potatoes, mushrooms, tomatoes, and peppers alternately onto 6 (12-inch) wooden skewers; place kabobs in a large shallow dish. Combine Italian dressing and next 4 ingredients in a small bowl; stir well. Brush over kabobs. Cover and marinate in refrigerator 4 hours.

Coat grill rack with cooking spray; place on grill over medium-hot coals. Place kabobs on rack, and cook 12 to 13 minutes or until vegetables are tender. Yield: 6 servings (78 calories per serving).

PROTEIN 2.6 FAT 0.9 (Saturated Fat 0.1) CARBOHYDRATE 16.0
FIBER 2.7 CHOLESTEROL 0 IRON 2.0 SODIUM 192 CALCIUM 23

GARDEN VEGETABLE TOSS

1 cup water
2 cups peeled, diced turnip
2 cups diced carrot
1 (10-ounce) package frozen English peas, thawed
½ cup unsweetened orange juice
¼ cup water
1½ teaspoons cornstarch
1 tablespoon chopped fresh chives
½ teaspoon chicken-flavored bouillon granules
¼ teaspoon salt

Place 1 cup water in a saucepan; bring to a boil. Add turnip and carrot; cover, reduce heat, and simmer 5 minutes. Add peas; cover and cook 15 minutes or until vegetables are tender. Drain; keep warm.

Combine orange juice, ¼ cup water, and cornstarch in a saucepan. Add chives, bouillon granules, and salt. Cook over medium heat until thickened and bubbly, stirring constantly. Pour over vegetables; toss gently. Yield: 10 servings (49 calories per ½-cup serving).

PROTEIN 2.1 FAT 0.2 (Saturated Fat 0) CARBOHYDRATE 10.2
FIBER 2.6 CHOLESTEROL 0 IRON 0.7 SODIUM 153 CALCIUM 24

ITALIAN STUFFED SQUASH

2 medium-size yellow squash
Vegetable cooking spray
½ cup chopped fresh mushrooms
3 tablespoons chopped green onions
2 tablespoons chopped green pepper
¼ cup frozen egg substitute, thawed
2 tablespoons fine, dry breadcrumbs
1 tablespoon chopped ripe olives
1½ teaspoons chopped fresh basil
1½ teaspoons chopped fresh oregano
1½ teaspoons chopped fresh thyme
¼ teaspoon freshly ground pepper
¼ cup (1 ounce) shredded part-skim mozzarella cheese

Prick squash several times with a fork. Bake at 325° for 25 minutes or until tender; cool slightly. Cut squash in half lengthwise; scoop out pulp, leaving ¼-inch-thick shells. Set shells aside. Drain pulp; mash.

Coat a nonstick skillet with cooking spray; place over medium-high heat until hot. Add mushrooms, green onions, and green pepper; sauté until tender. Combine mashed squash, mushroom mixture, egg substitute, and next 6 ingredients in a small bowl. Spoon into squash shells; sprinkle with cheese. Place in an 8-inch square baking dish. Bake at 325° for 25 minutes. Yield: 4 servings (72 calories per serving).

PROTEIN 5.2 FAT 2.2 (Saturated Fat 0.9) CARBOHYDRATE 8.8
FIBER 2.3 CHOLESTEROL 4 IRON 1.5 SODIUM 120 CALCIUM 90

SPICED APRICOT-PEARS

4 medium-size ripe pears (about 1¾ pounds)
⅓ cup dried apricots
1½ cups cranberry-apple juice
1 cup water
⅛ teaspoon ground ginger
⅛ teaspoon ground coriander
⅛ teaspoon ground cinnamon

Core pears; cut in half lengthwise. Place pear halves and apricots in a large nonstick skillet; pour cranberry-apple juice and water over fruit. Bring to a boil; cover, reduce heat, and simmer 10 minutes. Uncover and simmer an additional 10 minutes or until pears are tender.

Drain pears and apricots, reserving juice mixture. Place pears, cut side up, in an 11- x 7- x 2-inch baking dish; set aside.

Place apricots, 2 tablespoons reserved juice mixture, ginger, coriander, and cinnamon in container of an electric blender; top with cover, and process until smooth. Spoon apricot mixture evenly into centers of pear halves; pour 1 cup reserved juice mixture over pears. Bake at 325° for 15 minutes or until thoroughly heated. Serve with a slotted spoon. Yield: 8 servings (98 calories per serving).

PROTEIN 0.6 FAT 0.4 (Saturated Fat 0) CARBOHYDRATE 24.9
FIBER 2.4 CHOLESTEROL 0 IRON 0.6 SODIUM 6 CALCIUM 17

SAUCED FRUIT COMPOTE

3 medium bananas, peeled and sliced
1 tablespoon lemon juice
1 (16-ounce) can apricots in juice, drained
1 (16-ounce) can pear halves in juice, drained
1 (15¼-ounce) can pineapple chunks in juice, drained
1 (15-ounce) can unsweetened applesauce
¼ teaspoon ground cinnamon

Arrange sliced banana in a single layer in an 8-inch square baking dish; sprinkle lemon juice over banana.

Combine apricots, pears, pineapple, and applesauce; toss gently. Spoon over banana. Cover and bake at 350° for 25 minutes; uncover and bake an additional 10 minutes. Sprinkle with cinnamon, and serve warm. Yield: 8 servings (108 calories per serving).

PROTEIN 1.1 FAT 0.5 (Saturated Fat 0.1) CARBOHYDRATE 27.5
FIBER 4.2 CHOLESTEROL 0 IRON 0.7 SODIUM 8 CALCIUM 15

PINEAPPLE-GLAZED FRUIT

1 cup peeled, sliced banana (about 2 medium)
2 purple plums, pitted and sliced
2 cups fresh pineapple chunks
1 teaspoon brown sugar
¼ cup unsweetened pineapple juice
½ teaspoon ground cinnamon

Layer banana slices, plum slices, and pineapple chunks in a shallow 1½-quart baking dish. Sprinkle with brown sugar; drizzle pineapple juice over fruit. Sprinkle cinnamon evenly over fruit. Bake, uncovered, at 400° for 15 to 20 minutes or until thoroughly heated. Yield: 7 servings (74 calories per ½-cup serving).

PROTEIN 0.7 FAT 0.5 (Saturated Fat 0.1) CARBOHYDRATE 18.6
FIBER 2.2 CHOLESTEROL 0 IRON 0.4 SODIUM 1 CALCIUM 10

Loaded with tender chunks of meat and a garden's harvest, Turkey-Vegetable Stew (page 228) boasts of home-style flavor.

Soups & Stews

CHILLED BLUEBERRY SOUP

3 cups water, divided
4 cups fresh blueberries
3 tablespoons lemon juice
3 tablespoons crème de cassis
2 tablespoons Triple Sec or other orange-flavored
  liqueur
2 tablespoons honey
2 (1-inch) sticks cinnamon
2 tablespoons cornstarch
1 tablespoon plus 2 teaspoons low-fat sour cream
Orange zest (optional)

Combine 2½ cups water and next 6 ingredients in a large saucepan. Bring to a boil; cover, reduce heat, and simmer 15 minutes. Combine cornstarch and remaining ½ cup water, stirring until smooth. Add cornstarch mixture to blueberry mixture; bring to a boil. Boil 1 minute, stirring constantly. Remove from heat; let cool 15 minutes. Remove and discard cinnamon sticks.

Pour blueberry mixture into container of an electric blender or food processor; top with cover, and process until mixture is smooth. Cover and chill thoroughly.

To serve, ladle soup into individual bowls. Top each serving with 1 teaspoon sour cream. Garnish with orange zest, if desired. Yield: 5 cups (148 calories per 1-cup serving).

PROTEIN 1.4   FAT 0.5   (Saturated Fat 0.1)   CARBOHYDRATE 37.0
FIBER 5.2   CHOLESTEROL 0   IRON 0.3   SODIUM 14   CALCIUM 8

SPICED CHERRY SOUP

1 (16-ounce) package frozen sweet cherries,
  thawed
2½ cups water
¾ cup unsweetened apple juice
½ cup sugar
1 (3-inch) stick cinnamon
2 tablespoons plus 1 teaspoon cornstarch
3 tablespoons water

Combine first 5 ingredients in a medium saucepan. Bring to a boil; cover, reduce heat, and simmer 15 minutes.

Combine cornstarch and 3 tablespoons water; stir well. Add to cherry mixture; cook over low heat 2 minutes, stirring frequently. Transfer to a large bowl. Cover and chill thoroughly. Remove and discard cinnamon stick. To serve, ladle soup into individual bowls. Yield: 5½ cups (79 calories per ½-cup serving).

PROTEIN 0.5   FAT 0.4   (Saturated Fat 0.1)   CARBOHYDRATE 19.4
FIBER 1.0   CHOLESTEROL 0   IRON 0.2   SODIUM 1   CALCIUM 7

CREAM OF CELERY SOUP

Vegetable cooking spray
2 teaspoons vegetable oil
1 (8-ounce) package sliced fresh mushrooms
1 cup chopped onion
2¾ cups thinly sliced celery
2 cups water
¼ cup chopped fresh parsley
1½ teaspoons chicken-flavored bouillon granules
½ teaspoon dried whole sage
⅛ teaspoon ground white pepper
3½ tablespoons all-purpose flour
2 cups skim milk, divided
2 tablespoons sliced almonds, toasted

Coat a Dutch oven with cooking spray; add oil. Place over medium-high heat until hot. Add mushrooms and onion; sauté until tender. Stir in celery and next 5 ingredients. Bring to a boil; cover, reduce heat, and simmer 15 minutes, stirring occasionally.

Combine flour and ¼ cup milk; stir until smooth. Add flour mixture and remaining 1¾ cups milk to mushroom mixture; stir well. Cook over medium heat until slightly thickened and bubbly, stirring constantly. Ladle soup into individual bowls; sprinkle evenly with toasted almonds. Yield: 1½ quarts (101 calories per 1-cup serving).

PROTEIN 5.3   FAT 3.6   (Saturated Fat 0.5)   CARBOHYDRATE 13.4
FIBER 2.1   CHOLESTEROL 2   IRON 1.2   SODIUM 291   CALCIUM 136

Colorful Cream of Carrot Soup can be an appetizing start to your dinner party.

CREAM OF CARROT SOUP

Vegetable cooking spray
1 tablespoon reduced-calorie margarine
2 pounds carrots, scraped and thinly
   sliced
1¼ cups chopped onion
1 cup sliced celery
3 cups canned low-sodium chicken broth,
   undiluted
1 cup 1% low-fat milk
¼ teaspoon salt
Fresh chives (optional)

Coat a Dutch oven with cooking spray; add margarine. Place over medium-high heat until margarine melts. Add carrot, onion, and celery; sauté 10 minutes. Add chicken broth; bring to a boil. Cover, reduce heat, and simmer 20 minutes. Remove from heat, and let cool 10 minutes.

Transfer mixture in batches to container of an electric blender or food processor; top with cover, and process until smooth. Return puree to pan. Stir in milk and salt. Cook over medium heat just until thoroughly heated (do not boil). Ladle soup into individual bowls. Garnish with fresh chives, if desired. Yield: 7 cups (94 calories per 1-cup serving).

PROTEIN 2.9   FAT 1.8   (Saturated Fat 0.4)   CARBOHYDRATE 16.6
FIBER 4.3   CHOLESTEROL 1   IRON 0.7   SODIUM 173   CALCIUM 85

FRESH BROCCOLI SOUP

2 pounds fresh broccoli
1 cup chopped onion
¾ cup diced carrot
½ cup chopped celery
1 cup water
2 tablespoons reduced-calorie margarine
2½ tablespoons all-purpose flour
2½ cups 1% low-fat milk
1½ cups canned low-sodium chicken broth, undiluted
3 ounces light process cheese, cubed
½ teaspoon pepper
½ teaspoon low-sodium Worcestershire sauce
¼ teaspoon salt

Trim off large leaves of broccoli, and remove tough ends of lower stalks. Wash broccoli thoroughly, and coarsely chop.

Place broccoli in a large Dutch oven; add water to a depth of 1 inch. Bring to a boil; cover, reduce heat, and simmer 15 minutes or until broccoli is tender, stirring occasionally. Drain and set aside.

Combine onion, carrot, celery, and 1 cup water in a small saucepan. Bring to a boil; reduce heat, and simmer 20 minutes or until vegetables are tender. Remove from heat, and let cool slightly. Transfer vegetables and water to container of an electric blender or food processor; top with cover, and process until smooth.

Melt margarine in pan over medium heat; add flour. Cook 1 minute, stirring constantly with a wire whisk. Gradually add milk, stirring constantly; cook until thickened and bubbly, stirring constantly. Add broccoli, pureed vegetables, chicken broth, and remaining ingredients; stir well. Cook over low heat until cheese melts, stirring constantly. Yield: 9 cups (129 calories per 1-cup serving).

PROTEIN 9.1 FAT 3.9 (Saturated Fat 1.4) CARBOHYDRATE 16.7
FIBER 4.7 CHOLESTEROL 8 IRON 1.2 SODIUM 321 CALCIUM 169

BEAN AND VEGETABLE SOUP

½ pound dried pinto beans
4 cups water
¼ cup Burgundy or other dry red wine
1 cup chopped onion
1 cup chopped green pepper
1 cup sliced celery
1 cup sliced carrot
¼ cup minced fresh parsley
2 cloves garlic, minced
2 teaspoons chicken-flavored bouillon granules
½ teaspoon dried whole thyme
¼ teaspoon ground red pepper
1 (14½-ounce) can no-salt-added whole tomatoes, undrained and chopped
1½ cups sliced fresh okra

Sort and wash beans; place beans in a large Dutch oven. Cover with water to a depth of 2 inches above beans; let soak overnight. Drain beans well. Combine beans, 4 cups water, and next 10 ingredients in pan; bring to a boil. Cover, reduce heat, and simmer 1 hour or until beans are tender, stirring occasionally.

Remove 2 cups of vegetable mixture from pan, using a slotted spoon. Place in container of an electric blender or food processor; top with cover, and process until smooth.

Return pureed mixture to pan; add chopped tomato and sliced okra, stirring well. Bring to a boil; cover, reduce heat, and simmer 20 minutes or until okra is tender. Ladle soup into individual bowls. Yield: 2½ quarts (109 calories per 1-cup serving).

PROTEIN 6.0 FAT 0.6 (Saturated Fat 0.1) CARBOHYDRATE 21.3
FIBER 4.0 CHOLESTEROL 0 IRON 2.1 SODIUM 189 CALCIUM 67

CHICKEN PEPPER POT

Vegetable cooking spray
4 (4-ounce) skinned, boned chicken breast halves,
 cut into 1-inch pieces
1 cup finely chopped purple onion
1 cup finely chopped green pepper
1 serrano pepper, seeded and finely chopped
2 cups canned low-sodium chicken broth,
 undiluted
1½ cups water
½ cup dry sherry
1 tablespoon lemon juice
1¾ cups sliced carrot
1½ cups peeled, cubed potato
1 cup peeled, cubed turnip
1 teaspoon chicken-flavored bouillon granules
½ teaspoon dried whole thyme
¼ teaspoon dried whole oregano
¼ teaspoon pepper
⅛ teaspoon ground red pepper

Coat a large Dutch oven with cooking spray; place over medium-high heat until hot. Add chicken pieces, and sauté until lightly browned.

Remove chicken pieces from pan; drain and pat dry with paper towels. Wipe drippings from pan with a paper towel.

Coat pan with vegetable cooking spray; place over medium-high heat until hot. Add purple onion, chopped green pepper, and chopped serrano pepper; sauté until tender.

Add chicken, chicken broth, water, sherry, and lemon juice to purple onion mixture, stirring well to combine. Stir in carrot and remaining ingredients. Bring chicken mixture to a boil; cover, reduce heat, and simmer 1 hour or until vegetables are tender. Yield: 2 quarts (145 calories per 1-cup serving).

PROTEIN 14.8 FAT 1.9 (Saturated Fat 0.5) CARBOHYDRATE 16.3
FIBER 2.7 CHOLESTEROL 35 IRON 1.4 SODIUM 162 CALCIUM 32

HEARTY PORK AND CABBAGE SOUP

1½ pounds lean boneless pork loin
Vegetable cooking spray
1 cup chopped onion
1 cup chopped sweet red pepper
2 cloves garlic, minced
2 cups canned no-salt-added chicken broth,
 undiluted
2 cups water
1 cup peeled, diced red potato
1 cup peeled, diced rutabaga
1 cup diced carrot
¼ cup chopped fresh parsley
1 tablespoon chopped fresh thyme
1 tablespoon chopped fresh marjoram
¼ teaspoon salt
¼ teaspoon pepper
2 bay leaves
2 cups thinly sliced cabbage
1 cup thinly sliced celery

Trim fat from pork; cut pork into 1-inch cubes. Coat a large Dutch oven with cooking spray; place over medium heat until hot. Add pork; cook until pork is browned on all sides, stirring frequently. Drain and pat dry with paper towels. Wipe drippings from pan with a paper towel.

Coat pan with vegetable cooking spray; place over medium-high heat until hot. Add onion, red pepper, and garlic; sauté until vegetables are tender.

Add pork, chicken broth, and next 10 ingredients, stirring well. Bring mixture to a boil; cover, reduce heat, and simmer 45 minutes. Add sliced cabbage and sliced celery; cover and cook an additional 15 minutes. Remove and discard bay leaves. Ladle soup into individual bowls. Yield: 9 cups (185 calories per 1-cup serving).

PROTEIN 16.4 FAT 8.3 (Saturated Fat 2.6) CARBOHYDRATE 10.5
FIBER 2.2 CHOLESTEROL 49 IRON 1.5 SODIUM 159 CALCIUM 39

Chock-full of fresh vegetables and shrimp, a bowl of Saffron-Shrimp Soup with Sourdough Croutons makes a filling lunch or dinner.

SAFFRON-SHRIMP SOUP WITH SOURDOUGH CROUTONS

Olive oil-flavored vegetable cooking spray
1 cup chopped onion
1 cup chopped green pepper
1 cup chopped sweet red pepper
2 cloves garlic, minced
3 cups water
1 cup no-salt-added tomato juice
½ cup Chablis or other dry white wine
1⅔ cups peeled, seeded, and chopped tomato
¼ cup minced fresh parsley
1 teaspoon chicken-flavored bouillon granules
¼ teaspoon crushed saffron
¼ teaspoon crushed red pepper
¾ pound medium-size fresh shrimp, peeled
　and deveined
Sourdough Croutons

Coat a large Dutch oven with cooking spray; place over medium-high heat until hot. Add onion, green pepper, sweet red pepper, and minced garlic; sauté until tender.

Add water and next 7 ingredients; bring to a boil. Cover, reduce heat, and simmer 30 minutes. Add shrimp, stirring well. Simmer, uncovered, an additional 10 minutes, or until shrimp are done. Ladle soup into individual bowls. Top each serving evenly with Sourdough Croutons. Yield: 1½ quarts (137 calories per 1-cup serving).

Sourdough Croutons

3 (1-ounce) slices sourdough bread (½ inch thick)
2 teaspoons olive oil
¼ teaspoon garlic powder

Cut bread into ½-inch cubes; set aside. Combine olive oil and garlic powder in a small bowl, stirring well. Add bread cubes, and toss gently to coat well. Arrange bread cubes in a single layer in a 15- x 10- x 1-inch jellyroll pan. Bake at 275° for 30 to 35 minutes or until golden, stirring after 15 minutes. Remove from oven, and let cool completely. Yield: 1⅔ cups.

PROTEIN 11.6   FAT 3.2   (Saturated Fat 0.4)   CARBOHYDRATE 16.7
FIBER 2.1   CHOLESTEROL 65   IRON 2.5   SODIUM 291   CALCIUM 52

AUTUMN BEEF STEW

1½ pounds lean boneless round steak (½ inch thick)
Vegetable cooking spray
1½ cups coarsely chopped onion
1 cup sliced fresh mushrooms
2½ cups water
1 cup cranberry juice cocktail
½ cup Burgundy or other dry red wine
1½ teaspoons beef-flavored bouillon granules
½ teaspoon dried whole rosemary
¼ teaspoon dried whole thyme
¼ teaspoon ground allspice
¼ teaspoon pepper
2 cups peeled, seeded, and coarsely chopped acorn squash
2 cups sliced parsnips
2 tablespoons chopped fresh parsley

Trim fat from steak; cut steak into 1-inch pieces. Coat a large Dutch oven with cooking spray; place over medium-high heat until hot. Add steak; cook until browned on all sides, stirring frequently. Drain and pat dry with paper towels. Wipe drippings from pan with a paper towel.

Coat pan with cooking spray; place over medium-high heat until hot. Add onion and mushrooms; sauté until tender. Add steak, 2½ cups water, and next 7 ingredients, stirring well. Bring to a boil; cover, reduce heat, and simmer 1 hour and 15 minutes. Add squash and parsnips; cover and simmer 35 to 40 minutes or until meat and vegetables are tender. Ladle

soup into individual bowls. Sprinkle each serving with ¾ teaspoon parsley. Yield: 2 quarts (195 calories per 1-cup serving).

PROTEIN 19.4   FAT 5.7   (Saturated Fat 1.9)   CARBOHYDRATE 16.7
FIBER 1.7   CHOLESTEROL 52   IRON 2.6   SODIUM 226   CALCIUM 36

BEEF AND BARLEY STEW

1 pound lean boneless top round steak (½ inch thick)
Vegetable cooking spray
1 cup chopped onion
1 cup sliced celery
1 cup sliced carrot
2 cloves garlic, minced
3 cups water
1½ cups no-salt-added tomato juice
¼ cup pearl barley, uncooked
1 tablespoon low-sodium Worcestershire sauce
2 teaspoons beef-flavored bouillon granules
1 teaspoon paprika
½ teaspoon dried whole marjoram
¼ teaspoon pepper
1 cup frozen English peas, thawed
1 cup sliced fresh mushrooms

Trim fat from steak; cut steak into ½-inch cubes. Coat a Dutch oven with cooking spray; place over medium-high heat until hot. Add steak; cook until browned on all sides, stirring frequently. Drain and pat dry with paper towels. Wipe drippings from pan with a paper towel.

Coat pan with cooking spray; place over medium-high heat until hot. Add onion, celery, carrot, and garlic; sauté until tender. Add steak, 3 cups water, and next 7 ingredients; stir well. Bring to a boil; cover, reduce heat, and simmer 1½ hours. Add peas and mushrooms; cover and cook an additional 15 minutes or until vegetables are tender. Yield: 7 cups (187 calories per 1-cup serving).

PROTEIN 19.4   FAT 3.9   (Saturated Fat 1.1)   CARBOHYDRATE 18.5
FIBER 3.9   CHOLESTEROL 42   IRON 2.5   SODIUM 363   CALCIUM 30

CHUCK WAGON STEW

1 pound lean boneless round steak (½ inch thick)
Vegetable cooking spray
2 cups coarsely chopped carrot
1 medium onion, cut into eighths
2¼ cups cubed red potato
1 (14½-ounce) can no-salt-added whole tomatoes, undrained and chopped
1 cup water
1 cup brewed coffee
2 tablespoons molasses
1 tablespoon low-sodium Worcestershire sauce
1 teaspoon beef-flavored bouillon granules
½ teaspoon dried whole thyme
½ teaspoon dried whole marjoram
¼ teaspoon hot sauce
1 bay leaf
1 (15-ounce) can pinto beans, undrained

Trim fat from steak; cut steak into 1-inch pieces. Coat a Dutch oven with cooking spray; place over medium-high heat until hot. Add steak; cook until browned on all sides, stirring frequently. Drain and pat dry with paper towels. Wipe drippings from pan with a paper towel.

Coat pan with vegetable cooking spray; place over medium-high heat until hot. Add carrot and onion; sauté until carrot is slightly browned. Return steak to pan. Add potato and next 10 ingredients, stirring well to combine. Bring to a boil; cover, reduce heat, and simmer 1 hour and 15 minutes or until potato and steak are tender.

Add pinto beans, and stir well. Cover and simmer an additional 15 minutes. Remove and discard bay leaf. Yield: 2½ quarts (154 calories per 1-cup serving).

PROTEIN 12.5 FAT 2.5 (Saturated Fat 0.8) CARBOHYDRATE 20.6
FIBER 1.6 CHOLESTEROL 24 IRON 2.7 SODIUM 318 CALCIUM 54

BEEF AND PUMPKIN STEW

1½ pounds lean boneless round steak (½ inch thick)
Vegetable cooking spray
2 cups chopped onion
1 cup sliced celery
¼ cup chopped fresh parsley
4 cups water
1 tablespoon low-sodium Worcestershire sauce
1 teaspoon beef-flavored bouillon granules
½ teaspoon dried whole thyme
½ teaspoon dried whole marjoram
¼ teaspoon pepper
1 bay leaf
2 cups cubed fresh pumpkin
1 (10-ounce) package frozen mixed vegetables, thawed
2 tablespoons plus 2 teaspoons unsalted toasted pumpkin seeds

Trim fat from steak; cut steak into 1-inch pieces. Coat a large Dutch oven with cooking spray; place over medium-high heat until hot. Add steak; cook until browned on all sides, stirring frequently. Drain and pat dry with paper towels. Wipe drippings from pan with a paper towel.

Return steak to pan; add onion and next 9 ingredients, stirring well to combine. Bring to a boil; cover, reduce heat, and simmer 1 hour and 20 minutes. Add pumpkin and mixed vegetables. Cover and simmer 10 minutes or until steak and vegetables are tender. Remove and discard bay leaf. Ladle stew into individual serving bowls. Sprinkle each serving with 1 teaspoon pumpkin seeds. Yield: 2 quarts (229 calories per 1-cup serving).

PROTEIN 25.1 FAT 8.8 (Saturated Fat 2.7) CARBOHYDRATE 12.2
FIBER 2.9 CHOLESTEROL 63 IRON 3.9 SODIUM 209 CALCIUM 40

BRUNSWICK STEW

3 (4-ounce) skinned, boned chicken breast halves
2 cups water
3 tablespoons chopped fresh parsley
½ teaspoon salt
½ teaspoon dried whole thyme
1 bay leaf
1½ cups diced potato
1 cup sliced celery
1 medium onion, sliced
1 (14½-ounce) can no-salt-added whole tomatoes, undrained and chopped
1 (10-ounce) package frozen baby lima beans, thawed
1 (10-ounce) package frozen whole kernel corn, thawed
2 teaspoons low-sodium Worcestershire sauce
½ teaspoon pepper
¼ teaspoon garlic powder
¼ teaspoon ground red pepper

Trim excess fat from chicken breast halves. Place chicken, 2 cups water, chopped parsley, salt, thyme, and bay leaf in a large Dutch oven. Bring chicken mixture to a boil; cover, reduce heat, and simmer 20 minutes or until chicken is done.

Remove chicken breasts from broth; shred chicken breasts, and place in a medium bowl. Set aside. Remove and discard bay leaf.

Skim and discard fat from broth; return chicken to pan. Add diced potato, sliced celery, onion, chopped tomato, lima beans, and corn, stirring well to combine.

Add Worcestershire sauce and remaining ingredients; stir well. Bring mixture to a boil; cover, reduce heat, and simmer 2 hours, stirring frequently. Yield: 2 quarts (177 calories per 1-cup serving).

PROTEIN 14.9 FAT 1.5 (Saturated Fat 0.4) CARBOHYDRATE 26.6
FIBER 2.7 CHOLESTEROL 26 IRON 2.1 SODIUM 250 CALCIUM 51

PORK STEW MEXICALI

1 pound lean boneless pork shoulder (½ inch thick)
Vegetable cooking spray
1 cup chopped onion
1 cup chopped green pepper
1 jalapeño pepper, seeded and chopped
2 cloves garlic, minced
½ pound fresh tomatillos
1 (14½-ounce) can no-salt-added whole tomatoes, undrained and chopped
1 (10-ounce) can tomatoes and green chiles
1 cup water
2 tablespoons chopped fresh cilantro
2 tablespoons golden tequila
½ teaspoon ground cumin
½ teaspoon dried whole oregano
¼ teaspoon salt
¼ teaspoon pepper
1 cup frozen whole kernel corn, thawed
¼ cup sliced ripe olives

Trim fat from pork; cut pork into ½-inch cubes. Coat a large Dutch oven with cooking spray; place pan over medium-high heat until hot. Add pork, and cook until browned on all sides, stirring frequently. Drain pork, and pat dry with paper towels. Wipe drippings from pan with a paper towel.

Coat pan with cooking spray; place over medium-high heat until hot. Add onion, green pepper, jalapeño pepper, and garlic; sauté until tender.

Remove and discard husks from tomatillos; chop tomatillos. Add pork, tomatillos, chopped tomato, and next 8 ingredients. Bring to a boil; cover, reduce heat, and simmer 30 minutes or until pork is tender. Stir in corn. Cover and cook 10 minutes or until corn is tender. Add olives; cook 5 minutes or until thoroughly heated. Yield: 7 cups (190 calories per 1-cup serving).

PROTEIN 13.9 FAT 9.4 (Saturated Fat 2.8) CARBOHYDRATE 12.6
FIBER 1.9 CHOLESTEROL 46 IRON 2.2 SODIUM 444 CALCIUM 52

TURKEY-VEGETABLE STEW

2 (10½-ounce) cans low-sodium chicken broth,
   undiluted
1 (14½-ounce) can no-salt-added whole tomatoes,
   undrained and chopped
1½ cups sliced carrot
1 cup sliced celery
¾ cup chopped onion
¾ cup water
1 tablespoon chopped fresh basil
2 tablespoons no-salt-added tomato paste
¼ teaspoon salt
¼ teaspoon pepper
¼ teaspoon hot sauce
2 cloves garlic, minced
2½ cups chopped, cooked turkey breast (skinned
   before cooking and cooked without salt)
1 (10-ounce) package frozen English
   peas, thawed
1 (10-ounce) package frozen okra, thawed

Combine chicken broth, tomatoes, carrot, celery,
onion, water, basil, and tomato paste in a large Dutch
oven. Add salt and next 3 ingredients, stirring well
to combine. Bring to a boil; cover, reduce heat, and
simmer 30 minutes.

Stir in turkey, peas, and okra; simmer, uncovered,
10 minutes or until thoroughly heated. Yield: 9 cups
(184 calories per 1-cup serving).

PROTEIN 15.4 FAT 1.1 (Saturated Fat 0.3) CARBOHYDRATE 26.6
FIBER 2.1 CHOLESTEROL 31 IRON 1.9 SODIUM 295 CALCIUM 74

ROBUST VEGETABLE STEW

1 (15-ounce) can garbanzo beans, drained
1 (14½-ounce) can no-salt-added whole tomatoes,
   undrained and chopped
2 cups peeled, cubed potato
2 cups diced carrot
1 cup sliced celery
½ cup dried lentils
½ cup finely chopped onion
2¼ cups water
1 (13¾-ounce) can no-salt-added beef broth,
   undiluted
¼ cup Burgundy or other dry red wine
1 tablespoon low-sodium Worcestershire sauce
2 teaspoons chili powder
1 teaspoon ground cumin
½ teaspoon dried whole oregano
¼ teaspoon ground red pepper
½ cup plus 1 tablespoon (2¼ ounces) shredded
   40% less-fat Cheddar cheese
Chopped fresh cilantro (optional)

Combine first 15 ingredients in a Dutch oven. Bring
to a boil; cover, reduce heat, and simmer 1 hour or
until lentils are tender.

Ladle stew into individual bowls; sprinkle each
serving with 1 tablespoon cheese. Garnish with
chopped fresh cilantro, if desired. Yield: 9 cups (174
calories per 1-cup serving).

PROTEIN 9.0 FAT 2.2 (Saturated Fat 0.8) CARBOHYDRATE 31.2
FIBER 4.6 CHOLESTEROL 4 IRON 2.9 SODIUM 302 CALCIUM 108

*Save the best for last; (clockwise
from top) Chocolate-Espresso Angel
Food Cake (page 243), Jewelled
Raspberry Tartlets (page 241),
and Pink Grapefruit Ice (page 236)
are memorable endings for almost
any meal.*

Desserts

CARAMELIZED APPLES WITH SUGAR-GLAZED YOGURT

8 Granny Smith apples (about 3¾ pounds), peeled and cored
¼ cup reduced-calorie margarine, divided
⅓ cup sugar, divided
½ teaspoon ground cinnamon
¼ teaspoon ground nutmeg
¼ teaspoon ground allspice
⅛ teaspoon ground cloves
Vegetable cooking spray
Yogurt Sauce
3 tablespoons plus 1 teaspoon brown sugar

Cut each apple into 8 wedges; cut each wedge into 3 pieces. Pat apple dry with paper towels.

Melt 2 tablespoons margarine in a large nonstick skillet. Add half of the apple, and sauté 2 minutes. Gradually add half of the sugar, and cook 8 to 10 minutes or until apple is tender and lightly browned, stirring frequently. Remove from skillet, and set aside. Repeat with remaining margarine, apple, and sugar.

Combine cinnamon, nutmeg, allspice, and cloves; stir well. Sprinkle over apple; toss gently. Spoon evenly into 10 (6-ounce) custard cups coated with cooking spray. Spoon Yogurt Sauce evenly over apple mixture.

Place custard cups on a baking sheet. Sprinkle each with 1 teaspoon brown sugar. Broil 5½ inches from heat 2 minutes or until sugar melts. Serve immediately. Yield: 10 servings (190 calories per serving).

Yogurt Sauce

4 ounces light process cream cheese product
3 tablespoons sugar
1 cup plain nonfat yogurt
2 teaspoons grated lemon rind
1 tablespoon fresh lemon juice

Beat cream cheese and sugar at high speed of an electric mixer until light and fluffy. Gradually add yogurt, beating at low speed. Stir in lemon rind and lemon juice. Yield: 1¾ cups.

PROTEIN 2.7 FAT 5.5 (Saturated Fat 1.7) CARBOHYDRATE 35.4
FIBER 3.5 CHOLESTEROL 7 IRON 0.3 SODIUM 127 CALCIUM 71

APPLE-OATMEAL CRUMBLE

7 large Granny Smith apples (about 3⅛ pounds), peeled, cored, and cut into ½-inch-thick wedges
½ cup firmly packed brown sugar
1 tablespoon cornstarch
2 tablespoons lemon juice
1 teaspoon ground cinnamon
1 teaspoon vanilla extract
½ teaspoon ground nutmeg
½ teaspoon ground allspice
½ cup plus 2 tablespoons regular oats, uncooked
¼ cup reduced-calorie margarine, cut into chunks
¼ cup firmly packed brown sugar
2 tablespoons all-purpose flour
Vegetable cooking spray

Combine first 8 ingredients in a large bowl; toss well. Let stand 20 minutes, stirring occasionally.

Position knife blade in food processor bowl; add oats. Pulse 3 or 4 times. Add margarine, ¼ cup brown sugar, and flour; pulse 3 or 4 times or until mixture resembles coarse meal.

Place apple mixture in a 13- x 9- x 2-inch baking dish coated with cooking spray; sprinkle oat mixture evenly over apple mixture. Cover and bake at 400° for 35 minutes; uncover and bake an additional 20 minutes or until apple is tender and topping is lightly browned. Serve warm. Yield: 10 servings (178 calories per serving).

PROTEIN 1.1 FAT 3.7 (Saturated Fat 0.5) CARBOHYDRATE 37.6
FIBER 3.5 CHOLESTEROL 0 IRON 1.0 SODIUM 49 CALCIUM 25

APRICOT-BAKED BANANAS

1 cup dried apricots
¾ cup white port
1 teaspoon grated lemon rind
¼ cup sugar
¾ cup water
½ teaspoon vanilla extract
½ teaspoon almond extract
8 small ripe bananas, peeled
¼ cup sliced almonds, toasted

Place apricots in a bowl; add boiling water to cover. Let stand 30 minutes; drain. Place apricots in a small saucepan; add port and lemon rind. Bring to a boil; reduce heat, and simmer 15 minutes or until tender.

Place apricot mixture in container of an electric blender or food processor; top with cover, and process until pureed. Add sugar, ¾ cup water, and flavorings; pulse 2 or 3 times or until well blended.

Fold 8 (18- x 12-inch) sheets of aluminum foil in half crosswise. Twist ends of each sheet to form a boat-like packet. Place 1 banana in each; drizzle apricot mixture evenly over bananas. Fold tops of packets to seal securely. Bake at 425° for 15 minutes or until thoroughly heated. Place packets on dessert plates; open packets, and sprinkle with almonds. Serve immediately. Yield: 8 servings (228 calories per serving).

PROTEIN 2.9 FAT 2.7 (Saturated Fat 0.4) CARBOHYDRATE 53.1
FIBER 5.1 CHOLESTEROL 0 IRON 1.7 SODIUM 19 CALCIUM 31

BLUEBERRY CRUMBLE

8 cups fresh or frozen blueberries, thawed
⅓ cup all-purpose flour
3 tablespoons sugar
3 tablespoons brown sugar
1 teaspoon grated lemon rind
¼ cup plus 2 tablespoons lemon juice
Vegetable cooking spray
½ cup all-purpose flour
¼ cup sugar
¼ cup firmly packed brown sugar
¼ cup reduced-calorie margarine

Combine first 6 ingredients in a large bowl; toss well. Spoon mixture into a 13- x 9- x 2-inch baking dish coated with cooking spray.

Combine ½ cup flour, ¼ cup sugar, and ¼ cup brown sugar. Cut in margarine with a pastry blender until mixture resembles coarse meal. Sprinkle over blueberry mixture. Bake at 350° for 50 minutes or until golden. Yield: 12 servings (163 calories per serving).

PROTEIN 1.6 FAT 2.9 (Saturated Fat 0.4) CARBOHYDRATE 35.3
FIBER 4.9 CHOLESTEROL 0 IRON 0.8 SODIUM 45 CALCIUM 14

RUM-MARINATED CANTALOUPE

¼ cup sugar
2 tablespoons lemon juice
2 tablespoons rum
1 tablespoon lemon marmalade
4 cups cantaloupe balls

Combine sugar, lemon juice, and rum in a small saucepan; bring to a boil. Reduce heat, and simmer 1 minute, stirring constantly. Remove from heat, and add marmalade, stirring until marmalade melts.

Place melon balls in a medium bowl; add marmalade mixture, and toss gently. Cover and refrigerate at least 4 hours.

Spoon melon balls evenly into 8 individual dessert bowls; drizzle evenly with marmalade mixture. Yield: 8 servings (63 calories per ½-cup serving).

PROTEIN 0.8 FAT 0.3 (Saturated Fat 0.1) CARBOHYDRATE 15.8
FIBER 1.1 CHOLESTEROL 0 IRON 0.2 SODIUM 9 CALCIUM 11

 THE BETA CAROTENE EDGE
Beta carotene is thought to protect against certain types of cancer and new findings show it might be a hedge against heart disease, too. In one study, scientists found that 50 milligrams of beta carotene (about equal to 2 cups of cooked carrots) every other day offered protection against early death from cardiovascular disease.

ITEM	AMOUNT	BETA CAROTENE (milligrams)
Apricots	3 raw	1.7
Apricots	10 dried halves	1.5
Broccoli	½ cup cooked	1.8
Butternut squash	½ cup cooked	3.3
Cantaloupe	½ medium	5.2
Carrots	½ cup cooked	11.5
Collard greens	½ cup cooked	2.1
Mango	1 raw	4.9
Papaya	1 raw	3.7
Pumpkin	½ cup canned	16.1
Spinach	½ cup cooked	4.4
Sweet potatoes	½ cup mashed	13.0

CHERRIES IN RED WINE

1½ cups Burgundy or other dry red wine
⅓ cup sugar
1 tablespoon peeled, minced gingerroot
1 (3-inch) stick cinnamon
10 black peppercorns
6 (2- x ¼-inch) strips lemon rind
2 (16-ounce) packages frozen unsweetened sweet
  cherries, thawed

Combine first 6 ingredients in a large saucepan.
Bring to a boil. Add cherries; cover, reduce heat, and
simmer 5 minutes or until cherries are tender. Transfer
cherries to a bowl, using a slotted spoon.

Return wine mixture to a boil; cook over medium-
high heat 15 minutes, stirring frequently. Remove from
heat; strain through a fine sieve. Pour mixture over
cherries. Cover and refrigerate at least 4 hours. Yield:
8 servings (87 calories per ½-cup serving).

PROTEIN 1.1 FAT 0.5 (Saturated Fat 0.1) CARBOHYDRATE 21.5
FIBER 0.3 CHOLESTEROL 0 IRON 0.8 SODIUM 5 CALCIUM 18

HONEYDEW WITH
HONEY-GINGER SAUCE

¼ cup honey
2 tablespoons fresh lime juice
2 tablespoons brandy
1 tablespoon slivered crystallized ginger
4 cups honeydew melon balls
Lime rind curls (optional)

Heat honey in a small saucepan over medium-low
heat until warm; add lime juice and brandy. Cook until
thoroughly heated, stirring occasionally. Remove from
heat, and stir in ginger.

Place ½ cup melon balls in each of 8 dessert bowls;
drizzle honey mixture evenly over melon balls. Garnish with lime rind curls, if desired. Yield: 8 servings
(67 calories per ½-cup serving).

PROTEIN 0.5 FAT 0.1 (Saturated Fat 0) CARBOHYDRATE 17.9
FIBER 0.8 CHOLESTEROL 0 IRON 0.3 SODIUM 10 CALCIUM 8

FRESH FRUIT MÉLANGE WITH
STRAWBERRY SAUCE

2 fresh ripe peaches, peeled and sliced
2 tablespoons lemon juice
Strawberry Sauce
2 cups diced fresh pineapple
2 medium kiwifruit, peeled and cut into ¼-inch
  slices
1 cup fresh strawberries, halved

Combine peaches and lemon juice in a small bowl;
toss gently.

Spoon Strawberry Sauce evenly onto 6 individual
dessert plates. Arrange peaches, pineapple, kiwifruit,
and strawberries evenly over sauce. Serve immediately. Yield: 6 servings (135 calories per serving).

Strawberry Sauce

2 cups fresh strawberries
2 tablespoons sugar
¼ cup red currant jelly

Position knife blade in food processor bowl; add
strawberries and sugar. Process 1 to 2 minutes or until
smooth; set aside.

Melt jelly in a small saucepan over medium heat,
stirring constantly. Add pureed strawberry mixture,
stirring well. Cover mixture and chill thoroughly. Yield:
1⅔ cups.

PROTEIN 1.3 FAT 0.7 (Saturated Fat 0.1) CARBOHYDRATE 33.5
FIBER 4.2 CHOLESTEROL 0 IRON 0.8 SODIUM 3 CALCIUM 25

WINE-POACHED PEACHES WITH
BLACKBERRY SAUCE

1 cup Riesling or other dry white wine
1 cup unsweetened orange juice
⅓ cup sugar
4 large fresh peaches (about 1¾ pounds), peeled
  and halved
Blackberry Sauce
Fresh mint sprigs (optional)

Combine first 3 ingredients in a large nonstick skillet. Bring to a boil; reduce heat, and simmer 5 minutes. Arrange peaches in skillet; cover, reduce heat, and simmer 10 minutes or until peaches are tender. Remove from heat; cool slightly. Cover and chill thoroughly.

Remove peaches from liquid, using a slotted spoon; discard liquid. Place peaches, cut side down, on a flat cutting surface. Cut lengthwise slits in peaches to within ½ inch of one end, forming a fan. Spoon 2 tablespoons Blackberry Sauce onto each dessert plate. Place fanned peaches over sauce. Garnish with mint sprigs, if desired. Yield: 8 servings (154 calories per serving).

Blackberry Sauce

2 cups fresh blackberries
¼ cup sugar
¼ cup lemon marmalade
1 tablespoon blackberry brandy

Press blackberries through a sieve; discard seeds. Combine sugar and marmalade in a small saucepan. Cook over low heat until sugar dissolves and marmalade melts. Remove from heat, and stir in strained blackberries. Add brandy, and stir well. Cover and chill thoroughly. Yield: 1 cup.

PROTEIN 1.1   FAT 0.2   (Saturated Fat 0)   CARBOHYDRATE 38.6
FIBER 3.9   CHOLESTEROL 0   IRON 0.5   SODIUM 4   CALCIUM 24

SPICED PEACH CRUNCH

8 medium-size fresh peaches (about 3½ pounds), peeled and cut into ½-inch-thick slices
⅓ cup sugar
1 tablespoon cornstarch
2 tablespoons peach brandy
2 tablespoons lemon juice
¾ cup regular oats, uncooked
¼ cup all-purpose flour
¼ cup firmly packed brown sugar
¼ cup reduced-calorie margarine, cut into chunks and chilled
3 tablespoons unsweetened shredded coconut
½ teaspoon ground cinnamon
¼ teaspoon freshly grated nutmeg

Combine first 5 ingredients in a large bowl; toss well. Let stand 20 minutes, stirring occasionally.

Position knife blade in food processor bowl; add oats. Pulse 3 or 4 times. Add flour and remaining ingredients; pulse 4 or 5 times or until mixture resembles coarse meal.

Place peach mixture in an 11- x 7- x 2-inch baking dish; sprinkle oat mixture evenly over peaches. Cover and bake at 400° for 15 minutes; uncover and bake an additional 30 minutes or until peaches are tender and oat topping is crisp. Serve warm. Yield: 10 servings (174 calories per serving).

PROTEIN 2.2   FAT 4.4   (Saturated Fat 1.4)   CARBOHYDRATE 33.9
FIBER 2.7   CHOLESTEROL 0   IRON 0.8   SODIUM 47   CALCIUM 16

TIPS FOR HEALTHY EATING

If stress, a hectic schedule, or social influences have hindered your plans to eat healthier, here are a few easy-to-manage suggestions to get you back on track.

• Give yourself an hour for each meal; it takes the body at least 20 minutes to register being full.
• Sit down to a meal with a plate and eating utensils; eating on the move or eating straight from the container can lead to overeating, not to mention indigestion.
• Turn off the television, put away the books or newspaper, and give full attention to the meal at hand. Mealtime is meant to be savored and enjoyed; it should not be littered with distractions.
• Start the day with a healthy breakfast. Skipping the first meal of the day can lead to an overactive appetite at the next.
• Stock the cupboards and refrigerator with high-carbohydrate snacks that have a lean profile: fresh fruits, nonfat yogurt, raw vegetables, pretzels, or air-popped popcorn.
• Reward yourself for good progress with a movie, a good book, or flowers—anything but food.
• Take the fat out of meals in small but significant ways. Trim visible fats from meats, season vegetables with lemon juice and herbs, and switch to lower fat versions of favorite foods.

STEAMED PEARS WITH HONEY AND CURRANTS

4 medium-size ripe pears (about 1⅔ pounds)
¼ cup boiling water
1½ tablespoons currants
¼ cup honey
¾ teaspoon ground cinnamon
⅛ teaspoon ground nutmeg
⅛ teaspoon ground cloves
1 tablespoon lemon juice

Cut a 1-inch cap from the top of each pear. Core pear, cutting to, but not through the bottom.

Combine boiling water and currants in a small bowl. Let stand 15 minutes. Drain well.

Combine honey, cinnamon, nutmeg, and cloves in a small saucepan; stir well. Cook over medium heat until thoroughly heated. Remove from heat; stir in currants and lemon juice. Spoon honey mixture evenly into each pear; top with pear caps.

Place a glass bowl in center of a steaming rack in a large Dutch oven; add just enough water to fill pan below rack. Place pears upright in bowl. Bring water to a boil; cover, reduce heat, and simmer 20 to 25 minutes or until pears are tender. Remove from heat, and let stand 15 minutes. Remove bowl from pan, and let pears cool in liquid. Cover and chill thoroughly.

Spoon 2 tablespoons chilled liquid onto each of 4 individual dessert plates; place pears on liquid. Drizzle 1 tablespoon chilled liquid over each pear. Yield: 4 servings (180 calories per serving).

PROTEIN 0.9   FAT 0.9   (Saturated Fat 0.1)   CARBOHYDRATE 47.0
FIBER 4.7   CHOLESTEROL 0   IRON 0.8   SODIUM 3   CALCIUM 30

HONEY-ORANGE STRAWBERRIES

½ cup frozen orange juice concentrate, thawed
2 tablespoons honey
4 cups fresh ripe strawberries, quartered
Fresh mint sprigs (optional)

Combine orange juice concentrate and honey in a small bowl. Pour over strawberries, tossing gently to coat. Spoon mixture evenly into 8 individual dessert bowls. Garnish with mint sprigs, if desired. Yield: 8 servings (65 calories per ½-cup serving).

PROTEIN 0.9   FAT 0.3   (Saturated Fat 0)   CARBOHYDRATE 15.9
FIBER 1.9   CHOLESTEROL 0   IRON 0.3   SODIUM 1   CALCIUM 15

FLUFFY ORANGE CHIFFON

⅔ cup evaporated skimmed milk
1 envelope unflavored gelatin
1 cup fresh orange juice
1 teaspoon grated orange rind
3 tablespoons powdered sugar

Refrigerate milk at least 8 hours. Sprinkle gelatin over orange juice in a small nonaluminum saucepan; let stand 1 minute. Cook over medium heat, stirring constantly, until gelatin dissolves. Remove from heat, and stir in orange rind. Cool completely.

Place milk in a large chilled bowl; beat at high speed of an electric mixer until soft peaks form. Gradually add powdered sugar, 1 tablespoon at a time, beating until stiff peaks form. Gently fold in orange juice mixture. Spoon into individual serving dishes; chill until set. Yield: 9 servings (40 calories per ½-cup serving).

PROTEIN 2.3   FAT 0.1   (Saturated Fat 0)   CARBOHYDRATE 7.7
FIBER 0.1   CHOLESTEROL 1   IRON 0.1   SODIUM 23   CALCIUM 58

 HOW MUCH SHOULD YOU WEIGH?
Sometimes people's standards of "ideal" body weight are too stringent. While using the following formula to see how much you should weigh, remember that people vary in frame size. Subtract 10 percent from the total if you are small-boned; if you have a large frame, add 10 percent. WOMEN: Allow 100 pounds for the first 5 feet of height. Next, add 5 pounds for each additional inch. If you are 5'6" tall, for example, you should weigh about 130 pounds.
MEN: Allow 106 pounds for the first 5 feet of height. Next, add 6 pounds for each additional inch. A man who is 5'10" tall should weigh about 166 pounds.

Your friends will rave about Ginger Crème Caramel, a creamy, rich-tasting dessert.

GINGER CRÈME CARAMEL

¾ cup sugar
¼ cup water
¼ teaspoon cream of tartar
2½ cups 1% low-fat milk
1¼ cups frozen egg substitute, thawed
½ cup sugar
2 tablespoons minced crystallized ginger

Combine first 3 ingredients in a small saucepan; stir well. Cook over medium-low heat until sugar dissolves, stirring constantly. Bring to a boil; cook, without stirring, until mixture is caramel-colored or candy thermometer reaches 340°.

Remove from heat, and immediately pour mixture into an 8-inch round cake pan, tilting to coat bottom evenly; set aside.

Place milk in a heavy saucepan; cook over medium heat until thoroughly heated. Combine egg substitute and ½ cup sugar in a medium bowl; stir with a wire whisk until well blended. Gradually add warm milk, stirring well. Stir in ginger. Pour into prepared pan.

Place pan in a 13- x 9- x 2-inch baking pan; pour hot water into baking pan to a depth of 1 inch. Place in a 350° oven. Reduce heat to 325°, and bake 1 hour or until knife inserted halfway between center and edge comes out clean. Remove pan from water, and let cool on a wire rack. Cover and chill overnight. Unmold onto a serving platter. Yield: 8 servings (175 calories per serving).

PROTEIN 6.2   FAT 0.8   (Saturated Fat 0.5)   CARBOHYDRATE 36.4
FIBER 0   CHOLESTEROL 3   IRON 1.0   SODIUM 102   CALCIUM 109

ORANGE-APRICOT CUSTARD

2½ cups skim milk
1 (8-ounce) carton frozen egg substitute, thawed
½ cup apricot nectar
¼ cup sugar
1 tablespoon grated orange rind

Combine all ingredients in a large bowl. Beat at medium speed of an electric mixer until smooth. Pour mixture evenly into 8 (6-ounce) custard cups. Place custard cups in two 9-inch square baking pans; pour hot water into pans to a depth of 1 inch. Bake at 350° for 50 to 55 minutes or until a knife inserted in center comes out clean. Remove custard cups from water. Chill thoroughly. Yield: 8 servings (74 calories per ½-cup serving).

PROTEIN 5.5   FAT 0.1   (Saturated Fat 0.1)   CARBOHYDRATE 12.8
FIBER 0.1   CHOLESTEROL 2   IRON 0.6   SODIUM 83   CALCIUM 106

CRANBERRY SORBET

3 cups frozen cranberries, thawed
⅔ cup sugar
2 cups water
1¼ cups cranberry-apple juice
1 teaspoon grated lemon rind
3 tablespoons fresh lemon juice

Combine cranberries and sugar in a medium saucepan; cook over medium-low heat 16 to 18 minutes or until cranberry skins pop and mixture thickens, stirring frequently. Remove from heat. Press cranberry mixture through a sieve; discard skins and seeds. Combine cranberry mixture, water, and remaining ingredients; stir well.

Pour into freezer can of a 2-quart hand-turned or electric freezer. Freeze according to manufacturer's instructions. Let ripen 1 hour, if desired. Scoop sorbet into individual dessert bowls. Serve immediately. Yield: 6½ cups (68 calories per ½-cup serving).

PROTEIN 0.1   FAT 0.1   (Saturated Fat 0)   CARBOHYDRATE 17.7
FIBER 0.3   CHOLESTEROL 0   IRON 0.1   SODIUM 1   CALCIUM 4

PINK GRAPEFRUIT ICE

½ cup sugar
1¾ cups water
3 cups fresh pink grapefruit juice
2 tablespoons grenadine syrup
Fresh mint sprigs (optional)

Combine sugar and water in a small saucepan. Bring to a boil; cook over medium heat until sugar dissolves, stirring constantly. Boil 5 minutes without stirring. Remove from heat, and let cool slightly.

Combine sugar mixture, grapefruit juice, and grenadine syrup; stir well. Cover and chill thoroughly.

Pour mixture into freezer can of a 2-quart hand-turned or electric freezer. Freeze according to manufacturer's instructions. Let ripen 1 hour, if desired. Scoop into individual dessert bowls. Garnish with fresh mint sprigs, if desired. Serve immediately. Yield: 5 cups (69 calories per ½-cup serving).

PROTEIN 0.4   FAT 0.1   (Saturated Fat 0)   CARBOHYDRATE 17.2
FIBER 0   CHOLESTEROL 0   IRON 1.5   SODIUM 1   CALCIUM 5

PINK LEMONADE ICE MILK CAKE

1 (16-ounce) round angel food cake
3 cups vanilla ice milk, softened
½ cup plus 1 tablespoon frozen pink lemonade
   concentrate, unthawed
1 cup chopped fresh strawberries

Slice cake horizontally into 3 layers; set aside.

Combine softened ice milk, pink lemonade concentrate, and chopped strawberries in a large bowl; stir well. Place bottom layer of angel food cake in an 8-inch tube pan; spread half of ice milk mixture over cake, and top with middle layer of cake. Freeze 30 minutes. Spread remaining ice milk mixture over middle layer of cake, and top with remaining cake layer. Cover and freeze 4 hours or until firm. Slice into wedges. Yield: 16 servings (129 calories per serving).

PROTEIN 2.6   FAT 1.2   (Saturated Fat 0.7)   CARBOHYDRATE 27.8
FIBER 0.3   CHOLESTEROL 3   IRON 0.2   SODIUM 62   CALCIUM 62

Ripe peaches provide fresh summertime flavor to every spoonful of Peach Ice Milk.

PEACH ICE MILK

3 cups mashed ripe peaches (about 10 small
    peaches)
⅓ cup sugar
½ cup frozen egg substitute, thawed
½ cup sugar
1½ tablespoons all-purpose flour
Dash of salt
3 cups 1% low-fat milk
2 teaspoons vanilla extract

Combine peaches and ⅓ cup sugar; stir well. Let stand 15 minutes.

Beat egg substitute at medium speed of an electric mixer until foamy. Combine ½ cup sugar, flour, and salt in a small bowl; stir well. Gradually add flour mixture to egg substitute, beating well. Add milk, and mix well. Cook in a large saucepan over medium-low heat, stirring constantly, until mixture is slightly thickened. Remove from heat, and let cool. Add peach mixture and vanilla; stir well. Cover mixture and chill thoroughly.

Pour mixture into freezer can of a 5-quart hand-turned or electric freezer. Freeze according to manufacturer's instructions. Let ripen 1 hour, if desired. Scoop ice milk into individual dessert bowls. Serve immediately. Yield: 2 quarts (89 calories per ½-cup serving).

PROTEIN 2.7 FAT 0.5 (Saturated Fat 0.3) CARBOHYDRATE 18.9
FIBER 0.8 CHOLESTEROL 2 IRON 0.3 SODIUM 43 CALCIUM 61

LEMON FROZEN YOGURT

1½ teaspoons unflavored gelatin
¼ cup fresh lemon juice
2 (8-ounce) cartons plain nonfat yogurt
⅓ cup sugar
1 teaspoon grated lemon rind
3 egg whites
⅛ teaspoon cream of tartar
½ cup sugar
¼ cup water

Sprinkle gelatin over lemon juice in a small saucepan; let stand 1 minute. Cook over low heat, stirring constantly, until gelatin dissolves.

Combine yogurt, ⅓ cup sugar, and lemon rind, stirring until sugar dissolves. Add gelatin mixture, stirring well. Set aside.

Beat egg whites and cream of tartar at high speed of an electric mixer until stiff peaks form.

Combine ½ cup sugar and water in a small saucepan. Bring to a boil; cook, without stirring, until candy thermometer registers 238° (about 7 minutes).

Gradually pour sugar mixture in a thin stream over beaten egg whites while beating constantly at high speed. Continue to beat until egg white mixture is cool and set.

Fold yogurt mixture into egg white mixture; pour mixture into freezer can of a 2-quart hand-turned or electric freezer. Freeze according to manufacturer's instructions. Let ripen 1 hour, if desired. Scoop yogurt into individual dessert bowls. Serve immediately. Yield: 4½ cups (108 calories per ½-cup serving).

PROTEIN 4.5 FAT 0.1 (Saturated Fat 0.1) CARBOHYDRATE 23.0
FIBER 0 CHOLESTEROL 1 IRON 0.1 SODIUM 60 CALCIUM 102

LAYERED SHERBET DESSERT

½ cup vanilla wafer crumbs (about 14 wafers)
½ cup crisp rice cereal
¼ cup reduced-calorie margarine, melted
3 cups raspberry sherbet, softened
3 cups lime sherbet, softened
3 cups orange sherbet, softened

Combine first 3 ingredients; stir well. Firmly press crumb mixture evenly over bottom of a 9-inch springform pan. Bake at 350° for 15 minutes. Remove from oven, and cool completely.

Spread raspberry sherbet evenly over crust; cover and freeze until firm. Repeat procedure with lime sherbet and orange sherbet. Cover and freeze at least 4 hours or until firm.

To serve, carefully remove sides of springform pan. Slice dessert into wedges. Serve immediately. Yield: 14 servings (188 calories per serving).

PROTEIN 1.5 FAT 4.6 (Saturated Fat 1.4) CARBOHYDRATE 36.5
FIBER 0 CHOLESTEROL 3 IRON 0.2 SODIUM 133 CALCIUM 57

CINNAMON APPLE SKILLET COBBLER

¼ cup plus 3 tablespoons sugar, divided
1 tablespoon margarine
6 Granny Smith apples (about 2¾ pounds), peeled, cored, and cut into 8 wedges each
2 tablespoons cornstarch
1 teaspoon ground cinnamon
2 teaspoons grated lemon rind, divided
¾ cup all-purpose flour
½ teaspoon baking powder
3 tablespoons margarine, melted
2 teaspoons vinegar

Combine ¼ cup sugar and 1 tablespoon margarine in a 10-inch cast-iron skillet; cook over medium heat 5 minutes or until mixture is golden, stirring frequently.

Combine apples, cornstarch, cinnamon, and 1 teaspoon lemon rind; toss gently. Layer apple mixture in skillet; sprinkle with 2 tablespoons sugar.

Combine flour, baking powder, remaining 1 tablespoon sugar, and remaining 1 teaspoon lemon rind in a bowl, stirring well. Combine melted margarine and vinegar; add to flour mixture. Stir with a fork just until dry ingredients are moistened. Shape into a ball.

Place dough between 2 sheets of heavy-duty plastic wrap. Roll dough into a 10½-inch circle. Remove top sheet of plastic wrap; invert over apple mixture. Remove remaining sheet of plastic wrap. Cut slits in pastry for steam to escape. Bake at 375° for 45 minutes or until apples are tender and crust is golden. Yield: 8 servings (211 calories per serving).

PROTEIN 1.4   FAT 6.2   (Saturated Fat 1.1)   CARBOHYDRATE 39.5
FIBER 3.6   CHOLESTEROL 0   IRON 0.7   SODIUM 86   CALCIUM 25

 ROW YOUR BOAT

Whether you do it on land or in the water, rowing is an excellent way to get in shape. As you start in the forward position, the simple but strenuous motion of moving the body backward (by extending the legs and pulling on the oars or rowing machine levers) utilizes the muscles of the shoulders, arms, chest, back, and legs.

Returning to the starting position reworks some of these same muscles as well as a few additional leg and abdominal muscles. Because it works major muscle groups and can burn 300 to 500 calories per hour, rowing is what fitness experts call a total body workout.

APPLE CRÊPES WITH APRICOT SAUCE

1 (6-ounce) bag dried apricots
2 cups water
½ cup sugar
3 tablespoons brandy
½ teaspoon vanilla extract
½ cup boiling water
1½ tablespoons currants
1½ tablespoons margarine
2¾ cups peeled, chopped Granny Smith apple
1½ tablespoons sugar
⅛ teaspoon ground cinnamon
½ teaspoon grated lemon rind
Light Crêpes

Combine first 4 ingredients in a saucepan; bring to a boil. Partially cover, reduce heat, and simmer 25 minutes or until apricots are tender. Remove from heat, and stir in vanilla. Pour mixture into container of an electric blender or food processor; top with cover, and process until smooth. Cover and chill thoroughly.

Combine boiling water and currants in a small bowl; let stand 10 minutes. Drain currants, and set aside.

Melt margarine in large nonstick skillet over high heat; add apple. Gradually add 1½ tablespoons sugar, stirring constantly until apple is lightly browned and crisp-tender. Remove from heat; stir in reserved currants, cinnamon, and lemon rind.

To serve, spoon apple mixture evenly over half of each Light Crêpe, and fold crêpes over. Spoon apricot sauce evenly onto individual dessert plates; place crêpes on sauce. Serve immediately. Yield: 10 servings (206 calories per serving).

Light Crêpes

¾ cup plus 2 tablespoons all-purpose flour
½ teaspoon sugar
Dash of salt
¾ cup skim milk
¼ cup water
¼ teaspoon vanilla extract
⅓ cup frozen egg substitute, thawed
1 tablespoon margarine, melted
Vegetable cooking spray

Combine first 6 ingredients in a medium bowl; beat at medium speed of an electric mixer until batter is smooth. Add egg substitute, and beat well. Stir in margarine. Refrigerate batter 1 hour. (This allows flour particles to swell and soften so that crêpes will be light in texture.)

Coat a 6-inch nonstick skillet with cooking spray; place over medium heat just until hot, not smoking. Pour 2 tablespoons batter into pan; quickly tilt pan in all directions so batter covers bottom of pan in a thin film. Cook 1 minute or until lightly browned.

Lift edge of crêpe to test for doneness. Crêpe is ready for flipping when it can be shaken loose from pan. Flip crêpe, and cook about 30 seconds on other side. (This side is usually spotty brown and is the side on which the filling is placed.)

Place crêpes on a towel to cool. Stack crêpes between layers of wax paper to prevent sticking. Repeat procedure until all batter is used. Yield: 10 crêpes.

PROTEIN 3.3   FAT 3.7   (Saturated Fat 0.6)   CARBOHYDRATE 42.2
FIBER 2.5   CHOLESTEROL 0   IRON 1.6   SODIUM 83   CALCIUM 41

Hardly anyone can resist the home-baked freshness of Deep-Dish Cherry Pie.

DEEP-DISH CHERRY PIE

1 cup sifted cake flour
1 tablespoon sugar
½ teaspoon baking powder
¼ cup margarine
2 tablespoons water
Vegetable cooking spray
4 (16-ounce) cans tart cherries in water
⅔ cup sugar
⅓ cup cornstarch
1 teaspoon ground cinnamon
½ teaspoon almond extract

Combine first 3 ingredients in a bowl; cut in margarine with a pastry blender until mixture resembles coarse meal. Sprinkle water, 1 tablespoon at a time, over surface; stir with a fork until dry ingredients are moistened. Shape dough into a ball.

Place dough between 2 sheets of heavy-duty plastic wrap. Roll dough to a 12-inch circle. Remove top sheet of plastic wrap; invert pastry into a deep-dish 10-inch pieplate coated with cooking spray, and remove remaining sheet of plastic wrap. Fold edges under and flute, if desired.

Drain cherries, reserving 1¼ cups liquid. Set cherries aside. Combine reserved cherry liquid, ⅔ cup sugar, and cornstarch in a large saucepan, stirring well. Cook over medium heat until thickened and bubbly, stirring constantly. Gently stir in cherries, cinnamon, and almond extract.

Pour cherry mixture into prepared pastry shell. Shield crust, and bake at 400° for 20 minutes. Reduce heat to 375°; bake, unshielded, 25 to 30 minutes or until filling is hot and bubbly. Serve pie warm or at room temperature. Yield: 10 servings (204 calories per serving).

PROTEIN 1.7   FAT 4.7   (Saturated Fat 0.8)   CARBOHYDRATE 37.8
FIBER 0.5   CHOLESTEROL 0   IRON 2.1   SODIUM 78   CALCIUM 15

FRESH STRAWBERRY PIE

1¼ cups plus 1 tablespoon sifted cake flour
1 tablespoon sugar
½ teaspoon baking powder
¼ teaspoon salt
2 tablespoons plus 1½ teaspoons margarine
2 tablespoons Nêufchatel cheese
2 tablespoons plus 2 teaspoons ice water
1 tablespoon plus 2 teaspoons lemon juice, divided
7½ cups sliced fresh strawberries, divided
¼ cup sugar
1½ teaspoons unflavored gelatin
3 tablespoons cold water
¾ cup frozen strawberry daiquiri fruit juice
   concentrate, thawed
3 tablespoons cornstarch
¼ cup water

Combine first 4 ingredients in a large bowl; cut in margarine and Nêufchatel cheese with a pastry blender until mixture resembles coarse meal and is pale yellow (about 3½ minutes). Combine ice water and 2 teaspoons lemon juice; sprinkle, 1 tablespoon at a time, over flour mixture. Toss with a fork until dry ingredients are moistened and mixture is crumbly.

Gently press mixture to a 4-inch circle on heavy-duty plastic wrap. Roll to a 12½-inch circle between 2 sheets of heavy-duty plastic wrap. Remove top sheet of plastic wrap; invert pastry into a 10-inch pieplate. Remove remaining sheet of plastic wrap. Fold edges under and flute. Prick bottom of pastry with a fork. Line with foil; fill with pie weights. Bake at 400° for 12 minutes or until golden; cool completely on a wire rack.

Position knife blade in food processor bowl; add 1½ cups strawberries. Process until smooth. Toss remaining 6 cups strawberries with ¼ cup sugar in a bowl.

Sprinkle gelatin over 3 tablespoons cold water in a medium saucepan; let stand 1 minute. Add pureed strawberries, fruit juice concentrate, and remaining 1 tablespoon lemon juice; cook over medium heat until gelatin dissolves. Combine cornstarch and ¼ cup water, stirring until smooth; add to gelatin mixture. Cook over medium heat 2 minutes or until thickened and glossy, stirring constantly; cool slightly. Stir in sliced strawberry mixture. Spoon mixture into prepared pastry shell. Cover and chill at least 4 hours. Yield: 10 servings (192 calories per serving).

PROTEIN 2.3 FAT 3.7 (Saturated Fat 0.5) CARBOHYDRATE 38.2
FIBER 3.0 CHOLESTEROL 1 IRON 1.4 SODIUM 115 CALCIUM 30

JEWELLED RASPBERRY TARTLETS

2 cups plain nonfat yogurt
1¾ cups regular oats, uncooked
¼ cup firmly packed brown sugar
2 tablespoons all-purpose flour
¼ cup reduced-calorie margarine, melted
Vegetable cooking spray
1 (8-ounce) package Nêufchatel cheese, softened
¼ cup sugar
1 teaspoon grated lemon rind
1 tablespoon fresh lemon juice
¾ cup reduced-calorie apple spread
3 cups fresh raspberries

Line a colander or sieve with a double layer of cheesecloth that has been rinsed out and squeezed dry; allow cheesecloth to extend over edge of colander. Spoon yogurt into colander; fold edges of cheesecloth over yogurt. Place in a large bowl; refrigerate 12 hours. Scrape yogurt into a bowl; discard liquid.

Position knife blade in food processor bowl; add oats, brown sugar, and flour. Process until finely ground. Add margarine; process until combined.

Press 3 tablespoons oat mixture on bottom and ½ inch up sides of each of 10 (4-inch) tartlet pans coated with cooking spray. Bake at 350° for 15 minutes or until golden. Cool completely on wire racks.

Beat Nêufchatel cheese at medium speed of an electric mixer until smooth. Add sugar; beat well. Stir in drained yogurt, lemon rind, and lemon juice. Spoon evenly into prepared crusts. Place apple spread in a small saucepan; bring to a boil, stirring with a wire whisk until smooth. Arrange raspberries evenly over tarts. Brush with warm apple spread. Cover and chill 3 hours. Yield: 10 tartlets (241 calories each).

PROTEIN 7.6 FAT 9.6 (Saturated Fat 4.0) CARBOHYDRATE 32.8
FIBER 4.1 CHOLESTEROL 18 IRON 1.2 SODIUM 171 CALCIUM 128

KIWIFRUIT AND BANANA TART

1¼ cups regular oats, uncooked
3 tablespoons shredded coconut
3 tablespoons brown sugar
1½ tablespoons all-purpose flour
¼ cup reduced-calorie margarine
Vegetable cooking spray
2 egg whites
½ cup sugar
¼ cup water
⅛ teaspoon cream of tartar
½ cup 1% low-fat cottage cheese
4 ounces Nêufchatel cheese, softened
1 teaspoon grated lime rind
1 tablespoon fresh lime juice
3 kiwifruit, peeled and cut into
    ¼-inch-thick slices
2 medium-sized bananas, peeled and
    cut into ¼-inch-thick slices
¼ cup lime-shred marmalade

Position knife blade in food processor bowl; add first 4 ingredients, and process until mixture is ground. Add margarine, and process until combined. Press oat mixture into bottom and ½ inch up sides of an 11-inch tart pan coated with cooking spray. Bake at 350° for 15 minutes or until golden. Remove from oven, and let cool on a wire rack.

Beat egg whites at high speed of an electric mixer until stiff peaks form. Combine sugar, water, and cream of tartar in a small saucepan. Bring to a boil; cook, without stirring, until candy thermometer registers 238° (about 7 minutes).

Gradually pour sugar mixture in a thin stream over beaten egg whites while beating constantly at high speed. Continue to beat until egg white mixture is cool and set.

Place cottage cheese in processor bowl; process until smooth. Add Nêufchatel cheese, lime rind, and lime juice; process until blended. Transfer to a large bowl. Gently fold egg white mixture into cheese mixture. Spoon into prepared crust. Arrange kiwifruit and banana over tart.

Place marmalade in a small saucepan; bring to a boil, stirring constantly with a wire whisk until smooth.

Brush marmalade over fruit. Cover tart, and refrigerate at least 2 hours. Yield: 12 servings (186 calories per serving).

PROTEIN 4.6   FAT 6.0   (Saturated Fat 2.3)   CARBOHYDRATE 30.1
FIBER 2.2   CHOLESTEROL 8   IRON 0.8   SODIUM 129   CALCIUM 30

CHOCOLATE SOUFFLÉS

Vegetable cooking spray
½ cup plus 2½ tablespoons sugar, divided
¼ cup unsweetened cocoa
2 tablespoons cornstarch
1 teaspoon instant espresso powder
½ teaspoon ground cinnamon
1 cup skim milk
2 egg yolks, lightly beaten
5 egg whites
½ teaspoon cream of tartar

Coat 10 individual (¾-cup) soufflé dishes or custard cups with cooking spray. Sprinkle dishes evenly with 2½ tablespoons sugar, carefully shaking to coat bottom and sides of each dish; set aside.

Combine ¼ cup sugar and next 4 ingredients in a medium saucepan. Gradually add milk, stirring with a wire whisk until well blended. Cook over medium heat, stirring constantly, until mixture is thoroughly heated. Remove from heat. Gradually stir about one-fourth of hot mixture into egg yolks; add to remaining hot mixture, stirring constantly.

Beat egg whites and cream of tartar in a large bowl at high speed of an electric mixer until soft peaks form. Gradually add remaining ¼ cup sugar, 1 tablespoon at a time, beating until stiff peaks form.

Gently fold one-fourth of egg white mixture into chocolate mixture. Gently fold remaining egg white mixture into chocolate mixture. Spoon evenly into prepared dishes. Bake at 375° for 15 to 16 minutes or until soufflés are puffed. Serve immediately. Yield: 10 servings (98 calories per serving).

PROTEIN 3.8   FAT 1.6   (Saturated Fat 0.5)   CARBOHYDRATE 17.1
FIBER 0   CHOLESTEROL 44   IRON 0.6   SODIUM 53   CALCIUM 41

TRIPLE BERRY ANGEL FOOD SHORTCAKES

2 cups fresh blackberries
2 cups sliced fresh strawberries
1 cup fresh blueberries
3 tablespoons sugar
¾ cup nonfat sour cream
¼ cup plain nonfat yogurt
2 tablespoons sugar
Vegetable cooking spray
1 tablespoon sugar
5 egg whites
¾ teaspoon cream of tartar
¼ cup plus 2 tablespoons sugar
1 teaspoon fresh lemon juice
½ teaspoon almond extract
½ teaspoon vanilla extract
½ cup sifted cake flour
2 tablespoons sugar

Combine first 4 ingredients in a medium bowl; toss gently. Cover and chill thoroughly.

Combine sour cream, yogurt, and 2 tablespoons sugar in a small bowl. Cover and chill thoroughly.

Coat bottom and sides of 10 individual (½-cup) ovenproof molds or soufflé dishes with cooking spray.

Sprinkle evenly with 1 tablespoon sugar, carefully shaking to coat bottom and sides of each mold. Place on a large baking sheet, and set aside.

Beat egg whites in a large bowl at high speed of an electric mixer until foamy. Add cream of tartar, and beat until soft peaks form. Gradually add ¼ cup plus 2 tablespoons sugar, 1 tablespoon at a time, beating until stiff peaks form. Sprinkle lemon juice and flavorings over egg whites, and gently fold in.

Combine flour and 2 tablespoons sugar in a small bowl; stir well. Sift flour mixture over egg white mixture; gently fold in.

Spoon batter into prepared molds. Bake at 300° for 30 to 33 minutes or until lightly browned and top springs back when lightly touched. Remove from molds, and let cool on a wire rack.

To serve, place cakes on individual dessert plates. Spoon blackberry mixture evenly over each cake. Dollop each serving with sour cream mixture, and serve immediately. Yield: 10 servings (143 calories per serving).

PROTEIN 4.1 FAT 0.5 (Saturated Fat 0) CARBOHYDRATE 30.8
FIBER 3.5 CHOLESTEROL 0 IRON 0.7 SODIUM 60 CALCIUM 46

CHOCOLATE-ESPRESSO ANGEL FOOD CAKE

1¼ cups sifted cake flour
1¼ cups sugar, divided
⅓ cup unsweetened cocoa
1 teaspoon ground cinnamon
12 egg whites
1 teaspoon cream of tartar
1 tablespoon instant espresso powder
2 tablespoons warm water
1 teaspoon vanilla extract
1 tablespoon powdered sugar

Sift flour, ¾ cup sugar, cocoa, and cinnamon together 3 times; set aside.

Beat egg whites and cream of tartar in an extra-large bowl at high speed of an electric mixer until foamy. Gradually add remaining ½ cup sugar, beating

until soft peaks form. Sift flour mixture over egg white mixture, 2 tablespoons at a time; fold in gently after each addition. Combine espresso powder and water. Fold espresso mixture and vanilla into batter.

Spoon batter into an ungreased 10-inch tube pan; spread evenly with a spatula. Break large air pockets by cutting through batter with a knife.

Bake at 300° for 50 minutes or until cake springs back when lightly touched. Remove cake from oven; invert pan, and cool completely. Loosen cake from sides of pan, using a narrow metal spatula; remove from pan. Sift powdered sugar over cooled cake. Yield: 12 servings (148 calories per serving).

PROTEIN 5.0 FAT 0.4 (Saturated Fat 0.2) CARBOHYDRATE 31.0
FIBER 0.3 CHOLESTEROL 0 IRON 1.3 SODIUM 69 CALCIUM 10

GINGER-APPLE UPSIDE DOWN CAKE

¾ cup boiling water
¼ cup currants
2 Granny Smith apples, peeled and sliced
1½ teaspoons grated lemon rind
1 tablespoon lemon juice
½ teaspoon ground cinnamon
Vegetable cooking spray
2 tablespoons reduced-calorie margarine
3 tablespoons brown sugar
¼ cup margarine, softened
½ cup sugar
1 egg
½ cup molasses
1½ cups all-purpose flour
¾ teaspoon baking powder
¾ teaspoon baking soda
1 teaspoon ground cinnamon
1 teaspoon ground ginger
¼ teaspoon ground cloves
¾ cup hot water

Combine boiling water and currants in a small bowl; let stand 15 minutes. Drain well. Combine currants, apple, lemon rind, lemon juice, and ½ teaspoon cinnamon, stirring well; set aside.

Coat a 10-inch cast-iron skillet with cooking spray; add reduced-calorie margarine, and place over medium heat until margarine melts. Sprinkle brown sugar evenly over margarine. Remove skillet from heat, and arrange apple mixture evenly over brown sugar mixture; set aside.

Cream ¼ cup margarine in a medium bowl; gradually add sugar, beating at medium speed of an electric mixer until light and fluffy. Add egg, beating well. Stir in molasses.

Combine flour and next 5 ingredients, stirring well. Add flour mixture to creamed mixture alternately with ¾ cup hot water; beat until well blended.

Pour batter evenly over apple mixture in skillet. Bake at 350° for 35 to 40 minutes or until wooden pick inserted in center comes out clean. Let stand 5 minutes; invert cake onto a serving platter. Yield: 10 servings (240 calories per serving).

PROTEIN 2.7 FAT 7.0 (Saturated Fat 1.2) CARBOHYDRATE 43.2
FIBER 1.4 CHOLESTEROL 21 IRON 2.2 SODIUM 175 CALCIUM 94

ORANGE POPPY SEED CAKE

⅓ cup margarine, softened
¾ cup sugar
¼ cup frozen egg substitute, thawed
1 cup nonfat sour cream
2 teaspoons grated orange rind
2 cups sifted cake flour
1 teaspoon baking soda
½ teaspoon baking powder
¼ teaspoon salt
1 tablespoon poppy seeds
⅓ cup unsweetened orange juice
Vegetable cooking spray
⅓ cup sifted powdered sugar
2 teaspoons unsweetened orange juice

Cream margarine; gradually add sugar, beating at medium speed of an electric mixer until light and fluffy. Add egg substitute, sour cream, and orange rind; beat until well blended.

Combine flour, baking soda, baking powder, salt and poppy seeds, stirring well. Add flour mixture to creamed mixture alternately with ⅓ cup orange juice, beginning and ending with flour mixture. Mix after each addition.

Pour batter into a 9-inch square baking pan coated with cooking spray. Bake at 350° for 35 minutes or until a wooden pick inserted in center of cake comes out clean.

Combine powdered sugar and 2 teaspoons orange juice. Drizzle over warm cake. Yield: 12 servings (188 calories per serving).

PROTEIN 3.4 FAT 5.5 (Saturated Fat 0.9) CARBOHYDRATE 30.8
FIBER 0.1 CHOLESTEROL 0 IRON 1.3 SODIUM 211 CALCIUM 60

BLUEBERRY CHEESECAKE SQUARES

½ cup graham cracker crumbs
Vegetable cooking spray
2 (8-ounce) packages Nêufchatel cheese
1 cup 1% low-fat cottage cheese
¼ cup plus 2 tablespoons sugar
2 teaspoons vanilla extract
3 eggs
1 (16-ounce) package frozen unsweetened
  blueberries, thawed
3 tablespoons sugar
1 teaspoon grated lemon rind
2 tablespoons fresh lemon juice
2 tablespoons cornstarch

Spread cracker crumbs evenly in a 13- x 9- x 2-inch baking dish coated with cooking spray. Position knife blade in food processor bowl; add Nêufchatel cheese, cottage cheese, ¼ cup plus 2 tablespoons sugar, and vanilla. Process until smooth. Add eggs, 1 at a time, and process just until blended. Carefully pour batter into prepared dish. Bake at 350° for 18 to 20 minutes or until mixture is almost set. Remove from oven, and let cool 30 minutes on a wire rack.

Combine blueberries, 3 tablespoons sugar, lemon rind, and lemon juice in a large saucepan. Add cornstarch, and stir well. Bring to a boil, stirring constantly. Cook 1 minute or until mixture is thickened, stirring constantly. Remove from heat, and let cool slightly. Spoon blueberry mixture over cheesecake. Cover and chill at least 6 hours. Yield: 18 servings (147 calories per serving).

PROTEIN 5.5 FAT 7.5 (Saturated Fat 4.2) CARBOHYDRATE 14.6
FIBER 0.9 CHOLESTEROL 55 IRON 0.4 SODIUM 188 CALCIUM 34

ORANGE MARMALADE CHEESECAKE

2 (16-ounce) cartons plain nonfat yogurt
Vegetable cooking spray
5 (2-inch-diameter) gingersnaps, crushed
2 (8-ounce) packages Nêufchatel cheese, softened
½ cup sugar
2 eggs
4 egg whites
2 tablespoons frozen orange juice concentrate,
  thawed
1 tablespoon grated orange rind
1 teaspoon orange extract
½ cup low-sugar orange marmalade, melted
Orange rind curls (optional)

Line a colander or sieve with a double layer of cheesecloth that has been rinsed out and squeezed dry; allow cheesecloth to extend over edge of colander. Spoon yogurt into colander, and fold edges of cheesecloth over to cover yogurt. Place colander in a large bowl; refrigerate 12 hours. Scrape yogurt into a bowl, using a rubber spatula; discard liquid.

Coat a 10-inch springform pan with cooking spray. Sprinkle crushed gingersnaps evenly over bottom of springform pan.

Position knife blade in food processor bowl. Add Nêufchatel cheese and sugar; process until light and fluffy. Add drained yogurt, and process until smooth. Add eggs, egg whites, orange juice concentrate, orange rind, and orange extract; process until mixture is well blended.

Spoon mixture over crushed gingersnaps. Bake at 350° for 35 minutes (center will be soft but will firm when chilled). Remove from oven, and let cool to room temperature on a wire rack. Cover and chill 4 hours or until set.

Spread marmalade evenly over top of cheesecake. Garnish with orange rind curls, if desired. Cover and chill 1 hour or until marmalade is set. Yield: 14 servings (182 calories per serving).

PROTEIN 9.1 FAT 8.8 (Saturated Fat 5.2) CARBOHYDRATE 16.3
FIBER 0 CHOLESTEROL 57 IRON 0.4 SODIUM 208 CALCIUM 167

Clockwise from top right: Crispy Oatmeal Cookies and Black-Eyed Susans are nourishing cookies that will be enjoyed by young and old alike.

BLACK-EYED SUSANS

¼ cup margarine, softened
¼ cup sugar
¼ cup firmly packed brown sugar
½ cup creamy peanut butter
¼ cup frozen egg substitute, thawed
2 teaspoons warm water
¾ teaspoon vanilla extract
1 cup all-purpose flour
¼ teaspoon baking soda
¼ teaspoon salt
Vegetable cooking spray
1 tablespoon semisweet chocolate morsels

Cream margarine in a medium bowl; gradually add sugar and brown sugar, beating at medium speed of an electric mixer until mixture is light and fluffy. Add peanut butter, egg substitute, warm water, and vanilla; beat well.

Combine flour, baking soda, and salt, stirring well. Gradually add flour mixture to creamed mixture, mixing well.

Press dough from a cookie press onto cookie sheets coated with cooking spray, using a flower-shaped disk. Place a chocolate morsel in center of each cookie. Bake at 350° for 9 minutes or until lightly browned. Remove from cookie sheets, and cool completely on wire racks. Yield: 34 cookies (62 calories each).

PROTEIN 1.6   FAT 3.5   (Saturated Fat 0.7)   CARBOHYDRATE 6.5
FIBER 0.3   CHOLESTEROL 0   IRON 0.3   SODIUM 61   CALCIUM 6

CRISPY OATMEAL COOKIES

½ cup margarine, softened
½ cup sugar
½ cup firmly packed brown sugar
½ cup frozen egg substitute, thawed
1 teaspoon vanilla extract
1½ cups all-purpose flour
1 teaspoon baking powder
¾ teaspoon baking soda
¼ teaspoon salt
1¾ cups quick-cooking oats, uncooked
1½ cups corn flakes cereal
Vegetable cooking spray

Cream margarine; gradually add sugars, beating at medium speed of an electric mixer until light and fluffy. Add egg substitute and vanilla; beat well.

Combine flour and next 3 ingredients, stirring well. Add flour mixture to creamed mixture, mixing well. Stir in oats and cereal.

Drop dough by level tablespoonfuls, 2 inches apart, onto cookie sheets coated with cooking spray. Bake at 350° for 12 to 14 minutes. Remove from cookie sheets, and let cool completely on wire racks. Yield: 4 dozen (63 calories each).

PROTEIN 1.2 FAT 2.2 (Saturated Fat 0.4) CARBOHYDRATE 9.7
FIBER 0.4 CHOLESTEROL 0 IRON 0.5 SODIUM 67 CALCIUM 12

ORANGE-SPICE COOKIES

⅓ cup margarine, softened
⅔ cup sugar
¼ cup frozen egg substitute, thawed
1 tablespoon light-colored corn syrup
2 cups all-purpose flour
1 teaspoon baking soda
1 teaspoon ground ginger
1 teaspoon ground cinnamon
¼ teaspoon ground cloves
1½ teaspoons grated orange rind

Cream margarine; gradually add sugar, beating at medium speed of an electric mixer until light and fluffy. Add egg substitute and corn syrup; beat well. Combine flour and next 4 ingredients, stirring well. Gradually add flour mixture to creamed mixture, mixing well. Stir in orange rind.

Shape dough into a 15- x 1-inch log; wrap in plastic wrap, and refrigerate at least 4 hours. Unwrap log, and cut into ¼-inch slices. Place 2 inches apart on ungreased cookie sheets. Bake at 375° for 8 minutes or until lightly browned. Remove from cookie sheets, and let cool on wire racks. Yield: 4 dozen (42 calories each).

PROTEIN 0.6 FAT 1.3 (Saturated Fat 0.2) CARBOHYDRATE 6.9
FIBER 0.1 CHOLESTEROL 0 IRON 0.3 SODIUM 35 CALCIUM 6

VANILLA SLICE-AND-BAKE COOKIES

⅓ cup margarine, softened
⅔ cup sugar
¼ cup frozen egg substitute, thawed
2 teaspoons vanilla extract
2 cups plus 1 tablespoon all-purpose flour
½ teaspoon baking soda
¼ teaspoon salt
¾ cup crisp rice cereal
Vegetable cooking spray

Cream margarine; gradually add sugar, beating at medium speed of an electric mixer until light and fluffy. Add egg substitute and vanilla; beat well.

Combine flour, soda, and salt. Gradually add flour mixture to creamed mixture; mix well. Stir in cereal.

Divide dough into 2 equal portions; place each portion on a sheet of plastic wrap, and shape into an 8- x 1½-inch log. Wrap logs in plastic wrap, and freeze until firm.

Unwrap logs, and cut into ¼-inch slices. Place 1 inch apart on cookie sheets coated with cooking spray. Bake at 350° for 6 to 8 minutes or until lightly browned. Remove from cookie sheets, and let cool on wire racks. Yield: 64 cookies (32 calories each).

PROTEIN 0.5 FAT 1.0 (Saturated Fat 0.2) CARBOHYDRATE 5.2
FIBER 0.1 CHOLESTEROL 0 IRON 0.2 SODIUM 30 CALCIUM 3

Cooking Light 1993 Menu Plans

This plan for seven days of calorie-controlled meals provides a healthful approach to weight loss. Follow the plan precisely, or use it as a model for planning your own balanced meals by substituting foods of comparable calories and nutrients. Refer to the Calorie/Nutrient Chart on pages 250–261 for these values. The menu items marked with an asterisk are included in the menu or recipe sections and can be located in the Index. When planning your own menus, remember that of the total calories provided, at least 50 percent of the calories should be from carbohydrate, about 20 percent from protein, and no more than 30 percent from fat.

Most women can safely lose weight while eating 1,200 calories per day; most men can lose while eating 1,600. Once weight is lost, modify the menu plan according to the calories needed to maintain your ideal weight. If you feel that you are losing weight too slowly, keep in mind that eating fewer calories to speed up weight loss may rob you of the nutrients your body needs to stay healthy. Also, your metabolism may slow down to accommodate a limited food supply. Exercise is the key to speedier weight loss.

1200 calories		Day 1	1600 calories	
BREAKFAST				
1 each	127	*Carrot and Pineapple Muffins	2 each	254
1 teaspoon	17	Reduced-calorie margarine	2 teaspoons	34
½ cup	58	Apple juice	½ cup	58
1 cup	86	Skim milk	1 cup	86
	288			**432**
LUNCH				
1 serving	213	*Toasted Mozzarella Sandwiches	1 serving	213
		with Marinara Sauce		
1 cup	18	*Mixed Green Salad with	1 cup	18
		Raspberry Vinaigrette		
½ cup	103	*Glazed Waldorf Salad	½ cup	103
	334			**334**
DINNER				
1 serving	156	*Turkey-Vegetable Spiral	1 serving	156
½ cup	110	Brown rice	1 cup	220
½ cup	51	*Tarragon Brussels Sprouts	½ cup	51
—		*Herbed Garlic Bread	1 wedge	114
1 serving	180	*Steamed Pears with	1 serving	180
		Honey and Currants		
	497			**721**
SNACK				
3 cups	69	Air-popped popcorn	5 cups	115
	Total 1188			**Total 1602**
(Calories from Fat: 18%)			(Calories from Fat: 19%)	

1200 calories		Day 2	1600 calories	
BREAKFAST				
1 each	67	*Whole Wheat Buttermilk Pancakes	3 each	201
1 tablespoon	6	Reduced-calorie maple syrup	3 tablespoons	18
—		Reduced-calorie margarine	1 tablespoon	50
½ cup	56	Orange juice	½ cup	56
1 cup	86	Skim milk	1 cup	86
	215			**411**
LUNCH				
1 serving	252	*Grilled Turkey and Cheese	1 serving	252
		Sandwiches		
1 cup	166	*Dilled Pasta Salad	1 cup	166
½ cup	89	*Peach Ice Milk	½ cup	89
	507			**507**
DINNER				
1 serving	173	*Veal Patties Marsala	1 serving	173
½ cup	67	Boiled potatoes	½ cup	67
1 cup	24	Steamed broccoli	1 cup	24
—		Small kaiser roll	2 rolls	184
1 serving	87	*Cherries in Red Wine	1 serving	87
	351			**535**
SNACK				
1 cup	123	*Purple Cow	1 cup	123
	Total 1196			**Total 1576**
(Calories from Fat: 14%)			(Calories from Fat: 17%)	

1200 calories		Day 3	1600 calories	
BREAKFAST				
1 each	147	*Lemon-Raspberry Sweet Rolls	2 each	294
1 cup	59	Sliced honeydew	1 cup	59
1 cup	86	Skim milk	1 cup	86
	292			**439**
LUNCH				
1 serving	270	*Spicy Chicken Sandwiches	1 serving	270
1 cup	79	Fresh fruit cup	1 cup	79
1 tablespoon	19	*Cool Pineapple Dressing	2 tablespoons	38
	368			**387**
DINNER				
1 serving	294	*Blue Cheese-Stuffed	1 serving	294
		Sirloin Steak		
½ cup	147	*Four Grain Pilaf	½ cup	147
½ cup	22	Steamed green beans	½ cup	22
—		*Potato-Whole Wheat Cloverleaf Rolls	2 rolls	232
	463			**695**
SNACK				
1 pretzel	83	*Garlic-Mustard Soft Pretzels	1 pretzel	83
	Total 1206			**Total 1604**
(Calories from Fat: 22%)			(Calories from Fat: 21%)	

Day 4

1200 calories		Day 4	1600 calories	
		BREAKFAST		
1 each	99	*Citrus-Cranberry Twists	2 each	198
—		Grits	½ cup	73
—		Reduced-calorie margarine	1 teaspoon	17
½ cup	56	Orange juice	½ cup	56
1 cup	86	Skim milk	1 cup	86
	241			**430**
		LUNCH		
1 serving	247	*Layered Nacho Salad	1 serving	247
1 cup	109	*Poppy Seed Fruit Salad	1 cup	109
	356			**356**
		DINNER		
1 serving	243	*Glazed Pork Roast with Raisin Sauce	1 serving	243
1 serving	109	*Pumpkin Soufflé	1 serving	109
½ cup	62	Steamed green peas	1 cup	124
—		Brown-and-serve rolls	2 rolls	164
½ cup	68	*Cranberry Sorbet	½ cup	68
	482			**708**
		SNACK		
½ cup	110	*Nutty Cereal Snack	½ cup	110
	Total 1189			Total 1604
(Calories from Fat: 19%)			(Calories from Fat: 18%)	

Day 6

1200 calories		Day 6	1600 calories	
		BREAKFAST		
1 slice	134	*Banana-Date Loaf	1 slice	134
1 serving	79	*Cheese Grits Soufflé	2 servings	158
½ cup	47	Grapefruit juice	½ cup	47
1 cup	86	Skim milk	1 cup	86
	346			**425**
		LUNCH		
1 serving	227	*Harbor Salad	1 serving	227
5 crackers	140	*Caraway-Onion Crackers	6 crackers	168
½ cup	57	Seedless green grapes	½ cup	57
—		*Layered Sherbet Dessert	1 serving	188
	424			**640**
		DINNER		
1 serving	135	*Unsloppy Joes	1 serving	135
½ cup	43	*Festival Slaw	½ cup	43
1 serving	84	*Mexican Roasted Corn	1 serving	84
—		Vanilla ice milk	½ cup	92
	262			**354**
		SNACK		
4 each	172	*Sweet Wonton Snacks	4 each	172
	Total 1204			Total 1591
(Calories from Fat: 23%)			(Calories from Fat: 24%)	

Day 5

1200 calories		Day 5	1600 calories	
		BREAKFAST		
1 each	130	*Cardamom Yeast Waffles	2 each	260
1 tablespoon	18	*Peach-Raspberry Butter	2 tablespoons	36
1 cup	86	Skim milk	1 cup	86
	234			**382**
		LUNCH		
1 serving	235	*Chicken Salad Sandwiches Supreme	1 serving	235
½ cup	45	*Icy Hot Watermelon Salad	½ cup	45
1 cookie	63	*Crispy Oatmeal Cookies	3 cookies	189
—		Lime sherbet	½ cup	104
	343			**573**
		DINNER		
1 serving	246	*Italian Beef Pie	1 serving	246
1 serving	114	*Caesar Salad	1 serving	114
—		Whole wheat roll	1 roll	72
½ cup	108	*Lemon Frozen Yogurt	½ cup	108
	468			**540**
		SNACK		
4 chips	116	*Spicy Pita Chips	4 chips	116
	Total 1161			Total 1611
(Calories from Fat: 22%)			(Calories from Fat: 22%)	

Day 7

1200 calories		Day 7	1600 calories	
		BREAKFAST		
1 slice	84	*Miniature Brown Bread Loaves	2 slices	168
1 (8-oz) carton	127	Plain nonfat yogurt	1 (8-oz) carton	127
½ cup	22	Fresh strawberries	½ cup	22
	233			**317**
		LUNCH		
1 cup	154	*Chuck Wagon Stew	1 cup	154
1 wedge	84	Honey-Mustard Rye Rounds	1 wedge	84
½ cup	31	Carrot sticks	½ cup	31
1 serving	74	*Orange-Apricot Custard	1 serving	74
	343			**343**
		DINNER		
1 serving	193	*Sherried Roast Chicken	1 serving	193
1 serving	42	*Asparagus Dijon	1 serving	42
½ cup	149	*Fruited Wild Rice	½ cup	149
—		Hard rolls	2 rolls	312
1 serving	154	*Wine-Poached Peaches with Blackberry Sauce	1 serving	154
	538			**850**
		SNACK		
1 each	90	*Peanut Butter-Banana Pops	1 each	90
	Total 1204			Total 1600
(Calories from Fat: 14%)			(Calories from Fat: 12%)	

Calorie/Nutrient Chart

FOOD	APPROXIMATE MEASURE	FOOD ENERGY (CALORIES)	PROTEIN (GRAMS)	FAT (GRAMS)	SATURATED FAT (GRAMS)	CARBOHYDRATE (GRAMS)	FIBER (GRAMS)	CHOLESTEROL (MILLIGRAMS)	IRON (MILLIGRAMS)	SODIUM (MILLIGRAMS)	CALCIUM (MILLIGRAMS)
Apple											
Fresh, with skin	1 medium	81	0.2	0.5	0.08	21.0	4.3	0	0.2	0	10
Juice, unsweetened	½ cup	58	0.1	0.1	0.02	14.5	0.2	0	0.5	4	9
Applesauce, unsweetened	½ cup	52	0.2	0.1	0.01	13.8	1.8	0	0.1	2	4
Apricot											
Fresh	1 each	18	0.4	0.1	0.01	4.1	0.8	0	0.2	0	5
Canned, in juice	½ cup	58	0.8	0.0	0.00	15.0	0.5	0	0.4	5	15
Canned, in light syrup	½ cup	75	0.7	0.1	—	19.0	0.5	—	0.3	1	12
Canned, peeled, in water	½ cup	25	0.8	0.0	0.00	6.2	1.7	0	0.6	12	9
Dried, uncooked	1 each	17	0.3	0.0	0.00	4.3	0.5	0	0.3	1	3
Nectar	½ cup	70	0.5	0.1	0.01	18.0	0.8	0	0.5	4	9
Artichoke											
Whole, cooked	1 each	53	2.6	0.2	0.04	12.4	1.1	0	1.6	79	47
Hearts, cooked	½ cup	37	1.8	0.1	0.03	8.7	0.8	0	1.1	55	33
Arugula	3 ounces	21	2.2	0.5	—	3.1	—	0	—	23	136
Asparagus, fresh, cooked	½ cup	23	2.3	0.3	0.06	4.0	0.9	0	0.6	4	22
Avocado	1 medium	322	3.9	30.6	4.88	14.8	4.2	0	2.0	20	22
Bacon											
Canadian-style	1 ounce	45	5.8	2.0	0.63	0.5	0.0	14	0.2	399	2
Cured, broiled	1 ounce	163	8.6	14.0	4.93	0.2	0.0	24	0.5	452	3
Turkey, cooked	1 ounce	60	4.0	4.0	—	8.0	—	20	—	400	—
Bamboo shoots, cooked	½ cup	7	0.9	0.1	0.03	1.1	0.4	0	0.1	2	7
Banana											
Mashed	½ cup	101	1.1	0.5	0.20	25.8	3.2	0	0.3	1	7
Whole	1 medium	109	1.2	0.5	0.22	27.6	3.5	0	0.4	1	7
Barley											
Dry	½ cup	352	9.9	1.2	0.24	77.7	15.6	0	2.5	9	29
Cooked	½ cup	97	1.8	0.3	0.07	22.2	—	0	1.0	2	9
Basil, fresh, raw	¼ cup	1	0.1	0.0	—	0.1	—	0	0.1	0	3
Bean sprouts, raw	½ cup	16	1.6	0.1	0.01	3.1	0.6	0	0.5	3	7
Beans, cooked and drained											
Black	½ cup	114	7.6	0.5	0.12	20.4	3.6	0	1.8	1	23
Cannellini	½ cup	112	7.7	0.4	0.06	20.2	3.2	0	2.6	2	25
Garbanzo	½ cup	134	7.3	2.1	0.22	22.5	2.9	0	2.4	6	40
Great Northern	½ cup	132	9.3	0.5	0.16	23.7	3.8	0	2.4	2	76
Green, fresh	½ cup	22	1.2	0.2	0.40	4.9	1.1	0	0.8	2	29
Green, canned, regular pack	½ cup	14	0.8	0.1	0.01	3.1	0.9	0	0.5	171	18
Kidney or red	½ cup	112	7.7	0.4	0.06	20.2	3.2	0	2.6	2	25
Lima, frozen, baby	½ cup	94	6.0	0.3	0.06	17.5	4.8	0	1.8	26	25
Pinto, canned	½ cup	94	5.5	0.4	0.08	17.5	2.6	0	1.9	184	44
Wax, canned	½ cup	14	0.8	0.1	0.01	3.1	0.8	0	0.5	171	18
White	½ cup	127	8.0	0.6	0.15	23.2	3.9	0	2.5	2	65
Beef, trimmed of fat											
Flank steak, broiled	3 ounces	207	21.6	12.7	5.43	0.0	0.0	60	2.2	71	5
Ground, extra-lean, broiled	3 ounces	218	21.5	13.9	5.46	0.0	0.0	71	2.0	60	6
Liver, braised	3 ounces	137	20.7	4.2	1.62	2.9	0.0	331	5.7	60	6
Round, bottom, braised	3 ounces	189	26.9	8.2	2.92	0.0	0.0	82	2.9	43	4
Round, eye of, cooked	3 ounces	156	24.7	5.5	2.12	0.0	0.0	59	1.7	53	4
Round, top, lean, broiled	3 ounces	162	27.0	5.3	1.84	0.0	0.0	71	2.4	52	5
Sirloin, broiled	3 ounces	177	25.8	7.4	3.03	0.0	0.0	76	2.9	56	9

Dash (—) indicates insufficient data available.

FOOD	APPROXIMATE MEASURE	FOOD ENERGY (CALORIES)	PROTEIN (GRAMS)	FAT (GRAMS)	SATURATED FAT (GRAMS)	CARBOHYDRATE (GRAMS)	FIBER (GRAMS)	CHOLESTEROL (MILLIGRAMS)	IRON (MILLIGRAMS)	SODIUM (MILLIGRAMS)	CALCIUM (MILLIGRAMS)
Beets											
Fresh, diced, cooked	½ cup	26	0.9	0.4	0.01	5.7	0.8	0	0.5	42	9
Canned, regular pack	½ cup	31	0.8	0.1	0.02	7.5	0.7	0	0.5	201	16
Beverages											
Beer	12 fluid ounces	146	1.1	0.0	0.00	13.1	0.7	0	0.1	18	18
Beer, light	12 fluid ounces	95	0.7	0.0	0.00	4.4	—	0	0.1	10	17
Brandy, bourbon, gin, rum, vodka, or whiskey, 80 proof	1 fluid ounce	65	0.0	0.0	0.00	0.0	0.0	0	0.0	0	0
Champagne	6 fluid ounces	135	0.5	0.0	0.00	2.1	0.0	0	0.9	7	5
Club soda	8 ounces	0	0.0	0.0	0.00	0.0	0.0	0	—	48	11
Coffee, black	1 cup	5	0.2	0.0	0.00	0.9	—	0	1.0	5	5
Coffee liqueur	1 fluid ounce	99	0.0	0.1	0.03	13.9	—	0	0.0	2	0
Cognac brandy	1 fluid ounce	69	—	—	—	—	—	0	—	—	—
Crème de menthe liqueur	1 tablespoon	110	0.0	0.1	0.00	12.3	—	0	0.0	1	0
Sherry, sweet	1 fluid ounce	39	0.1	0.0	—	2.0	0.0	0	0.1	4	2
Vermouth, dry	1 fluid ounce	35	0.0	0.0	0.00	1.6	0.0	0	0.1	5	2
Vermouth, sweet	1 fluid ounce	45	0.0	0.0	0.00	4.7	0.0	0	0.1	8	2
Wine, port	6 fluid ounces	279	0.2	0.0	0.00	21.3	0.0	0	0.7	7	7
Wine, red	6 fluid ounces	121	0.4	0.0	0.00	0.5	0.0	0	1.4	18	12
Wine, white, dry	6 fluid ounces	117	0.2	0.0	0.00	1.1	0.0	0	0.9	7	16
Blackberries, fresh	½ cup	37	0.5	0.3	0.01	9.2	5.3	0	0.4	0	23
Blueberries, fresh	½ cup	41	0.5	0.3	0.02	10.2	3.3	0	0.1	4	4
Bouillon, dry											
Beef-flavored cubes	1 cube	3	0.1	0.0	—	0.2	—	—	—	400	—
Beef-flavored granules	1 teaspoon	10	0.5	1.1	0.30	0.5	—	—	—	945	—
Chicken-flavored cubes	1 cube	10	0.2	0.2	—	1.1	—	1	0.1	1152	—
Chicken-flavored granules	1 teaspoon	10	0.5	1.1	0.30	0.5	—	—	—	819	—
Bran											
Oat, dry, uncooked	½ cup	153	8.0	3.0	0.28	23.5	6.0	0	2.6	1	31
Oat, unprocessed	½ cup	114	8.0	3.3	0.62	30.8	7.4	0	2.5	2	27
Wheat, crude	½ cup	65	4.7	1.3	0.19	19.4	12.7	0	3.2	1	22
Bread											
Bagel, plain	1 each	161	5.9	1.5	0.21	30.5	1.2	—	1.4	196	23
Biscuit, homemade	1 each	127	2.3	6.4	1.74	14.9	0.6	2	0.6	224	65
Bun, hamburger or hot dog	1 each	136	3.2	3.4	0.52	22.4	0.1	13	0.8	112	19
Cornbread	2-ounce square	154	3.5	6.0	3.36	21.1	1.2	56	0.7	273	96
English muffin	1 each	182	5.9	3.6	1.93	30.9	0.8	32	1.5	234	41
French	1 slice	73	2.3	0.5	0.16	13.9	0.6	1	0.6	145	11
Light, wheatberry or 7-grain	1 slice	40	2.0	1.0	—	7.0	2.8	0	0.7	105	20
Pita, whole wheat	1 medium	122	2.4	0.9	0.10	23.5	4.4	0	4.4	—	39
Pumpernickel	1 slice	76	2.8	0.4	0.05	16.4	1.8	0	0.7	176	26
Raisin	1 slice	66	1.6	0.7	0.16	13.4	0.9	1	0.3	91	18
Rye	1 slice	61	2.3	0.3	0.04	13.0	1.5	0	0.4	139	19
White	1 slice	67	2.2	0.8	0.19	12.6	0.5	1	0.6	127	18
Whole wheat	1 slice	56	2.4	0.7	0.12	11.0	2.1	1	0.5	121	23
Breadcrumbs											
Fine, dry	½ cup	196	6.3	2.2	0.52	36.7	2.1	2	1.7	368	61
Seasoned	½ cup	214	8.4	1.5	—	41.5	0.3	—	1.9	1590	59
Breadstick, plain	1 each	17	0.4	0.5	—	2.7	—	—	0.2	20	1
Broccoli, fresh, chopped, cooked or raw	½ cup	12	1.3	0.1	0.02	2.3	1.4	0	0.4	12	21
Broth											
Beef, canned, diluted	1 cup	31	4.8	0.7	0.34	2.6	0.0	24	0.5	782	0
Beef, no-salt-added	1 cup	22	0.5	0.0	0.00	1.9	0.0	0	0.0	7	0
Chicken, low-sodium	1 cup	22	0.4	0.0	—	2.0	0.0	0	0.0	4	0
Chicken, no-salt-added	1 cup	16	1.0	1.0	—	0.0	—	—	—	67	—
Brussels sprouts, fresh, cooked	½ cup	30	2.0	0.4	0.08	6.8	3.4	0	0.9	16	28
Bulgur, uncooked	½ cup	239	8.6	0.9	0.16	53.1	12.8	0	1.7	12	24

FOOD	APPROXIMATE MEASURE	FOOD ENERGY (CALORIES)	PROTEIN (GRAMS)	FAT (GRAMS)	SATURATED FAT (GRAMS)	CARBOHYDRATE (GRAMS)	FIBER (GRAMS)	CHOLESTEROL (MILLIGRAMS)	IRON (MILLIGRAMS)	SODIUM (MILLIGRAMS)	CALCIUM (MILLIGRAMS)
Butter											
Regular	1 tablespoon	102	0.1	11.5	7.17	0.0	0.0	31	0.0	117	3
Whipped	1 tablespoon	68	0.1	7.7	4.78	0.0	0.0	21	0.0	78	2
Cabbage											
Bok choy	1 cup	9	1.0	0.1	0.02	1.5	0.7	0	0.6	45	73
Common varieties, raw, shredded	½ cup	8	0.4	0.1	0.01	1.9	0.8	0	0.2	6	16
Cake, without frosting											
Angel food	2-ounce slice	147	3.2	0.1	—	33.7	0.0	0	0.2	83	54
Pound	1-ounce slice	305	3.6	17.5	10.19	33.7	0.4	134	0.5	245	27
Sponge, cut into 12 slices	1 slice	183	3.6	5.0	1.48	30.8	0.3	221	0.8	99	44
Yellow, cut into 12 slices	1 slice	190	2.8	7.5	1.92	28.0	0.3	40	0.2	157	79
Candy											
Fudge, chocolate	1 ounce	113	0.8	3.4	—	21.3	0.1	0	0.3	54	22
Gumdrops	1 ounce	98	0.0	0.2	0.03	24.8	0.0	0	0.1	10	2
Hard	1 each	27	0.0	0.0	0.00	6.8	0.0	0	0.1	2	1
Jelly beans	1 ounce	104	0.0	0.1	0.09	26.4	0.0	0	0.3	3	3
Milk chocolate	1 ounce	153	2.4	8.7	5.13	16.4	—	7	0.4	23	58
Cantaloupe, raw, diced	½ cup	28	0.7	0.2	0.12	6.7	0.9	0	0.2	7	9
Capers	1 tablespoon	4	0.4	0.0	—	0.6	—	0	—	670	—
Carambola (starfruit)	1 medium	42	0.7	0.4	—	9.9	1.5	0	0.3	3	5
Carrot											
Raw	1 medium	31	0.7	0.1	0.02	7.3	2.3	0	0.4	25	19
Cooked, sliced	½ cup	33	0.8	0.1	0.22	7.6	1.4	0	0.4	48	22
Juice, canned	½ cup	66	1.6	0.2	0.05	15.3	1.6	0	0.8	48	40
Catsup											
Regular	1 tablespoon	18	0.3	0.1	0.01	4.3	0.3	0	0.1	178	4
No-salt-added	1 tablespoon	15	0.0	0.0	—	4.0	—	—	—	6	—
Reduced-calorie	1 tablespoon	7	0.0	0.0	—	1.2	—	—	0.0	3	0
Cauliflower											
Raw, flowerets	½ cup	12	1.0	0.1	0.01	2.5	1.2	0	0.3	7	14
Cooked, flowerets	½ cup	15	1.2	0.1	0.02	2.8	1.4	0	0.2	4	17
Caviar	1 tablespoon	40	3.9	2.9	0.07	0.6	0.0	94	—	240	—
Celeriac, raw, shredded	½ cup	30	1.2	0.2	0.06	7.2	1.0	0	0.5	78	34
Celery, raw, diced	½ cup	10	0.4	0.1	0.02	2.2	1.0	0	0.2	52	24
Cereal											
Bran flakes	½ cup	64	2.5	0.4	0.06	15.3	2.7	0	5.6	182	10
Bran, whole	½ cup	104	6.0	1.5	0.12	32.7	14.9	0	6.7	387	30
Corn flakes	½ cup	44	0.9	0.0	0.00	9.8	0.1	0	0.7	140	0
Crispy rice	½ cup	55	0.9	0.1	—	12.4	0.2	0	0.3	103	3
Granola	½ cup	242	5.8	8.9	—	34.7	—	—	1.8	66	29
Puffed wheat	½ cup	22	0.9	0.1	0.01	4.8	0.2	0	0.3	0	2
Raisin bran	½ cup	77	2.7	0.5	—	18.6	3.4	0	3.0	179	9
Shredded wheat miniatures	½ cup	76	2.3	0.5	0.08	17.0	2.0	0	0.9	2	8
Toasted oat	½ cup	44	1.7	0.7	0.13	7.8	0.4	0	1.8	123	19
Whole-grain wheat flakes	½ cup	79	1.9	0.2	0.04	18.6	1.4	0	0.6	150	6
Cheese											
American, processed	1 ounce	106	6.3	8.9	5.58	0.5	0.0	27	0.1	405	175
American, processed, light	1 ounce	50	6.9	2.0	—	1.0	0.0	—	—	407	198
American, processed, skim	1 ounce	69	6.0	4.0	—	2.0	0.0	15	—	407	198
Blue	1 ounce	100	6.1	8.1	5.30	0.7	0.0	21	0.1	395	150
Brie	1 ounce	95	5.9	7.8	4.94	0.1	0.0	28	0.1	178	52
Camembert	1 ounce	85	5.6	6.9	4.33	0.1	0.0	20	0.1	239	110
Cheddar	1 ounce	114	7.0	9.4	5.98	0.4	0.0	30	0.2	176	204
Cheddar, 40% less-fat	1 ounce	71	5.0	4.1	2.40	6.0	—	15	0.1	195	192
Cheddar, light, processed	1 ounce	50	6.9	2.0	—	1.0	0.0	—	—	442	198
Cheddar, reduced-fat, sharp	1 ounce	86	8.3	5.4	3.15	1.2	—	19	0.1	205	251

Dash (—) indicates insufficient data available.

FOOD	APPROXIMATE MEASURE	FOOD ENERGY (CALORIES)	PROTEIN (GRAMS)	FAT (GRAMS)	SATURATED FAT (GRAMS)	CARBOHYDRATE (GRAMS)	FIBER (GRAMS)	CHOLESTEROL (MILLIGRAMS)	IRON (MILLIGRAMS)	SODIUM (MILLIGRAMS)	CALCIUM (MILLIGRAMS)
Cheese (continued)											
Colby, reduced-fat	1 ounce	85	8.2	5.5	3.23	0.7	—	19	0.1	163	223
Cottage, dry curd, no-salt-added	½ cup	62	12.5	0.3	0.20	1.3	0.0	5	0.2	9	23
Cottage, nonfat	½ cup	70	15.0	0.0	0.00	3.0	—	5	—	419	60
Cottage, low-fat (1% milk-fat)	½ cup	81	14.0	1.1	0.72	3.1	0.0	5	0.2	459	69
Cottage, low-fat (2% milk-fat)	½ cup	102	15.5	2.2	1.38	4.1		9	0.2	459	77
Cottage (4% milk-fat)	½ cup	108	13.1	4.7	2.99	2.8	0.0	16	0.1	425	63
Cream, light	1 ounce	62	2.9	4.8	2.86	1.8	—	16	0.0	160	38
Farmer	1 ounce	40	4.0	3.0	—	1.0	—	—	—	—	30
Feta	1 ounce	75	4.0	6.0	4.24	1.2	0.0	25	0.2	316	139
Fontina	1 ounce	110	7.3	8.8	5.44	0.4	0.0	33	0.1	—	156
Gouda	1 ounce	101	7.1	7.8	4.99	0.6	0.0	32	0.1	232	198
Gruyère	1 ounce	117	8.4	9.2	5.36	0.1	0.0	31	—	95	287
Monterey Jack	1 ounce	106	6.9	8.6	5.41	0.2	0.0	22	0.2	152	211
Monterey Jack, reduced-fat	1 ounce	83	8.4	5.4	3.15	0.5	—	19	0.1	181	227
Mozzarella, part-skim	1 ounce	72	6.9	4.5	2.86	0.8	0.0	16	0.1	132	183
Mozzarella, whole milk	1 ounce	80	5.5	6.1	3.73	0.6	0.0	22	0.0	106	147
Muenster	1 ounce	104	6.6	8.5	5.42	0.3	0.0	27	0.1	178	203
Neufchâtel	1 ounce	74	2.8	6.6	4.20	0.8	0.0	22	0.1	113	21
Parmesan, grated	1 ounce	129	11.8	8.5	5.40	1.1	0.0	22	0.3	528	390
Provolone	1 ounce	100	7.2	7.5	4.84	0.6	0.0	20	0.1	248	214
Ricotta, lite	1 ounce	20	3.0	1.0	0.60	1.0	—	4	—	20	34
Ricotta, nonfat	1 ounce	20	4.0	0.0	—	2.0	—	3	—	15	48
Ricotta, part-skim	1 ounce	39	3.2	2.2	1.39	1.5	0.0	9	0.1	35	77
Romano, grated	1 ounce	110	9.0	7.6	4.85	1.0	0.0	29	—	340	302
Swiss	1 ounce	107	8.1	7.8	5.04	1.0	0.0	26	0.0	74	272
Swiss, reduced-fat	1 ounce	85	9.6	5.0	2.78	0.5	—	18	0.1	44	334
Cherries											
Fresh, sweet	½ cup	52	0.9	0.7	0.16	12.0	1.7	0	0.3	0	11
Sour, in light syrup	½ cup	94	0.9	0.1	0.03	24.3	0.1	0	1.7	9	13
Sour, unsweetened	½ cup	39	0.8	0.2	0.05	9.4	1.8	0	0.2	2	12
Chicken, skinned, boned, and roasted											
White meat	3 ounces	147	26.1	3.8	1.07	0.0	0.0	72	0.9	65	13
Dark meat	3 ounces	174	23.3	8.3	2.26	0.0	0.0	79	1.1	79	13
Liver	3 ounces	134	20.7	4.6	1.56	0.7	0.0	537	7.2	43	12
Chili sauce	1 tablespoon	18	0.4	0.1	0.03	4.2	0.1	0	0.1	228	3
Chives, raw, chopped	1 tablespoon	1	0.1	0.0	0.00	0.1	0.1	0	0.0	0	2
Chocolate											
Chips, semisweet	¼ cup	215	1.7	15.2	—	24.2	0.4	0	1.1	1	13
Sweet	1 ounce	150	1.2	9.9	—	16.4	0.1	0	0.4	9	27
Syrup, fudge	1 tablespoon	62	0.9	2.6	1.55	10.1	0.1	2	0.2	17	24
Unsweetened, baking	1 ounce	141	3.1	14.7	8.79	8.5	0.7	0	2.0	1	23
Chutney, apple	1 tablespoon	41	0.2	0.0	—	10.5	—	—	0.2	34	5
Cilantro, fresh, minced	1 tablespoon	1	0.1	0.0	0.00	0.3	0.2	0	0.2	1	5
Clams											
Raw	½ cup	92	15.8	1.2	0.12	3.2	0.0	42	17.3	69	57
Canned, drained	½ cup	118	20.4	1.6	0.15	4.1	0.0	54	22.4	90	74
Cocoa powder, unsweetened	1 tablespoon	24	1.6	0.7	0.44	2.6	—	0	0.9	2	8
Coconut											
Fresh, grated	1 cup	460	4.3	43.5	38.61	19.8	11.7	0	3.2	26	18
Dried, sweetened, shredded	1 cup	463	2.7	32.8	29.08	44.0	4.9	0	1.8	242	14
Dried, unsweetened, shredded	1 cup	526	5.5	51.4	45.62	18.8	4.2	0	2.6	30	21
Cookies											
Brownie	2-ounce bar	243	2.7	10.1	3.13	39.0	—	10	1.3	153	25
Chocolate	1 each	72	1.0	3.4	0.90	9.4	0.0	13	0.4	61	18
Chocolate chip, homemade	1 each	69	0.9	4.6	—	6.8	0.2	7	0.3	30	7
Fortune	1 each	23	0.3	0.2	—	5.0	0.1	—	0.1	—	1
Gingersnaps	1 each	36	0.5	1.3	0.33	5.4	0.0	3	0.4	11	14
Oatmeal, plain	1 each	57	0.9	2.7	0.68	7.2	0.4	9	0.3	46	13

FOOD	APPROXIMATE MEASURE	FOOD ENERGY (CALORIES)	PROTEIN (GRAMS)	FAT (GRAMS)	SATURATED FAT (GRAMS)	CARBOHYDRATE (GRAMS)	FIBER (GRAMS)	CHOLESTEROL (MILLIGRAMS)	IRON (MILLIGRAMS)	SODIUM (MILLIGRAMS)	CALCIUM (MILLIGRAMS)
Cookies *(continued)*											
Sugar wafers	1 each	47	0.6	2.4	0.48	5.9	0.0	7	0.1	61	4
Vanilla creme	1 each	83	0.8	3.6	—	12.1	—	—	0.4	61	3
Vanilla wafers	1 each	17	0.2	0.9	0.17	2.1	0.0	2	0.1	22	2
Corn											
Fresh, kernels, cooked	½ cup	89	2.6	1.0	0.16	20.6	3.0	0	0.5	14	2
Cream-style, regular pack	½ cup	92	2.2	0.5	0.08	23.2	1.5	0	0.5	365	4
Cornmeal											
Degermed, yellow	1 cup	505	11.7	2.3	0.31	107.2	7.2	0	5.7	4	7
Self-rising	1 cup	407	10.1	4.1	0.58	85.7	—	0	7.0	1521	440
Cornstarch	1 tablespoon	31	0.0	0.0	0.00	7.3	0.1	0	0.0	1	0
Couscous, cooked	½ cup	100	3.4	0.1	0.03	20.8	—	0	0.3	4	7
Crab											
Blue, cooked	3 ounces	87	17.2	1.5	0.19	0.0	0.0	85	0.8	237	88
Imitation	3 ounces	87	10.2	1.1	—	8.7	0.0	17	0.3	715	11
King, cooked	3 ounces	82	16.5	1.3	0.11	0.0	0.0	45	0.6	912	50
Crackers											
Butter	1 each	17	0.0	1.0	—	2.0	—	—	0.1	32	4
Graham, plain	1 square	30	0.5	0.5	—	5.5	—	—	0.2	48	1
Melba rounds, plain	1 each	11	0.4	0.2	—	2.0	—	—	0.1	34	0
Saltine	1 each	13	0.3	0.4	—	2.1	—	—	0.1	43	5
Whole wheat	1 each	33	0.7	1.3	0.33	4.7	0.3	0	0.0	60	0
Cranberry											
Fresh, whole	½ cup	23	0.2	0.1	0.01	6.0	0.6	0	0.1	0	3
Juice cocktail, reduced-calorie	½ cup	22	0.0	0.0	0.00	5.6	—	0	0.0	4	11
Juice cocktail, regular	½ cup	75	0.0	0.1	0.00	19.2	—	0	0.2	5	4
Sauce, sweetened	¼ cup	105	0.1	0.1	0.01	26.9	0.2	0	0.1	20	3
Cream											
Half-and-half	1 tablespoon	20	0.4	1.7	1.08	0.7	0.0	6	0.0	6	16
Sour	1 tablespoon	31	0.5	3.0	1.88	0.6	0.0	6	0.0	8	17
Sour, nonfat	1 tablespoon	10	1.0	0.0	—	1.0	—	0	—	10	—
Sour, reduced-calorie	1 tablespoon	20	0.4	1.8	1.12	0.6	0.0	6	0.0	6	16
Whipping, unwhipped	1 tablespoon	51	0.3	5.5	3.43	0.4	0.0	20	0.0	6	10
Creamer, non-dairy, powder	1 teaspoon	11	0.1	0.7	0.64	1.1	0.0	0	0.0	4	16
Croutons, seasoned	1 ounce	139	3.0	5.0	—	18.9	—	—	0.3	—	20
Cucumbers, raw, whole	1 medium	32	1.3	0.3	0.08	7.1	2.4	0	0.7	5	34
Currants	1 tablespoon	25	0.4	0.0	0.00	6.7	0.1	0	0.3	1	8
Dandelion greens, raw	1 cup	25	1.5	0.4	—	5.1	0.9	0	1.7	42	103
Dates, pitted, unsweetened	5 each	114	0.8	0.2	0.08	30.5	3.6	0	0.5	1	13
Doughnut											
Cake type	1 each	156	1.8	7.4	1.92	20.6	0.5	24	0.5	200	16
Plain, yeast	1 each	166	2.5	10.7	2.60	15.1	0.9	10	0.6	94	15
Egg											
White	1 each	16	3.4	0.0	0.00	0.3	0.0	0	0.0	52	2
Whole	1 each	77	6.5	5.2	1.61	0.6	0.0	213	0.7	66	25
Yolk	1 each	61	2.8	5.2	1.61	0.3	0.0	213	0.6	7	23
Substitute	¼ cup	30	6.0	0.0	0.00	1.0	—	0	1.1	90	20
Eggplant, cooked without salt	½ cup	13	0.4	0.1	0.02	3.2	0.5	0	0.2	1	3
Extract, vanilla	1 teaspoon	15	0.0	0.0	—	1.5	0.0	0	0.0	0	0
Fennel, leaves, raw	½ cup	13	1.2	0.2	—	2.3	0.2	0	1.2	4	45
Figs											
Fresh	1 medium	37	0.4	0.2	0.03	9.9	1.9	0	0.2	1	18
Dried	1 each	48	0.6	0.2	0.04	12.2	3.2	0	0.4	2	27

Dash (—) indicates insufficient data available.

FOOD	APPROXIMATE MEASURE	FOOD ENERGY (CALORIES)	PROTEIN (GRAMS)	FAT (GRAMS)	SATURATED FAT (GRAMS)	CARBOHYDRATE (GRAMS)	FIBER (GRAMS)	CHOLESTEROL (MILLIGRAMS)	IRON (MILLIGRAMS)	SODIUM (MILLIGRAMS)	CALCIUM (MILLIGRAMS)
Fish, cooked											
Cod	3 ounces	89	19.4	0.7	0.14	0.0	0.0	47	0.4	66	12
Flounder	3 ounces	100	20.5	1.3	0.31	0.0	0.0	58	0.3	89	15
Grouper	3 ounces	100	21.1	1.1	0.25	0.0	0.0	40	1.0	45	18
Haddock	3 ounces	95	20.6	0.8	0.14	0.0	0.0	63	1.1	74	36
Halibut	3 ounces	119	22.7	2.5	0.35	0.0	0.0	35	0.9	59	51
Mackerel	3 ounces	134	20.1	5.4	1.53	0.0	0.0	62	0.6	56	11
Perch	3 ounces	100	21.1	1.0	0.20	0.0	0.0	98	1.0	67	87
Pollock	3 ounces	96	20.0	1.0	0.20	0.0	0.0	82	0.2	99	5
Pompano	3 ounces	179	20.1	10.3	3.83	0.0	0.0	54	0.6	65	37
Salmon, sockeye	3 ounces	184	23.2	9.3	1.63	0.0	0.0	74	0.5	56	6
Scrod	3 ounces	89	19.4	0.7	0.14	0.0	0.0	47	0.4	66	12
Snapper	3 ounces	109	22.4	1.5	0.31	0.0	0.0	40	0.2	48	34
Sole	3 ounces	100	20.5	1.3	0.31	0.0	0.0	58	0.3	89	15
Swordfish	3 ounces	132	21.6	4.4	1.20	0.0	0.0	43	0.9	98	5
Trout	3 ounces	128	22.4	3.7	0.71	0.0	0.0	62	2.1	29	73
Tuna, canned in oil, drained	3 ounces	168	24.8	7.0	1.30	0.0	0.0	15	1.2	301	11
Tuna, canned in water	3 ounces	111	25.2	0.4	0.14	0.0	0.0	—	2.7	303	10
Flour											
All-purpose, unsifted	1 cup	455	12.9	1.2	0.19	95.4	3.4	0	5.8	2	19
Bread, sifted	1 cup	495	16.4	2.3	0.33	99.4	—	0	6.0	3	21
Cake, sifted	1 cup	395	8.9	0.9	0.14	85.1	—	0	8.0	2	15
Rye, light, sifted	1 cup	374	8.6	1.4	0.15	81.8	14.9	0	1.8	2	21
Whole wheat, unsifted	1 cup	407	16.4	2.2	0.39	87.1	15.1	0	4.7	6	41
Frankfurter											
All-meat	1 each	138	4.9	12.6	4.63	1.1	0.0	22	0.5	482	5
Chicken	1 each	113	5.7	8.6	—	3.0	—	44	0.9	603	42
Turkey	1 each	103	5.6	8.5	2.65	1.1	—	42	0.8	488	60
Fruit bits, dried	1 ounce	93	1.3	0.0	—	20.0	—	0	0.5	24	—
Fruit cocktail, canned, packed in juice	½ cup	57	0.6	0.0	0.00	14.6	0.8	0	0.2	5	10
Garlic, raw	1 clove	4	0.2	0.0	0.00	1.0	0.0	0	0.1	1	5
Gelatin											
Flavored, prepared with water	½ cup	81	1.5	0.0	—	18.6	0.0	0	0.0	54	0
Unflavored	1 teaspoon	10	2.6	0.0	—	0.0	—	—	—	3	—
Ginger											
Fresh, grated	1 teaspoon	1	0.0	0.0	0.00	0.3	0.0	0	0.0	0	0
Crystallized	1 ounce	96	0.1	0.1	—	24.7	0.2	0	6.0	17	65
Grape juice, concord	½ cup	60	0.0	0.0	—	14.9	—	—	0.0	11	4
Grapefruit											
Fresh	1 medium	77	1.5	0.2	0.03	19.3	1.5	0	0.2	0	29
Juice, unsweetened	½ cup	47	0.6	0.1	0.02	11.1	0.0	0	2.5	1	9
Grapes, green, seedless	1 cup	114	1.1	0.9	0.30	28.4	2.6	0	0.4	3	18
Grits, cooked	½ cup	73	1.7	0.2	0.40	15.7	—	0	0.8	0	0
Ham											
Cured, roasted, extra-lean	3 ounces	123	17.8	4.7	1.54	1.3	0.0	45	1.3	1023	7
Reduced-fat, low-salt	3 ounces	104	15.3	4.2	—	1.8	—	42	—	658	—
Hominy, white or yellow	½ cup	58	1.2	0.7	0.10	11.4	2.0	0	0.5	168	8
Honey	1 tablespoon	64	0.1	0.0	0.00	17.5	0.0	0	0.1	1	1
Honeydew, raw, diced	1 cup	59	0.8	0.2	0.08	15.6	1.5	0	0.1	17	10
Horseradish, prepared	1 tablespoon	6	0.2	0.0	0.01	1.4	0.1	0	0.1	14	9
Hot sauce, bottled	¼ teaspoon	0	0.0	0.0	—	0.0	—	0	0.0	9	0
Ice, cherry	½ cup	82	0.2	0.0	—	10.3	—	—	—	0	—
Ice cream											
Vanilla, regular	½ cup	134	2.3	7.2	4.39	15.9	0.0	30	0.0	58	88
Vanilla, gourmet	½ cup	175	2.0	11.8	7.37	16.0	0.0	44	0.1	54	75
Ice milk, vanilla	½ cup	92	2.6	2.8	1.76	14.5	0.0	9	0.1	52	88

FOOD	APPROXIMATE MEASURE	FOOD ENERGY (CALORIES)	PROTEIN (GRAMS)	FAT (GRAMS)	SATURATED FAT (GRAMS)	CARBOHYDRATE (GRAMS)	FIBER (GRAMS)	CHOLESTEROL (MILLIGRAMS)	IRON (MILLIGRAMS)	SODIUM (MILLIGRAMS)	CALCIUM (MILLIGRAMS)
Jams and Jellies											
Regular	1 tablespoon	54	0.1	0.0	0.01	14.0	0.2	0	0.2	2	4
Reduced-calorie	1 tablespoon	29	0.1	0.0	—	7.4	—	0	0.0	16	1
Jicama	1 cup	49	1.6	0.2	0.07	10.5	0.7	0	0.7	7	18
Kiwifruit	1 each	44	1.0	0.5	0.08	8.9	2.6	0	0.4	0	20
Kumquat	1 each	12	0.2	0.0	0.00	3.1	0.7	0	0.1	1	8
Lamb											
Ground, cooked	3 ounces	241	21.0	16.7	6.91	0.0	—	82	1.5	69	19
Leg, roasted	3 ounces	162	24.1	6.6	2.35	0.0	—	76	1.8	58	7
Loin or chop, broiled	3 ounces	184	25.5	8.3	2.96	0.0	—	81	1.7	71	16
Lard	1 tablespoon	116	0.0	12.8	5.03	0.0	0.0	12	0.0	0	0
Leeks, bulb, raw	½ cup	32	0.8	0.2	0.03	7.3	0.6	0	1.0	10	31
Lemon											
Fresh	1 each	22	1.3	0.3	0.04	11.4	0.4	0	0.6	3	66
Juice	1 tablespoon	3	0.1	0.0	0.01	1.0	—	0	0.0	3	2
Lemonade, sweetened	1 cup	99	0.2	0.0	0.01	26.0	0.2	0	0.4	7	7
Lentils, cooked	½ cup	115	8.9	0.4	0.05	19.9	4.0	0	3.3	2	19
Lettuce											
Belgian endive	1 cup	14	0.9	0.1	0.02	2.9	—	0	0.5	6	—
Boston or Bibb, shredded	1 cup	7	0.7	0.1	0.02	1.3	0.4	0	0.2	3	—
Curly endive or escarole	1 cup	8	0.6	0.1	0.02	1.7	0.4	0	0.4	11	26
Iceberg, chopped	1 cup	7	0.5	0.1	0.01	1.1	0.5	0	0.3	5	10
Radicchio, raw	1 ounce	7	0.4	0.1	—	1.3	—	0	—	6	6
Romaine, chopped	1 cup	9	0.9	0.1	0.01	1.3	1.0	0	0.6	4	20
Lime											
Fresh	1 each	20	0.4	0.1	0.01	6.8	0.3	0	0.4	1	21
Juice	1 tablespoon	4	0.1	0.0	0.00	1.4	—	0	0.0	0	1
Lobster, cooked, meat only	3 ounces	83	17.4	0.5	0.09	1.1	0.0	61	0.3	323	52
Luncheon meats											
Bologna, all meat	1 slice	90	3.3	8.0	3.01	0.8	0.0	16	0.4	289	3
Deviled ham	1 ounce	78	4.3	6.7	—	0.0	0.0	—	0.3	—	1
Salami	1 ounce	71	3.9	5.7	2.29	0.6	0.0	18	0.8	302	4
Turkey ham	1 ounce	34	5.5	1.2	0.45	0.3	—	19	0.4	286	2
Turkey pastrami	1 ounce	33	5.4	1.2	0.43	0.1	—	18	0.4	283	2
Lychees, raw	1 each	6	0.1	0.0	—	1.6	0.0	0	0.0	0	0
Mango, raw	½ cup	54	0.4	0.2	0.05	14.0	1.2	0	0.1	2	8
Margarine											
Regular	1 tablespoon	101	0.1	11.4	2.23	0.1	0.0	0	0.0	133	4
Reduced-calorie, stick	1 tablespoon	50	0.1	5.6	0.93	0.1	0.0	0	0.0	139	3
Marshmallows, miniature	½ cup	73	0.5	0.0	0.00	18.5	0.0	0	0.4	9	4
Mayonnaise											
Regular	1 tablespoon	99	0.2	10.9	1.62	0.4	0.0	8	0.1	78	2
Nonfat	1 tablespoon	12	0.0	0.0	—	3.0	—	0	0.0	190	—
Reduced-calorie	1 tablespoon	44	0.1	4.6	0.70	0.7	0.0	6	0.0	88	1
Milk											
Buttermilk	1 cup	98	7.8	2.1	1.35	11.7	0.0	10	0.1	257	284
Buttermilk, nonfat	1 cup	88	8.8	0.8	0.64	12.0	—	8	—	256	288
Chocolate, low-fat 1%	1 cup	158	8.1	2.5	1.55	26.1	0.1	8	0.6	153	288
Chocolate, low-fat 2%	1 cup	180	8.0	5.0	3.10	25.8	0.1	18	0.6	150	285
Condensed, sweetened	1 cup	982	24.2	26.3	16.77	166.5	0.0	104	0.5	389	869
Evaporated, skim, canned	1 cup	200	19.3	0.5	0.31	29.1	0.0	10	0.7	294	742
Low-fat, 1% fat	1 cup	102	8.0	2.5	1.61	11.6	0.0	10	0.1	122	300
Low-fat, 2% fat	1 cup	122	8.1	4.7	2.93	11.7	0.0	20	0.1	122	298
Nonfat dry	⅓ cup	145	14.5	0.3	0.20	20.8	0.0	8	0.1	214	503

Dash (—) indicates insufficient data available.

FOOD	APPROXIMATE MEASURE	FOOD ENERGY (CALORIES)	PROTEIN (GRAMS)	FAT (GRAMS)	SATURATED FAT (GRAMS)	CARBOHYDRATE (GRAMS)	FIBER (GRAMS)	CHOLESTEROL (MILLIGRAMS)	IRON (MILLIGRAMS)	SODIUM (MILLIGRAMS)	CALCIUM (MILLIGRAMS)
Milk *(continued)*											
Powder, malted, chocolate	1 tablespoon	84	1.1	0.7	—	18.4	—	—	0.3	47	13
Skim	1 cup	86	8.3	0.4	0.28	11.9	0.0	5	0.1	127	301
Whole	1 cup	149	8.0	8.1	5.05	11.3	0.0	34	0.1	120	290
Millet, cooked	½ cup	143	4.2	1.2	0.21	28.4	—	0	0.8	2	4
Mint, fresh, raw	¼ cup	1	0.1	0.0	—	0.1	—	0	0.1	0	4
Molasses, cane, light	1 tablespoon	52	0.0	0.0	—	13.3	0.0	0	0.9	3	34
Mushrooms											
Fresh	½ cup	9	0.7	0.1	0.02	1.6	0.5	0	0.4	1	2
Canned	½ cup	19	1.5	0.2	0.02	3.9	—	0	0.6	—	—
Shiitake, dried	1 each	14	0.3	0.0	0.01	2.6	0.4	0	0.1	0	0
Mussels, blue, cooked	3 ounces	146	20.2	3.8	0.02	6.3	0.0	48	5.7	314	28
Mustard											
Dijon	1 tablespoon	18	0.0	1.0	—	1.0	0.0	0	—	446	—
Prepared, yellow	1 tablespoon	12	0.7	0.7	0.03	1.0	0.2	0	0.3	196	13
Nectarine, fresh	1 each	67	1.3	0.6	0.07	16.1	2.2	0	0.2	0	7
Nuts											
Almonds, chopped	1 tablespoon	48	1.6	4.2	0.40	1.7	0.9	0	0.3	1	22
Cashews, dry roasted, unsalted	1 tablespoon	49	1.3	4.0	0.78	2.8	0.5	0	0.5	1	4
Hazelnuts, chopped	1 tablespoon	45	0.9	4.5	0.32	1.1	0.3	0	0.2	0	14
Macadamia, roasted, unsalted	1 tablespoon	60	0.6	6.4	0.96	1.1	0.1	0	0.1	1	4
Peanuts, roasted, unsalted	1 tablespoon	53	2.4	4.5	0.62	1.7	0.8	0	0.2	1	8
Pecans, chopped	1 tablespoon	50	0.6	5.0	0.40	1.4	0.5	0	0.2	0	3
Pine	1 tablespoon	52	2.4	5.1	0.78	1.4	0.1	0	0.9	0	3
Pistachio nuts	1 tablespoon	46	1.6	3.9	0.49	2.0	0.9	0	0.5	0	11
Walnuts, black	1 tablespoon	47	1.9	4.4	0.28	0.9	0.5	0	0.2	0	5
Oats											
Cooked	1 cup	145	6.1	2.3	0.42	25.3	2.1	0	1.6	374	19
Rolled, dry	½ cup	156	6.5	2.6	0.45	27.1	4.2	0	1.7	2	21
Oil											
Canola	1 tablespoon	117	0.0	13.6	0.97	0.0	0.0	0	0.0	0	0
Corn	1 tablespoon	121	0.0	13.6	1.73	0.0	0.0	0	0.0	0	0
Olive	1 tablespoon	119	0.0	13.5	1.82	0.0	0.0	0	0.1	0	0
Peanut	1 tablespoon	119	0.0	13.5	2.28	0.0	0.0	0	0.0	0	0
Safflower	1 tablespoon	121	0.0	13.6	1.24	0.0	0.0	0	0.0	0	0
Sesame	1 tablespoon	121	0.0	13.6	1.92	0.0	0.0	0	0.0	0	0
Okra, cooked	½ cup	26	1.5	0.1	0.04	5.8	0.6	0	0.3	4	50
Olives											
Green, stuffed	1 each	4	0.0	0.4	—	0.1	—	—	—	290	—
Ripe	1 medium	5	0.0	0.4	0.08	0.3	0.1	0	0.1	35	4
Onions											
Green	1 tablespoon	2	0.1	0.0	0.00	0.5	0.2	0	0.1	1	5
Raw, chopped	½ cup	32	1.0	0.1	0.02	7.3	1.6	0	0.2	3	17
Cooked, yellow or white	½ cup	23	0.7	0.1	0.02	5.3	—	0	0.1	2	12
Orange											
Fresh	1 medium	62	1.2	0.2	0.02	15.4	5.8	0	0.1	0	52
Juice	½ cup	56	0.8	0.1	0.01	13.4	0.2	0	0.1	1	11
Mandarin, canned, packed in juice	½ cup	46	0.7	0.0	0.00	12.0	0.1	0	0.4	6	14
Mandarin, canned, packed in light syrup	½ cup	77	0.6	0.1	0.02	20.4	0.1	0	0.5	8	9
Mandarin, canned, packed in water	½ cup	37	0.0	0.0	—	8.4	—	—	0.4	11	—
Oysters, raw	3 ounces	59	6.0	2.1	0.54	3.3	0.0	47	5.7	95	38
Papaya											
Fresh, cubed	½ cup	27	0.4	0.1	0.03	6.9	1.2	0	0.1	2	17
Nectar, canned	½ cup	71	0.3	0.3	0.06	18.1	—	0	0.4	6	13
Parsley, raw	1 tablespoon	1	0.1	0.0	0.00	0.3	0.2	0	0.2	1	5

FOOD	APPROXIMATE MEASURE	FOOD ENERGY (CALORIES)	PROTEIN (GRAMS)	FAT (GRAMS)	SATURATED FAT (GRAMS)	CARBOHYDRATE (GRAMS)	FIBER (GRAMS)	CHOLESTEROL (MILLIGRAMS)	IRON (MILLIGRAMS)	SODIUM (MILLIGRAMS)	CALCIUM (MILLIGRAMS)
Parsnips, cooked, diced	½ cup	63	1.0	0.2	0.04	15.1	2.1	0	0.4	8	29
Passion fruit	1 medium	17	0.4	0.1	—	4.2	2.0	0	0.3	5	2
Pasta, cooked											
Macaroni or lasagna noodles	½ cup	99	3.3	0.5	0.07	19.8	1.1	0	1.0	1	5
Medium egg noodles	½ cup	106	3.8	1.2	0.25	19.9	1.8	26	1.3	6	10
Rice noodles	½ cup	138	3.1	1.3	—	28.6	—	0	2.2	—	40
Spaghetti or fettuccine	½ cup	99	3.3	0.5	0.07	19.8	1.1	0	1.0	1	5
Spinach noodles	½ cup	100	3.8	1.0	0.15	18.9	1.4	0	1.8	22	46
Whole wheat	½ cup	100	3.7	1.4	0.18	19.8	2.5	0	1.0	1	12
Peaches											
Fresh	1 medium	37	0.6	0.1	0.01	9.7	1.4	0	0.1	0	4
Canned, packed in juice	½ cup	55	0.8	0.0	0.00	14.3	0.6	0	0.3	5	7
Canned, packed in light syrup	½ cup	69	0.6	0.0	0.00	18.6	0.4	0	0.5	6	4
Canned, packed in water	½ cup	29	0.5	0.1	0.01	7.5	0.4	0	0.4	4	2
Juice	½ cup	57	0.0	0.0	—	13.6	—	—	—	5	—
Peanut butter											
Regular	1 tablespoon	95	4.6	8.3	1.38	2.6	1.0	0	0.3	79	5
No-salt-added	1 tablespoon	95	4.6	8.3	1.38	2.6	1.0	0	0.3	3	5
Pear											
Fresh	1 medium	97	0.6	0.7	0.03	24.9	4.3	0	0.4	0	18
Canned, packed in juice	½ cup	62	0.4	0.1	0.00	16.0	1.1	0	0.3	5	11
Canned, packed in light syrup	½ cup	71	0.2	0.0	—	19.6	3.1	0	0.3	6	6
Nectar, canned	½ cup	64	0.4	0.2	—	16.1	0.4	—	0.1	1	4
Peas											
Black-eyed, cooked	½ cup	90	6.7	0.7	0.17	15.0	1.5	0	1.2	3	23
English, cooked	½ cup	62	4.1	0.2	0.04	11.4	3.5	0	1.2	70	19
Snow pea pods	½ cup	34	2.6	0.2	0.03	5.6	2.2	0	1.6	3	34
Split, cooked	½ cup	116	8.2	0.4	0.05	20.7	2.3	0	1.3	2	14
Peppers											
Chile, hot, green, chopped	1 tablespoon	4	0.2	0.0	0.00	0.9	0.2	0	0.1	1	2
Jalapeño, green	1 each	4	0.2	0.0	0.00	0.9	0.2	0	0.1	1	2
Sweet, raw, green, red, or yellow	1 medium	19	0.6	0.4	0.05	3.9	1.2	0	0.9	2	4
Phyllo strudel dough, raw	1 each	63	2.1	0.2	—	13.3	—	—	0.5	—	—
Pickle											
Dill, sliced	¼ cup	4	0.2	0.1	0.02	0.9	0.5	0	0.4	553	10
Relish, chopped, sour	1 tablespoon	3	0.1	0.1	—	0.4	0.2	0	0.2	207	4
Sweet, sliced	¼ cup	57	0.2	0.2	0.04	14.1	0.4	0	0.5	276	5
Pie, baked, 9-inch diameter, cut into 8 slices											
Apple, fresh	1 slice	409	3.3	15.3	5.22	67.7	3.5	12	0.8	229	37
Chocolate meringue	1 slice	354	6.8	13.4	5.38	53.8	0.5	109	1.2	307	130
Egg custard	1 slice	248	7.3	11.6	4.07	28.6	0.3	149	0.9	229	129
Peach	1 slice	327	3.2	11.0	2.74	55.1	0.8	0	1.0	339	35
Pecan	1 slice	478	5.8	20.3	4.31	71.1	0.5	141	2.4	324	51
Pumpkin	1 slice	181	4.0	6.8	2.24	27.0	0.8	61	1.1	210	78
Pimiento, diced	1 tablespoon	4	0.2	0.1	0.01	1.0	—	0	0.3	3	1
Pineapple											
Fresh, diced	½ cup	38	0.3	0.3	0.02	9.6	1.2	0	0.3	1	5
Canned, packed in juice	½ cup	75	0.5	0.1	0.01	19.6	0.9	0	0.3	1	17
Canned, packed in light syrup	½ cup	66	0.5	0.2	0.01	16.9	0.6	0	0.5	1	18
Juice, unsweetened	½ cup	70	0.4	0.1	0.01	17.2	0.1	0	0.3	1	21
Plum, fresh	1 medium	35	0.5	0.4	0.03	8.3	1.3	0	0.1	0	3
Popcorn, hot-air popped	1 cup	23	0.8	0.3	0.04	4.6	0.9	0	0.2	0	1
Poppy seeds	1 tablespoon	47	1.6	3.9	0.43	2.1	0.5	0	0.8	2	127
Pork, cooked											
Chop, center-loin	3 ounces	204	24.2	11.1	—	0.0	0.0	77	0.9	59	5
Roast	3 ounces	204	22.7	11.7	4.07	0.0	0.0	77	1.0	59	8

Dash (—) indicates insufficient data available.

FOOD	APPROXIMATE MEASURE	FOOD ENERGY (CALORIES)	PROTEIN (GRAMS)	FAT (GRAMS)	SATURATED FAT (GRAMS)	CARBOHYDRATE (GRAMS)	FIBER (GRAMS)	CHOLESTEROL (MILLIGRAMS)	IRON (MILLIGRAMS)	SODIUM (MILLIGRAMS)	CALCIUM (MILLIGRAMS)
Pork *(continued)*											
Sausage link or patty	1 ounce	105	5.6	8.8	3.06	0.3	0.0	24	0.3	367	9
Spareribs	3 ounces	338	24.7	25.7	10.00	0.0	0.0	103	1.5	79	40
Tenderloin	3 ounces	141	24.5	4.1	1.41	0.0	0.0	79	1.3	57	8
Potatoes											
Baked, with skin	1 each	218	4.4	0.2	0.05	50.4	3.6	0	2.7	16	20
Boiled, diced	½ cup	67	1.3	0.1	0.02	15.6	1.2	0	0.2	4	6
Potato chips											
Regular	10 each	105	1.3	7.1	1.81	10.4	1.0	0	0.2	94	5
No-salt-added	10 each	105	1.3	7.1	1.81	10.4	1.0	0	0.2	1	5
Pretzel sticks, thin	10 each	25	0.5	0.5	—	4.4	0.0	—	0.3	83	4
Prunes											
Dried, pitted	1 each	20	0.2	0.0	0.00	5.3	0.6	0	0.2	0	4
Juice	½ cup	91	0.8	0.0	0.00	22.3	1.3	0	1.5	5	15
Pumpkin											
Canned	½ cup	42	1.3	0.3	0.18	9.9	2.0	0	1.7	6	32
Seeds, dry	1 ounce	153	7.0	13.0	2.46	5.0	0.6	0	4.2	5	12
Radish, fresh, sliced	½ cup	10	0.3	0.3	0.01	2.1	0.3	0	0.2	14	12
Raisins	1 tablespoon	27	0.3	0.0	0.01	7.2	0.5	0	0.2	1	4
Raisins, golden	1 tablespoon	31	0.4	0.1	0.02	8.2	0.5	0	0.2	1	5
Raspberries											
Black, fresh	½ cup	33	0.6	0.4	0.01	7.7	5.0	0	0.4	0	15
Red, fresh	½ cup	30	0.6	0.3	0.01	7.1	4.6	0	0.3	0	14
Rhubarb											
Raw, diced	½ cup	13	0.5	0.1	0.02	2.8	0.4	0	0.1	2	52
Cooked, with sugar	½ cup	157	0.5	0.1	0.01	42.1	—	0	0.3	1	196
Rice, cooked without salt or fat											
Brown	½ cup	110	2.5	0.9	—	23.2	0.3	1	0.5	1	8
White, long-grain	½ cup	108	2.0	0.1	—	24.0	0.5	0	0.9	0	10
Wild	½ cup	83	3.3	0.3	0.04	17.5	—	0	0.5	2	2
Rice cake, plain	1 each	36	0.7	0.2	0.00	7.7	0.1	0	0.2	1	1
Roll											
Croissant	1 each	272	4.6	17.3	10.67	24.6	0.8	47	1.1	384	32
Hard	1 each	156	4.9	1.6	0.35	29.8	0.1	2	1.1	312	24
Kaiser, small	1 each	92	3.0	1.8	—	16.0	0.1	—	1.3	192	7
Plain, brown-and-serve	1 each	82	2.2	2.0	0.34	13.7	0.1	2	0.5	141	13
Whole wheat	1 each	72	2.3	1.8	0.51	12.0	0.8	9	0.5	149	16
Rutabaga, cooked, cubed	½ cup	29	0.9	0.2	0.02	6.6	0.9	0	0.4	15	36
Salad dressing											
Blue cheese	1 tablespoon	84	0.4	9.2	—	0.3	0.0	0	0.0	216	3
Blue cheese, low-calorie	1 tablespoon	59	0.9	5.8	1.40	0.8	—	11	0.1	171	24
French	1 tablespoon	96	0.3	9.4	—	2.9	0.0	8	0.1	205	6
French, low-calorie	1 tablespoon	20	0.0	0.0	0.00	4.0	—	0	—	120	—
Italian	1 tablespoon	84	0.1	9.1	—	0.6	0.0	0	0.0	172	1
Italian, no-oil, low-calorie	1 tablespoon	8	0.1	0.0	—	1.8	0.0	0	0.0	161	1
Thousand Island	1 tablespoon	59	0.1	5.6	0.94	2.4	0.3	—	0.1	109	2
Thousand Island, low-calorie	1 tablespoon	24	0.1	1.6	0.25	2.5	0.2	2	0.1	153	2
Salsa, commercial	1 tablespoon	3	0.1	0.0	—	0.5	—	—	0.0	42	1
Salt, iodized	1 teaspoon	0	0.0	0.0	0.00	0.0	0.0	0	0.0	2343	15
Sauerkraut, canned	½ cup	22	1.1	0.2	0.04	5.0	1.3	0	1.7	780	35
Scallops, raw, large	3 ounces	75	14.3	0.6	0.07	2.0	0.0	28	0.2	137	20
Sesame seeds, dry, whole	1 teaspoon	17	0.5	1.5	0.21	0.7	0.1	0	0.4	0	29
Sherbet											
Lime or raspberry	½ cup	104	0.9	0.9	—	23.8	0.0	0	0.0	67	39
Orange	½ cup	135	1.1	1.9	1.19	29.3	0.0	7	0.1	44	52
Shortening	1 tablespoon	113	0.0	12.6	2.36	0.0	0.0	0	0.0	0	0

FOOD	APPROXIMATE MEASURE	FOOD ENERGY (CALORIES)	PROTEIN (GRAMS)	FAT (GRAMS)	SATURATED FAT (GRAMS)	CARBOHYDRATE (GRAMS)	FIBER (GRAMS)	CHOLESTEROL (MILLIGRAMS)	IRON (MILLIGRAMS)	SODIUM (MILLIGRAMS)	CALCIUM (MILLIGRAMS)
Shrimp											
Fresh, cooked, peeled, and deveined	3 ounces	84	17.8	0.9	0.25	0.0	0.0	166	2.6	191	33
Canned, drained	3 ounces	102	19.6	1.7	0.32	0.9	0.0	147	2.3	144	50
Soup, condensed, made with water											
Beef broth	1 cup	31	4.8	0.7	0.34	2.6	0.0	24	0.5	782	0
Chicken noodle	1 cup	75	4.0	2.4	0.65	9.3	0.2	7	0.7	1106	17
Chili, beef	1 cup	170	6.7	6.6	—	21.4	1.4	13	2.1	1035	43
Cream of chicken	1 cup	117	2.9	7.3	2.07	9.0	0.1	10	0.6	986	34
Cream of mushroom	1 cup	129	2.3	9.0	2.44	9.0	0.4	2	0.5	1032	46
Cream of potato	1 cup	73	1.7	2.3	1.22	11.0	—	5	0.5	1000	20
Onion	1 cup	58	3.7	1.7	—	8.2	—	0	0.7	1053	27
Tomato	1 cup	85	2.0	1.9	0.37	16.6	0.5	0	1.7	871	12
Vegetable, beef	1 cup	78	5.4	2.0	0.83	9.8	0.2	5	1.2	956	17
Soy sauce											
Regular	1 tablespoon	8	0.8	0.0	0.00	1.2	0.0	0	0.3	829	2
Low-sodium	1 tablespoon	6	0.0	0.0	0.00	0.0	—	0	0	390	—
Reduced-sodium	1 tablespoon	8	0.8	0.0	0.00	1.2	0.0	0	0.3	484	2
Spinach											
Fresh	1 cup	12	1.6	0.2	0.03	2.0	2.2	0	1.5	44	55
Canned, regular pack	½ cup	22	2.3	0.4	0.00	3.4	1.1	0	1.8	373	97
Cooked	½ cup	21	2.7	0.2	0.04	3.4	2.4	0	3.2	63	122
Squash, cooked											
Acorn	½ cup	57	1.1	0.1	0.03	14.9	1.2	0	1.0	4	45
Butternut	½ cup	41	0.8	0.1	0.02	10.7	1.2	0	0.6	4	42
Spaghetti	½ cup	22	0.5	0.2	0.05	5.0	1.0	0	0.3	14	16
Summer	½ cup	18	0.8	0.3	0.06	3.9	1.4	0	0.3	1	24
Squid, raw	4 ounces	104	17.7	1.6	0.41	3.5	0.0	264	0.8	50	36
Strawberries, fresh	1 cup	45	0.9	0.6	0.03	10.5	3.9	0	0.6	1	21
Sugar											
Granulated	1 tablespoon	48	0.0	0.0	0.00	12.4	0.0	0	0.0	0	0
Brown, packed	1 tablespoon	51	0.0	0.0	—	13.3	0.0	0	0.5	4	12
Powdered	1 tablespoon	29	0.0	0.0	0.00	7.5	0.0	0	0.0	0	0
Sunflower kernels	¼ cup	205	8.2	17.8	1.87	6.8	2.4	0	2.4	1	42
Sweet potatoes											
Whole, baked	½ cup	103	1.7	0.1	0.02	24.3	3.0	0	0.4	10	28
Mashed	½ cup	172	2.7	0.5	0.10	39.8	4.9	0	0.9	21	34
Syrup											
Chocolate-flavored	1 tablespoon	49	0.6	0.2	0.00	11.0	—	0	0.3	12	3
Corn, dark or light	1 tablespoon	60	0.0	0.0	0.00	15.4	0.0	0	0.8	14	9
Maple, reduced-calorie	1 tablespoon	30	0.0	0.2	0.00	7.8	0.0	0	0.0	41	0
Pancake	1 tablespoon	50	0.0	0.0	0.00	12.8	0.0	0	0.2	2	20
Taco shell	1 each	52	0.7	2.8	—	5.9	—	—	—	62	—
Tangerine											
Fresh	1 medium	38	0.5	0.1	0.02	9.6	1.6	0	0.1	1	12
Juice, unsweetened	½ cup	53	0.6	0.2	0.02	12.5	0.1	0	0.2	1	22
Tapioca, dry	1 tablespoon	32	0.0	0.0	—	8.4	0.1	0	0.2	0	2
Tofu											
Firm	4 ounces	164	17.9	9.9	1.43	4.9	1.4	0	11.9	16	232
Soft	4 ounces	60	7.0	3.0	—	2.0	—	0	1.4	5	100
Tomato											
Fresh	1 medium	26	1.0	0.4	0.06	5.7	1.6	0	0.6	11	6
Cooked	½ cup	30	1.3	0.3	0.04	6.8	0.9	0	0.7	13	10
Juice, regular	1 cup	41	1.8	0.1	0.02	10.3	0.9	0	1.4	881	22
Juice, no-salt-added	1 cup	41	1.8	0.1	0.02	10.3	0.9	—	1.4	24	22
Paste, regular	1 tablespoon	14	0.6	0.1	0.02	3.1	0.7	0	0.5	129	6
Paste, no-salt-added	1 tablespoon	11	0.5	0.0	—	2.6	—	—	0.2	6	4

Dash (—) indicates insufficient data available.

FOOD	APPROXIMATE MEASURE	FOOD ENERGY (CALORIES)	PROTEIN (GRAMS)	FAT (GRAMS)	SATURATED FAT (GRAMS)	CARBOHYDRATE (GRAMS)	FIBER (GRAMS)	CHOLESTEROL (MILLIGRAMS)	IRON (MILLIGRAMS)	SODIUM (MILLIGRAMS)	CALCIUM (MILLIGRAMS)
Tomato (continued)											
Sauce, regular	½ cup	37	1.6	0.2	0.03	8.8	1.8	0	0.9	741	17
Sauce, no-salt-added	½ cup	40	1.2	0.0	—	9.2	1.6	—	—	24	—
Stewed, canned	½ cup	30	0.9	1.1	0.20	5.2	0.2	0	0.4	187	10
Whole, canned, peeled	½ cup	22	0.9	0.0	—	5.2	0.8	—	0.5	424	38
Whole, canned, no-salt-added	½ cup	22	0.9	0.0	—	5.2	0.8	—	0.5	15	38
Tortilla											
Chips, plain	10 each	135	2.1	7.3	1.05	16.0	0.2	0	0.7	24	3
Corn, 6″ diameter	1 each	67	2.1	1.1	0.12	12.8	1.6	0	1.4	53	42
Flour, 6″ diameter	1 each	111	2.4	2.3	0.56	22.2	0.9	0	0.8	0	27
Turkey, skinned, boned, and roasted											
White meat	3 ounces	134	25.3	2.7	0.87	0.0	0.0	59	1.1	54	16
Dark meat	3 ounces	159	24.3	6.1	2.06	0.0	0.0	72	2.0	67	27
Smoked	3 ounces	126	20.4	4.9	1.45	0.0	0.0	48	2.3	586	9
Turnip greens, cooked	½ cup	14	0.8	0.2	0.04	3.1	2.2	0	0.6	21	99
Turnips, cooked, cubed	½ cup	14	0.6	0.1	0.01	3.8	1.6	0	0.2	39	17
Veal, cooked											
Ground	3 ounces	146	20.7	6.4	2.59	0.0	—	88	0.8	71	14
Leg	3 ounces	128	23.9	2.9	1.04	0.0	—	88	0.8	58	5
Loin	3 ounces	149	22.4	5.9	2.19	0.0	—	90	0.7	82	18
Vegetable juice cocktail											
Regular	1 cup	46	1.5	0.2	0.03	11.0	0.5	0	1.0	883	27
Low-sodium	1 cup	48	2.4	0.2	—	9.7	—	—	1.7	48	34
Venison, roasted	3 ounces	134	25.7	2.7	1.06	0.0	—	95	3.8	46	6
Vinegar, distilled	1 tablespoon	2	0.0	0.0	0.00	0.8	0.0	0	0.0	0	0
Water chestnuts, canned, sliced	½ cup	35	0.6	0.0	0.01	8.7	0.4	0	0.6	6	3
Watercress, fresh	½ cup	2	0.4	0.0	0.00	0.2	0.4	0	0.0	7	20
Watermelon, raw, diced	1 cup	51	1.0	0.7	0.35	11.5	0.9	0	0.3	3	13
Wheat bran, crude	1 tablespoon	8	0.6	0.2	0.02	2.4	1.6	0	0.4	0	3
Wheat germ	1 tablespoon	26	1.7	0.7	0.12	3.7	1.1	0	0.5	1	3
Whipped cream	1 tablespoon	26	0.2	2.8	1.71	0.2	0.0	10	0.0	3	5
Whipped topping, non-dairy, frozen	1 tablespoon	15	0.1	1.2	1.02	1.1	0.0	0	0.0	1	0
Wonton wrappers	1 each	6	0.2	0.1	0.03	0.9	0.0	5	0.1	12	1
Worcestershire sauce											
Regular	1 tablespoon	12	0.3	0.0	0.00	2.7	0.0	0	0.0	147	15
Low-sodium	1 tablespoon	12	0.0	0.0	0.00	3.0	—	0	—	57	—
Yeast, active, dry	1 package	20	2.6	0.1	0.01	2.7	2.2	0	1.1	4	3
Yogurt											
Coffee and vanilla, low-fat	1 cup	193	11.2	2.8	1.84	31.3	0.0	11	0.2	150	388
Frozen, low-fat	½ cup	99	3.0	2.0	1.41	18.0	—	10	—	35	100
Frozen, nonfat	½ cup	82	3.4	0.0	0.00	18.1	—	0	—	60	129
Fruit varieties, low-fat	1 cup	225	9.0	2.6	1.68	42.3	0.2	9	0.1	120	313
Plain, low-fat	1 cup	143	11.9	3.5	2.27	16.0	0.0	14	0.2	159	415
Plain, nonfat	1 cup	127	13.0	0.4	0.26	17.4	0.0	5	0.2	173	452
Zucchini											
Raw	½ cup	9	0.7	0.1	0.02	1.9	0.3	0	0.3	2	10
Cooked, diced	½ cup	17	0.7	0.1	0.01	4.1	0.5	0	0.4	3	14

Source of Data:

Computrition, Inc., Chatsworth, California. Primarily comprised of *Composition of Foods: Raw, Processed, Prepared*. Agriculture Handbook No. 8 Series. United States Department of Agriculture, Human Nutrition Information Service, 1976–1990.

Recipe Index

Kiwifruit
  Mélange with Strawberry Sauce,
    Fresh Fruit, 232
  Tart, Kiwifruit and Banana, 242

Lamb
  Chops, Grilled Lamb, 162
  Chops, Peppered Raspberry Lamb, 52
  Chops, Teriyaki Lamb, 163
  Diane, Lamb, 161
  Leg of Lamb, Coffee-Glazed, 163
  Rack of Lamb, Mustard-Crusted, 88
  Steaks, Hearty Lamb, 163
  Thai Lamb, Cabbage-Wrapped, 100
Lasagna
  Potato Lasagna, 144
  Turkey Lasagna, 175
Lemon
  Bread, Lemon-Apricot Soda, 108
  Lemonade, Cherry, 51
  Molds, Lemon-Saffron Rice, 185
  Rolls, Lemon-Raspberry Sweet, 115
  Tea, Sparkling Lemon-Mint, 45
  Yogurt, Lemon Frozen, 238
Lime Parfaits, Key West, 66
Lobster
  Casseroles, Individual Lobster, 126
  Tails with Mustard Vinaigrette,
    Chilled Lobster, 126

Mangoes
  Ice Milk, Pineapple-Mango, 69
  Sauce, Halibut with Mango, 119
Melons
  Cantaloupe, Rum-Marinated, 231
  Cantaloupe Soup, Chilled, 41
  Honeydew with Honey-Ginger
    Sauce, 232
  Punch, Melonade, 103
  Salad, Poppy Seed Fruit, 182
  Salsa, Southwest Melon, 207
  Watermelon Salad, Icy Hot, 182
Mint
  Carrots, Minted Pineapple, 213
  Chutney, Minted Fruit, 210
  Squash with Mint, Mixed, 71
Muffins
  Blueberry Muffins, Miniature, 39
  Carrot and Pineapple Muffins, 107
  Pumpkin Muffins, Whole Grain-, 107
  Zucchini Corn Muffins, 45
Mushrooms
  Pasta Toss, Mushroom-, 136
  Pâté, Mushroom, 94
  Pesto, Roasted Herbed Chicken with
    Mushroom, 172
  Sauce, Swordfish with Mushroom and
    Tomato, 123

Mustard
  Aioli, Stone Crab Claws with
    Mustard-Fennel, 100
  Asparagus Dijon, 212
  Carrots, Maple-Mustard, 56
  Dressing, Tart Mustard, 191
  Lamb, Mustard-Crusted Rack of, 88
  Pork Chops, Mustard-Tarragon
    Baked, 164
  Pretzels, Garlic-Mustard Soft, 110
  Rounds, Honey-Mustard Rye, 113
  Sauce, Currant-Mustard, 207
  Trout Dijon, 123
  Vinaigrette, Chilled Lobster Tails
    with Mustard, 126

Oatmeal
  Bread, Toasted Oat-Wheat, 114
  Cake, Oatmeal Snack, 51
  Cookies, Crispy Oatmeal, 247
  Crumble, Apple-Oatmeal, 230
  Loaf, Hearty Oat and Grain, 109
Olive Dip, Nacho, 94
Onions
  Caramelized Onions, 95
  Casserole Loaf, Fennel-Onion, 113
  Crackers, Caraway-Onion, 106
Oranges
  Cake, Orange Poppy Seed, 244
  Cheesecake, Orange Marmalade, 245
  Chiffon, Fluffy Orange, 234
  Cookies, Orange-Spice, 247
  Cups, Frozen Orange, 51
  Custard, Orange-Apricot, 236
  Dressing, Citrus, 192
  Dressing, Orange Cream, 180
  Greens Orlando, Citrus and, 65
  Strawberries, Honey-Orange, 234
  Tenderloin, Cinnamon-Orange
    Pork, 166
  Vegetables, Orange-Glazed
    Mixed, 215

Pancakes
  Black Forest Pancakes, 35
  Maple-Pumpkin Pancakes, 34
  Pineapple-Yogurt Pancakes, 35
  Potato Pancake with Corn Chili, 146
  Whole Wheat Buttermilk
    Pancakes, 106
Pastas. See also specific types.
  Cannelloni, Veal and Chicken, 138
  Capellini with Clam Sauce, 137
  E Fagioli, Pasta, 139
  Garlic Pasta Appetizer, 70
  Mushroom-Pasta Toss, 136
  Ravioli with Cilantro-Tomato
    Sauce, 140

Rigatoni, Tomato and Herb, 136
Rotelle with Broccoli, 136
Salad, Dilled Pasta, 187
Spicy Tuna-Pasta Toss, 45
Spinach Pasta, Basic, 134
Tortellini with Zucchini and
  Sun-Dried Tomatoes, 139
Vermicelli with Beef and Vegetables,
  Korean, 138
Peaches
  Butter, Peach-Raspberry, 209
  Compote, Praline Peach, 60
  Crunch, Spiced Peach, 233
  Freeze, Fuzzy Navel, 102
  Ice Milk, Peach, 237
  Poached Peaches with Blackberry
    Sauce, Wine-, 232
  Sundaes, Gingered Peach, 45
Peanut Butter
  Black-Eyed Susans, 246
  Dressing, Peanut Butter Fruit, 192
  Pops, Peanut Butter-Banana, 202
Pears
  Cinnamon Pears, 33
  Compote, Sauced Fruit, 218
  Poached Pears with Vanilla Custard
    Sauce, Wine-, 71
  Salad, Festive Cranberry-Pear, 180
  Sandwiches, Pear and Brie, 194
  Sauce, Custard-Pear, 204
  Spiced Apricot-Pears, 218
  Steamed Pears with Honey and
    Currants, 234
  Tenderloins, Brandy-Pear Pork, 165
Peas
  Hopping John, Southwest, 150
  Roll-Ups, Sugar Snap, 77
  Salad, Texas Caviar, 187
  Stir-Fry, Snow Pea-Carambola, 216
  Vegetable Toss, Garden, 217
Pecans
  Coffee, Chocolate-Pecan, 49
  Compote, Praline Peach, 60
Peppers
  Chicken Pepper Pot, 223
  Chile
    Rellenos, Chicken Chiles, 168
    Stuffed Chile Bites, 95
    Stuffed Green Chiles with Yellow
      Pepper Sauce, 143
  Focaccia, Pepper-Topped, 112
  Jalapeño Chicken Breasts, 169
  Kabobs, Grilled Vegetable, 217
  Mahimahi with Papaya and Roasted
    Red Pepper, 120
  Stuffed Peppers, Vegetable-, 215
  Terrine, Sweet Red Pepper, 99
  Wedges, Spicy Pepper, 97

Subject Index

Meats, 15. *See also* specific types.
  fat content in, 158
  luncheon, 172
  nutrients in, 158
  recommended servings of, 15
Metabolism
  effects of dieting on, 83
  and exercise, 18
  muscles and, 18
Milk and milk products, 15. *See also*
  Dairy products.
  recommended servings of, 15
Minerals. *See* specific types.
Monounsaturated fat, 176
Motion sickness, ginger and, 110
Muscles, 19, 239
  exercises for, 14, 21
  strengthening of, 14, 18, 20, 239

National Association for Sports and
  Physical Education, 11
National Cancer Institute, 9, 16
National Cholesterol Education
  Program, 8
National Fisheries Institute, 121
National Institutes of Health (NIH), 8,
  10, 23
Nutmeg, 25
Nutrients, 17. *See also* specific types.
  balanced mix of, 7, 16, 92
  daily percentages of different, 17, 30,
    92, 248
Nutrients, computer analysis of, 17
  calories, 17
  carbohydrates, 17
  cholesterol, 17
  daily amounts of, 17
  fat, 17
  protein, 17
  saturated fat, 17
  sodium, 17
Nutrition
  children and, 37
  symbol, 14
Nutrition Labeling and Education Act, 26

Oat bran, 8
  benefits of, 8
  consumption of, 147
Oats, 147
Olive oil, saturated fat content
  of, 176
Osteoporosis, prevention
  of, 11, 19
Oxidation, 10

Papaya, beta carotene content
  of, 231
Peppercorns, 25
Phosphorus, source of, 132
Physical education, 11
Platelets, 8
Polyps, prevention of, 9
Portion control, weight loss
  and, 89
Protein, 15
  calories in, 15, 17
  computer analysis of, 17
  daily amounts of, 17
  percentage suggestions on, 17,
    30, 92
  sources of, 132, 151
Pumpkin, beta carotene content
  of, 231

Quinoa, 132

Racewalking, 124
  benefits of, 124
Rapeseed plant, 176
Recipe modification, 24
Recommended Dietary Allowances
  (RDAs), 17
Red pepper, 25
Rowing, 239
  benefits of, 239

Saffron, 25
Salt, 172. *See also* Sodium.
  children and, 37
Saturated fat, 7, 92, 176
  labeling for, 26
  polyps and intake of, 9
  recommentations for, 15, 16, 17,
    30, 92
  reducing intake of, 9, 15, 16, 92
  sources of, 9, 16, 176
Shellfish. *See* specific types.
Shrimp, 121
  butterflying of, 101
Smoking
  high-density lipoproteins (HDLs)
    and, 8
Snacks, high-carbohydrate, 233
Sodium
  computer analysis of, 17
  daily amounts of, 17
  reducing intake of, 172
  sources of excess, 172

Spices, 25. *See also* specific types.
  benefits of, 110
Spinach, beta carotene content
  of, 16, 231
Spot reducing, 19, 194
Starch, beans and indigestible, 151
Step aerobics, 20
  benefits of, 20
Strength training, 18, 20
  benefits of, 18
  exercises for, 21
Stress, 23
  exercise and, 23
Stretching, 18, 20
  benefits of, 18
  exercises for, 20
Sugar, children and, 37
Sulforaphane, 10

Target heart rate (THR), 18, 63
  to determine, 63

U.S. Department of Agriculture (USDA),
  10, 11, 15, 16, 17, 110
U.S. Public Health Service, 14
Unsaturated fat, 92

Veal, 158
Vegetable oil, 176. *See also* specific
  types.
Vegetables, 15. *See also* specific types.
  recommended servings of, 15, 16
Vitamins
  vitamin A, 9, 10, 16
  vitamin Bs, 132
  vitamin C, 9, 10, 16
  vitamin E, 9, 10, 16, 132

Walking, 14, 124, 187
Warm-up phase, 20
  in exercise program, 20
Weight control, 19, 23, 83, 89, 194, 234
  back pain and, 137
  blood pressure and, 9
  calorie requirement for, 17, 83
  exercise and, 9, 11, 19, 83, 194
  fat intake and, 8, 15, 16
  fiber intake and, 16, 77
  formula for, 234
  gallbladder disease and, 199
  heart disease and, 8
Wine, heart disease and consumption
  of, 9
Workout. *See* Exercise, program of.

Acknowledgments and Credits

Oxmoor House wishes to thank the following individuals and merchants:

Annieglass, Santa Cruz, CA

Barbara Eigen Arts, Jersey City, NJ

Blenko, Milton, VA

Bridges Antiques, Birmingham, AL

Bromberg's, Birmingham, AL

California Tropics, Carpinteria, CA

Carriage Antique Village, Birmingham, AL

Cassis & Co., New York, NY

Christine's, Birmingham, AL

Cooseman's, Los Angeles, CA

Country Workshop Marketing, Wyncote, PA

Dansk International Designs Ltd., Mount Kisco, NY

Deruta of Italy, New York, NY

Epicure Imports, New York, NY

Fioriware, Zanesville, OH

Frankie Engel Antiques, Birmingham, AL

Fresh World Produce, Birmingham, AL

Gien, New York, NY

Goldsmith/Corot, Inc., New York, NY

Gorham, Providence, RI

Haldon, Irving, TX

J.R. Brooks and Son, Inc., Homestead, FL

Le Jacquard Français, Charlottesville, VA

The Loom Co., New York, NY

Maralyn Wilson Gallery, Birmingham, AL

N.S. Gustin, Atlanta, GA

Sasaki, Secaucus, NJ

Tile Unlimited, Inc., Birmingham, AL

Tavel Strawberry Farms, Warrior, AL

Valley Bakery, Fresno, CA

Vietri, Hillsborough, NC

Timothy Weber, Tuscaloosa, AL

Wedgwood-Waterford, Wall, NJ

Wilton Armetale, Mount Joy, PA

Photographers

Ralph Anderson: frontispiece, pages 13, 17, 20, 21, 24, 25, 26, 27, 29, 31, 32, 34, 36, 38, 40, 43, 44, 46, 52, 54, 57, 58, 61, 64, 67, 70, 72, 75, 76, 78, 81, 84, 87, 167, 195, 200, 206, 211, 216, 221, 224, 229, 237, 246

Jim Bathie: front cover, back cover, pages 6, 48, 50, 91, 93, 96, 98, 101, 103, 105, 108, 111, 117, 120, 122, 125, 129, 131, 132, 135, 138, 141, 142, 145, 150, 153, 156, 160, 162, 165, 171, 174, 177, 179, 181, 186, 193, 197, 203, 209, 214, 219, 235, 240

Photo Stylists

Kay E. Clarke: front cover, back cover, pages 6, 48, 50, 91, 93, 98, 103, 105, 108, 111, 117, 120, 122, 125, 129, 131, 135, 141, 142, 145, 150, 153, 156, 160, 162, 165, 171, 174, 177, 179, 181, 186, 214, 219, 235

Virginia R. Cravens: frontispiece, pages 13, 17, 24, 25, 26, 27, 29, 31, 32, 34, 36, 38, 40, 43, 44, 46, 52, 54, 57, 58, 61, 64, 67, 70, 72, 75, 76, 78, 81, 84, 87, 167, 193, 195, 197, 200, 203, 206, 209, 211, 216, 221, 224, 229, 237, 240, 246